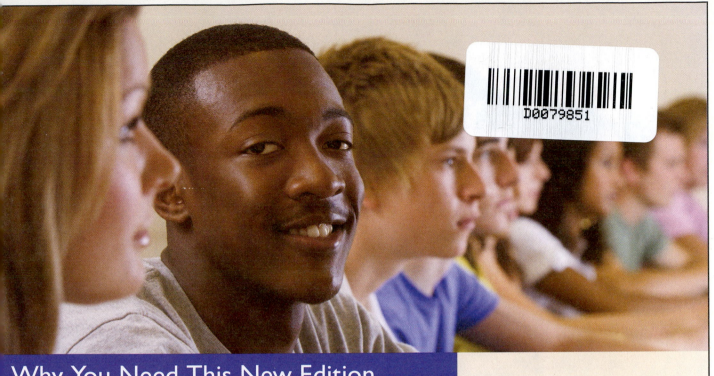

Why You Need This New Edition

See the Future of Group Communication Studies with *Working in Groups*, Sixth Edition

Since its first edition, *Working in Groups* has led the study of group communication by introducing new research, new topics, new features, and new skills. The Sixth Edition of *Working in Groups* continues to innovate while retaining its intellectual rigor, practical focus, and commitment to student learning.

- New! *Follow the Research* features in every chapter highlight new research that helps explain why and how we behave and work in groups.

- New! Remember This features in every chapter provide authoritative quotations or comments to help students remember key ideas and critical research.

- New! Two Video Scenarios applicable to chapter content are highlighted in every chapter.

- Contemporary approaches to group roles, listening, and leadership reflect up-to-date research. Updated topic coverage focuses on effectively working in virtual groups and successfully managing groupthink, meetingthink, and disruptive group members.

- Unsurpassed treatment of virtual groups and technology, including related Virtual Groups features in every chapter, helps students apply group theory, methods, and skills to the work of virtual groups.

- Revised group dialectics approach—emphasizing the book's continuing theme of balance—better explains how group members balance and negotiate the contradictory tensions they encounter while working together to achieve a common goal.

- A thoroughly updated set of ready-to-use ancillary materials for instructors includes a comprehensive *Instructor's Manual*, *Test Bank*, PowerPoint Slides, and text-specific Video Scenarios written by and/or closely supervised by the authors.

PEARSON

Sixth Edition

Working in Groups

Communication Principles and Strategies

Isa N. Engleberg
Prince George's Community College

Dianna R. Wynn
Nash Community College

PEARSON

Boston   Columbus   Indianapolis   New York   San Francisco   Upper Saddle River
Amsterdam   Cape Town   Dubai   London   Madrid   Milan   Munich   Paris   Montréal   Toronto
Delhi   Mexico City   São Paulo   Sydney   Hong Kong   Seoul   Singapore   Taipei   Tokyo

Editor-in-Chief, Communication: Karon Bowers
Senior Acquisitions Editor: Melissa Mashburn
Development Editor: Elsa Peterson
Associate Development Editor: Corey Kahn
Assistant Editor: Stephanie Chaisson
Editorial Assistant: Megan Hermida
Marketing Manager: Blair Zoe Tuckman
Senior Digital Editor: Paul DeLuca
Digital Editor: Lisa Dotson
Photo Researcher: PreMediaGlobal/Carolyn Arcabascio
Permissions Research: Boston/Joanna Green
Project Coordination, Text Design, and Electronic Page Makeup: Integra
Senior Cover Design Manager/Cover Designer: Nancy Danahy
Cover Photo: Cirque du Soleil perform "Varekai" at the Royal
    Albert Hall, London, 3rd January 2010. © Nathan King/Alamy.
Procurement Specialist: Mary Ann Gloriande
Printer/Binder: R.R. Donnelley & Sons/Willard
Cover Printer: Lehigh-Phoenix Color Corporation/Hagerstown

Credits and acknowledgments for material borrowed from other sources and reproduced, with permission, in this textbook appear on page 361.

Library of Congress Cataloging-in-Publication Data

Engleberg, Isa N.
    Working in groups: communication principles and strategies/Isa N. Engleberg
    and Dianna R. Wynn. — 6th ed.
        p. cm.
    Includes bibliographical references and index.
    ISBN-13: 978-0-205-02937-2
    ISBN-10: 0-205-02937-X
1. Group relations training.   2. Small groups.   3. Communication in small
groups.   I. Wynn, Dianna.   II. Title.
    HM1086.E53 2013
    302'.14—dc23

                                                                            2011023721

10 9 8 7 6 5 4 3 2—RRD/W—15 14 13

PEARSON

www.pearsonhighered.com

ISBN 10: 0-205-02937-X
ISBN 13: 978-0-205-02937-2

Brief Contents

Detailed Contents

6 *Verbal and Nonverbal Communication in Groups* 123

12 *Technology and Virtual Groups*   266

Web Chapter: Parliamentary Procedure   W-1
Available at www.pearsonhighered.com/engleberg

Guide to Features

Chapter	Case Study	Ethics in Groups	Follow the Research	Groups in Balance	Theory in Groups	Virtual Groups
Chapter 1: Introduction to Group Communication	• The Study Group Dilemma	• The National Communication Association Credo for Ethical Communication	• What Is the Ideal Group Size?	• Create Synergy • Enjoy Their Work • Empower Members	• Systems Theory • Relational Dialectics Theory	• Using Technology to Communicate
Chapter 2: Group Development	• Nice to Meet You, Too	• Ethical Group Norms	• Group Development Models • Beware of Unreasonable Norms	• Socialize Newcomers • Change Norms as Needed	• Goal Theory and Group Work	• Developmental Tasks
Chapter 3: Group Membership	• Taming Tony the Tiger	• Managing Manipulators	• Curbing Compulsive Communicators	• Adapt to Both High and Low Levels of Member Apprehension • Know When to Say No	• Belbin's Team-Role Theory	• Confidence with Technology
Chapter 4: Diversity in Groups	• No Offense Intended	• The Golden Rule May Not Apply in Diverse Groups	• Where Is Your Face in the U.S. Census? • Who Talks More—Women or Men?	• Seek Intellectual Diversity • Value Both Introverts and Extroverts	• Muted Group Theory	• Cultural Dimensions in Cyberspace
Chapter 5: Group Leadership	• The Leader in Sheep's Clothing	• Leadership • Integrity	• The Two Sides of "Great" Leadership	• Value Leadership and Followership	• The Evolution of Leadership Theory	• Sharing Leadership Functions
Chapter 6: Verbal and Nonverbal Communication in Groups	• How to Sink the Mayflower	• Sticks and Stones May Break Your Bones, but Words Can Hurt Forever	• Immediacy in Groups	• Speak "Silently" • Survive	• The Whorf Hypothesis	• Expressing Emotions Online
Chapter 7: Listening in Groups	• That's Not What I Said	• Self-Centered Roles and Listening	• Listening and Working • Memory Theory	• Ask Questions to Enhance Comprehension • Learn the Art of High-Context Listening	• The HURIER Listening Model	• Listening Online

Chapter 8: Conflict and Cohesion in Groups	• Sociology in Trouble	• The Group and the Golden Mean	• Does Diversity Enhance or Inhibit Group Cohesiveness?	• Know When and How to Apologize • Let Members Save Face	• Attribution Theory and Member Motives	• Conflict in Cyberspace
Chapter 9: Structured and Creative Problem Solving in Groups	• No More Horsing Around	• The Morality of Creative Outcomes	• Which Is Better—Brainstorming or the Nominal Group Technique?	• Avoid False Consensus	• The Functional Perspective and Group Problem Solving	• Adapting Decision-Making and Problem-Solving Methods
Chapter 10: Critical Thinking and Argumentation in Groups	• Slicing the Pie	• Ethical Argumentation	• Emotional Intelligence in Groups	• Document Sources of Evidence	• Argumentative and Aggressive Communication	• Think Critically About the Internet
Chapter 11: Planning and Conducting Meetings	• Monday Morning Blues	• Use Discretion When Taking Minutes	• Why Do Many Meetings Fail?	• Choose Good Meeting Places • Avoid Meeting-think • Pace the Meeting	• Chaos and Complexity Theories	• Meeting in Cyberspace
Chapter 12: Technology and Virtual Groups	• Virtual Misunder-standing	• The Ten Commandments for Computer Ethics	• Internet Addiction	• Negotiate the Dialectics of Virtual Groups • Use Netspeak, Netlingo, and Leet Appropriately • Take Advantage of Collaborative Presentation Technology	• Media Richness and Media Synchronicity Theories	• A Chapter-by-Chapter Review
Appendix: Group Presentations	• Team Challenge	• Respect Copyrights	• Adapting to Audience Opinions	• Welcome and Encourage Questions • Know When to Break the "Slide" Rules	• Aristotle's Ethos	• Mediated Presentations

Preface

One central question has always guided our research and writing for *Working in Groups*:

> ## What do college students enrolled in a group communication course *really* need to know?

Our guiding question led us to include both classic and current theories of group communication that focus on "how groups work" as well as practical group communication strategies and skills that emphasize "how to work in groups."

New to This Edition

The Sixth Edition of *Working in Groups* includes a variety of new features and key updates intended to continue a tradition of intellectual rigor, practical focus, and commitment to student learning.

- **Follow the Research** features in every chapter explain why and how we behave and work in groups with a focus on current research.
- **Remember This** features highlight key ideas and critical research with authoritative quotations and comments.
- **Video Scenarios** applicable to chapter content are now highlighted in every chapter.
- **Contemporary approaches** to group roles, listening, and leadership reflect the newest research. Updated topic coverage focuses on effectively working in virtual groups and successfully managing groupthink, meetingthink, and disruptive group members.
- **Expanded and updated treatment of virtual groups and technology** helps students apply group theory, methods, and skills to the work of virtual groups.
- A revised **group dialectics** approach emphasizes the book's continuing theme of balance while better explaining how group members balance and negotiate the contradictory tensions they encounter while working together to achieve a common goal.

Unified Perspective: Balance and Group Dialectics

Beginning with the first edition of *Working in Groups*, we have used the concept of **balance** as a central metaphor. A group that reaches a decision or completes a task is not in balance if group members end up disliking or mistrusting one another. A group that relies on two or three members to do all the work is not in balance. Effective groups balance factors such as task and social functions, individual and group needs, and leadership and followership.

We further developed the balance metaphor by introducing the concept of **group dialectics**—the interplay of opposing or contradictory forces inherent in group work. A dialectic approach examines how group members negotiate and resolve the tensions and pressures they encounter while working together to achieve a common goal. We apply contemporary theories and research to illuminate the nine group dialectics that characterize the delicate balance achieved by effective groups.

Group Dialectics

Individual Goals	↔	Group Goals
Conflict	↔	Cohesion
Conforming	↔	Nonconforming
Task Dimensions	↔	Social Dimensions
Homogeneous	↔	Heterogeneous
Leadership	↔	Followership
Structure	↔	Spontaneity
Engaged	↔	Disengaged
Open System	↔	Closed System

Comprehensive Topic Coverage

The Sixth Edition of *Working in Groups* strengthens the textbook's scholarship and applicability. Before reading further, flip through the detailed table of contents to get a feel for the depth and breadth of topic coverage. We include **classic and traditional group communication** subject matter, such as

- Group Development
- Member Diversity
- Verbal and Nonverbal Communication
- Decision Making and Problem Solving
- Group Norms and Roles
- Leadership Theories and Power
- Group Cohesiveness and Conflict
- Planning and Conducting Meetings

We also include **cutting-edge theories and topics** such as

- Group Dialectics and Balance
- "Team Talk" Strategies and Skills
- Communication Apprehension in Groups
- Belbin's Group Roles
- Group Goal Setting
- Group and Member Motivation
- Working in Virtual Groups
- Effective Argumentation in Groups
- Brownell's HURIER Listening Model
- Personality Traits in Groups
- Decision-Making Models
- 5M Model of Effective Leadership

Pedagogical Features

The Sixth Edition of *Working in Groups* includes pedagogical features that link the theories of group communication (how groups work) with communication strategies and skills (how to work in groups). Two of these features are new: **Follow the Research** and **Remember This**. Continuing pedagogical features include **Case Studies, Ethics in Groups, Groups in Balance, Theory in Groups,** and **Virtual Groups** as well as **Summary Study Guides, GroupWork** activities, and **Group Assessment** instruments at the end of each chapter.

Follow the Research

What Is the Ideal Group Size?

Research Question: What's the ideal size for a group working to achieve a common goal? Answer: It depends. It depends on member knowledge, attitudes, and skills; on the nature and needs of the task; and—most important of all—on the group's goal. Fortunately, researchers have looked at the group-size question and given us some useful guidelines:

• Groups of three to nine members are generally more productive.
• Groups of more than nine members are generally less productive.[6]

In general, the ideal group size for a *problem-solving* discussion is five to seven members. To avoid ties, an odd number of members is usually better than an even number.

Group communication scholar Susan Wheelan further defines the relationship of group size to group development and productivity. She concludes that groups of three to nine members are more effective than groups of ten or more members. As group size increases, cohesion and effective collaboration decreases, and members tend to divide into subgroups. In large groups, members are more argumentative, less unified, and more competitive than cooperative. Some members may feel left out or inconsequential. As a result, member satisfaction also decreases.[7]

Now, can you answer the question: What's the ideal size for a group working to achieve a common goal? Although there are always exceptions to most rules, you'd be wise to aim for three to nine members. When possible, follow Susan Wheelan's advice and limit "group size to the smallest number of members necessary to accomplish group goals."[8]

New Feature: Follow the Research

The new **Follow the Research** feature offers the latest in relevant academic research and answers commonly asked questions about the nature of effective group communication.

Examples of Follow the Research Features

- What Is the Ideal Group Size?
- Beware of Unreasonable Norms
- The Two Sides of "Great" Leadership
- Does Diversity Enhance or Inhibit Group Cohesiveness?
- Who Talks More— Women or Men?
- Curbing Compulsive Communicators
- Why Do Many Meetings Fail?
- Immediacy in Groups

New Feature: Remember This

Remember This

Group communication is the interaction of three or more interdependent members working to achieve a common goal.

Remember This, another new feature, highlights significant and memorable quotations and author excerpts in every chapter to help students identify and remember key ideas and critical research.

Examples of Remember This Features

- "The United States is the most individualistic culture in the world." —Geert Hofstede, *Culture's Consequences*
- "A meeting without an agenda is like a search party without a map." —Harvard Business School, *Running Meetings*
- "Effective leaders welcome disagreement. They do not suppress conflict, they rise and face it." —Jorge Correia Jesuino, *Understanding Group Behavior*
- "The way a team talks reveals where the team is coming from and where it is headed." —Anne Donnellon, *Team Talk*
- "Time and again, researchers find that the arguments group members make *matter*." —John Gastil, *The Group in Society*
- "Communication apprehension may be the single most important factor in predicting communication behavior in a small group." —James C. McCroskey and Virginia P. Richmond

New and Revised Feature: Case Studies and Related Video Scenarios

The Sixth Edition of *Working in Groups* provides case studies at the beginning of every chapter, followed by critical questions students should be able to discuss and answer after reading the chapter. The case studies questions do not offer a single or correct answer. Rather, they ask students to apply what they learn in the chapter to select what they believe is an appropriate response.

Six Video Scenarios that portray a case study or a similar situation are available on MySearchLab. Two Video Scenarios are highlighted in every chapter.

Examples of Case Study Features

- *That's Not What I Said.* What should a group of marketing students do when several members fail to listen to one another as they work on a major group project?

- *Monday Morning Blues.* How would you help a group that meets every two weeks on Monday afternoons even when there's no reason to have a meeting?

- *The Leader in Sheep's Clothing.* What would you do when the public face of your boss is gentle as a lamb, but his private behavior is unreasonable and ruthless?

- *Sociology in Trouble.* How would you manage a Sociology Department in which faculty members pursue personal rather than group goals that would ensure the department's success and survival?

Case Study
That's Not What I Said

A junior-level marketing class has been divided into four project teams. Each team must research and prepare a marketing proposal for a small business in the community. The members of Group 4 are Lilly, Wendy, Michael, John, and Peter.

Today, Group 4 is holding its eighth meeting at the usual time and place: 2:00 P.M. in Library Study Room 303B. Members are worried because they haven't finished the research portion of the project even though the due date for their marketing project and group presentation is three weeks away. It's now 2:15 and everyone is there except Lilly.

"Hi!" shouts a bright-eyed Lilly as she rushed into the room.

"Lilly," says John crisply, "before you get carried away with something else, please tell us that you brought the research we need in order to finish this part of the project report. At our last meeting, you said you'd have it done before today or, at the latest, would give it to us at today's meeting."

The other group members nod as John speaks. They are impressed with how well he addressed what had become an increasing group problem.

"Guess what?" Lilly throws her books down on the table and leans forward. "Jack is coming to visit this weekend! He didn't think he could get away until Thanksgiving break, but he just called—that's why I'm late—to say he got two days off. He's leaving in the morning to drive here!"

"That's great, Lilly," nods Peter, acknowledging Lilly's excitement and happiness. "But could we talk about your good news after the meeting? We have a lot to do today."

Lilly laughs. "Yeah, I know. Work, work, work and no play makes us dull boys and girls. You guys are worse task masters than our professor."

Michael looks up and takes out his earbuds. "What? Is there a problem here?"

Everyone rolls their eyes. "Go back to dreamland!" snaps Peter.

"That's says Wendy in a hopeful tone, "we need to go through your research and see whether we're ready to move ahead with our marketing plan."

"I'm just so excited," says a grinning Lilly. "Just two more days 'til he's here."

"Excuse me," John interrupts, "but what about the research? I didn't get any email from you with it attached. Did anyone? You said you'd have it by today. Come on, Lilly, this is not the first time you've let us down."

Lilly is no longer smiling. "That's not what I said. What I said was that I'd try to get it done by today. Look, it's not that big a deal. We can go ahead and work on the marketing plan with or without this research because there's nothing in it we don't already know. I'm still tweaking the data and I didn't have time to finish the graphics. We can add the research later and adjust the report."

Michael, who's been paying attention now that he's turned off his iPod, can no longer sit still. "Damn it, Lilly, you haven't been part of this group since day one. We're always waiting for you to show up. And when you take on a task, you either don't do it or finish it late. What's up with you? Don't you care?"

"Of course I care," Lilly retorts.

"Now," reminds Peter, "We know Lilly had some health problems early in the semester and we agreed to make some allowances for her. Certainly everyone knows that Lilly often comes up with some great ideas."

John throws up his hands, "Does that mean we have to make allowances when Jack shows up for two days of sex?"

The rest of the members wince and fear that he may have gone too far. "Out of line. Out of line," murmurs Michael in an audible whisper.

Lilly stands glaring at the group. "Well," she says, "if that's how all of you feel, I guess you don't need my work. Oh—and thanks for ruining my day." With that, Lilly picks up her books and strides out of the room.

The remaining group members look at one another in frustration and begin talking about whether they should suck it up and do Lilly's work or ask the professor if they can "fire" Lilly.

(continued)

149

Continuing and Revised Features

Working in Groups Video Scenarios

The *Working in Groups* Video Scenarios, available on MySearchLab, offer original case studies that highlight important group communication theories, strategies,

Planning the Playground   The Group Project

Before you read any further, visit Pearson's MyCommunicationLab website and watch this case study's video, "Planning the Playground." You may also want to watch the short video, "The Group Project," which illustrates Chapter 2 concepts. Each video comes with a set of study questions to keep in mind as you read this chapter.

and skills. Two specific videos are recommended for instructional use with every chapter. Instructors can use these videos to supplement classroom lectures and discussions, as the basis for exam questions, or as cases for analysis in student papers. The Sixth Edition of *Working in Groups* offers two new videos.

Video case studies include the following scenarios:

- *The Group Project.* A group of college students is having a difficult time finishing their group project and preparing for the group presentation in class.
- *Planning a Playground.* A group of community residents meets for the first time to discuss raising funds for a neighborhood playground. (The related case study, "Nice to Meet Your, Too" is included in Chapter 2).
- *The Politics of Sociology.* Members of a college's sociology department discuss possible course offerings for the next semester. (The related case study, "Sociology in Trouble," is included in Chapter 9.)
- *Helping Annie.* A school nurse has called a meeting with a psychiatrist and a social worker to discuss the best treatment plan for Annie, a high school student with possible depression and an eating disorder.
- *The Reunion.* Three family members have very different ideas about planning a family reunion.
- *Virtual Misunderstanding.* A project manager has organized a conference call with an offsite staff writer and designer to discuss a missed deadline for an important sales brochure. (The related case study, "Virtual Misunderstanding," is included in Chapter 12.)

▲ Groups in Balance...
Value *Both* Leadership and Followership

Who wants to be a follower? In the United States—the number one individualistic country in the world—we praise and value individual leaders. This admiration of leaders is not shared by all cultures. In collectivist cultures, standing out from the group is considered arrogant. Instead, loyal, hard-working followers are admired. In the United States, being a follower receives little praise. Garry Will captured this perception in his book, *Certain Trumpets: The Call of Leaders:*

Talk about the nobility of leaders, the need for them, our reliance on them, raises the clear suspicion that followers are not so noble, not needed—that there is something demeaning about being a follower. In that view, leaders only rise by sinking others to subordinate roles.[5]

Of course, in an *effective* group, none of these suspicions make sense. Leaders and followers share ideas and opinions. They collaborate to achieve a common goal. Followers have a say about where they are being led. After all, without followers, there would be no one to lead.

In Chapter 1, we identified the leadership↔followership dialectic as significant to group success. We emphasized that effective leaders have the confidence to put their egos aside and bring out the leadership in others.[6] Think of how many "ordinary" people came forward to take leadership roles during the horrific events of September 11, 2001. Office workers in the World Trade Center organized coworkers to carry injured colleagues down thousands of stairs. Local businesses worked cooperatively to provide food to workers during the rescue and recovery operation.[7] Other businesses donated office space to companies whose operations had been destroyed when the towers collapsed.[8] Despite the fact that Mayor Rudy Giuliani was widely credited and praised for his leadership during the crisis, there were hundreds of extraordinary followers doing what was needed to help the stricken New York City community recover from the emotional, physical, logistical, and financial shocks it suffered.

Groups in Balance

The **Groups in Balance** feature calls attention to group dialectics and the need to balance the contradictory forces inherent in all group work. The feature also examines the ways in which groups negotiate and resolve a variety of tensions using a both/and approach. Many of the **Groups in Balance** features are new or revised for the Sixth Edition.

Examples of **Groups in Balance** Features

- Groups in Balance… Create Synergy
- Groups in Balance… Seek Intellectual Diversity
- Groups in Balance… Avoid Meetingthink
- Groups in Balance… Value *Both* Introverts *and* Extroverts
- Groups in Balance… Avoid False Consensus
- Groups in Balance… Change Norms as Needed
- Groups in Balance… Socialize Newcomers
- Groups in Balance… Value *Both* Leadership *and* Followership

Theory in Groups
Relational Dialectics Theory

Communication scholars Leslie Baxter and Barbara Montgomery use the term *dialectics* to describe the complex and contradictory nature of personal relationships. Their **Relational Dialectics Theory** claims that relationships are characterized by ongoing, dialectic tensions between the multiple contradictions, complexities, and changes in human experiences.[30] The following pairs of common folk proverbs illustrate such contradictory, dialectic tensions:

"Opposites attract," but "Birds of a feather flock together."

"Two's company; three's a crowd," but "The more, the merrier."[31]

Rather than trying to prove that one of these contradictory proverbs is truer than the other—an *either/ or* response—relational dialectics takes a *both/and* approach. There are several ways to resolve relational dialectic tensions:

- You can choose different options for different situations or different points in time. *Example:* A group's monthly meeting always follows a highly structured agenda. When group members have difficulty coming up with a new ideas or possible solutions to a problem, however, you may set aside the agenda and do some unstructured brainstorming.
- You can choose one option and ignore the other. *Example:* Even though a group knows that two absent members would vote against a proposal they're discussing, they go ahead and make the decision anyway.

Generally, choosing one option over another is the *least* effective way to resolve relational dialectics because you or someone else must "give up" or "lose" one option over another. Engaging *both* options to some degree is usually a better way.

Theory in Groups

Every chapter of *Working in Groups* includes significant theories and research that explain why and how we behave and work in groups. Throughout this edition, we use the **Theory in Groups** feature to focus on why groups succeed or fail and how the strategies and skills in this book can enhance group effectiveness. Many of the theories in the Sixth Edition are revised or new to the textbook.

Examples of **Theory in Groups** Features

- Systems Theory
- Muted Group Theory
- Attribution Theory
- The Evolution of Leadership Theory
- Belbin's Team-Role Theory
- Goal Theory and Group Work
- Argumentative and Aggressive Communication
- Relational Dialectics Theory
- The HURIER Listening Model

Ethics in Groups
The Group and the Golden Mean

The ancient Greek philosopher Aristotle equates *ethics* with *virtue* (such as goodness, moral excellence, righteousness, and integrity). Aristotle explains that virtue can be destroyed by too little or too much of certain behaviors. For example, someone who runs away is a coward while someone who fears nothing is reckless. The virtue bravery is the mean between two extremes. Aristotle offered his "doctrine of the mean," also known as the "golden mean," as a practical way of looking at ethical behavior.[36] Ethical behavior is based on moderation and appropriateness. If, for example, you face an ethical decision, you should select an *appropriate* response somewhere between the two extremes of expressing mild annoyance and uncontrolled rage. Thus, if a group member says something that angers you, according to the golden mean, you should find an appropriate response somewhere between screaming back at the other person in anger or simply giving in. It may be much more appropriate and productive to state in a strong, but reasoned tone that you disagree. Aristotle maintained that anyone can become angry—that is easy. But to be angry at the right things, with the right people, to the right degree, at the right time, for the right purpose, and in the right way—is worthy of praise.[37] For Aristotle, being "brutally honest" in all situations is not an ethical virtue because your honesty may do more harm than good.[38]

In examining the nature and consequences of group conflict, Aristotle's golden mean represents a desirable balance of two dialectic extremes. Consider how the following table illustrates dialectic tensions and the golden mean for three of Aristotle's virtues.[39]

Dialectic Tension	Golden Mean
Cowardice ↔ Rashness	Courage
Shyness ↔ Shamelessness	Humbleness
Boastfulness ↔ Understatement	Truthfulness

Ethics in Groups

Every chapter includes an **Ethics in Groups** feature that examines the many ethical issues that frequently arise when interdependent members interact to achieve a group goal.

Examples of **Ethics in Groups** Features

- The National Communication Association Credo for Ethical Communication
- Leadership Integrity
- The Morality of Creative Outcomes
- The Ten Commandments for Computer Ethics
- Ethical Group Norms
- Ethical Argumentation
- The Group and the Golden Mean

Virtual Groups

In each chapter, the **Virtual Groups** feature guides readers in the use of technology to help achieve group goals in face-to-face settings as well as in virtual groups.

Examples of Virtual Groups Features

- Cultural Dimensions in Cyberspace
- Developmental Tasks
- Thinking Critically About the Internet
- Sharing Leadership Functions
- Listening Online
- Conflict in Cyberspace
- Mediated Presentations

Summary Study Guide

At the end of every chapter, a **Summary Study Guide** reviews the major concepts in the chapter. Readers should be able to explain and apply summary statements to a variety of group situations and contexts.

GroupWork

The **GroupWork** feature at the end of each chapter provides several new and revised activities that demonstrate and/or apply chapter principles. In addition to including additional class activities, the *Instructor's Manual* gives directions for expanding each GroupWork feature into interactive collaborative exercises.

Examples of GroupWork Features

- Classroom Norms
- The Least-Preferred Co-Worker Scale
- What Is Your Decision-Making Style?
- Disrupting Disruptive Behavior
- Conflict Awareness Log
- Group Attraction Survey
- Practice Paraphrasing
- Analyze the Arguments

Group Assessment

The **Group Assessment** feature at the end of each chapter provides several new and revised instruments for evaluating student and group understanding of textbook theories, strategies, and skills. Additional assessment instruments are provided in the *Instructor's Manual*.

Examples of **Group Assessment** Features

- Group Communication Competencies Survey
- Auditing Team Talk
- Are You Ready to Lead?
- Argumentative Scale
- Identifying Cultural Dimensions

- Personal Report of Communication Apprehension (PRCA-24)
- How Do *You* Respond to Conflict?
- Problem-Solving Competencies

Group Assessment

Auditing Team Talk

Directions: Circle the term that best describes the extent to which the members of your group engage in productive team talk.

When your group communicates . . .			
1. Do members use plural pronouns rather than singular ones?	Often	Sometimes	Rarely
2. Do members use language that acknowledges shared needs?	Often	Sometimes	Rarely
3. Do members solicit opinions and express the need for cooperation?	Often	Sometimes	Rarely
4. Do members talk to one another on equal terms?	Often	Sometimes	Rarely
5. Do members use casual language, nicknames, and/or slang?	Often	Sometimes	Rarely
6. Do members express empathy and liking?	Often	Sometimes	Rarely
7. Do members express interest in solving problems?	Often	Sometimes	Rarely
8. Do members use a nonthreatening tone and nonjudgmental language?	Often	Sometimes	Rarely
9. Do members paraphrase one another?	Often	Sometimes	Rarely
10. Do members ask what-if questions?	Often	Sometimes	Rarely
11. Do members propose objective criteria for solutions?	Often	Sometimes	Rarely
12. Do members summarize areas of agreement?	Often	Sometimes	Rarely

Scoring: Analyze your group's team talk by looking at the number of times you circled "Often," "Sometimes," and "Rarely." The more times you circled "Often," the more likely it is that your group engages in productive team talk. The more times you circled "Rarely," the more likely it is that talk inhibits the progress and success of your group.

For a more accurate assessment of team talk in your group, each member should complete the questionnaire and share their responses. Is there a consistent response to each question? Can members identify specific examples of team talk within the group? If there are significant disagreements on several questions, the members of your group may benefit from a discussion about the nature of their team talk.

Glossary

Key words, phrases, and the names of theories are printed in **bold** in the chapters. These terms and phrases are defined in the Glossary at the back of the book.

Glossary

abdicrat A group member whose need for control is not met; an abdicrat is submissive and avoids responsibility.

abstract word A word that refers to an idea or concept that cannot be perceived by your five senses.

accommodation conflict style An approach to conflict in which a person gives in to other group members, even at the expense of his or her own goals.

achievement norm A norm that determines the quality and quantity of work expected from group members.

action item An item in the written minutes of a meeting that identifies the member responsible for an assigned task.

ad hominem attack The fallacy of making an irrelevant attack against a person's character rather than a substantive response to an issue or argument.

adjourning stage The group development phase in which a group has achieved its common goal and begins to disengage or disband.

A-E-I-O-U Model A conflict resolution model with five steps: *A*ssume that other members mean well; *E*xpress your feelings; *I*dentify your goal; clarify expected *O*utcomes; and achieve mutual *U*nderstanding.

affection need The need to express and receive warmth or to be liked.

affective conflict A type of conflict that reflects the emotions stirred by interpersonal disagreements, differences in personalities and communication styles, and conflicting core values and beliefs.

agenda An outline of the items to be discussed and the tasks to be accomplished at a meeting.

aggressiveness Critical, insensitive, combative, or abusive behavior that is motivated by self-interest at the expense of others.

aggressor A group member who puts down other members to get what she or he wants (a self-centered role).

antecedent phase The first phase of new member socialization in which the newcomer's beliefs and attitudes, culture, traits, and prior experiences are identified.

anticipatory phase The second phase of new member socialization in which group members determine if a newcomer meets the group's expectations in terms of characteristics and motives.

appeal to authority The fallacy of using the opinions of a supposed expert when in fact the person has no particular expertise in the area under consideration.

appeal to popularity The fallacy of claiming that an action or belief is acceptable because many people do it or believe it.

appeal to tradition The fallacy of claiming that people should continue a certain course of action because that is the way it has always been done.

arbitration A conflict resolution method that involves a third party who, after considering all sides in a dispute, decides how to resolve the conflict.

argument A claim supported by evidence and reasons for accepting it.

argumentation The use of critical thinking to advocate a position, examine competing ideas, and influence others.

argumentativeness The willingness to argue with others and take public positions on controversial issues.

assertiveness Speaking up and acting in your own best interests without denying the rights and interests of others.

assimilation phase The fourth phase of new member socialization in which a newcomer becomes fully integrated into the group and works toward the common group goal.

asynchronous communication Electronic communication that does not occur simultaneously or in real time; communication that is linear and not interactive.

Supplements Package

Name of Supplement	Availability	Instructor or Student Supplement	Description
Instructor's Manual and Test Bank	Online	Instructor Supplement	The *Instructor's Manual* is text-specific, comprehensive, easy to use, and written by the authors and Todd Allen of Geneva College. The *Instructor's Manual* includes the following resources: • An introduction to group communication studies and pedagogy • Sample syllabi • Ready-to-use group assignments • Ready-to-use assessment instruments • Service learning assignment and assessment instruments • Chapter-by-chapter activities with accompanying teaching tips • An instructor's resource library • A guide to using the *Working in Groups* Video Scenarios The *Test Bank* contains multiple-choice, true/false, and essay questions for each chapter. Test questions are referenced by difficulty level to assist with question selection.
MyTest	Online	Instructor Supplement	**MyTest** is a flexible, online test-generating software that includes all questions found in the *Test Bank*. Computerized software allows instructors to create their own personalized exams, edit any of the existing test questions, and even add new questions. Other special features of this program include random generation of test questions, creation of alternate versions of the same test, scrambling of question sequence, and test preview before printing. This resource is available at www.pearsonmytest.com (access code required).
PowerPoint™ Presentation Package	Online	Instructor Supplement	Created by Susan M. Ward of Delaware County Community College, the text's **PowerPoint™ Presentation Package** includes slides and sample lecture notes for each chapter of *Working in Groups*. Many of the images from the book are also included. Available for download at www.pearsonhighered.com/irc (access code required).
Pearson's Group Communication Study Site	Online	Student Supplement	This open-access student website features **small group communication study materials,** including a complete set of practice tests (multiple-choice, true/false, and essay questions) for all major topics. Students will also find web links to valuable sites for further exploration of major topics. The site can be accessed at http://www.pearsonsmallgroups.com.
MySearchLab® with eText	Online	Instructor & Student Supplement	**MySearchLab with eText** features access to the EBSCO Content Select database and Associated Press news feeds, and step-by-step tutorials offering overviews of the writing and research process.

MySearchLab®

Proven. Engaging. Trusted.

MySearchLab is an interactive website that features an eText, access to the EBSCO ContentSelect database and Associated Press news feeds, and step-by-step tutorials that offer complete overviews of the entire writing and research process. **MySearchLab** is designed to amplify a traditional course in numerous ways or to administer a course online. Additionally, **MySearchLab** offers **course-specific tools** to enrich learning and help students succeed.

eTEXT: Identical in content and design to the printed text, the Pearson eText provides access to the book wherever and whenever it is needed. Students can take notes and highlight, just like with a traditional book.

MediaShare: This comprehensive file upload tool allows students to post speeches, outlines, visual aids, video assignments, role plays, group projects, and more in a variety of formats including video, Word documents, PowerPoint, and Excel. Structured much like a social networking site, MediaShare can help promote a sense of community among students. Uploaded files are available for viewing, commenting, and grading by instructors and class members in face-to-face and online course settings. Integrated video capture functionality allows students to record video directly from a webcam to their assignments, and allows instructors to record videos via webcam in class or in a lab and attach them directly to a specific student and/or assignment. Instructors also can upload files as assignments for students to view and respond to directly in MediaShare. Grades can be imported into most learning management systems, and robust privacy settings allow instructors and students to ensure a secure learning environment.

Video Clips: Videos related to key text content are included on the site. These clips will allow students to gain a deeper, more nuanced understanding of basic communication principles.

Online Quizzes: Chapter quizzes test student comprehension and are automatically graded. Grades flow directly to an online gradebook.

Chapter-specific Content: Each MySearchLab chapter contains Learning Objectives and Flashcards. Flashcards review important terms and concepts from each chapter online. Students can search by chapter or within a glossary and also access drills to help them prepare for quizzes and exams. Flashcards can be printed or exported to your mobile device. These chapter resources can be used to enhance comprehension, help students review key terms, prepare for tests, and retain what they have learned.

A MySearchLab with eTEXT access code is no additional cost when packaged with new print copies of this text. To get started, contact your local Pearson Publisher's Representative at www.pearsonhighered.com/replocator.

Acknowledgments

Although the title page of *Working in Groups* puts our names front and center, this project would never have seen the light of day without the talent, dedication, and creativity of our publishing team. We are particularly grateful to the group of production editors, graphic designers, photo editors, copy editors, and behind-the-scenes technicians who transformed a manuscript into an engaging, cutting-edge textbook: at Integra-Chicago, Heather Johnson, Managing Editor, Jessica Werley, Project Manager, and Emily Friel, Design Manager; and at PreMedia Global, Carolyn Arcabascio, Image Researcher.

We extend very special thanks to Karon Bowers, our dynamic, multitasking Editor in Chief at Pearson, whose wise advice, problem-solving ability, flexibility, creative spirit, and friendship have supported and sustained us through this and other textbook projects. We also welcome our new editor, Melissa Mashburn, who joined us as Senior Acquisitions Editor midway through this project. She immediately became our sounding board and quality assurance expert in the production process. And, as always, we extend heartfelt thanks to Jerry Higgins, our dependable sales representative and loyal friend.

We extend our gratitude to Assistant Editor Stephanie Chaisson for helping us expertly shepherd this textbook and to Associate Development Editor Corey Kahn for transforming our ancillaries into a multitude of useful formats.

We are grateful to our Digital Editor Lisa Dotson for all her work and creativity on the MySearchLab website.

A great deal of credit for this Sixth Edition of *Working in Groups* goes to Elsa Peterson, our resourceful and supportive Development Editor, whose professionalism, innovative ideas, and kindness made all the difference—especially when one of us lost a lot more than textbook documents in a North Carolina tornado. Thanks, Elsa, for seeing us through thick and thin. We are also grateful to Marketing Manager Blair Tuckman and her team. Without her help, this book would have neither caught the eyes of the faculty who will adopt it nor the attention of the students who will use it to become more effective and ethical communicators.

In addition to our publishing team, we enjoyed, learned a great deal from, and made needed changes based on the advice of our conscientious reviewers, whose excellent suggestions and comments enriched every edition of *Working in Groups*:

Todd Allen, Geneva College
Audrey Wilson Allison, Kennesaw State University
Diane Auten, Allan Hancock College
Amy Bippus, California State University, Long Beach
Kevin James Brown, Oregon Institute of Technology
Susan S. Easton, Rollins College
Dennis S. Gouran, Penn State University
Nancy Hoar, Western New England College
Bernadette Kapocias, Southwestern Oregon Community College

Nan Gesche Larsen, University of Minnesota
Suzanne Southerland, Clark College
Roxane Sutherland, Clark College
Jenna Yeager, Towson University

We are particularly indebted to the students and faculty members who have shared their opinions and provided valuable suggestions and insights about our teaching and our textbooks. They are the measure of all things.

Isa Engleberg and Dianna Wynn

About the Authors

Isa Engleberg, professor *emerita* at Prince George's Community College in Maryland, is a past president of the National Communication Association. In addition to writing six college textbooks in communication studies and publishing more than three dozen articles in academic journals, she earned the Outstanding Community College Educator Award from the National Communication Association and the President's Medal from Prince George's Community College for outstanding teaching, scholarship, and service. Her professional career spans appointments at all levels of higher education as well as teaching abroad.

Dianna Wynn is a professor at Nash Community College in North Carolina. Previously she taught at Midland College in Texas and Prince George's Community College in Maryland, where students chose her as the Outstanding Teacher of the Year. She has co-authored two communication textbooks and written articles in academic journals. In addition to teaching, she has many years of experience as a trial consultant, assisting attorneys in developing effective courtroom communication strategies.

chapter 1

Introduction to Group Communication

Chapter Outline

Case Study

The Study Group Dilemma

Grace has always wanted to be a pediatric nurse. When she was accepted into the nursing program at a local college, she looked forward to studying for her dream job. Her first day in Anatomy and Physiology class, however, turned her hopes into fears. Her professor explained that every student must learn and understand the significance of more than 15,000 terms. As she looked around the classroom, she could see that many of the other new nursing majors seemed just as stunned as she was.

After class was over, she walked down the hallway with four students from class. The mood was gloomy. After an uncomfortable period of silence, one of the other students suggested that they form a study group. Grace had her doubts. She thought, "A study group will just take up a lot of my time and energy, with no guarantee that it will help me earn a good grade. As much as I'd like to get to know these students better, I can probably learn more by studying alone. Besides, what if we don't get along? What if I end up doing most of the work or the others don't show up?"

Grace's concerns—like those of many people—are understandable. Groups use a lot of time, energy, and resources. In some cases, a single person can accomplish just as much or more by working alone. And even if a study group has the potential to aid learning, it also has the potential for interpersonal conflicts and long-lasting resentments.

When you finish reading this chapter, you should be able to answer the following critical thinking questions about this case study:

1   If you were in Grace's position, would you have similar concerns about spending valuable time and energy in a study group? What factors would you consider in deciding whether to join?

2   What communication strategies should a study group use to ensure that members are satisfied with the group experience?

3   Which dialectic tensions are most likely to affect how well Grace and her study group achieve their goals?

4   Is it ethical for a study group to work together to improve their chances of earning a good grade when other students in the same class study alone? If yes, why? If no, why not?

The Group Project

The Reunion

Before you read any further, visit Pearson's MyCommunicationLab website and watch the short videos "The Group Project" and "The Reunion," which illustrate Chapter 1 concepts. Each video comes with a set of study questions to keep in mind as you read this chapter.

Succeeding in Groups

All of us work in groups. We work in groups at school and on the job; with family members, friends, and colleagues; in diverse locations, from sports fields and battlefields to courtrooms and classrooms; face to face, by telephone, and through electronic communication channels. Whereas individual achievement was once the measure of personal success, success in today's complex world depends on the ability to work in groups. Researchers Steve Kozlowski and Daniel Ilgen describe our profound dependence on groups:

> Teams of people working together for a common cause touch all of our lives. From everyday activities like air travel, fire fighting, and running the United Way drive to amazing feats of human accomplishments like climbing Mt. Everest and reaching for the stars, teams are at the center of how work gets done in modern times.[1]

Working in groups may be the most important skill you learn in college. A study commissioned by the Association of American Colleges and Universities (AAC&U) asked employers to rank essential learning outcomes needed by college graduates entering the workplace. In two of four major categories ("Intellectual and Practical Skills" and "Personal and Social Responsibility"), the top-ranked outcome was "teamwork skills and the ability to collaborate with others in diverse group settings." Recent graduates ranked the same learning outcomes as top priorities.[2] A business executive in the same study wrote that they look for employees who "are good team people over anything else. I can teach the technical."[3] In another major study, employers identified group-related communication skills as more important than written communication, proficiency in the field of study, and computer skills.[4]

Before reading any further, take a brief look at the Group Assessment survey at the end of this chapter on page 23. How well do you stack up against the list of group competencies?

Defining Group Communication

When does a collection of people become a group? Do people talking in an elevator or discussing the weather at an airport constitute a group? Are the members of a church congregation listening to a sermon or fans cheering at a baseball game a group? Although the people in these examples may look like a group, they are not necessarily working for or with other members. We define **group communication** as the interaction of three or more interdependent members working to achieve a common goal.

In this textbook, we use the terms *group* and *team* interchangeably. A group of friends organizing an annual block party can be just as diligent, organized, and productive as a corporate team organizing a stockholders' meeting. Even though we don't call a football team a football group or a group of family members a team (unless they're playing a sport or game together), we can say that all of these people are interdependent and interact in order to achieve a common goal.

Remember This

Group communication is the interaction of three or more interdependent members working to achieve a common goal.

Figure 1.1   Components of Group Communication

Key Elements of Group Communication

Now, let's break down our definition into the essential components of group communication (see Figure 1.1).

Three or More Members.   The saying "two's company, three's a crowd" recognizes that a conversation between two people is fundamentally different from a three-person discussion. If two people engage in a conversation, Jill communicates with Jack and Jack communicates with Jill. But if a third person is added, the dynamics change: A third person can be the listener who judges and influences the content and style of the conversation. She or he can listen while the other two talk, support or criticize one or both, offer alternatives, and contribute to a tie-breaking decision if the other two people can't agree.

As the size of a group increases, the number of possible interactions (and potential misunderstandings) increases even faster. For example, a group with five members has the potential for 90 different types of interaction; a group with seven members has the potential for 966 different types of interaction.[5]

Many organizations have learned the importance of creating groups in a size most likely to achieve specific goals. For example, many successful megachurches in the United States may have thousands of members in their congregations, but small groups are the key to their success. Church members are encouraged to

Follow the Research

What Is the Ideal Group Size?

Research Question: What's the ideal size for a group working to achieve a common goal? Answer: It depends. It depends on member knowledge, attitudes, and skills; on the nature and needs of the task; and—most important of all—on the group's goal. Fortunately, researchers have looked at the group-size question and given us some useful guidelines:

- Groups of three to nine members are generally more productive.
- Groups of more than nine members are generally less productive.[6]

In general, the ideal group size for a *problem-solving* discussion is five to seven members. To avoid ties, an odd number of members is usually better than an even number.

Group communication scholar Susan Wheelan further defines the relationship of group size to group development and productivity. She concludes that groups of three to nine members are more effective than groups of ten or more members. As group size increases, cohesion and effective collaboration decreases, and members tend to divide into subgroups. In large groups, members are more argumentative, less unified, and more competitive than cooperative. Some members may feel left out or inconsequential. As a result, member satisfaction also decreases.[7]

Now, can you answer the question: What's the ideal size for a group working to achieve a common goal? Although there are always exceptions to most rules, you'd be wise to aim for three to nine members. When possible, follow Susan Wheelan's advice and limit "group size to the smallest number of members necessary to accomplish group goals."[8]

create or join tightly knit groups of five to seven people who meet in a member's home to pray and support one another in times of need. Worshipers match their interests with those of other group members—new parents, retired accountants, mountain bike riders—and use their commonalities as the basis for religious discussions, member support, and volunteer projects. Thus, while successful megachurches boast large congregations that share a common belief system, they rely on the motivation and comfort of small groups to strengthen their religious faith.[9]

Interaction.　**Interaction** requires communication among group members who use verbal and nonverbal messages to generate meanings and establish relationships.[10] Communication allows members to share information and opinions, make decisions and solve problems, and develop interpersonal relationships. The way in which group members communicate does more than reveal group dynamics; it creates them.[11] Members learn which behaviors are appropriate and inappropriate, and which communication rules govern the interaction among members. Regardless of whether group members are meeting face to face or in cyberspace, group communication requires interaction.

Interdependence.　**Interdependence** means that each group member is affected and influenced by the actions of other members. A successful interdependent group functions as a cohesive team in which every member is responsible for doing his or her part. The failure of a single group member can adversely affect the entire group. For example, if one student in a study group fails to read an assigned chapter, the entire group will be unprepared for questions related to the subject matter covered in that chapter. There are not many tasks that can be accomplished by a group without information, advice, support, and assistance from all interdependent members.

Working.　Work is the physical or mental effort you use when trying to accomplish something. That "something" can be a social goal such as getting friends together for a surprise party, a family goal such as deciding jointly where to go on vacation, a

Theory in Groups

Systems Theory

Systems Theory examines how interdependent factors affect one another. In communication studies, Systems Theory recognizes that "communication does not take place in isolation, but rather necessitates a communication system."[12]

Every group we describe in this textbook is a **system**, a collection of interacting, interdependent elements working together to form a complex whole that adapts to a changing environment. However, groups are not the only systems in our lives. For example, in biology, we study the digestive system, the nervous system, and the immune system. We also know that when one part of a biological system fails, the consequences can be serious or even deadly. We

praise the democratic system of government, marvel at our solar system, and hope that our computer system doesn't crash.

Systems Theory tells us a great deal about the nature of groups and helps prepare us for the tensions—both predictable and unpredictable—that characterize the work of a group and its members. It also helps us understand the behavior of groups and their members. For example, groups make decisions, solve problems, produce products, and implement programs that affect people within and outside the group. If one member fails to cooperate or contribute, the entire group may suffer. On the other hand, a group benefits if members suggest creative solutions to a problem.

medical team's goal such as planning training sessions for improving patient care, or a management goal in which members develop a strategic plan for their organization.

The title of this textbook, *Working in Groups*, focuses on the ways in which members work with one another to achieve a common goal. *Working* in a group is not about hard labor or exhausting effort. Rather, when we work effectively in groups, we join others in a productive and motivating experience in which members combine their talents and energy to achieve a worthy goal.

Common Goal. Group members come together for a reason. Their collective reason or goal defines and unifies the group. A **goal** is the purpose or objective toward which group work is directed. The label—goal, objective, purpose, mission, assignment, or vision—doesn't matter. Without a common goal, groups would wonder: Why are we meeting? Why should we care or work hard? Where are we going?

While some groups have the freedom to develop their own goals, other groups are assigned a goal. For example, a gathering of neighbors may meet to discuss ways of reducing crime in the neighborhood. Nursing students may form a study group to prepare for an upcoming exam. On the other hand, a marketing instructor may assign a semester-long project to a group of students to assess their ability to develop a marketing campaign. A chemical company may assemble a group of employees from various departments and ask them to develop recommendations for safer storage of hazardous chemicals. Whatever the circumstances, effective groups work to accomplish a common goal.

> ### Remember This
>
> In their book, *TeamWork*, Carl Larson and Frank LaFasto observe that effective groups have "a clear, elevated goal."[13] Goals guide action, set standards for measuring success, provide a focus for resolving conflict, and motivate members.

Types of Groups

Groups, like their individual members, have diverse characteristics and goals. Although a basketball team, a study group, a corporate board of directors, and a homecoming committee all meet our definition of a group, each one has unique features and functions.

The Green Bay Packers have won more championships than any other team in National Football League history. How do the Packers exemplify the definition of group communication: the interaction of three or more interdependent members working to achieve a common goal?

Figure 1.2   Types of Groups

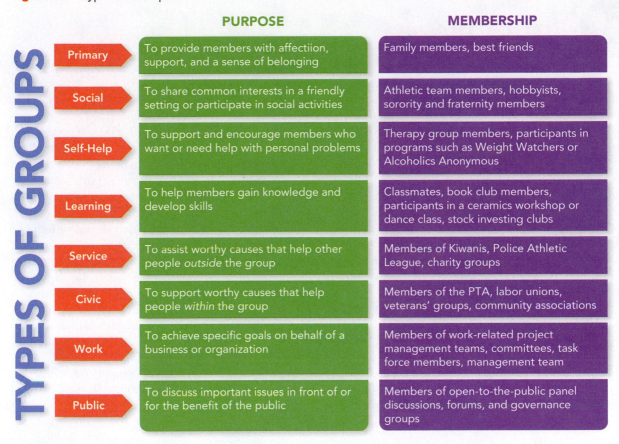

TYPES OF GROUPS		PURPOSE	MEMBERSHIP
	Primary	To provide members with affectiion, support, and a sense of belonging	Family members, best friends
	Social	To share common interests in a friendly setting or participate in social activities	Athletic team members, hobbyists, sorority and fraternity members
	Self-Help	To support and encourage members who want or need help with personal problems	Therapy group members, participants in programs such as Weight Watchers or Alcoholics Anonymous
	Learning	To help members gain knowledge and develop skills	Classmates, book club members, participants in a ceramics workshop or dance class, stock investing clubs
	Service	To assist worthy causes that help other people *outside* the group	Members of Kiwanis, Police Athletic League, charity groups
	Civic	To support worthy causes that help people *within* the group	Members of the PTA, labor unions, veterans' groups, community associations
	Work	To achieve specific goals on behalf of a business or organization	Members of work-related project management teams, committees, task force members, management team
	Public	To discuss important issues in front of or for the benefit of the public	Members of open-to-the-public panel discussions, forums, and governance groups

We have sorted the most common types of groups into eight categories: primary groups, social groups, self-help groups, learning groups, service groups, civic groups, work groups, and public groups (see Figure 1.2). These categories range from the most personal and informal types of groups to more formal types. You can identify each type of group by observing its purpose (why the group meets) and its membership (who is in the group).

The eight types of groups in Figure 1.2 are not absolute categories. Many groups overlap. A Girl Scout belongs to both a social group and a learning group, whereas the scout leaders who operate under the direction of the national association belong to both a service group and a work group.

The last two types of groups in Figure 1.2—work groups and public groups— serve the interests of organizations and public audiences. Their goal may be as complex as reengineering a global corporation or as simple as reporting their progress at a weekly staff meeting. If you are employed, you probably belong to several work groups. You may be a member of a production team or a work crew. You may be part of a sales staff, service department, management group, or research team.

Public group members interact in front of or for the benefit of the public. Although public groups may engage in information sharing, decision making, or problem solving, they are also concerned with making a positive impression on a public audience. In Appendix A, we recommend strategies and skills for developing and delivering effective presentations when serving in a public group.

Virtual Groups

Using Technology to Communicate

Instead of—or in addition to—meeting face to face, many groups interact virtually. A **virtual group** uses technology to communicate, often across time, distance, and organizational boundaries. One key aspect of virtual group communication is that it can take place synchronously and/or asynchronously. **Synchronous communication** occurs simultaneously and in real time. Audioconferences, videoconferences, text conferences, and computer-mediated meeting systems such as webinars allow for synchronous interaction. **Asynchronous communication** is electronic communication that does not occur simultaneously or in real time. Messages sent via email, voice mail, and electronic bulletin boards are asynchronous.

In the spring of 2010, when the airspace above Europe shut down due to ash clouds from Iceland's Eyjafjallajökull volcano, the disruption in travel led to an increase in business teleconferencing. Even though the biggest fans of phone conferences acknowledge that virtual groups are not always the best substitute for face-to-face meetings, the volcano's activity motivated many organizations to replace an expensive (and, in some cases, seriously delayed) business trip with a convenient virtual meeting.[14] Even without the incentive of an erupting volcano, "organizations are no longer confined to team efforts that assemble people from the same location or the same time zone. Indeed, small groups of people from two or more locations and time zones routinely convene for collaborative purposes."[15]

Virtual groups are complex. Members may come from different organizations, cultures, time zones, and geographic locations—not to mention the many technological variables they may encounter. For example, different group members may have different levels of experience and knowledge in using the virtual medium; they may also have computer systems with different capabilities, such as an older or newer version of the software being used for group communication. As a result, virtual groups develop a different group dynamic from those meeting face to face.[16]

Chapter 12, "Technology and Virtual Groups," discusses the unique issues these groups face. In most chapters, we offer additional recommendations on how to work effectively in virtual group environments.

Advantages and Disadvantages of Working in Groups

If you're like most people, there have probably been times when you have suffered through a long, boring meeting run by an incompetent leader. Perhaps you have lost patience with a group that couldn't accomplish a simple task that you could easily do by yourself. Even so, the potential advantages of working in effective groups far outweigh the disadvantages.

Let's begin acknowledging several certainties about the advantages of group work. There is no question that some tasks are impossible for one person to complete. Prehistoric people joined groups to hunt large, ferocious animals and to protect their nomadic family clans. Today we form groups to build skyscrapers and rocket ships, to perform life-saving surgery and classical symphonies, and to play football games and clean up oil spills.

We also rely on smaller groups in our day-to-day circumstances to make decisions and solve problems. Do these groups do a better job than one person can? If the group is poorly organized, lacks a clear goal, has unmotivated members with limited or inappropriate knowledge and skills, the answer is no. But when groups work effectively, efficiently, and ethically, they have the potential to outperform individuals working alone and can make significant contributions to the quality of our lives. The critical question is not, "Are groups better than individuals?" Rather, we must ask ourselves this: "How can we make sure that our groups are effective?"[17] That question drives the content of this textbook. As we note in Figure 1.3, the potential advantages far outweigh the potential disadvantages.

Figure 1.3 Advantages and Disadvantages of Working in Groups

Advantages	Disadvantages
Superior Resources	More Time, Energy, and Resources
Member Satisfaction	Conflict
Learning	People Problems
Cultural Understanding	
Creativity	
Civic Engagement	

Advantages

When a task is fairly simple and routine (write a memo, total the receipts), it may be more efficient for an individual working alone to accomplish the task. If one person knows the answer to a question or if the task requires a specialized expert, then a single person may be better equipped to get the job done. However, when the task is complex and the answers are unclear, a group has the potential to do the job more effectively.

Superior Resources.   Every group member brings a wide variety of resources to a group. Each member has different life experiences and unique perspectives, ideas, and information about a variety of issues. When group members share what they know and what they believe, the group's knowledge base is enriched.[18] These collective perspectives, ideas, and information are likely to result in better-informed, more meaningful, and more effective group decision making and problem solving.[19] With rare exceptions, a group will have more and better resources to call upon than an individual working alone.

Member Satisfaction.   The social benefits of group work can be just as important as task achievement. People belong to and work in groups because groups give them the opportunity to make friends, socialize, receive peer support, and feel part of a unified and successful team. Not surprisingly, the more opportunities group members have to communicate with one another, the more satisfied they are with the group experience.

Learning.   An added advantage of working in groups is the amount of learning that takes place. Groups can enhance learning by sharing collective information, stimulating critical thinking, and challenging assumptions. A review of 168 studies of college students comparing cooperative, group-based learning with traditional approaches indicates that collaborative learning promotes higher individual achievement in knowledge acquisition, retention, accuracy, creativity in problem solving, and higher-level reasoning.[20] New members learn from veterans, and amateurs learn from experts. Not only do members learn more about the topics they discuss, but they also learn more about how to work as a group.

Cultural Understanding. Working effectively in groups requires that you understand, respect, and adapt to differences in members' skills, experiences, opinions, and behavior as well as differences in gender, age, race, nationality, ethnicity, religion, status, and worldviews. By recognizing, appreciating, and adapting to member differences, you can become a more effective communicator in your group, and in your community, your studies, your work, and your travels within this country or throughout the world. Chapter 4, "Diversity in Groups," examines the ways in which member similarities and differences benefit groups.

Creativity. Not only do groups perform better than individuals working alone, they can also generate more innovative ideas and creative solutions. As MIT management professor Peter Senge writes, "If you want something really creative done, you ask a team to do it—instead of sending one person off to do it on his or her own."[21]

Lee Towe, author of *Why Didn't I Think of That? Creativity in the Workplace,* writes that the "key to creativity is the mental flexibility required to mix thoughts from our many different experiences."[22] When you mix your thoughts with those of other group members, you increase the group's creative potential. In addition to providing a creative multiplier effect by tapping more information, more brainpower, and more insights, groups have "awesome superiority" when trying to unleash creativity and solve challenging problems.[23]

Civic Engagement. In recent years, many educational institutions have implemented service-learning programs as a way of connecting students to the community in which they live and work. Rather than confining the study of group communication to the classroom, service learning provides student groups with opportunities to use the strategies and skills they learn in class as they work together toward achieving a genuine, community-based goal.[24] Sara Chudnovsky Weintraub, an expert in service learning, claims that "service-learning projects [or any community-based group projects] help engage students in meaningful experiences that bridge the gap between theory and practice."[25]

Whether you participate in a service-learning group project, organize a neighborhood watch group, or join a city task force, learning effective group communication skills will help you serve your community with dedication and skill.

Disadvantages

The advantages of working in groups occur when groups are working efficiently and effectively. The disadvantages are more likely to occur when working in a group is not the appropriate way to achieve a goal, when members do not work to their full potential, or when problems interfere with group members' willingness and ability to communicate. The most common complaints about working in groups concern the amount of time, energy, and resources expended by groups and the conflicts and people problems that can arise.

More Time, Energy, and Resources. Working in groups costs time, energy, and resources. The 3M Corporation examined the many factors that affect the cost of meetings, including the hourly wages of group members, the wages of those who help prepare for meetings, the cost of materials used in meetings, and overhead costs. Here's its conclusion: The 3M Corporation spends a staggering $78.8 million annually for meetings.[26] A Microsoft survey concludes that nonproductive meetings, poor communication, and hazy group objectives gobble up two of every five workdays. In another study, workers report that they spend an average of 5.6 hours a week in meetings and rate 69 percent of those meetings as "ineffective."[27] We spend a lot of time in groups; if that time and effort are wasted, we are throwing away valuable resources. In Chapter 11, "Planning and Conducting Meetings," we offer several strategies for making meetings more productive and satisfying.

Conflict.   Very few people enjoy or seek out conflict. However, when group members work together to achieve a common goal, there is always the potential for disagreement. Unfortunately, those who disagree may be seen as aggressive and disruptive. As a result, some people will do almost anything to avoid conflict and confrontation. They may go out of their way to avoid working in groups, even though, "in a good discussion, arguing our different viewpoints might lead to clarifying and reconciling them."[28] Yet because of apprehension about conflict, some people avoid meetings in which controversial issues are scheduled for discussion, or they are unwilling to express their opinions. In Chapter 8, "Conflict and Cohesion in Groups," we recommend specific conflict management strategies that address different types and styles of conflict.

People Problems.   As much as we may want others to share our interests, viewpoints, and willingness to work, there is always the potential for individual group members to create problems. Like anyone else in our daily lives, group members can be stubborn, lazy, and even cruel. When deciding whether to work in a group, we often consider whether we want to spend time working with certain members.

Members who lack confidence or who are unprepared may have little to contribute. To avoid conflict or extra work, some members may go along with the group or play "follow the leader" rather than search for the best solution to a problem. Strong, domineering members can put so much pressure on others that dissent is stifled. Although no one wants to work with a group of unpleasant members, there may be circumstances in which people problems cannot be avoided. Fortunately, the upcoming chapters in this textbook provide a wide range of effective strategies and skills for conducting successful and efficient meetings, for managing the inevitable conflicts that arises in groups, and for coping with and overcoming inappropriate member behavior.

 ## Groups in Balance...

Create Synergy

When three or more interdependent group members interact and work toward a common goal, they have the potential to create a synergistic system. **Synergy** is a term that describes the cooperative interaction of several factors that result in a combined effect greater than the total of all individual contributions. In other words, the whole is greater than the sum of its individual parts. The term *synergy* comes from the Greek word *synergos,* meaning "working together." Synergy does not occur when people work alone; it occurs only when people work together.

Effective groups are synergistic. Baseball teams without superstars have won the World Series. Companies whose executives earn modest salaries have surpassed other companies in which CEOs are paid millions of dollars. Ordinary groups have achieved extraordinary results.

Synergy occurs when the knowledge, talents, and dedication of group members merge into a force that surpasses anything group members could have produced without cooperative interaction.

The Nature of Group Communication

Beyond the basic components and types of groups, two concepts can help you to better understand the complex nature of group communication: (1) the critical functions of communication theories, strategies, skills and (2) the group communication process.

Theories, Strategies, and Skills

Management expert Peter Senge and his colleagues believe that theories, strategies, and skills are inseparable components of effective organizations.[29] Throughout this textbook, we examine the theories, strategies, and skills needed to promote and balance group productivity and member satisfaction.

- A **theory** is a statement that tries to explain or predict events and behavior. Group communication theories help us understand what is occurring in a group and why a group succeeds or fails.
- A **strategy** is a method, guideline, or technique for dealing with the issues and problems that arise in groups. Effective strategies are based on theories. Without theories, you won't know why a particular strategy works in one situation and fails in another.
- A **skill**, in the context of group work, is a specific ability that helps a group carry out or achieve its common goal. Communication skills are the most important skills available to group members. Like strategies, skills are most effective when their use is based on theories.

Although an effective group member can tell you what strategies and skills you should use, you may have no idea why the strategies work or how to do the required skills. In our eagerness to solve problems or achieve a group's goal, we may rely on easy-to-use skills that do not address the causes of a problem or help us achieve the goal. Using skills without an understanding of communication strategies and theories can make the process of working in groups inefficient, ineffective, and frustrating for all members.

The Group Communication Process

Central to group communication is the notion of *interaction.* That is, members must communicate with one another as they work together toward achieving a common goal. Communication is complex when just two people interact, and the process becomes more complicated when additional people are involved. At its most fundamental level, the group communication process includes six basic elements common to all forms of human communication; these are illustrated in Figures 1.4 and 1.5.

Figure 1.4   The Group Communication Process

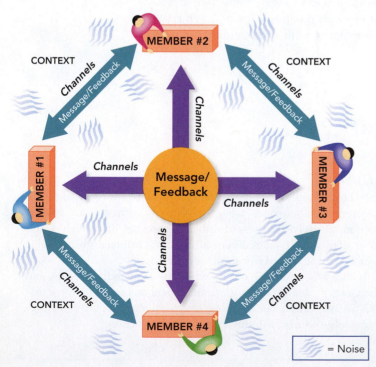

= Noise

Figure 1.5   Basic Elements of Group Communication

Basic Elements of Group Communication	Description	Group Examples
Members	People with distinct knowledge,experiences, personality traits, attitudes, skills, and cultural backgrounds who are recognized as belonging to the group	A surgical team includes one or more surgeons, an anesthesiologist, and function-specific surgical nurses.
Messages	The expression of ideas, information, opinions, and/or feelings that generate meaning	Group members take on a variety of communicative roles such as asking for or giving information and opinions, praising other members, and alleviating tension with friendly humor.
Context	The physical and psychological environment in which a group communicates, including factors such as group size, working conditions, and the relationships among members	A study group meeting in the college cafeteria communicates in a different context than a corporate marketing team holding a videoconference with international clients.
Channels	The media through which group members share messages using one or more of their five senses in face-to-face or mediated settings	Group members may respond by nodding and smiling, scowling and frowning; by expressing their opinions and reactions; by looking attentive or bored.
Feedback	Verbal or nonverbal responses or reactions to a message that help members assess how well others receive and interpret their messages	Group members may nod or scowl when someone makes a suggestion; may vote against a proposal; may look attentive when they agree and smile when pleased.
Noise	Any external (sounds, room conditions) or internal (attitudes, beliefs, and values) factors that interfere with how well members express themselves or interpret the messages of others	*External Noise:* Hallway sounds, hot/cold room, poor lighting, uncomfortable seating. *Internal Noise:* biases, worried thoughts, anger, fatigue, hunger, headaches

Balance: The Guiding Principle of Group Work

At the heart of this book is an important guiding principle: An ideal group succeeds because it achieves balance. **Balance** describes a state of equilibrium in which no significant factor dominates or interferes with other factors. In group communication, the group's common goal is the point on which members must balance many factors. A group that makes a decision or completes an assigned task is not in balance if group members end up hating one another. A group that relies on one or two members to do all the work is not in balance. Effective groups balance factors such as the group's task and social functions, individual and group needs, and the responsibilities of leadership and followership. Achieving balance requires an understanding of the interplay of the contradictory forces that operate in all groups.

Groups in Balance

All of us balance competing options every day. Should you work or play? Should you spend or save? Should you eat a big bowl of ice cream or a fresh salad? These kinds of tensions are best resolved by taking a *both/and* approach rather than an *either/or* perspective. For example, if you're lucky, you may *both* have a job that pays well *and* enjoy it as much as play. If you *both* spend wisely *and* save more, you can look forward to a more secure financial future. If you eat *both* small portions of ice cream *and* fresh salads, the result is a more balanced diet. Even in close personal relationships, a couple may *both* cherish their time together *and* respect each other's need for time apart. As you will see, this *both/and* approach also applies to achieving balance in group interactions.

Group Dialectics

We define **group dialectics** as the contradictory tensions groups experience as they work toward a common goal. Effective groups engage in a cooperative effort to balance group dialectics through effective communication strategies.

Although the word **dialectics** may be new to you, it captures the way in which successful groups balance competing pressures. It may help you to remember that the prefix *di-* means two, as in diagonal (joining two opposite points) or dialogue (a conversation between two people). Dialectics is a method for examining and resolving two contradictory or opposing ideas.

Successful groups balance dialectic tensions by using the *both/and* approach. For example, in some groups, you may *both* enjoy warm friendships with some members *and*

Theory in Groups

Relational Dialectics Theory

Communication scholars Leslie Baxter and Barbara Montgomery use the term *dialectics* to describe the complex and contradictory nature of personal relationships. Their **Relational Dialectics Theory** claims that relationships are characterized by ongoing, dialectic tensions between the multiple contradictions, complexities, and changes in human experiences.[30] The following pairs of common folk proverbs illustrate such contradictory, dialectic tensions:

"Opposites attract," *but* "Birds of a feather flock together."

"Two's company; three's a crowd," *but* "The more, the merrier."[31]

Rather than trying to prove that one of these contradictory proverbs is truer than the other—an *either/or* response—relational dialectics takes a *both/and* approach. There are several ways to resolve relational dialectic tensions:

- You can choose different options for different situations or different points in time. *Example:* A group's monthly meeting always follows a highly structured agenda. When group members have difficulty coming up with a new ideas or possible solutions to a problem, however, you may set aside the agenda and do some unstructured brainstorming.
- You can choose one option and ignore the other. *Example:* Even though a group knows that two absent members would vote against a proposal they're discussing, they go ahead and make the decision anyway.

Generally, choosing one option over another is the *least* effective way to resolve relational dialectics because you or someone else must "give up" or "lose" one option over another. Engaging *both* options to some degree is usually a better way.

Figure 1.6 Group Dialectics

Group Dialectics	Balancing Group Dialectics
Individual Goals ↔ Group Goals	Members' personal goals are *balanced* with the group's common goal.
Conflict ↔ Cohesion	The value of constructive conflict is *balanced* with the need for unity and cohesiveness.
Conforming ↔ Nonconforming	A commitment to group norms and standards is *balanced* with a willingness to differ and change.
Task Dimensions ↔ Social Dimensions	The responsibility and motivation to complete tasks are *balanced* with promoting member relationships.
Homogeneous ↔ Heterogeneous	Member similarities are *balanced* with member differences in skills, roles, personal characteristics, and cultural perspectives.
Leadership ↔ Followership	Effective and ethical leadership is *balanced* with committed and responsible followership.
Structure ↔ Spontaneity	The need for structured procedures is *balanced* with the need for innovative and creative thinking.
Engaged ↔ Disengaged	Member energy and labor are *balanced* with the group's need for rest and renewal.
Open System ↔ Closed System	External support and recognition are *balanced* with internal group solidarity and rewards.

effectively cope with members who are difficult. Your group may want *both* a stable, predictable process in some situations *and* the freedom to experiment and change in other circumstances. In Figure 1.6 we present nine dialectic tensions that are balanced in effective groups.[32]

Individual Goals ↔ Group Goals.   A group will not function well—or at all—if members focus entirely on their individual goals rather than on the group's common goal. When a group agrees upon a clear and important goal, members can pursue both individual *and* group goals as long as their personal goals do not undermine the group goal. For example, if you join a group because you're interested in forming a romantic attachment with another member, you may strongly support the group or its goal, because, hopefully, it will impress the person you desire.

In the best of groups, your personal goals support the group's common goal. If you do not share the group's goal, you may become frustrated or try to undermine the group. In ideal groups, members negotiate their personal needs and interests to achieve a balance between the dialectic tension of being an independent member in an interdependent group.

Successful groups learn to balance the competing and contradictory forces that operate in all groups. How does a cheerleading squad balance dialectic factors such as the squad's task and social functions, individual and group needs, the responsibilities of leadership and followership, and the homogeneous and heterogeneous characteristics of group members?

Conflict ⟷ Cohesion. Conflict is unavoidable in effective groups. How else can members express disagreements that may lead to better solutions? How else can groups ensure that ethical standards are upheld? Groups without constructive conflict are groups without the means to analyze the wisdom of their decisions. At the same time, groups also benefit from cohesion—the mutual attraction that holds the members of a group together. All for one and one for all! Cohesive groups are committed and unified, but they are also willing to engage in conflict. Chapter 9, "Conflict and Cohesion in Groups," examines the conflict–cohesiveness dialectic in detail.

Conforming ⟷ Nonconforming. Group norms (accepted standards of behavior) affect the quality and quantity of work by group members. Dialectic tensions can arise, however, when one or more members challenge a group norm or standard. At the same time, constructive criticism that promotes a group's goal can contribute to group effectiveness. In Chapter 2, "Group Development," we explore the ways in which group norms address the need for both conformity and nonconformity.

Task Dimensions ⟷ Social Dimensions. The best groups negotiate the task/social dialectic by balancing work with pleasure. A group's **task dimension** focuses on the job—the goal or product of group effort. The **social dimension** is concerned with people—the interpersonal relationships among group members. Thus, a group discussing a department's budget primarily focuses on its task. If, however, at the end of the meeting, the group surprises a member with a cake in celebration of her birthday, the group's focus shifts to the social dimension. More often, groups exhibit both task and social dimensions when they get the job done in a way that makes everyone feel socially accepted and valued.

When groups balance work and play, they are more productive. Think of how frustrating it is to work on a group task when members don't get along. Think of how disappointing it is to work with friends who don't take a task seriously or don't make significant contributions. The old saying "All work and no play makes Jack [or Jill] a dull boy [or girl]" certainly applies to groups. On the other hand, all play and no work can make you unemployed.[33]

Homogeneous ⟷ Heterogeneous. The prefixes *homo* and *hetero* come from the Greek language. *Homo* means "same or similar"; *hetero* means "different." Thus, a **homogeneous group** is composed of members who are the same or very similar to one another, and a **heterogeneous group** includes members who are different from one another. Not surprisingly, there is no such thing as a purely homogeneous group because no two members can be exactly the same. Certainly some groups are more homogeneous than heterogeneous. For example, the Black Caucus in the U.S. Congress will be more homogeneous than the Congress as a whole. The legal team representing a client will be more homogeneous in terms of education, income, professional experience, and lifestyle than the jury selected to hear the case. In Chapter 4, "Diversity in Groups," we emphasize that every person on this earth—and thus every member of a group—is different. And that's a good thing. If every group member were exactly alike, the group would not achieve much more than

Groups of teenagers meet monthly as part of the Joint 13-17 Project that helps impoverished Jewish families in Argentina. The project provides a social assistance network for members of the Jewish community. How would you describe this type of group in terms of its task and social dimensions?

one member working alone. At the same time, similarities assure members that they share some common characteristics, traits, and attitudes.

Leadership ⟷ Followership.   Chapter 5, "Group Leadership," examines the components and challenges of effective leadership. Here, we only note that effective leadership is not a solo task—it requires competent and responsible followers. Effective leaders have the confidence to put their egos aside and bring out the leadership in others.[34] When group members assume specific leadership functions, the group has achieved an optimum balance of leadership and followership.

Structure ⟷ Spontaneity.   In Chapter 10, "Structured and Creative Problem Solving in Groups," we quote group communication scholar Marshall Scott Poole, who describes procedures as "the heart of group work [and] the most powerful tools we have to improve the conduct of meetings."[35] Structured procedures help groups balance participation, resolve conflicts, organize discussions, and solve problems. If a group becomes obsessed with rigid procedures, however, it misses out on the benefits of spontaneity and creativity. Whether it's just "thinking outside the box" or organizing a creative problem-solving session, groups can reap enormous benefits by encouraging innovation and "what-if" thinking. Effective groups balance the need for structure with time for spontaneous and creative thinking.

Engaged ⟷ Disengaged.   The engaged–disengaged dialectic has two dimensions—one related to the amount of activity, the other related to the level of commitment. Groups often experience two opposite types of activities: high-energy, nonstop action relieved by periods of relaxation and renewal. Effective groups understand that racing toward a distant finish line may only exhaust group members and leave some sitting on the sidelines. At the same time, low energy and inaction will accomplish nothing. Balancing the urge to run with the need for rest and renewal challenges most groups.

Groups in Balance...

Enjoy Working Together

Have you or a group you're in ever been totally caught up in what you were doing, wholly focused on it, and also able to perform at a very high level with ease?[36] If your answer is *yes*, you have had an **optimal group experience**. When groups provide optimal experiences, members are highly motivated. They are committed and inspired. Creative thinking comes easily and working on the task is pleasurable. Hard work is energizing rather than exhausting. Some groups find the optimal experience so pleasurable that they'd rather do group work than relax or socialize.[37]

To achieve this optimal level of motivation, you and your group must negotiate several dialectic tensions. First, you must have a worthy goal that motivates *both* individual members *and* the group as a whole. You must balance *both* task *and* social dimensions by encouraging members to complete tasks and by promoting strong interpersonal relationships. You must *both* support and reward member engagement *and* accommodate members who need to disengage by pausing, recharging, and relaxing.

Sometimes, high-energy action is unstoppable because group members are extremely motivated, personally committed, and appropriately rewarded for their work. Stopping to recharge or relax would only frustrate a group with pent-up energy. At the other end of the dialectic spectrum, groups that plod through problems with little enthusiasm may be unmotivated, uncaring, and unrewarded for their work. Asking them to pick up speed would only increase their resentment.

Open System ↔ Closed System.   Although all groups are systems, effective groups maintain a balance by moving between open and closed systems. When a group functions as an open system, it welcomes input from and interaction with its environment. That input can be the opinions of nongroup members, information from outside research, or challenges from competing groups. When a group functions as a closed system, it guards its boundaries and discourages input or interaction with the outside. Depending on the situation, a group may open its boundaries and welcome input or close them to protect the group and its work. Effective groups understand that there are times when they must function as an open system and other times when they must close the door and work in private. For example, a hiring committee may function as an open system in order to recruit candidates and research their backgrounds. When they have finished this process, they meet privately and confidentially to evaluate the candidates and make a hiring recommendation.

Ethics Group Communication

Ethics requires an understanding of whether behaviors meet agreed-upon standards of right and wrong.[38] Ethical questions—Are we doing the right thing? Is he dishonest? Is she tolerant of different viewpoints?—arise whenever we communicate because communication has consequences. What you say and do can help or hurt both group members and other people who are affected by the group's decisions and actions.

Ethics in Balance

Initially, you may think that the "rules" of ethical behavior are absolute: "Thou shalt not steal," or "Thou shalt not tell a lie." Is it ethical, however, to steal a loaf of bread if

Groups in Balance...

Empower Members

Group empowerment is a documented dimension of successful groups and teams. **Empowerment** describes a shift in power and authority in a group so that members assume responsibility for their work. Rather than relying on a senior manager, boss, or designated leader to direct their work, empowered groups have the authority to make relevant decisions and carry out their work effectively.[39]

A study by management expert Bradley L. Kirkman explains that empowered groups are more successful and generally share four characteristics:[40]

- *Potency.* The group believes it has the power and ability to achieve its common goal.

- *Meaningfulness.* The group believes that its common goal is important, valuable, and worthwhile.
- *Autonomy.* The group is optimistic about achieving its goal because it has the freedom to make decisions and implement those decisions.
- *Impact.* The group believes that its work produces significant benefits for other people and organizations.

Not surprisingly, members of empowered groups feel powerful and able to control how the group works toward achieving its goal.[41] Empowered groups enjoy a sense of excitement about their work. Members genuinely respect and like one another. They also look forward to working with one another to achieve common goals.

your family is starving? Is it acceptable to lie if telling the truth would do more harm than good? There are often dialectic tensions involved in making ethical decisions.

The ancient Greek philosopher Aristotle offered his "doctrine of the mean"[42] (*mean* as in "a point between extremes," not *mean* as in "nasty" or "cruel"). He suggested that when you face an ethical decision, you should select an *appropriate* reaction somewhere between two extremes—such as a response somewhere between expressing mild annoyance at one extreme and uncontrolled rage at the other extreme. Aristotle maintained that anyone can become angry—that is easy. But to be angry at the right things, with the right people, to the right degree, at the right time, for the right purpose, and in the right way is worthy of praise.[43]

Ethical questions arise whenever you work in groups. Is it ethical to share gossip about a job candidate in order to make sure a group doesn't hire that person? Is it acceptable to tell exaggerated, heartbreaking stories about children who go hungry every day to persuade a group to financially support a local food bank? Is it fair for some group members to boycott a meeting because they are strongly opposed to the politics of a person who has been invited to participate in the meeting? Aristotle would tell us to avoid a yes or no answer. An ethical group and its members seek an appropriate and ethical *both/and* response. Throughout this textbook, we provide regular features about group ethics that address issues that you and your group will face as you work collectively toward a common goal.

Credo for Ethical Communication

The National Communication Association (NCA) provides a credo for ethical communication.[44] In Latin, the word *credo* means "I believe." Thus, an ethics credo is a belief statement about what it means to be an ethical communicator. All of these ethical principles apply to working in groups. Ethical communication requires an understanding of the tensions that operate in all groups as well as a desire to communicate in a way that meets agreed-upon standards of right and wrong.

Ethics in Groups

The National Communication Association Credo for Ethical Communication

Preamble

Questions of right and wrong arise whenever people communicate. Ethical communication is fundamental to responsible thinking, decision making, and the development of relationships and communities within and across contexts, cultures, channels, and media. Moreover, ethical communication enhances human worth and dignity by fostering truthfulness, fairness, responsibility, personal integrity, and respect for self and others. We believe that unethical communication threatens the well-being of individuals and the society in which we live. Therefore we, the members of the National Communication Association, endorse and are committed to practicing the following principles of ethical communication

Principles of Ethical Communication

- We advocate truthfulness, accuracy, honesty, and reason as essential to the integrity of communication.

- We endorse freedom of expression, diversity of perspective, and tolerance of dissent to achieve the informed and responsible decision making fundamental to a civil society.

- We strive to understand and respect other communicators before evaluating and responding to their messages.

- We promote access to communication resources and opportunities as necessary to fulfill human potential and contribute to the well-being of families, communities, and society.

- We promote communication climates of caring and mutual understanding that respect the unique needs and characteristics of individual communicators.

- We condemn communication that degrades individuals and humanity through distortion, intimidation, coercion, and violence, and through the expression of intolerance and hatred.

- We are committed to the courageous expression of personal conviction in pursuit of fairness and justice.

- We advocate sharing information, opinions, and feelings when facing significant choices while also respecting privacy and confidentiality.

- We accept responsibility for the short- and long-term consequences of our own communication and expect the same of others.

Summary Study Guide

Succeeding in Groups

- Working in groups is an inescapable part of everyday life; most people spend a considerable amount of time and energy working in groups.
- Many employers view group-related skills as more important than written communication skills, proficiency in the field of study, and computer skills.

Defining Group Communication

- Group communication is the interaction of three or more interdependent people working to achieve a common goal.
- A clear goal is the most significant factor separating successful groups from unsuccessful groups.
- Types of groups include primary, social, self-help, learning, service, civic, work, and public groups.
- Virtual groups rely on technology to communicate synchronously and/or asynchronously.

Advantages and Disadvantages of Working in Groups

- Advantages: superior performance, greater member satisfaction, learning, cultural sensitivity, creative thinking, and civic engagement.
- Disadvantages: the amount of time, energy, and resources expended by groups; the potential for interpersonal conflicts and people problems.

The Nature of Group Communication

- Understanding and applying theories, strategies, and skills are inseparable components in learning about group communication.
- Basic elements of the group communication process: members, messages, channels, feedback, noise, and context.
- Groups are complex systems in which the actions of individual members affect everyone in the group as well as the outcome of group work.

Balance: The Guiding Principle of Group Work

- Group dialectics represent the balance between competing and contradictory components of group work by taking a *both/and* approach to resolving such tensions.
- The nine group dialectics: individual goals ↔ group goals; conflict ↔ cohesion; conforming ↔ nonconforming; task dimensions ↔ social dimensions; homogeneous ↔ heterogeneous; leadership ↔ followership; structure ↔ spontaneity; engaged ↔ disengaged; open system ↔ closed system.

Ethics and Group Communication

- The National Communication Association (NCA) Credo for Ethical Communication sets forth guiding principles to assess how well communication behaviors meet agreed-upon standards of right and wrong.

GroupWork

The Ethics Credo in Action

Directions: Review the preamble and principles in the NCA Credo for Ethical Communication. The following table lists each of the ethical principles with an example to demonstrate its application to groups. Consider the principle and the example, then work with your group to supply a second example that demonstrates your understanding of each principle. The example can be a situation you have experienced personally, or it can be taken from current events or from history.

Applying the Credo for Ethical Communication to Working in Groups

Credo for Ethical Communication Principles	Examples of Application to Working in Groups	Student Group Example
1. Truthfulness, accuracy, honesty, and reason are essential for ethical communication.	Groups should urge members to accurately quote and cite the sources of researched information.	
2. Freedom of expression, diversity of perspective, and tolerance of dissent are fundamental to a civil society.	Groups should create a supportive climate in which members feel free to express their ideas, opinions, and feelings.	
3. Ethical communicators understand and respect others before evaluating and responding to their messages.	Group members should strive to understand one another's messages before making judgments.	
4. Access to communication resources and opportunities are necessary to fulfill human potential and contribute to the well-being of families, communities, and society.	When working in virtual groups, group members should have access to similar equipment and software.	
5. Ethical communicators promote climates of caring and mutual understanding that respect the unique needs and characteristics of individual communicators.	Groups should respect and adapt to members whose cultural backgrounds are different than the majority of group members.	
6. Ethical communicators condemn communication that degrades individuals and humanity through distortion, intimidation, coercion, and violence, and through the expression of intolerance and hatred.	Group members should not tolerate statements that belittle or stereotype other group members.	
7. Ethical communicators express their personal convictions in pursuit of fairness and justice.	Group members should be encouraged to express well-informed and reasonable arguments.	
8. Ethical communicators share information, opinions, and feelings when facing significant choices while also respecting privacy and confidentiality.	Group leaders should keep members informed about their individual progress in private and in confidence.	
9. Ethical communicators accept responsibility for the short- and long-term consequences of their own communication and expect the same of others.	Group members who are justly criticized for disrupting group process should accept the consequences of their actions.	

Group Assessment

Group Communication Competencies Survey

Directions: On a 5-point scale, where 5 is "extremely important" and 1 is "not at all important," rate the following types of group competencies in terms of their importance for becoming a *highly effective* group member. Please circle one number for each item. When you are finished, ask yourself this question: How competent am *I* in the "extremely important" areas?

If time is available, form groups of five to seven students. Each group should identify five or six items that, in the group's collective opinion, are the most important group communication competencies. When all of the groups have identified their top items, a group representative should write them on the board or be prepared to share them verbally.

Member and Group Competencies	Extremely Important	Very Important	Somewhat Important	Not Very Important	Not at All Important
1. Understand the group communication process.	5	4	3	2	1
2. Reduce your nervousness when speaking in a discussion or meeting.	5	4	3	2	1
3. Understand, respect, and adapt to diverse group members.	5	4	3	2	1
4. Communicate openly and ethically.	5	4	3	2	1
5. Carry out critical task roles (ask questions, summarize ideas) and/or social roles (encourage and support members).	5	4	3	2	1
6. Influence group members to change their attitudes and/or behavior.	5	4	3	2	1
7. Use and interpret nonverbal communication effectively.	5	4	3	2	1
8. Develop clear group goals.	5	4	3	2	1
9. Listen appropriately and effectively to other members.	5	4	3	2	1
10. Intervene appropriately to resolve member and group problems.	5	4	3	2	1
11. Develop good interpersonal relationships with group members.	5	4	3	2	1
12. Manage and resolve interpersonal conflicts.	5	4	3	2	1
13. Develop and follow a well-organized meeting agenda.	5	4	3	2	1
14. Actively contribute to group discussions.	5	4	3	2	1
15. Use gestures, body language, and eye contact effectively.	5	4	3	2	1

(continued)

16. Demonstrate strong leadership skills.	5	4	3	2	1
17. Research and share important ideas and information with group members.	5	4	3	2	1
18. Use visual aids and presentation software effectively.	5	4	3	2	1
19. Plan and conduct effective meetings.	5	4	3	2	1
20. Use appropriate procedures for group decision making and problem solving.	5	4	3	2	1
21. Ask questions to clarify ideas and get needed information.	5	4	3	2	1
22. Motivate group members.	5	4	3	2	1
23. Use assertiveness strategies and skills confidently and effectively.	5	4	3	2	1
24. Respect and adapt to group norms (standards of behavior).	5	4	3	2	1
25. Prepare and deliver effective presentations or oral reports.	5	4	3	2	1
26. Use appropriate and effective words in a group discussion.	5	4	3	2	1
27. Use parliamentary procedure effectively and fairly in meetings.	5	4	3	2	1
28. Use effective technologies and skills to communicate in virtual groups.	5	4	3	2	1
29. Develop and present valid arguments and opinions in a group discussion.	5	4	3	2	1
30. Provide appropriate emotional support to group members.	5	4	3	2	1
31. Other strategies or skills:					
a. _____	5	4	3	2	1
b. _____	5	4	3	2	1
c. _____	5	4	3	2	1

Group Development

Chapter Outline

Case Study

Nice to Meet You, Too

A group of community volunteers meets for the first time to plan and raise funds for building a neighborhood playground. Although Dave, Betty, Ray, Bill, and Aisha live in the same community, they don't know one another well or at all. They begin the meeting by introducing themselves. They all smile a lot, but communication seems a bit stiff and awkward. Betty's handshake connects to other members only at her fingertips, while Ray and Bill offer firm handshakes. As Aisha introduces herself, she giggles and runs a hand through her long hair. Dave sits at the head of the table and chairs the meeting.

Aisha has come to the meeting well prepared. She hesitantly raises her hand to speak, and Dave recognizes her. She reports that, according to her research, a simple playground can range from $5,000 to $50,000. She suggests that $35,000 would be a good target budget. Bill starts to respond by saying, "Well, uh…" but when he sees that Ray has raised his hand, he concludes with "Go ahead." Ray says, "Oh, I was going to say—ah—I've looked it over a bit—$35,000 is—ah—I don't know—I guess that would be good, but I think we should stay as high as we can." Bill now responds with "Ah—I was thinking just the opposite—kind of—we should go lower—uh…." Dave interrupts and suggests that they go with the $35,000 Aisha proposed, just to get started. Bill seems a bit annoyed with Dave's suggestion, but doesn't say anything.

Dave notes that regardless of the cost, they need to discuss ways of raising money for the playground. At this point Aisha begins taking notes. Betty says, "Well—it worked at our church—in the other city where I lived…we had great bake sales—twice a year." Ray politely tells Betty that a bake sale is a great idea, but that it may not raise enough funds. The rest of the group grimaces and ignores Betty's offer to run a bake sale. Aisha then asks if group members know anyone who works for a foundation that might donate some of the money. Betty reveals that she has a dear friend who is actively involved in a large, local foundation. The group sits up and pays a lot more attention to Betty. Ray even jokes that maybe the foundation can help with the bake sale, too. Everyone laughs.

Only three minutes of the meeting have gone by. The group has a lot more to discuss but members have slowly become better acquainted with one another and have a better feeling about how they will work together and get along.

When you finish reading this chapter, you should be able to answer the following critical thinking questions about this case study:

1 What verbal and nonverbal behaviors demonstrated the forming stage of group development?

2 In your opinion, which members are most likely to compete for status and influence in the storming stage?

3 What strategies did group members use or should they have used to decrease primary tension?

4 What, if any, dialectic tensions will affect how well this group achieves its goal and how well members get along with one another?

Planning the Playground

The Group Project

Before you read any further, visit Pearson's MyCommunicationLab website and watch this case study's video, "Planning the Playground." You may also want to watch the short video, "The Group Project," which illustrates Chapter 2 concepts. Each video comes with a set of study questions to keep in mind as you read this chapter.

Group Development Stages

How do you behave when you attend the first meeting of a new group? Do you march into the room briskly, extend your hand to the first person you see, and say "Hi, I'm (your name)—Nice to meet you"? Or do you pause at the door, check things out as you move into the room, and look for a suitable moment to introduce yourself? Like many people, you may choose the second, more cautious entrance. Welcome to the world of group development! In this chapter, we examine how groups form and evolve as they try to balance the complex and contradictory dialectic tensions inevitable in group work.

Follow the Research

Group Development Models

Group development research began in the early 1950s and continues to this day. Dozens of theoretical models describe how a group moves through several "passages" during its lifetime.[1] By observing the behavior of groups and their members in a variety of settings and circumstances, researchers have identified distinct phases that groups experience as members work with one another to achieve a common goal. They also suggested that most groups need to move through at least four stages in order to achieve maximum effectiveness.[2]

The table to the right summarizes three major group development models. Although each model uses different words to describe the process, the descriptions of group development are strikingly similar.

All three of these development models are linear: They describe development stages as small changes that follow one another in a fixed path.[3] However, many groups don't move through each successive stage systematically or as though they are running a clearly marked obstacle course. Most groups work through a stage until circumstances motivate them to take on the challenges of another stage. Factors such as "changes in membership, external demands, and changes in leader-

ship" may slow development or push a group back to a previous stage.[4]

Group communication scholar Marshall Scott Poole suggests that the stages described in most theoretical models may be "ideal" steps, but that groups often stray from the ideal.[5] For example, a very large, new group may have difficulty getting itself going, whereas a smaller group whose members have previously worked together may skip or move quickly through the early stages. Also, if a group's goal is unclear, the result can be wasted time, member frustration, and unproductive work. If, however, the group's goal is clear and members are cooperative, the group is more likely to move through the stages with ease.

Group Development Models

Bruce Tuckman[6]	• Forming
	• Storming
	• Norming
	• Performing
	• Adjourning
B. Aubrey Fisher[7]	• Orientation
	• Conflict
	• Emergence
	• Reinforcing
Susan Wheelan[8]	• Dependency and Inclusion
	• Counterdependency and Fight
	• Trust and Structure
	• Work and Productivity
	• Termination

There are recognizable milestones in the lives of most groups. Like individuals, groups move through stages as they develop and mature. An "infant" group behaves differently than a group that has worked together for a long time and has matured into an "adult." A group's ability to "grow up" directly affects how well its members work together to achieve a common goal.

Bruce W. Tuckman, an educational psychologist, identified four discrete stages in the life cycle of groups—forming, storming, norming, and performing.[9] He and Mary Ann Jensen later refined the model by adding a fifth stage—adjourning.[10] In this chapter, we use **Tuckman's Group Development Stages** model (see Figure 2.1) because it is well recognized in communication and business management literature, it is easy to remember, and it remains one of the most comprehensive models of group development relevant to *all* types of groups.[11]

Figure 2.1 Tuckman's Group Development Stages

Forming	Storming	Norming	Performing	Adjourning
Members are socially cautious and polite.	Members compete for status and openly disagree.	Members resolve status conflicts and establish norms.	Members assume appropriate roles and work productively.	Members disengage and relinquish responsibilities.

Forming Stage

When you join a group, you rarely know what to expect. Will everyone get along together and work hard? Will you make a good first impression? Will this be a positive group experience or a nightmare? Most people enter a new group with caution.

During the initial **forming stage**, members carefully explore *both* their personal goals *and* the group's goal. They may be tentative and somewhat uncomfortable about working with a group of strangers or unfamiliar colleagues. They try to understand their tasks, test personal relationships, and determine what behaviors are acceptable. Although little gets done during this orientation phase, members need this time to become acquainted with one another and to assess the group's goal. At this point in the group development process, "the most important job…is not to build a better rocket or debug…a new software product or double sales—it is to orient itself to itself."[12]

Primary Tension. Group communication scholar Ernest G. Bormann describes **primary tension** as the social unease and stiffness that accompanies the getting-acquainted stage in a new group.[13] Because most members of a new group want to create a good first impression, they tend to be overly polite with one another. Members don't interrupt one another, and there may be long, awkward pauses between comments. When members do speak, they often speak softly and avoid expressing strong opinions. Although laughter may occur, it is often strained, inappropriate, or uncomfortable. When the group starts its discussion, the topic may be small talk about sports, the weather, or a recent news event.

A group that experiences primary tension may talk less, provide little in the way of ideas and opinions, and be perceived as ineffective. Before a group can work efficiently and effectively, members should try to reduce primary tension. In some groups, primary tension lasts for only a few minutes. In less fortunate groups, primary tension may continue for months, but eventually it should decrease as members come to feel more comfortable with one another.

> ### Remember This
> "Early socialization experiences have a long-term impact on newcomers' satisfaction, performance, and intention to stay in a group."[14]

Groups in Balance...

Socialize Newcomers

In some instances you will be a newcomer to an already well established group. Not surprisingly, your experiences in other groups affect how you adapt to and communicate with new group members. Understanding the socialization process can help you reduce the uncertainty that accompanies every new group experience.

In the context of group communication, **socialization** refers to "the process by which an individual acquires the social knowledge and skills necessary to assume an organizational role."[15] The socialization process is important in groups because "positive socialization creates stronger commitments to confront and balance the multiple issues and tensions involved in participating in group activities."[16] Carolyn Anderson and her colleagues describe the ways in which group members move through five phases as they experience the socialization process:

1. **Antecedent phase.** A newcomer brings beliefs and attitudes, cultural dimensions, needs and motives, communication skills, personality traits, knowledge, and prior group experiences to a new group. These factors can influence how well the group accepts the newcomer: If the group needs and values what the newcomer has to offer, socialization will be faster and easier.

2. **Anticipatory phase.** Members of an established group have expectations about newcomers. They may look for someone with certain types of knowledge or communication skills. They may

have heard that the newcomer shares their beliefs and attitudes. Socialization is more likely to succeed if the newcomer's characteristics and motives align with the group's expectations.

3. **Encounter phase.** During the encounter phase, newcomers try to fit in by adjusting to group expectations, assuming needed roles, communicating effectively, and finding an appropriate balance between individual goals and the group's goals.

4. **Assimilation phase.** During this phase, newcomers become fully integrated into the group's culture. Established members and newcomers blend into a comfortable state of working together to achieve common goals.

5. **Exit phase.** Some groups, such as families, may never disband, although they change as new members join and others leave. Working groups manage this process by giving departing members a warm send-off and welcoming new members who take their place. Regardless of the reason (whether positive or negative), leaving an established group can be a difficult experience.[17]

Generally, newcomers can gain acceptance by asking the group for help or information, offering assistance to other group members, and conforming to group norms.[18] Socialization in groups is a give-and-take process in which members and groups come together to satisfy needs and accomplish goals.

Resolving Primary Tension.   Although primary tension often disappears quickly and naturally as group members get to know one another and gain confidence, some groups need direct intervention to relieve this early form of tension.

Recognizing and discussing primary tension is one way of breaking its cycle. A perceptive member may purposely behave in a way that counteracts primary tension, such as talking in a strong voice, looking involved and energized, sticking to the group's topic, and expressing an opinion. Here are some additional suggestions for resolving primary tension:

- Be positive and energetic. Smile. Nod in agreement. Laugh. Exhibit enthusiasm.
- Be patient and open-minded, knowing that primary tension should decrease with time.
- Be prepared and informed before your first meeting so you can help the group focus on its task.

Storming Stage

After spending some time in the forming stage, group members realize that "being nice" to one another may not accomplish very much, particularly when there are critical issues to address and problems to solve. As a group gradually moves from the forming stage to the storming stage, disagreements arise.

In the **storming stage,** groups address the conflict↔cohesion dialectic and the leadership↔followership dialectic. Some members lose their patience with forming stage niceties, while others begin competing with one another to determine their status and to establish group roles. During this stage, group members may become argumentative and emotional. As the group tries to get down to business, the most confident members begin to compete for both social acceptance and leadership. They openly disagree on issues of substance. It is still too early in the group's existence, however, to predict the outcome of such competition.

Many groups try to skip this stage in order to avoid competition and conflict. However, storming is a necessary part of a group's development. Without it, a group may fail to establish productive member roles, appropriate leadership responsibilities, and clear goals.

Secondary Tension.   The frustrations and personality conflicts experienced by group members as they compete for acceptance and achievement within a group are the source of what Bormann calls **secondary tension.**[19] Whereas primary tension arises from lack of confidence, secondary tension emerges when members have gained enough confidence to become assertive and even aggressive as they pursue positions of power and influence. Conflicts can result from disagreements over issues, conflicts in values, or an inability to deal with disruptive members. Regardless of the causes, a group cannot hope to achieve its common goal without managing secondary tension.

The signs of secondary tension are almost the direct opposite of those of primary tension. There is a high level of energy and agitation. The group is noisier, more dynamic, and physically active. Members speak in louder voices, interrupting and overlapping one another so that two or three people may be speaking at the same time. Members sit up straight, lean forward, or squirm in their seats. Everyone is alert and listening intently.

Resolving Secondary Tension.   Members of successful groups develop ways to handle this phase in a group's development. Often, one or two members will joke about the tension. The resulting laughter is likely to ease the stress. If secondary tension threatens to disable a group, someone needs to bring up secondary tension as an issue that the group needs to recognize and minimize by focusing on the group's goal. As was the case with primary tension, members should be patient and open-minded, knowing that secondary tension should decrease with time. In some cases, members will work outside the group setting to discuss the personal difficulties and anxieties of group members. Dealing with secondary tension can be difficult and even painful. However, when a group successfully resolves interpersonal problems, it can become an effective and cohesive work group.

| Primary Tension | Secondary Tension |

Most groups experience some form of primary and secondary tension during the forming and storming stages. In fact, a little bit of tension is a good thing. It can motivate a group toward action and increase a group's sensitivity to feedback. Effective groups learn to balance the need for both conflict and cohesion. As group communication scholars Donald Ellis and Aubrey Fisher point out, "the successful and socially healthy group is not characterized by an absence of social tension, but by successful management of social tension."[20]

Norming Stage

During the forming and storming stages, groups lack balance; they are either too cautious or too confrontational. Once a group moves to the **norming stage,** members resolve these early tensions and learn to work as a committed and unified team. "Group members accept the group and accept the idiosyncrasies of fellow members."[21] As members begin to build trust in one another, they are more willing to disagree and express opinions. They develop methods for achieving group goals and establish norms and "rules of engagement." "Communication becomes more open and task oriented" as "members solidify positive working relationships with each other."[22]

There is more order and direction during this third stage of group development. Members have begun to balance a wide range of group dialectics, with special emphasis on norms (conforming↔nonconforming), task requirements (structure↔spontaneity), and adapting to member characteristics (homogeneous↔heterogeneous).

Performing Stage

When a group reaches the **performing stage,** members are fully engaged and eager to work. Roles and responsibilities are fluid; they adapt and change according to group needs and task requirements. In this stage, group identity, loyalty, and morale are generally high. When groups reach the performing stage, members focus their energies on both the task and social dimensions of group work as they make major decisions and solve critical problems. Just about everyone shares in and supports a unified effort to achieve a common goal. Although disagreements occur, they are usually resolved intelligently and amicably. During this stage, "interaction patterns reflect virtually no tension; rather, the members are jovial, loud, boisterous, laughing, and verbally backslapping each other."[23]

Chapter 9, "Structured and Creative Problem Solving in Groups," offers strategies that help groups solve problems and make decisions effectively during the performing stage.

Adjourning Stage

When a group reaches the **adjourning stage,** it has usually achieved its common goals and may begin to disband.[24] Groups end their work and their existence for many reasons. After achieving a goal or completing an assigned task, a group may

Virtual Groups

Developmental Tasks

Most group development theories assume that members interact face to face at the same time and in the same place. This assumption does not apply when describing development stages in virtual groups. Two developmental features of virtual groups require added attention:

- The planning, organization, and use of technology add components to each stage of group development.
- Members' technical expertise, attitudes about, and confidence with technology can all affect how groups move through group development stages.

Forming Stage

During the forming stage of virtual groups, members begin to develop codes of virtual conduct, to review software and hardware requirements, and to raise and answer questions about how they will use technology to accomplish the group's goals. Because resolving this stage is critical to group development, some virtual groups arrange a face-to-face meeting before going online, especially when members "do not know each other and the project or work is complex and requires a high degree of interaction. Face-to-face orientation meetings also help orient groups when the task is new and ambiguous."[25]

Storming Stage

During a virtual group's storming stage, members must deal with the added complication imposed by the virtual environment. In addition to expressing opinions and debating substantive issues, the group may encounter technical problems and different levels in member expertise. For example, whereas some members can tolerate and adjust to a bad phone connection or slow online response rate, for other members—perhaps a non-native English speaker, a member who is hearing impaired, or a slow typist—these challenges can make interaction difficult or unintelligible. What should the group do if technical systems are not compatible, or if some members are technically unskilled or apprehensive about using advanced technology? Virtual groups must solve technical problems if they hope to address task-related issues and move beyond the storming stage.

Norming Stage

In the norming stage, virtual groups define members' roles, resolve conflicts, solve most technical problems, and accept the group's norms for interaction. They will be ready to focus on the task. They will also resolve issues related to differences in time, distance, technology, member cultures, and organizational environments. At this point, the group is ready to begin working virtually and effectively.

Performing Stage

Once a virtual group reaches the performing stage, members engage in ongoing virtual interaction and encourage equal participation by all members. They have overcome or adjusted to technical roadblocks and have become comfortable with the virtual media used by the group.

Adjourning Stage

Finally, a group may rely on virtual communication to blunt the separation anxiety that comes with the adjourning stage. If a group has matured and performed well, its members will be reluctant to give up their relationships with their colleagues. Even if a virtual group no longer operates in an official capacity, members may continue to use technological media to consult and interact with one another.

have no reason to continue. In other cases, individual members leave a group for personal or professional reasons or to seek out and join another group.

When an entire group disbands, most members experience the stress that comes with relinquishing group responsibilities. They also confront relational issues such as how to retain friendships with other members.[26] Although members are often proud of what they've achieved, they may also feel a sense of loss when the group dissolves. When groups adjourn, the dialectic balance shifts from engagement to disengagement. Some writers describe this fifth stage as "mourning," which recognizes the loss felt by group members.[27]

Group Goals

An effective group has *both* a clear understanding of its goal *and* a belief that its goal is meaningful and worthwhile.[28] In a three-year study of characteristics that explain how and why effective groups develop, Carl Larson and Frank LaFasto found "a clear and elevated goal" to be the top attribute on the list.[29] The Apollo Moon Project, initiated during the Kennedy administration, is a good example. Which goal is more motivating: "To be leaders in space exploration" or "To land a man on the moon by the end of the 1960s"? Fortunately, NASA adopted the second goal, and its simple words were both clear and inspiring.[30] Any old goal is not enough.

Clear, elevated goals challenge group members and give them the opportunity to excel—both as individuals and as a group. Here is how Larson and LaFasto describe what happens when groups work to achieve such goals:

> [Groups] lose their sense of time. They discover to their surprise that it's dark outside and they worked right through the supper hours. The rate of communication among team members increases dramatically, even to the point that individuals call each other at all hours of the night because they can't get something out of their minds. There is a sense of great excitement and feelings of elation whenever even minor progress is made toward the goal.[31]

Establishing Group Goals

If your group is given what someone *else* thinks is a clear and elevated goal, group members may not be impressed or inspired. However, if your group develops its *own* goal, the motivation of members to achieve that goal is heightened.[32] This increase in motivation occurs because group-based goal setting produces a better balance of member and group needs, a better understanding of the group actions needed to achieve the goal, and a better appreciation of how individual members can contribute to group action. Moreover, when group members set the group's goals, the process can create a more interdependent, cooperative, and cohesive environment in which to work.[33]

Group goals should be both specific and challenging. Specific goals lead to higher performance than do generalized goals. For example, telling a group to "do your best"

Rescue teams, NASA astronauts, surgical teams, mountain climbers, and sports teams work together to achieve a goal. What are the characteristics of an effective group goal?

in choosing someone for a job is a generalized goal. A specific goal would be: Review the candidates for the job, recommend three top candidates, and include a list of each top candidate's strengths and weaknesses.

Setting a specific, clear, and elevated goal benefits *every* group. You don't have to be a NASA scientist or a corporate executive to set impressive goals. Even if your only task is to participate in a graded classroom discussion, your group should take the time to develop a set of appropriate goals. For example, in many group communication classes, instructors require students to participate in a problem-solving discussion. The group usually chooses its topic, creates a discussion agenda, and demonstrates its preparation and group communication skills in class. This is nothing like "landing a man on the moon." Yet even a classroom discussion can be more effective if the group establishes a clear, elevated goal, such as "Our group and every member will earn an A on this assignment." In order to achieve this goal, your group will have to do many things: Choose a meaningful discussion topic, prepare a useful agenda, research the topic thoroughly, make sure that every member is well prepared and ready to contribute, and demonstrate effective group communication skills during the discussion.

A clear, elevated goal does more than set your sights on an outcome; it helps your group decide how to get there. Figure 2.2 summarizes some questions to ask in deciding on goals.

Figure 2.2   Questions for Setting Group Goals

Questions for Setting Group Goals
Regardless of the circumstances or the setting, your group will benefit by asking six questions about your goals:[34]
1. **Clarity.** Is the goal clear, specific, and observable if achieved?
2. **Challenge.** Is the goal difficult, inspiring, and thought provoking?
3. **Commitment.** Do members see the goal as meaningful, realistic, and attainable? Are they dedicated to achieving the goal?
4. **Compatibility.** Can *both* group *and* individual goals be achieved?
5. **Cooperation.** Does the goal require cooperation among group members?
6. **Cost.** Does the group have adequate resources, such as time and materials, to achieve the goal?

Balancing Group Goals and Hidden Agendas

As we noted in Chapter 1, a group will *not* function well—or at all—if members only focus on their personal goals rather than on the group's common goal. When a group agrees on a clear and important goal, members can pursue both group *and* individual goals, as long as their personal goals do not undermine the group goal.

Theory in Groups

Goal Theory and Group Work

Researchers Edwin Locke and Gary Latham emphasize the value of setting group goals and methods for accomplishing those goals. Their research establishes a strong relationship between how difficult and specific a goal is and how well people work to achieve it. Likewise, having a goal that's too easy is not a strong motivator. For example, if you set out merely to pass a difficult college course, you may not work hard or feel proud of the results if you succeed. If you strive for an A or B, however, you will work harder, be proud of your work, and, if you succeed, enjoy the rewards that come with achieving an enviable grade in a notoriously "killer" course.

Locke and Latham conclude that groups function best when their goals are (1) specific, (2) hard but realistic, (3) accepted by members, (4) used to evaluate performance, (5) linked to feedback and rewards, (6) set by members and groups, and (7) framed to promote member growth.[35]

Effective goal setting does more than raise group productivity and improve work quality. It also clarifies group and member expectations, increases satisfaction with individual and group performance, and enhances members' self-confidence, pride, and willingness to accept future challenges. Difficult or challenging goals, provided the group accepts them as worthwhile, can lead to greater effort and persistence than do easy goals.[36]

When, however, a member's goal is kept private and is different from the group's common goal, the result is a **hidden agenda.** Hidden agendas represent what people really want rather than what they say they want. Hidden agendas can disrupt the flow of communication. When they become more important than a group's goal, the result can be group frustration and failure because real issues and concerns may be buried while pseudoarguments dominate the discussion.

A student reported this incident in which a hidden agenda disrupted a group's deliberations:

> I was on a student government board that decides how college activities funds should be distributed to student clubs and intramural teams. About halfway through the process, I became aware that several members were active in intramural sports. By the time I noticed their pro-sports voting pattern, they'd gotten most of what they wanted. You wouldn't believe the bizarre reasons they came up with to cut academic clubs while fully supporting the budgets of athletic teams. What made me mad was that they didn't care about what most students wanted; they only wanted to make sure that *their* favorite teams were funded.

If unrecognized and unresolved during the forming stage, hidden agendas can permeate and infect *all* stages of group development. Effective groups deal with hidden agendas by recognizing them and trying to resolve them whenever they occur. If a group member is hesitant to get involved in the group process, or if the group's progress is unusually slow, look for hidden agendas. A question such as "What seems to be hanging us up here?" may encourage members to reveal some of their private concerns. Recognizing the existence of hidden agendas may be sufficient to keep a group moving from one stage to another in its development.

Individual Goals   Group Goals

Even when you recognize the existence of hidden agendas, some of them cannot and should not be shared because they may create an atmosphere of distrust. Not many people would want to deal with the following revelation during a group discussion: "I only joined this group because I thought it would look good on my résumé." Recognizing hidden agendas means knowing that some of them can and should be confronted, whereas others need not be shared with the group.

Groups can resolve the dialectic tensions caused by hidden agendas through early agreement on the group's goals and careful planning of the group's process. Sociologists Rodney Napier and Matti Gershenfeld suggest discussing hidden agendas during the early stages of group development.[37] Initial discussion could include some of the following questions:

- What are the group's goals?
- Does the leader have any personal concerns or goals that differ from these?
- Do any members have any personal concerns or goals that differ from these?
- What outcomes do members expect?

Group Norms

One factor that influences a group's successful passage from the forming to the performing stage is the creation of norms. Communication scholar Patricia Andrews defines **norms** as "sets of expectations held by group members concerning what kinds of behaviors or opinions are acceptable or unacceptable, good or bad, right or wrong, appropriate or inappropriate."[38] Norms serve several important purposes to ensure positive interaction among group members. Group norms:

- express the values of the group.
- help the group to function smoothly.
- define appropriate social behavior.
- help the group survive.[39]

Norms are the group's rules. They affect how members behave, dress, speak, and work. For example, the norms for the members of a company's sales team might include meeting before lunch, applauding one another's successes, and staying late at work without complaining. Without norms, accomplishing group goals would be difficult. There would be no agreed-upon way to organize and perform work.

Some norms, however, can work against a group and its goals. If group norms place a premium on friendly and peaceful discussions, group members may be reluctant to voice disagreement or share bad news. If group norms permit members to arrive late and leave early, meetings may not have enough members to make important decisions. Norms that do not support a group's goal can prevent the group from succeeding.

Group norms are powerful predictors of group behavior. According to Nicky Hayes, a British psychologist, "Group norms are intangible and often difficult to express in words, but that doesn't mean that they are not real. People who belong to groups often try very hard to conform to their group's norms—because the price of failure may be exclusion from the group, or even ridicule."[40]

Types of Norms

There are two general types of group norms—explicit and implicit. Because **explicit norms** are put in writing or are stated verbally, they are easy to recognize. Explicit norms are often imposed on a group. The group leader may have the authority to determine work rules. A large group or organization may have standard procedures that it expects everyone to follow. For example, the workers in a customer service department may be required to wear name badges. The staff members may have recommended this rule, the supervisor may have ordered this "custom," or the company may have established a policy regarding employee identification.

Implicit norms are rarely discussed or openly communicated. As a result, they are not as easy to recognize. Generally, they evolve as members interact with one another. For example, it may take new group members several weeks to learn that meetings begin 15 minutes later than scheduled. Even seating arrangements may be governed by implicit norms: Almost all of us have been unsettled when we walked into a classroom and discovered someone sitting at "our" desk. Although not a word is spoken, offending members may sense that they have violated an implicit norm, whether or not they understand what that norm is. Members who fail to "get it" may be considered insensitive or clueless.

Regardless of whether norms are openly communicated or implicitly understood, they can be divided into four categories: interaction norms, procedural norms, status norms, and achievement norms (see Figure 2.3). **Interaction norms** determine how group members communicate with one another and reveal what types of communication behavior are appropriate in a group. **Procedural norms** dictate how the group operates. Knowing these norms will help you adapt to the rules and procedures the group typically follows. **Status norms** identify the levels of influence among group members and help explain how status (prestige, respect, influence) is determined. **Achievement norms** determine the quality and quantity of work expected from group members. They can help you make decisions about how much time and energy should be devoted to working with a particular group.

Figure 2.3 Types of Norms

	Interaction Norms	Procedural Norms	Status Norms	Achievement Norms
Key Question	What communication behavior is appropriate?	How does the group operate?	Who has power and control?	What are the group's standards?
Implicit Norms	We tend to use the pronouns *we*, *us*, and *our* rather than *I*, *me*, and *my*.	Everyone turns off cell phones and other technologies during meetings.	The group leader always sits at the head of the table.	Everyone shows up on time or early for our scheduled meetings.
Explicit Norms	The group leader is responsible for making sure that everyone gets a chance to speak.	We always get an agenda in advance and use it during our meetings.	When a group vote is tied, the leader casts the deciding vote.	All members *must* have full references for any reports or research they cite.

In Chapter 1, we noted that dialectic tensions can arise when one or more members challenge the group's norms or standards. At the same time, constructive criticism that promotes a group's goal can contribute to group effectiveness. As you read about the conformity↔nonconformity dialectic, think of the ways in which you can help your group resolve this common tension.

Conformity

Group norms function only to the extent that members conform to them. **Conformity** occurs when group members adopt attitudes and actions that a majority favors or that adhere to the group's social norms.[41] We learn the value of conformity at a young age. In the classroom, children learn that standing in line and raising their hands are expected behaviors. On the playground, children who refuse to play by the rules may find themselves playing alone.

Although some group members may have reasons for ignoring or wanting to change norms, most groups pressure their members to conform. You are more likely to conform to norms when one or more of the following factors are present:

- You want to continue your membership in the group.
- You have a lower status than other group members and don't want to risk being seen as an upstart.
- You feel obligated to conform.
- You get along with and like working with the other group members.
- You may be punished for violating norms and/or rewarded for compliance.[42]

Nonconformity

Members decide whether they will or will not conform to group norms. **Nonconformity** occurs when a member behaves counter to the expectations of the group. Although conformity to norms is essential to the functioning of a group,

Follow the Research

Beware of Unreasonable Norms

Groups can exert enormous pressure to conform. Two classic (and disturbing) studies illustrate our tendency to conform to unreasonable norms.[43]

During the 1960s, Stanley Milgram of Yale University designed a series of experiments to find out whether people would obey commands from a stranger who tells them to inflict what seems to be considerable pain on another person. Subjects were told by the supposed experimenter to administer painful electric shocks to a research associate if the associate answered a question incorrectly. In fact, *no* shock was given, but the associates were trained to writhe in pain, scream, and pound on walls. Even though these behaviors convinced the subjects that they were causing enormous pain, very few subjects refused to increase the shocks as directed by an experimenter. In this case, pressure from an authority figure outweighed individual judgment and morality.

In another famous study conducted in the early 1970s, Philip Zimbardo created a realistic-looking prison in a Stanford University basement in which

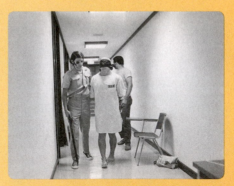

Student "guard" and "prisoner" form Zimbardo's prison experiment.

student subjects were assigned to play the role of prison guard or prisoner for several days. Very quickly, the prison guards used their power and became increasingly abusive and cruel. After a brief period of rebellion, the prisoners became passive, demoralized, and depressed. Zimbardo halted the experiment because it was "out of control" and causing psychological and physical damage to the subjects.[44]

Figure 2.4   Dealing with Nonconformity

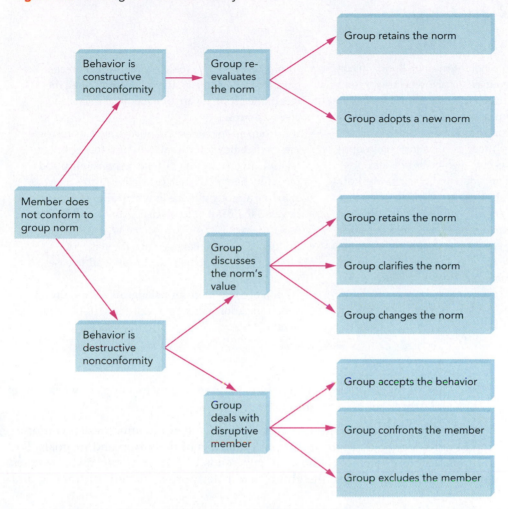

nonconformity can improve group performance when members have legitimate concerns and alternative suggestions. Figure 2.4 presents the process for dealing with nonconformity in a decision tree format.

Constructive nonconformity occurs when a member resists a norm while still working to promote a group goal. Constructive nonconformity is occasionally needed and valuable. Movies, television shows, and books have championed the holdout juror, the stubbornly honest politician, and the principled but disobedient soldier or crew member. Sometimes there is so much pressure for group members to conform that they need a nonconformist to shake up the process, to provide critical feedback, and to create doubt about what had been a confident but wrong decision. Nonconformity can serve a group well if it prevents members from ignoring important information or making a poor decision. The following statements are examples of constructive nonconformity:

- "I know we always ask the newest group member to take minutes during the meeting, but we may be losing the insight of an experienced member and skilled note taker by continuing this practice."

Remember This

Effective groups balance the benefits of both conformity and nonconformity.

Ethics in Groups

Ethical Group Norms

Group communication scholar Ernest G. Bormann contends that ethical dilemmas surface whenever groups face unavoidable dialectic tensions.[45] Group norms can present ethical dilemmas when they serve unethical purposes. In some groups, norms exclude people because of race, gender, age, or personal philosophy. When group norms restrict members' freedom of expression, an ethical member should object to the norm and try to change it. If all else fails, ethical members may publicly renounce the group or quit in protest.

A group and its members have ethical responsibilities. We offer some conclusions based on Bormann's advice and urge you to meet these standards as you interact with group members to achieve a common goal:[46]

- When you join a group, focus on the group's goals rather than your own.

- If someone asks you to do something unethical, object or decline the assignment—and make the rest of the group aware of the ethical issues and consequences.
- If a group adopts unethical norms, such as restricting the free flow of information or refusing to include diverse members, take responsibility and push for changes to such restrictive norms.
- Promote a group climate in which all members can develop their full potential as individuals of worth and dignity.
- Build group cohesiveness, raise the status of others, volunteer to help the group, and release social tensions.
- As you become more knowledgeable about group communication, develop a well-thought-out code of ethics.

- "I have to question devoting my time to these weekly meetings if we continue to take three hours to get through a routine agenda."

In contrast, **destructive nonconformity** occurs when a member resists conforming to norms without regard for the best interests of the group and its goals. For example, a group member who routinely sends and responds to text messages during meetings in spite of the group's clear disapproval is both distracting and annoying.

Nonconformity of either type provides a group with an opportunity to examine its norms. When members deviate, the group may have to discuss the value of a particular norm and subsequently choose to change it, clarify it, or continue to accept it. At the very least, nonconforming behavior helps members recognize and understand the norms of the group. For instance, if a member is reprimanded for criticizing an office policy, other members will learn that the boss should not be challenged. Some groups may attempt to correct nonconforming members or change their norms as a result of constructive nonconformity.

While most groups can handle an occasional encounter with a renegade, dealing with highly disruptive members is another story. Fortunately, several strategies can help a group deal with a member whose disruptive behavior becomes destructive. The methods discussed in the following subsections begin with efforts to accommodate a disruptive member and escalate to a more permanent solution. A group can accept, confront, or even exclude the troublesome member.

Accept.   In some cases, a group will accept and put up with disruptive nonconformity. Acceptance is not the same as approval; it involves learning to live with disruptive behavior. When the disruption is not critical to the group's ultimate success, or when the member's positive contributions far outweigh the inconvenience and annoyance of putting up with the behavior, a group may allow the disruptive behavior to continue. For example, a member who is always late for meetings but puts in more than her fair share of work may find her tardy behavior accepted as an unavoidable fact of group life.

Confront.   Another strategy for dealing with disruptive nonconformity is confrontation, particularly when a member's behavior is impossible to accept or ignore and when it threatens the success of a group and its members. At first, rather than singling out the disruptive member, you may address the entire group about the issue by talking in general terms about coming to meetings prepared and on time, not interrupting others while they're speaking, or criticizing ideas rather than people. However, when a member becomes "impossible," groups may confront the perpetrator in several ways. At first, members may direct a lot of attention to the wayward member in an attempt to reason with him or her. They may even talk about him or her during the course of the discussion: "Barry, it's distracting and disrupts our discussion when you answer your cell phone in meetings. Please turn it off." Although such attention can be intimidating and uncomfortable for the nonconforming member, it may not be sufficient to overcome the problem.

Group norms express group values, help groups function efficiently, and define appropriate social behavior. Why does constructive nonconformity also help a group achieve its common goal?

As an alternative to a public confrontation, there may be value in discussing the problem with the disruptive member outside the group setting. A frank and open conversation between the disruptive member and the leader or a trusted member of the group may uncover the causes of the problem as well as solutions for it. Some nonconforming members may not see their behavior as disruptive and, as a result, may not understand why the group is ignoring, confronting, or excluding them. Taking time to talk with a disruptive member in a nonthreatening setting can solve both a personal and a group problem.

Exclude.   When all else fails, a group may exclude disruptive members. Exclusion can take several forms. During discussions, group members can turn away from problem members, ignore their comments, or refuse to make eye contact. Exclusion might mean assigning disruptive members to unimportant, solo tasks or ones that will drive them away. Finally, a group may be able to expel unwanted members. Being asked to leave a group or being barred from participating is a humiliating experience that all but the most stubborn members would prefer to avoid.

Rather than covering up for disrupters and noncontributors, effective groups deal with such members. As Jon Katzenback and Douglas Smith wrote in *The Discipline of Teams*, "Sometimes that requires replacing members, sometimes it requires punishing them, and sometimes it requires working with them. [An effective group] does whatever it takes to eliminate disruptive behavior and ensure productive contributions from all of its members."[47]

Groups in Balance...

Change Norms as Needed

When norms do not meet the needs of a group or its members, new ones should be established. Some norms may be too rigid, others too vague. Some norms may have outlived their usefulness. Finding an appropriate balance between old, rigid, or useless norms and creating new norms presents a challenge to every group. Effective groups learn how to change norms in order to prevent or curb recurring disruptions or problems. Norms can be difficult to change, especially when they are implicit or unspoken. Changes in group norms typically occur as the result of the following conditions or behaviors:

- Contagious behavior, as in dress style and speech patterns

- Suggestions or actions of high-status members
- Suggestions or actions of highly confident members
- Suggestions of consultants
- Group discussion and decision making (for explicit norms)
- Continued interaction (for implicit norms)[48]

When group norms do not help a group achieve its purpose, some members may resist changes simply because change can be disruptive and threatening. Fear of change, however, should be weighed against fear of failure. Effective groups know when to hold on to tried-and-true norms and when to change them. The natural development of most groups requires changes in goals, membership, and norms.

Group Motivation

The word *motivate* comes from a French word, *motif*, which means "causing to move." Thus, if you motivate someone, you give that person a cause, or reason, to act. Group motivation provides the inspiration and incentives that move group members to work together to achieve a common goal. Without motivation, we may know what we need to do and even how to do it, but we lack the will and energy to do it.

In *Intrinsic Motivation at Work*, Kenneth Thomas explains the critical differences between two ways of using rewards to motivate group members. Most us of are familiar with the **extrinsic rewards** that come from the external environment (a boss, a business, an organization) and usually take the form of money, benefits, job perks, and special privileges. Thomas notes that extrinsic rewards rarely motivate group members. Rather, the rewards that motivate group members are **intrinsic rewards** that come from the group itself—pride in the work, the praise of others, a sense of personal accomplishment.[49] Every group has the potential to make group work an optimal experience for members by using Thomas's four categories of motivators to energize and reinforce an entire group (see Figure 2.5).[50]

A Sense of Meaningfulness

The shared feeling that the group is pursuing a meaningful goal creates a **sense of meaningfulness.** Highly motivated groups believe that the job is worth doing and that they are capable of getting it done. Whether your group is setting out to climb Mt. Everest, planning a homecoming rally, or establishing a new product line, make sure there is a clear and elevated goal supported by every member of the group. You can also promote a sense of meaningfulness in your group by meeting members' needs and adapting to their personality types. If you are leading a group, give group members feedback that tells them whether their efforts are contributing to the group's goal.[51]

Figure 2.5   Thomas's Intrinsic Motivators in Action

A Sense of Choice

Motivated groups feel they have a **sense of choice**—the shared feeling that the group has the power and ability to make decisions about how to organize and do its job. In addition to focusing on the group goal, group members should select agreed-upon strategies for achieving the goal. Every member knows what she or he is expected to do. Members communicate frequently in an effort to share information, discuss issues, and make decisions.[52] If you are the group's leader, you can promote a sense of choice by encouraging members to make decisions about how the group does its work and accept the inevitability of making mistakes when exploring innovative approaches. When group members have the power to make decisions, they are motivated by a greater sense of personal control and responsibility.

A Sense of Competence

The shared feeling that your group is doing good, high-quality work creates a **sense of competence.** Motivated groups need more than a clear goal and strategies for achieving that goal. They also need competent group members who are ready, willing, and able to perform the tasks necessary to achieve their common goal. You can promote a sense of competence in your group by providing constructive feedback to group members and listening to their feedback, complimenting member abilities and achievements, and setting high standards for yourself and the group.

A Sense of Progress

Motivated groups must feel a **sense of progress**—the shared feeling that the group is accomplishing something. "How are we doing?" is an important question for all groups. It's difficult for members to stay motivated if they have no idea whether the group is making progress toward its goal. A well-chosen, structured goal should be measurable. Motivated groups "create good, objective measurements that people can relate to their specific behavior."[53] A group can provide a sense of progress by tracking and measuring progress; monitoring and, if needed, finding ways to sustain group motivation; and celebrating group accomplishments.

Summary Study Guide

Group Development Stages

- According to Tuckman and Jensen, the life cycle of groups has five discrete stages—forming, storming, norming, performing, and adjourning.
- During the forming stage, many groups experience primary tension, the social unease that accompanies the getting–acquainted stage in a new group.
- During the storming stage, secondary tensions often emerge as members pursue positions of power and influence.
- Virtual groups must take into account their members' technical expertise, attitudes about, and confidence with technology in order to move through group development stages efficiently and effectively.
- The process of socializing newcomers in a group moves through five phases: antecedent, anticipatory, encounter, assimilation, and exit.

Group Goals

- An effective group has *both* a clear understanding of its goal *and* a belief that its goal is meaningful and worthwhile.
- Effective group goals require attention to their clarity, challenge, commitment, compatibility, cooperation, and cost.
- Locke and Latham's Goal Theory claims that groups function best when their goals are specific, challenging, accepted, used to evaluate performance, and promote member growth.
- Hidden agendas occur when a member's private goal conflicts with the group's goal.

Group Norms

- Norms are expectations held by group members concerning acceptable behavior; norms can be explicit or implicit.
- Norms can be classified as interaction, procedural, status, and achievement norms.
- Constructive nonconformity occurs when a member resists a norm while still working to promote a group goal. Destructive nonconformity occurs when a member resists conforming to norms without regard for the best interests of the group and its goal.
- When members engage in destructive nonconformity a group can accept, confront, and even exclude disruptive members.

Group Motivation

- Group motivation provides the inspiration and incentives that move group members to work together to achieve a common goal.
- Members are motivated when they have a sense of meaningfulness, a sense of choice, a sense of competence, and a sense of progress.

GroupWork

Classroom Norms

Directions: Form a group of three to five members and discuss some of the norms in your classes. List at least five implicit norms and at least five explicit norms that operate in some of your classes. When you have identified examples of each type of norm, rank the norms in terms of their usefulness in ensuring quality instruction and effective learning. Do all of the norms that the group listed contribute to a positive classroom experience? Should some of the existing norms be modified? Are there any additional norms needed in some classes?

Explicit Classroom Norms	Your Ranking	Implicit Classroom Norms	Your Ranking
Example: The syllabus states that no makeup work is allowed without a legitimate written excuse.		*Example:* When students come in late, they tiptoe to the closest available seat near the door.	
1.		1.	
2.		2.	
3.		3.	
4.		4.	
5.		5.	

Group Assessment

How Good Is Your Goal?

Directions: For each of the following questions, circle Yes or No to assess the goals of a group you belong to or belonged to in the past. Each time you circle a No response, consider how the goal or situation could have been improved.

1. Does the group have a goal?	Yes	No
2. Is the goal specific?	Yes	No
3. Do group members understand the goal?	Yes	No
4. Do group members believe the goal is worthwhile?	Yes	No
5. Is the goal achievable?	Yes	No
6. Are the resources available to achieve the goal?	Yes	No
7. Is the goal sufficiently challenging to group members?	Yes	No
8. Are all group members committed to the goal?	Yes	No
9. Do all group members understand their contribution to the goal?	Yes	No
10. Does the goal require group cooperation?	Yes	No
11. Does the group recognize any individual hidden agendas?	Yes	No
12. Has the group resolved any hidden agendas?	Yes	No
13. Will group members receive feedback about their progress toward the goal?	Yes	No
14. Is there a reward for achieving the group's goal?	Yes	No
15. When achieved, is the goal observable or measurable?	Yes	No

16. What could you and your group members do to improve their ability to achieve the groups' goal?

_____

_____

_____

chapter **3**

Group Membership

Chapter Outline

Group Member Needs
Schutz's Theory of Interpersonal Needs
Balancing Individual and Group Needs

Member Roles
Benne and Sheats Functional Group Roles
Belbin's Team Roles

Member Confidence
Communication Apprehension

Strategies for Reducing Communication
Apprehension
Strategies for Helping Apprehensive
Members

Member Assertiveness
Balancing Passivity and Aggression
Assertiveness Skills

Case Study

Taming Tony the Tiger

Anthony (Tony the Tiger) Tarantella is a conscientious and assertive man who has always liked working in groups. In addition to being a member of a large family and group of friends, he enjoys playing Tuesday night basketball games on a neighborhood team and making Saturday morning food deliveries for Meals on Wheels. At work, Tony manages the sales and advertising department for a small business. For the last 20 years, his group experiences have been positive and enjoyable.

In the last few years, however, he has sensed a change in his feelings and commitment to several groups. The members of his basketball team often miss games, saying they're too tired, too busy, or too injured to play. His solo drives to deliver Meals on Wheels have become lonely. On the job, he seems to have less time to complete more work. His young and less experienced colleagues respect his expertise, but he no longer gets a boost from working with them.

Tony understands that things have changed. His family has grown up, and he has less control over their lives. Some of his close friends have moved out of the neighborhood. Retirement has claimed several of his best coworkers. He also recognizes that his way of working may not be in sync with the work styles of others. He can tell that some staff members don't like his insistence on establishing clear schedules and meeting all deadlines. He knows he becomes aggravated and critical when a basketball game is cancelled, a Meals on Wheels schedule is changed, or someone makes a last-minute request for an advertisement. He finds himself losing patience with his wife and kids when they change plans without telling him. To make matters worse, everyone knows he's frustrated, but he can't seem to tone down his judgmental reactions. A few times, he's lost his temper over small issues and had to apologize for his behavior. Tony decides he needs to take a good look at himself to help figure out how to recapture his commitment to group work.

When you finish reading this chapter, you should be able to answer the following critical thinking questions about this case study:

1   What needs motivate Tony's participation in groups? To what extent are those needs met in his current job?

2   What roles does Tony assume in his group, and how do these roles affect his attitude and behavior as a group member?

3   How can Tony balance his interaction style and become more assertive than aggressive?

4   Which dialectic tensions help explain the problems Tony is experiencing as he works in groups?

Helping Annie

The Politics of Sociology

Before you read any further, visit Pearson's MyCommunicationLab website and watch the short videos "Helping Annie" and "The Politics of Sociology," which illustrate Chapter 3 concepts. Each video comes with a set of study questions to keep in mind as you read this chapter.

Group Member Needs

Most of us join groups because they satisfy specific needs. For example, some people join volunteer fire departments or participate in neighborhood watch programs to safeguard their community. College students often join campus clubs and societies to be with friends or make new ones. Job applicants may decline an offer if they view members of the work team as unpleasant. In many cases, you may join a group to meet a need separate from the group's goal. For instance, a young attorney might join a local civic organization in an effort to meet prospective clients. A retiree may volunteer as a teacher's aide to feel productive and appreciated.[1]

Although many psychologists have studied human needs and offered theories to explain their impact, the work of Will Schutz focuses on the interpersonal needs of *group* members. His work explains why we join, stay in, and even leave groups.

Schutz's Theory of Interpersonal Needs

William Schutz developed a **Fundamental Interpersonal Relationship Orientation (FIRO) Theory** that focuses on three needs that most of us share to some degree: the needs for inclusion, for control, and for affection (see Figure 3.1 on page 50). Schutz maintains that we join groups in order to satisfy one or more of these needs.[2] As you will see, ideal group members meet these needs by finding a balance between two extremes.

The Need for Inclusion.   An **inclusion need** represents our desire to belong, to be involved, and to be accepted. For some group members, the need for inclusion is strong—they want to fit in and be appreciated by other members. For other group members, the need for inclusion is less important—they are quite content to work without significant involvement in the group. When a group meets a member's inclusion need, the result is what Schutz calls a **social member**—a person who enjoys working with people but is also comfortable working alone.

When inclusion needs are *not* met, members do not feel accepted; they do not fit in with the group and may engage in undersocial behavior or oversocial behavior. An **undersocial member** feels unworthy or undervalued by the group and may withdraw and become a loner. Because these people believe that no one values them, they try not to be noticed and thus avoid being hurt. An **oversocial member** tries to attract attention to compensate for feelings of inadequacy. Such members seek companionship for all activities because they can't stand being alone. They try to impress other members with what and whom they know.[3]

Dealing with undersocial and oversocial members requires group behavior that satisfies inclusion needs. Making new members feel welcome and veteran members feel valued requires a careful balance between the needs of the members and the needs of the group.

The Need for Control.   **Control need** refers to whether we feel competent, confident, and free to make our own decisions. The need for control is often expressed by a member who wants to be the group's leader. For some members, the need for control is strong—they want to take charge of the group and influence members. For other group members, the need for control is less important—they are quite content to be followers and let others lead. When a group meets a member's control need, the result is what Schutz calls a **democratic member**—a person who has no

Figure 3.1   Schutz's Fundamental Interpersonal Relationship Orientation (FIRO) Theory

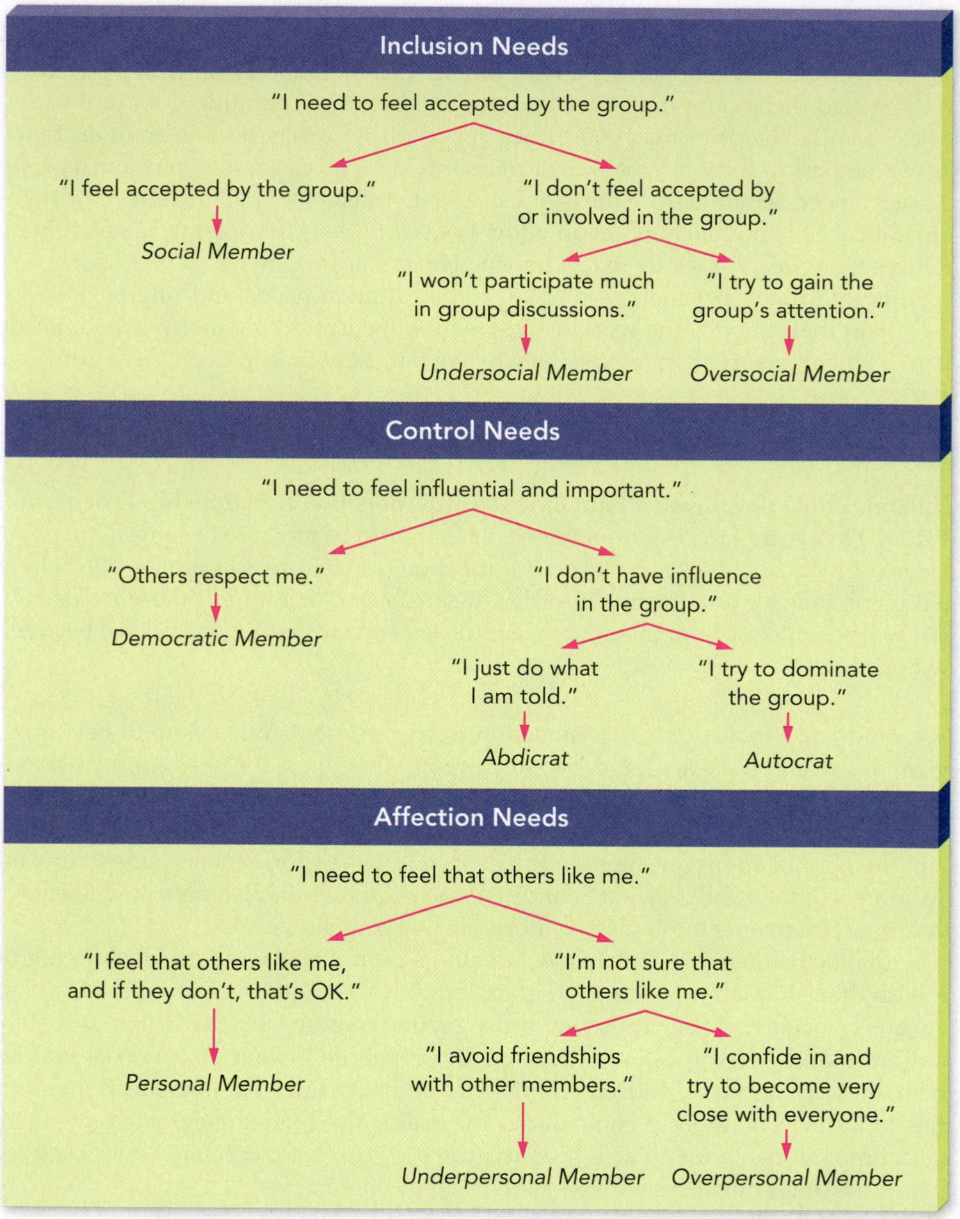

Inclusion Needs

"I need to feel accepted by the group."

"I feel accepted by the group." → *Social Member*

"I don't feel accepted by or involved in the group."

"I won't participate much in group discussions." → *Undersocial Member*

"I try to gain the group's attention." → *Oversocial Member*

Control Needs

"I need to feel influential and important."

"Others respect me." → *Democratic Member*

"I don't have influence in the group."

"I just do what I am told." → *Abdicrat*

"I try to dominate the group." → *Autocrat*

Affection Needs

"I need to feel that others like me."

"I feel that others like me, and if they don't, that's OK." → *Personal Member*

"I'm not sure that others like me."

"I avoid friendships with other members." → *Underpersonal Member*

"I confide in and try to become very close with everyone." → *Overpersonal Member*

problems with power and control and who feels just as comfortable giving orders as taking them. Such members are often excellent leaders because they can exercise control when needed, but they put the group's goals ahead of their own needs.

Unmet control needs can result in the emergence of an abdicrat or an autocrat. Each type manifests control needs through opposite behaviors. An **abdicrat** wants control but is reluctant to pursue it. Abdicrats are often submissive members because they have no hope of having any control in the group. Generally, they do what they are told and avoid responsibilities. The **autocrat** tries to take control by dominating the group. Autocrats often criticize other members and try to force their decisions on the group.[4]

Dealing with abdicrats and autocrats requires granting members a sense of control appropriate to their needs. Giving members responsibility for and leadership of special projects or tasks may satisfy their need for control. For example, asking a member to chair a highly visible and important subcommittee may satisfy that person's control need.

The Need for Affection.

An **affection need** reflects our desire to be liked by others.[5] Members with strong affection needs seek close friendships and expressions of warmth from others. As was the case with inclusion and control, some group members have a high need for affection—they want to be liked and develop strong friendships with group members. For others, the need for affection is less important—they don't need to be liked to be a productive group member. When a group meets a member's affection need, the result is what Schutz calls a **personal member**—a person who has no emotional problems dealing with group members. While preferring to be liked, an ideal personal member is secure enough to function in a group where social interaction and affection are not high priorities.

When affection needs are not met, members do not feel liked; they become uncomfortable in the group setting. Reactions to this deficit fall into two categories: underpersonal behavior and overpersonal behavior. **Underpersonal members** believe no one likes them; they may establish only superficial relationships with other members. They may appear aloof and uninvolved, and when pressed, they rarely share their honest feelings or opinions. An **overpersonal member** tries to get close to everyone and seeks intimate friendships despite the disinterest of other members. Such members are often too talkative, too personal, and too confiding.[6]

Dealing with underpersonal and overpersonal members requires expressions of fondness and friendliness to those who need affection. Expressing liking to new members and taking the time to communicate affection to long-standing members take extra effort, but these actions can convert unsatisfied participants into ideal personal members.

Throughout history and in all cultures, people have joined and relied on groups to satisfy important needs. What kinds of needs are satisfied by belonging to and working in public service groups such as firefighters, police officers, and emergency medical teams?

Balancing Individual and Group Needs

Using Schutz's FIRO theory to improve a group's performance requires a balanced approach that helps members meet *both* inclusion, control, and affection needs *and* the group's need for productive interaction. For example, a member who seeks attention or tries to impress other members may have a strong inclusion need. Rather than giving up on or criticizing an undersocial or oversocial member, you can help satisfy members' inclusion needs by praising their good work. When members have strong control needs but are not capable enough or eligible to lead a group, you may be able to satisfy *both* their need for control *and* the need to advance the group's goal by asking them to lead a special project. Praising and rewarding effective group behavior can help group members feel included, competent, and well liked.

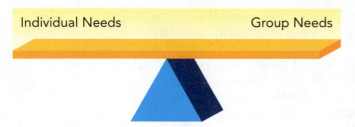

There are reasons to be cautious, however, about using FIRO theory to explain and predict group behavior. Undersocial behavior may not reflect an unmet inclusion need; the member may be quite comfortable and happy working alone. Overpersonal behavior may not reflect an unmet affection need; such behavior may represent an enthusiastic effort to create a positive social climate for the group.

Member Roles

When a group member exhibits a unique set of skills or behavior patterns that serve specific functions within the group, that member has assumed a **role**.[7] For example, a group may rely on one member to generate enthusiasm for the group's work and promote teamwork, while another plays the role of harmonizer by reconciling disagreements, reducing tension, and calming anxious members. Both of these roles serve valuable group functions.

Benne and Sheats Functional Group Roles

Most group communication textbooks—including this one—present a list of group roles identified by Kenneth Benne and Paul Sheats in their classic 1948 essay.[8] In addition to describing how each role helps or hinders groups from achieving a common goal, they explain that members may temporarily adopt a role that suits a particular situation or may take on a permanent role. Thus, if you know the most about the discussion topic, your primary function might be that of Information Giver. When members strongly disagree about an important issue, your group may look to you as its Harmonizer. And if a member assumes the role of Dominator, several group members may try to counteract such behavior by taking on positive roles such as Coordinator, Tension Releaser, and Compromiser. What's critical, claim Benne and Sheats, is finding a *balance* of appropriate roles based on the group's progress toward achieving its goals.[9]

The Benne and Sheats roles fall into three functional categories: group task roles, group maintenance roles, and self-centered roles. Group **task roles** affect a group's ability to achieve its common goal by focusing on behaviors that help get the job done.

Group **maintenance roles** affect how group members get along with one another while pursuing a shared goal. They are concerned with building relationships and keeping the group cohesive and cooperative. **Self-centered roles** put individual needs ahead of the group's goal and other members' needs. On this and the next two pages, each functional role is categorized, named, described, and illustrated with a statement that might be heard from a member assuming such a role.

Group Task Roles

1. **Initiator–contributor.** Proposes ideas and suggestions; provides direction for the group; gets the group started.
   "Let's begin by looking at the problem from the client's point of view."

2. **Information seeker.** Asks for needed facts and figures; requests explanations and clarification of ideas; makes the group aware of information gaps.
   "How can we decide on a policy for students with disabilities without knowing more about the new federal laws and regulations?"

3. **Opinion seeker.** Asks for others' opinions; tests for group opinions and consensus; tries to discover what others believe or feel about an issue.
   "Lyle, what do you think? Will it work?"

4. **Information giver.** Provides the group with relevant information; researches, organizes, and presents needed information.
   "I checked with our diversity officer, and she said...."

5. **Opinion giver.** States personal beliefs and interpretations; shares feelings; offers analysis and arguments.
   "I don't agree that radio ads are the answer because they'll use up our entire promotional budget."

6. **Elaborator.** Helps explain ideas and suggestions by providing examples or summaries or by describing the consequence of a decision or action.
   "We've been trying to analyze this problem for the last hour. Perhaps a few examples can help us clarify the problem."

7. **Coordinator.** Pulls ideas together and suggestions together; tries to coordinate the activities of various members or subgroups.
   "Beth and Karla—what does your subcommittee recommend?"

8. **Orienter.** Summarizes what has been said and what has occurred; raises questions about the direction the discussion is taking in relationship to the group agenda and its goal.
   "I think we're getting a bit carried away. Remember, we are only trying to come up with suggestions at this point, not make a final decision.

9. **Evaluator–critic.** Assesses ideas, arguments, and suggestions; functions as the group's critical thinker; diagnoses task and procedural problems.
   "I think we've forgotten something here. These building figures don't take into account monthly operating costs, such as utilities and maintenance."

10. **Energizer.** Motivates group members to do their best; helps create enthusiasm for the task and, if needed, a sense of urgency; serves as the group's "cheerleader."
    "This is incredible! We may be the first department to come up with such a unique and workable solution to this problem."

11. **Procedural technician.** Assists with preparation for meetings; suggests agenda items; makes room arrangements; provides materials and equipment.

"Don't forget—if you have handouts for your presentation, you need to email them to me at least two days in advance."

12. **Recorder.** Keeps and provides accurate written records of a group's major ideas, suggestions, and decisions.
"Maggie, please repeat your two deadline dates so I can get them into the minutes."

Group Maintenance Roles

1. **Encourager–supporter.** Praises and agrees with group members; provides recognition and person-to-person encouragement; listens empathically.
"The information you found has been a big help. Thanks for taking all that time to find it."

2. **Harmonizer.** Helps resolve conflicts; mediates differences among group members; emphasizes teamwork and the importance of everyone getting along.
"I know we're starting to get on each other's nerves, but we're almost done. Let's put aside our differences and finish up."

3. **Compromiser.** Offers suggestions that minimize differences; helps the group reach consensus; searches for solutions that are acceptable to everyone.
"It looks as though no one is going to agree on this one. Maybe we can improve the old system rather than trying to come up with a brand new way of doing it."

4. **Tension releaser.** Alleviates tension with friendly humor; breaks the ice and cools hot tempers; monitors tension levels and tries to relax the group.
"Can Karen and I arm wrestle to decide who gets the assignment?"

5. **Gatekeeper.** Monitors participation; encourages quiet members to speak and talkative members to stop speaking; tries to control the flow of communication.
"I think we've heard from everyone except Sophie, and I know she has strong feelings on this issue."

6. **Observer–commentator.** Explains what others are trying to say; monitors and interprets feelings and nonverbal communication; expresses group feelings; paraphrases other members.
"I sense that you two are not really disagreeing. Tell me if I'm wrong, but I think that both of you are saying that we should…"

7. **Follower.** Supports the group and its members; accepts others' ideas and assignments; serves as an attentive audience member.
"That's fine with me. Just tell me when it's due."

Self-Centered Roles

1. **Aggressor.** Puts down members to get what he or she wants; is sarcastic toward and critical of others; may take credit for someone else's work or idea.
"It's a good thing I had time to rewrite your report. There were so many mistakes in it, we would have been embarrassed by it."

2. **Blocker.** Stands in the way of progress; presents negative, disagreeable, and uncompromising positions; uses delaying tactics to derail an idea or proposal.

"There's no way I'm signing off on this idea if you insist on putting Gabriel in charge of the project."

3. **Dominator.** Prevents others from participating; asserts authority and tries to manipulate others; interrupts others and monopolizes discussion.
"That's crazy, Wanda. Right off the top of my head I can think of at least four major reasons why we can't do it your way. The first reason is…"

4. **Recognition seeker.** Boasts about personal accomplishments; tries to impress others and become the center of attention; pouts or disrupts the discussion if not getting enough attention.
"As the only person here to have ever won the company's prestigious top achiever award, I personally suggest that…"

5. **Clown.** Injects inappropriate humor or commentary into the group; seems more interested in goofing off than in working; distracts the group.
"Listen—I've been working on this outrageous impersonation of the boss. I've even got his funny walk down."

6. **Deserter.** Withdraws from the group; appears "above it all" and bored or annoyed with the discussion; remains aloof or stops contributing.
"I'm leaving now because I have to go to an important meeting."

7. **Self-confessor.** Seeks emotional support from the group; shares very personal feelings and problems with members; uses the group for emotional support rather than contributing to the group's goal.
"I had an argument with my boyfriend yesterday. I could really use some advice. Let me start at the beginning."

8. **Help-seeker.** Seeks sympathetic responses from the group; expresses insecurity, confusion, or inferiority.
"Look, how can you expect me to do this when I've broken up with the love of my life and will probably fail most of my classes?"

9. **Special interest pleader.** Speaks on behalf of an outside group or a personal interest; tries to influence group members to support nongroup interests.
"Let's hire my brother-in-law to cater our annual dinner. We'd get better food than the usual rubber chicken."

Belbin's Team Roles

Consider this question: Are some roles more essential than others? R. Meredith Belbin claims that groups work best when "there is a *balance* of primary roles and when team members *know* their roles, work to their strengths, and actively manage weaknesses."[10] However, three of the roles he describes are critical for effective group performance: Innovator (fosters creativity), Coordinator (helps a group organize its work in order to make good decisions), and Team Worker (promotes group collaboration and avoids friction).[11]

Understanding the functions of Belbin's roles helps groups analyze and improve their overall performance. For example, if there is conflict, a Team Worker and Coordinator are best equipped to help resolve the conflict. If the group is making a lot of mistakes, an Evaluator is most able to step in and point out errors. A new group may need a Shaper and Innovator to get started, but it needs a good Coordinator and Finisher when it gets tired and bogged down.[12]

Theory in Groups

Belbin's Team-Role Theory

Belbin's **Team-Role Theory** goes well beyond Benne and Sheats list of roles. After studying work groups for many years, he identified nine roles that lead to team success.[13] In addition to identifying nine essential roles, Belbin concluded that it is "not intellect, but balance" that is the key to group success. For example, a group without an Innovator (which Belbin visually portrays as a bright light bulb) may struggle to come up with the initial spark of a good idea, while too many Innovators produce a confusion of ideas, good and bad. Similarly, with no Shaper (which Belbin visually portrays as a whip), the group ambles along without drive or direction, missing deadlines. With too many Shapers, in-fighting can occur and morale is lowered.[14]

Belbin claims that group members seek out certain roles and that, in highly effective groups, members perform the roles that are most natural to them—those that are compatible with their personal characteristics and skills. As was the case with the Benne and Sheats roles, there are no such things as "pure" roles in Belbin's model. Most members assume a mix of roles depending on the needs of the group and its members.[15]

Belbin's Roles	Function	Characteristics
Coordinator/ Chairperson	Clarifies goals; helps allocate roles, responsibilities, and duties; articulates group conclusions	Calm, trusting, impartial, self-disciplined, mature, positive thinker, confident; decisive when necessary; may be seen as manipulative
Shaper	Seeks patterns in group work; pushes group toward agreement and decisions; challenges others	Energetic, high achiever, anxious, impatient, outgoing, argumentative, provocative, dynamic; can be abrasive
Innovator	Advances proposals and offers new and creative ideas; provides insights on courses of action	Creative, individualistic, serious and knowledgeable, unorthodox, intellectual; may disregard practical details and people
Resource Investigator	Explores opportunities, makes contacts, shares external information; negotiates with outsiders; responds well to challenges	Extroverted, curious, versatile, sociable, innovative, communicative, noisy and energetic; sometimes lazy
Monitor/ Evaluator	Analyzes problems and complex issues; monitors progress and prevents mistakes; assesses the contributions of others; sees all options; judges accurately	Sober, clever, discreet, detached, unemotional, prudent, not easily aroused; takes time to consider; rarely wrong; may appear cold
Implementer	Transforms talk and ideas into practical action; develops action plans for group members	Tough-minded, practical, tolerant, conscientious, conservative, methodical
Teamworker	Gives personal support and help to others; socially oriented and sensitive to others; resolves conflicts; calms the waters; serves as an in-group diplomat	Cooperative, sensitive, team-oriented, indecisive, deputy leader, gregarious, supportive; may sacrifice task for social goals; listens well
Completer/ Finisher	Emphasizes the need for meeting schedules, deadlines, and completing tasks; searches out errors	Perfectionist, persevering, conscientious, detail oriented, persistent, anxious; sometimes obnoxious
Specialist	Single-minded, self-starting, dedicated; provides unique or rare expertise and skills	Contributes in narrow area; dwells on technicalities; overlooks the "big picture"

The members of successful groups know how to identify appropriate roles for themselves and how to work with the roles that other group members adopt.[16] Group members should be "very clear about their roles," but they should also avoid the temptation of establishing inflexible roles.[17] Instead, they should seek balance by calling on group members' multiple talents.[18]

Member Confidence

Imagine the benefits and satisfaction of working with group members who have a positive and realistic perception about themselves and their abilities. Add to that personal attributes such as assertiveness, optimism, enthusiasm, affection, pride, independence, trust, the ability to handle criticism, and emotional maturity. These personal attributes describe a nearly perfect group member. Note that the same words are also found in dictionaries describing the characteristics of a person with confidence.[19]

Groups with confident members are more likely to succeed. They cope effectively with unexpected events, problematic behavior, and challenging assignments because their members have a positive, "can do" attitude. Fostering group and member confidence is much more than the power of positive thinking—it helps groups commit to ambitious goals and believe in their ability to meet them.[20]

Remember This

When member skills combine with a desire to contribute and an ability to collaborate, "the observable outcome is an elevated sense of confidence among team members."[21]

—Frank M. J. LaFasto and Carl Larson, When Teams Work Best

Communication Apprehension

Communication scholars have investigated the anxieties that people feel when they must speak to others in a variety of contexts. The result is a large body of research that has important implications for working in groups.

Communication scholar James McCroskey defines **communication apprehension** as "an individual's level of fear or anxiety associated with either real or anticipated communication with another person or persons."[22] About 20 percent of the U.S. population experience very high levels of communication apprehension. About 75 to 85 percent experience apprehension when faced with the prospect of making a presentation.[23] However, communication apprehension includes more than public speaking anxiety; it also encompasses fear of speaking in conversations, meetings, or group settings.

There are different levels of communication apprehension, depending on several factors, such as the personality of the speaker, the nature of the listeners, and the characteristics of the occasion or setting. For example, talking at a weekly staff meeting may be easy, but defending a department's actions at a meeting of company executives may generate high levels of anxiety.

James McCroskey and Virginia Richmond write that "it is not an exaggeration to suggest that CA [communication apprehension] may be the single most important factor in predicting communication behavior in a small group."[24] Consequently, it is not surprising that highly apprehensive people may avoid group communication or sit quietly in a group if they must be present.[25] Figure 3.2 on p. 58 lists some of the basic characteristics of group members with low and high apprehension.

Groups in Balance...

Adapt to *Both* High *and* Low Levels of Member Apprehension

At the end of this chapter, you'll find a self-test called the Personal Report of Communication Apprehension (PRCA). You might want to complete this questionnaire and follow the scoring instructions now, before you read the rest of this section. The Personal Report of Communication Apprehension instrument is the best available measure of traitlike communication apprehension; that is, it measures relatively enduring, personality-type orientations toward a given mode of communication across a wide variety of contexts.[26] In other words, your PRCA score is a relatively permanent trait that is not likely to change significantly unless you engage in some type of effective intervention or training to change it.

Effective groups learn to *both* support members who experience high levels of communication apprehension *and* tactfully curb low apprehensives who may talk too much or are oblivious to how other members feel about speaking.

Strategies for Reducing Communication Apprehension

If your PRCA score classifies you as an apprehensive speaker, or if you believe that your level of anxiety associated with talking in groups is unusually high, there are several effective strategies to help you reduce your level of fear.

Know That You Are Not Alone. Everyone has experienced communication apprehension in certain settings. If you dread the thought of communicating in a group or public setting, you are one of millions of people who feel the same way. Such feelings are normal. As you listen to other group members, don't assume that it is easy for them to talk. Several of them are probably experiencing the same level of fear and anxiety that you are.

Be Well Prepared. Although you cannot totally eliminate communication apprehension, you can boost your confidence by being well prepared for every group discussion. Many successful group members who experience high levels of communication apprehension spend extra time making sure that they are well prepared to participate in a scheduled discussion or meeting. Well-prepared

Figure 3.2 Communication Apprehension in Groups

Members with High Apprehension May . . .	Members with Low Apprehension May . . .
• avoid group participation. • talk less often. • agree with others rather than voice disagreement. • smile and giggle inappropriately. • fidget. • use awkward phrases as fillers, such as "well," "uh," "you know." • have difficulty following a discussion.	• initiate discussions. • speak more often. • assert themselves and their beliefs. • become group leaders. • strategically choose when to speak and when to remain silent. • appear more confident. • dominate a discussion or talk compulsively.

members know more about the topic and have a clear idea of the positions they support. As a result, they have more to contribute when they are asked to participate. Being well prepared will not completely eliminate anxiety, but it can reduce a member's fear of being at a loss for relevant ideas and information when called upon to speak.

Learn Communication Skills. If you wanted to improve your tennis game, you would try to improve specific skills—perhaps your serve, your return, or your backhand shot. The same is true about communicating in groups: Learning and practicing specific skills can help you improve your ability to participate in groups. These skills are described throughout this textbook. Learning to become more sensitive to feedback, follow a group's agenda, or serve as an effective group leader and participant can give you the tools you need to succeed in a group discussion. Improving your communication skills will not erase communication apprehension, but it can reduce your level of anxiety.

Relax Physically. One reason we experience communication apprehension is that our bodies feel tense. Our hearts beat faster, our hands shake, and we're short of breath. This response is a natural one and may reflect excitement and eagerness as much as anxiety and fear. By learning to relax your body, you may also reduce your level of communication apprehension. For example, break the word *relax* into two syllables: *re* and *lax*. Inhale slowly through your nose while saying the sound *re* ("ree") silently to yourself. Then breathe out slowly while thinking of the sound *lax* ("laks"). Inhale and exhale three or four times while thinking, "Reee-laaax." By the time you finish, your pulse should be slower and—hopefully—you will also feel calmer.[28]

> ## Remember This
>
> Communication apprehension "may be the single most important factor in predicting communication behavior in a small group."[27]
>
> —James C. McCroskey and Virginia P. Richmond

Think Positively. You may be able to reduce apprehension by changing the way you *think* about communicating. Rather than thinking "They won't listen to me," try thinking "Because I'm so well prepared, I'll make a valuable contribution." **Cognitive restructuring** assumes that communication anxiety is caused by worrisome, irrational, and nonproductive thoughts about speaking to and with others (cognitions) that need modifying (restructuring).[29] Researchers who study emotions contend that thinking happy or sad thoughts can make you *feel* happy or sad.[30] So think positively and feel confident! Next time you feel anxious, tell yourself these positive statements: "My ideas are important," "I am well prepared," and "Nervousness gives me extra energy."[31]

Visualize Success. Closely related to cognitive restructuring is **visualization,** a technique that encourages you to think positively about communicating in groups. Many professional athletes improve their performance by finding a quiet place where they can relax and visualize themselves competing and winning.[32] You can do the same thing. Take time—*before* you meet with your group—to visualize yourself communicating effectively. Mentally practice the skills you need in order to succeed while also building a positive image of your effectiveness. When you can visualize or imagine yourself succeeding in a group and you can maintain a relaxed state at the same time, you will have broken your fearful response to communicating in groups.

Virtual Groups

Confidence with Technology

When groups use audioconferences or videoconferences, or participate in online or computer-mediated discussions, members' confidence may erode or improve, depending on the electronic medium and the personal preferences of members. In a videoconference, for example, members who experience high levels of communication apprehension may find themselves *more* nervous because they are "on television." Every word and movement is captured for all to see and hear.

When a conference moves online, two different kinds of anxiety come into play. The first is writing apprehension.[33] Because online interaction depends on *written* words, poor writers and those who experience writing apprehension find themselves anxious about and preoccupied with the task of writing rather than being focused on the group's goal.

Computer anxiety—a condition affecting as many as 50 percent of all Americans—is "a feeling of being fearful or apprehensive when using or considering the use of a computer."[34] Factors such as past failure, the nature of the task, and the use of a new computer application have the potential to affect every group member.[35] Fortunately, researchers have found that the more experience people have with computers, the less anxious they are.[36] The solution? Help anxious group members acquire and master computer skills, and their anxieties are likely to decrease. Also, "many

tried-and-true, face-to-face methods of confidence building still apply," such as letting group members know when they are doing a good job.[37]

There is, however, a flip side to the confidence coin when it's applied to online conferences and computer-mediated discussions. Some people are *more* confident when communicating via computer. A theory called **hyperpersonal communication** explains why some group members express themselves more competently and confidently in mediated settings than they do in face-to-face discussions.[38]

First, consider how you feel when communicating online. You have greater control over how you present yourself. An added confidence booster is the fact that your written message is separate from your appearance, your gender and race, your status, and your accent or dialect. None of these nonverbal factors is displayed in your message unless you choose to include remarks about them.

A second reason is that the online channel allows members to take the time to construct suitable replies. For example, depending on how soon you have been asked to reply to a question, you can consult a report or do research and sound like an expert.

Finally, online communication usually provides feedback that lets you know whether your message was received and interpreted as you intended. Confirming feedback reinforces confidence.[39]

Strategies for Helping Apprehensive Members

If your PRCA score classifies you as a low apprehensive, this puts you in a position to help the more apprehensive group members. Three strategies may help reduce other members' level of communication apprehension.

Provide Supportive and Constructive Feedback. All group members work more effectively when they receive supportive feedback. When apprehensive group members speak, smile and nod, listen patiently, and don't interrupt or let other members interrupt them.

Sometimes, however, feedback must address a problem. Here, you should provide constructive feedback as you describe your own feelings, thoughts, and

Communication apprehension can have a significant effect on group effectiveness because highly apprehensive members may be reluctant to participate in group discussions. What can you do to help members feel more confident about communicating in groups?

wants: "I'm a little frustrated with this discussion (feeling) because we seem to be avoiding the real issue (thought). Let's talk about what's really hanging us up (want)."[40] Expressing feedback constructively can increase your own credibility and other members' confidence while also moving the group forward. Use the following guidelines to provide supportive and constructive feedback:

- Focus on the behavior (rather than on the person).
- Describe the behavior (rather than judging it).
- Provide factual observations (rather than assumptions).
- Choose an appropriate time and place to contribute feedback (rather than ignoring the circumstances).
- Give supportive feedback to help others (rather than meeting your own needs).[41]

Encourage and Include Anxious Members.   Patience and understanding alone may not be enough to encourage a member who is too frightened to join in a discussion. Encouraging anxious members to speak up contributes to the group's overall success because quiet members often have important information and good ideas.[42] However, there are both effective and counterproductive ways to include someone. Confronting a reluctant speaker with a direct challenge—such as "Why in the world do you disagree with the rest of us?"—is not very helpful. It's much more effective to ask a question that you know the apprehensive person is able to answer and to encourage taking turns speaking.

Stop Talking.   Finally, the most obvious thing you can do to help those who have difficulty participating is to stop talking. If you know that other members have difficulty entering the discussion or interrupting someone who is speaking, try to curb your own comments so that others have a chance to contribute. Keep a careful

Follow the Research

Curbing Compulsive Communicators

In addition to the research on communication apprehension, Robert Bostrom and Nancy Grant Harrington have investigated the characteristics of compulsive talkers. Group members who talk too much can be just as much of a problem as members who don't speak. Compulsive talkers tend to dominate a discussion, speak more frequently than others, feel less inhibited, and experience lower levels of communication apprehension.[43] Compulsive talkers focus on expressing their own ideas and fail to listen to what others have to say.

Unfortunately, compulsive talkers are often unaware that their behavior is a problem. If you answer *yes* to several of the following questions, you may be a compulsive talker.[44]

- Do you speak significantly more than other group members?

- Do you direct the course of a group's discussion?
- Do you immediately take charge of a group?
- Do you forcefully express opinions on even minor issues?
- Do you speak for long periods of time without pausing?

A compulsive talker can frustrate group members by depriving them of a chance to express or respond to ideas during a discussion. One way to rein in a compulsive talker is to set ground rules or time limits for discussion. For example, you could say, "In order for us all to have a say, let's limit our comments on this issue to two minutes each." In other instances, it may simply be necessary to interrupt, "Sean, I appreciate your comments, but I would like to hear what others have to say on the matter."

eye on less-than-confident participants. Often you will see members take a breath as though they want to speak, only to be stifled by your continued comments or by the comments of others. When that happens, conclude your remarks and give that person an opportunity to speak.

Member Assertiveness

Remember This

Assertive group members have the confidence to stand up for themselves while interacting with others to achieve a group goal.

Assertiveness—speaking up and acting in your own best interests without denying the rights and interests of others[45]—has the potential to enhance the confidence and effectiveness of a group and its members. When expressed appropriately, assertive communication can also raise your level of confidence and reduce communication apprehension.

Assertive group members get along well with other members, are usually relaxed (as opposed to stressed) because they know how to handle most situations reasonably well, focus on the present rather than on past complaints or disappointments, and are confident about themselves and respectful of others.[46] How assertive are you? Take the quiz in Figure 3.3 to find out.

Even if you are a highly assertive group member, there are times when you may decide to be passive because an issue is unimportant or because the cost of getting your way is too high to achieve any benefits. In other situations, you may decide

Figure 3.3   Assertiveness Quiz[47]

Behavior	I usually act this way	I rarely act this way
1. When I make a mistake in a group, I admit it, apologize, and if possible, try to fix it.		
2. I speak up during group discussions when I have a question or believe I can answer another member's question.		
3. If a group member is not paying attention, having a side conversation, texting, or apparently daydreaming, I say something to get the member's attention back on task.		
4. If a group member says or does something that upsets me, I find an appropriate time to talk with the member about the problem.		
5. If a group member asks me to do a favor, but I'm very busy, I say that I cannot help out with making a big apology or making up an excuse.		
6. If a group member is rude or insulting to me or another member during a discussion, I interrupt and object to the behavior or insult.		
7. Generally, I look members in the eye when talking to them.		
8. If a group member justly criticizes me, I take time to analyze and correct the problem without becoming defensive.		
9. I express my emotions openly during group discussions.		
10. Even when I disagree with group members, I respect their right to express their opinions and feelings.		

to express yourself aggressively when an issue is very important and the benefits of achieving a particular goal outweigh the cost of interpersonal conflict. The key, again, is balance. You can choose assertiveness in some situations but decide to be passive or even aggressive in other situations depending on what is best for you and your group.

Balancing Passivity and Aggression

When members lack the will or skill to behave assertively, they may behave passively. **Passivity** is expressed when group members lack confidence and/or are reluctant to express their opinions and feelings. Passive members may experience high levels of communication apprehension, fear criticism from others, and do what they're told to do, even when they disagree with or dislike the order. They are rarely satisfied with their group experiences because they feel powerless and put-upon.

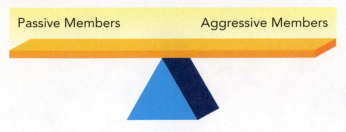

With **aggressiveness,** on the other hand, members act in their own self-interest at the expense of others. They are critical, insensitive, combative, and even abusive. They get what they want by taking over or by bullying other members into submission. As a consequence, they are often disliked and disrespected. In many cases, aggressive members behave this way because their needs are not met or they don't know how to express themselves assertively.

In some cases, passivity and aggression combine to create a third type of behavior—**passive-aggressive.** Passive-aggressive individuals rarely exhibit aggressive behavior, even though they lack respect for the rights of others. They also may appear confident rather than passive because they speak up and contribute. However, beneath the façade of effective participation lies a potentially destructive member. Passive-aggressives often get their way by undermining other members behind their backs, by behaving cooperatively but rarely following through with promised contributions, and by appearing to agree while privately planning an opposite action. For example, a passive-aggressive member may volunteer to work on a subcommittee but fail to do the work. A passive-aggressive member may appear to handle criticism calmly but then spread vicious rumors about the person who was critical.

The graph in Figure 3.4 demonstrates how group or member assertiveness represents a balance between passivity and aggression.[48] Group or member effectiveness increases as you move from passivity to assertiveness and then decreases as you move beyond assertiveness into aggressiveness.

Figure 3.4 Group Effectiveness and Member Assertiveness

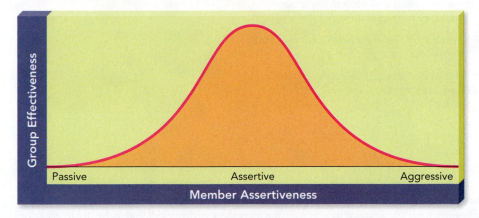

Assertiveness Skills

Regardless of how assertive you are, you can always improve your assertiveness skills. Building assertiveness skills incrementally can help you and your group increase in confidence while reducing social tensions. The following list includes both simple and complex skills for enhancing your assertiveness:

- Devote a significant amount of time to preparing for meetings.
- Enlist an assertive colleague who will make sure that you are recognized and given time to speak at meetings.
- Express your opinions clearly. Don't talk around the issue or ramble.
- Establish and maintain direct eye contact with individual group members.

Groups in Balance...

Know When and How to Say *No*

One of the most basic but difficult assertiveness skills is having the ability and confidence to say *no*. Randy Paterson, author of *The Assertiveness Workbook*, puts it this way: "If you cannot say *no*, you are not in charge of your own life."[49] Why, then, do so many people believe that if someone asks them to do something, they have to do it? Paterson offers several reasons:

- They won't accept my *no* and will expect me to do it anyway.
- They won't accept or like *me* if I say *no*.
- Given our relationship, I don't have the right or the courage to say *no*.[50]

Think of it this way: If someone said, "Can I have your car?" you'd say *no*, wouldn't you? What about "Would you write the group's paper and put everyone's name on it?" or "Can the group meet at your house on Sunday?"

Certainly there's nothing wrong with saying *yes* when the request is reasonable and you want to do it or you want to help someone. But what if you want to say *no*? Fortunately, there are several communication strategies and skills you can use to say *no*:

- Use assertive body posture. If you say *no* with your words, but signal *maybe* with your body, people will believe that you can be persuaded to do what they want.
- Decide on your wording. Use a clear statement, such as "No, I'm not willing to do that," rather than "Gee, I'm not sure…maybe another time."
- Don't apologize or make an excuse when it isn't necessary. Avoid statements such as "I'm sorry but I really can't…" or "I wish I could but… ."
- Don't ask permission to say *no*. Avoid saying, "Would it be okay if I didn't…?" or "Will you be upset if I say *no*?"
- Accept the consequences. Just as you have the right to say *no*, others have the right not to like it.[51]

- Assume an assertive body posture. Your body should be alert and focused in the direction of other speakers.
- Express your feelings as well as your thoughts. If you let group members see your emotions, your recommendations may be taken more seriously.
- Speak expressively—use volume, pitch, and rate to help your statements stand out.

Assertive group members reap many rewards. Generally, they are more satisfied with and proud of the work they do in groups. They are also more likely to become group leaders. Because assertive members respect the rights of others, they are well liked. There is much to be gained from exhibiting assertive behavior in groups, and first among those benefits is increased confidence.

High Need for Inclusion, Control, and Affection	Low Need for Inclusion, Control, and Affection
Task Roles	Maintenance Roles
High Communication Apprehesion	Low Communication Apprehesion
Assertiveness	Passivity; Aggressiveness

Ethics in Groups

Managing Manipulators

Manipulation describes the way people seek to influence and manage others, usually for self-centered reasons. For example, let's assume you have a high control need and that your experience and personality traits make you well suited for a leadership role you prize. By putting aside the rights and needs of group members, you enlist what you know about each member to get what *you* want, rather than what your group *needs*. If you know that some members have high inclusion needs, you may praise and reward them well beyond what they deserve so they feel valued—and beholden to you. If another member is highly apprehensive or reluctant to take on highly visible roles that require assertiveness, you may consign that member to a thankless or routine job. In these cases, you deceived some members and removed a potentially talented member from contributing in a meaningful way.

Now refer back to the list of Benne and Sheats group roles and consider just four of the *self-centered roles*: aggressor, blocker, dominator, and special interest pleader. These roles depend on a member's ability to manipulate, control, and motivate members to behave in a way that solely benefits the self-centered member.

The National Communication Association's Credo for Ethical Communication calls for a commitment to the "courageous expression of personal conviction in pursuit of fairness and justice."[52] Ethical group members have an obligation to assert themselves, not only to pursue their own goals, but also to prevent unjust or unethical behavior by others. For instance, the members of a medical team must have the courage to speak up if they believe that a patient is being given the wrong treatment. Whether your group is deciding how to trim a budget, determining the best candidate to hire, or developing a marketing campaign, each group member has the ethical responsibility to act assertively by expressing opposition to unethical group behavior and decisions.

Fortunately, the skillful use of assertiveness strategies can counteract such unethical behavior. Here are four strategies for dealing with a group member whose self-centered behavior seeks to manipulate others:[53]

1. **Identify the manipulative behavior.** What is the person doing to control you and other members? How did the manipulator criticize you and others? Be on the alert if you feel stressed or resentful when dealing with this member.
2. **Don't excuse or pardon the manipulator.** Don't fall for a manipulator who "plays the victim."
3. **Don't accept favors from manipulators**. You'll be expected to pay them back big time.
4. **Assert yourself.** Say *no* to manipulative demands. Encourage other members to do the same. In addition, use the following assertiveness techniques to deal with the manipulative behavior:

   • Distance yourself emotionally when dealing with the manipulator's comments and behaviors. Use logic instead of emotion when responding.
   • Challenge dishonest statements. Call out rudeness and offensive behavior.
   • Agree to disagree and/or change the subject.
   • Stand firm. Be prepared to use the "broken record" technique: Repeat yourself many times until the manipulator gets the point.
   • Enlist other group members to back you up when you take a stand and back them up when they confront a manipulator.

Summary Study Guide

Group Member Needs

- Schutz's FIRO Theory identifies three interpersonal needs (inclusion, control, and affection) that affect member behavior and group effectiveness.
- Whereas a social member's inclusion needs are met, undersocial or oversocial behavior may indicate that a member's inclusion needs are not met.
- Whereas a democratic member's control needs are met, control needs may not be met when members behave as abdicrats or autocrats.
- Whereas personal member's affection needs are met, underpersonal or overpersonal behavior may indicate that a member's affection needs are not met.

Member Roles

- When a group member exhibits a unique set of skills or behavior patterns that serve specific functions within the group, that member has assumed a role.
- Benne and Sheats divided group roles into three categories: group task roles (e.g., information seeker, coordinator, opinion giver, evaluator–critic), group maintenance roles (e.g., harmonizer, compromiser, tension releaser, gatekeeper), and self-centered roles (e.g., aggressor, blocker, dominator, special interest pleader).
- Belbin's Team-Role Theory identifies nine group roles: Coordinator/Chairperson, Shaper, Innovator, Resource Investigator, Monitor/Evaluator, Team Worker, Completer/Finisher, and Specialist.

Member Confidence

- Communication apprehension is an individual's level of fear or anxiety associated with either real or anticipated communication with another person or persons.
- The following strategies can help reduce communication apprehension: know that you are not alone, be well prepared, learn communication skills, relax physically, think positively (cognitive restructuring), and visualize success.
- The following strategies can help others reduce their level of communication apprehension: provide supportive and constructive feedback, encourage and include anxious members, and stop talking.

Member Assertiveness

- Assertiveness—speaking up and acting in your own best interests without denying the rights and interests of others—has the potential to enhance the confidence and effectiveness of a group and its members.
- Effective assertiveness seeks a balance between passivity and aggression, and avoids passive-aggressive behavior.
- Assertive group members know when and how to say "no" as well as when and how to manage manipulators.

GroupWork

Group Attraction Survey

Directions: Think of an effective group in which you currently work or in which you have worked in the past. Try to keep the group you select in mind as you complete this assessment instrument. The 15 statements to the right describe the possible reasons you joined or were attracted to your group. Indicate the degree to which each statement applies to you by marking whether you (5) strongly agree, (4) agree, (3) are undecided, (2) disagree, or (1) strongly disagree. Work quickly and record your first impression.

After completing your answers, form groups of five to seven students. Combine everyone's scores and then divide by the number of people in the group to arrive at the average score for each of the five attraction items. Discuss the following questions as a group or as a class:

- Did one or two items receive a much higher score than the others? If yes, why do you think these items topped the list?
- Did one or two of the items receive a lower average score than you would have anticipated?
- How do your scores compare to the group average? What does this say about the factors that do or do not attract you to group work?

Score Interpretation: A score of 12 or above in any category indicates that this source of attraction is an important reason that you joined and stay in this group. A score of 6 or below indicates that this source of attraction was not an important factor in joining this group and not a major reason for your staying in it. Examining your attraction to other groups in which you work may result in different scores.

____ 1. I like having authority and high status in the group.

____ 2. I want the other group members to act friendly toward me.

____ 3. Group members help one another solve personal problems.

____ 4. I am proud when the group achieves a goal or an objective.

____ 5. I try to be an active participant in group activities.

____ 6. Some group members are close friends.

____ 7. I become upset if group members waste time and effort.

____ 8. I like to do things with group members outside the group.

____ 9. Group members are excellent decision makers and problem solvers.

____ 10. Group members like me.

____ 11. I work hard to be a valuable group member.

____ 12. I try to influence the opinions and actions of group members.

____ 13. I like it when group members invite me to join their activities.

____ 14. I enjoy talking to group members, even when the conversation is unrelated to the group's goal.

____ 15. I try to get group members to do things the way I want them done.

Group Attraction	Scoring	Score
Seek task achievement	Add your responses to items 4, 7, and 9.	
Seek social interaction	Add your responses to items 3, 8, and 14.	
Seek inclusion	Add your responses to items 5, 11, and 13.	
Seek control	Add your responses to items 1, 12, and 15.	
Seek affection	Add your responses to items 2, 6, and 10.	
	Total Score	

Group Assessment

Personal Report of Communication Apprehension (PRCA-24)[54]

Directions: This instrument is composed of 24 statements concerning feelings about communication with other people. Indicate the degree to which each statement applies to you by marking whether you (1) strongly agree, (2) agree, (3) are undecided, (4) disagree, or (5) strongly disagree. Work quickly; record your first impression.

_____ 1. I dislike participating in group discussions.

_____ 2. Generally, I am comfortable while participating in group discussions.

_____ 3. I am tense and nervous while participating in group discussions.

_____ 4. I like to get involved in group discussions.

_____ 5. Engaging in a group discussion with new people makes me tense and nervous.

_____ 6. I am calm and relaxed while participating in a group discussion.

_____ 7. Generally, I am nervous when I have to participate in a meeting.

_____ 8. Usually I am calm and relaxed while participating in a meeting.

_____ 9. I am very calm and relaxed when I am called on to express an opinion at a meeting.

_____ 10. I am afraid to express myself at meetings.

_____ 11. Communicating at meetings usually makes me feel uncomfortable.

_____ 12. I am very relaxed when answering questions at a meeting.

_____ 13. While participating in a conversation with a new acquaintance, I feel very nervous.

_____ 14. I have no fear of speaking up in conversations.

_____ 15. Ordinarily I am very tense and nervous in conversations.

_____ 16. Ordinarily I am very calm and relaxed in conversations.

_____ 17. While conversing with a new acquaintance, I feel very relaxed.

_____ 18. I'm afraid to speak up in conversations.

_____ 19. I have no fear of giving a speech.

_____ 20. Certain parts of my body feel very tense and rigid while I am giving a speech.

_____ 21. I feel relaxed while giving a speech.

_____ 22. My thoughts become confused and jumbled when I am giving a speech.

_____ 23. I face the prospect of giving a speech with confidence.

_____ 24. While giving a speech, I get so nervous that I forget facts I really know.

Scoring: The PRCA permits computation of one total score and four subscores. The subscores are related to communication apprehension in each of four common communication contexts: group discussions, meetings, interpersonal conversations, and public speaking. To compute your scores, merely add or subtract your scores for each item as indicated here.

Scoring Formula

Group Discussions: 18 + scores for items 2, 4, and 6; minus scores for items 1, 3, and 5.

Meetings: 18 + scores for items 8, 9, and 12; minus scores for items 7, 10, and 11.

Interpersonal Conversations: 18 + scores for items 14, 16, and 17; minus scores for items 13, 15, and 18.

Public Speaking: 18 + scores for items 19, 21, and 23; minus scores for items 20, 22, and 24.

Subscores

_____ Group Discussions

_____ Meetings

_____ Interpersonal Conversations

_____ Public Speaking

To obtain your total score for the PRCA, simply add your four subscores together. Your score should be between 24 and 120. If your score is below 24 or above 120, you have made a mistake in computing the score. Scores for each of the four contexts (groups, meetings, interpersonal conversations, and public speaking) can range from a low of 6 to a high of 30. Any score above 18 indicates some degree of apprehension. If your score is above 18 for the public speaking context, you are like the overwhelming majority of Americans.

Norms for PRCA-24

	Mean	Standard Deviation
Total Score	65.5	15.3
Group	15.4	4.8
Meetings	16.4	4.8
Interpersonal	14.5	4.2
Public Speaking	19.3	5.1

Diversity in Groups

Chapter Outline

Case Study

No Offense Intended

The local arts council is proud of its diverse governing board. Born in Barbados, the male president chairs the chemistry department at a nearby liberal arts college. The vice president is a black female who retired from the local school system after 40 years of teaching high school music. The treasurer, a young black male with a master's degree in finance, was appointed by the county executive to oversee grant distribution. The secretary, a gay white male, has supported local arts programs for many years as a financial donor and fundraiser. The fifth member of the board is a white Jewish woman with a degree in theatre. The sixth member is a 25-year-old poet whose Japanese father and Chilean mother immigrated to the United States from Chile 30 years ago. You are the seventh member of the board.

During a long and heated discussion about revising the rules for awarding grant funds to artists and arts organizations, the exasperated treasurer announces, "Look, we've got to draft and implement a final solution to deal with the funding question." The Jewish woman gasps audibly. The secretary pauses in mid-sentence as he records the minutes of the meeting. Silence reigns.

The bewildered treasurer breaks the silence with "What's wrong?" The retired music teacher responds, "Don't you know the meaning of the *final solution*?" Then the Jewish woman says, "Please don't use the phrase *final solution*. You phrased your sentence almost exactly the way Hitler described his plan for exterminating the Jews." Another awkward silence.

As the seventh member of the arts council, what would you do?

When you finish reading this chapter, you should be able to answer the following critical thinking questions about this case study:

1   How does the diversity of the arts council's governing board help or hinder the group's ability to achieve its goals?

2   How, if at all, did generational differences influence group members' interpretation of the phrase *final solution*? Why or why not?

3   As a member of the governing board, how would *you* respond to the use of the phrase *final solution* and the resulting awkward silence in the group?

Helping Annie

The Politics of Sociology

Before you read any further, visit Pearson's MyCommunicationLab website and watch the short videos "Helping Annie" and "The Politics of Sociology," which illustrate Chapter 4 concepts. Each video comes with a set of study questions to keep in mind as you read this chapter.

A Balanced Approach to Group Diversity

Every person on this earth—and thus every member of a group—is different. Even identical twins have different experiences as well as different characteristics, abilities, and beliefs. Think about the many ways in which you differ from others by asking the following questions:

- Where did you grow up, and how did that influence who you are now?
- What aspects of your culture do you most appreciate and are you not likely to give up?[1]
- Which of your physical characteristics do you like or dislike?
- What are your interpersonal, intellectual, and physical skills?

Your answers to these questions reflect who you are and how you differ from other group members. These differences are not trivial. Your success, and that of your group, depends on your ability to handle the inevitable dialectic tensions that arise in diverse groups.

At the same time—and regardless of your culture, nationality, gender, religion, age, and abilities—you share more similarities than differences with others. The Institute for Global Ethics identifies seven core global values that transcend individual cultures and personal differences: love, truthfulness, fairness, freedom, unity, tolerance, responsibility, and respect for life.[2] And all of us smile when we're happy, blush when we're embarrassed, and cry when we're sad or in pain.[3]

James Surowiecki, author of *The Wisdom of Crowds*, explains that member diversity helps groups make better decisions because it "adds perspectives that would otherwise be absent."[4] James G. Marsh, an organizational theorist, explains that when groups are too much alike, they find it harder to keep learning because each member brings less and less new information to the table.[5] From these observations, it is clear that diversity is much more than accepting political correctness; instead, it offers advantages that are often essential to achieving a group's goals.

Follow the Research

Where Is *Your* Face in the U.S. Census?

According to the 2010 Census, the "face" of the United States continues to change in significant ways. More than half of the growth in the total U.S. population between 2000 and 2010 was due to increases in the Hispanic population. In 2000, Hispanics accounted for 35.3 million people and 13 percent of the population. In 2010, there were 50.5 million Hispanics in the United States, composing 16 percent of the total population. During the same period, the proportion of the non-Hispanic White population declined from 69 percent to 64 percent. Of all population groups, the Asian population had the fastest rate of growth and the non-Hispanic White population experienced the slowest growth. The Census Bureau notes that during the last ten years, the Hispanic population and the Asian population have grown considerably, in part due to relatively higher levels of immigration.[6]

The Census Bureau also reports that in 2010 Texas joined California, the District of Columbia, Hawaii, and New Mexico in having a "majority-minority" population with California leading the nation with the largest minority population (22.3 million).[7] Around the middle of this century, non-Hispanic white Americans will become one of the many minority groups living in the United States.[8] In other words, there will be no majority culture; group members will increasingly interact with classmates, neighbors, and colleagues from cultures different from their own.

Before going any further, we need to define the terms *culture* and *diversity*. **Culture** is "a learned set of shared interpretations about beliefs, values, and norms which affect the behaviors of a relatively large group of people."[9] Within most cultures, there are also groups of people—members of **co-cultures**—who coexist within the mainstream society yet remain connected to one another through their cultural heritage.[10] In the United States, Native American tribes are co-cultures, as are African Americans, Hispanic/Latino Americans, Asian Americans, Arab Americans, Irish Americans, and members of large and small religious groups. Given our broad definition of culture, a Nebraska rancher and a Boston professor can have very different cultural perspectives, as would a native Brazilian, an Indonesian Muslim, and a member of the Chippewa tribe.

Now let's compare the notion of culture to a broader concept: *diversity*. Diversity describes more than a person's country of origin, skin color, or ethnic heritage. When discussing group communication, we use the term **diversity** in its most general sense—the quality of being different. In just about every group, you will work with members whose physical characteristics, status, traits, values, and attitudes are different from yours. These distinctive characteristics include age, occupation, physical ability, marital status, personality preferences, and much more. Diversity exists in all groups.

In addition to differences in member cultures, a concept known as **deep diversity** describes characteristics that are much more difficult to observe, such as members' knowledge, skills, and abilities related to the demands of a group's task.[11]

 Groups in Balance...

Seek Intellectual Diversity

Let's assume you belong to a group whose members boast a higher-than-average IQ. You're eager and ready to roll because your group is so brilliant! There's just one problem: Smart groups do not always make smart decisions. Before you conclude that your group should look for a balance of *both* smart *and* dumb members, stop! Rather, your group should look for a balance of *both* smart, well-informed members *and* members with needed skills and diverse points of view.

Member diversity improves group performance and member satisfaction in many ways, including how well groups make "smart" decisions. Scott Page, a political scientist at the University of Michigan, studies groups and problem solving. Here's his conclusion:

On the group level, intelligence alone is not enough, because intelligence alone cannot guarantee you different perspectives on a problem.... Grouping only smart people together doesn't work that well because the smart people (whatever that

means) tend to resemble each other in what they can do.... Adding in a few people who know less, but have different skills, actually improves the group's performance.[12]

Think about the many intelligent people on a U.S. president's staff—and then consider some of the poor decisions made in the White House, for example, the failed U.S. invasion of Cuba in 1961, the Watergate conspiracy during the 1972 presidential election campaign, and the 2002 decision to go to war in Iraq. Then think about the well-educated, intelligent people who run U.S. corporations and consider some of their poor decisions—from denying they manufacture defective products to condoning or ignoring dishonest accounting practices. In Chapter 9, "Conflict and Cohesion in Groups," we examine Irving Janis's concept of *groupthink*, a phenomenon that describes the deterioration of group effectiveness that results from in-group pressure. As you will see, it takes a lot more than collective geniuses to avoid poor decision making.

A study by psychologist James Larson concludes that members of deeply diverse, heterogeneous groups widen the range of possible solutions to a problem, whereas homogeneous groups narrow the range of solutions they are likely to consider.[13] He adds that deeply diverse groups tend to perform better than the very best member in the group working alone. Deep diversity promotes synergy and, as a result, group productivity.[14]

Figure 4.1 illustrates three layers of diversity within every group member.[15] Your core personality—which permeates all the other layers—is at the center and represents your unique ways of experiencing, interpreting, and behaving in the world around you. The second layer represents internal dimensions over which you have no control. For example, you cannot change your race, age, or ethnicity. You may try to look younger or mask an accent, but you cannot change the number of years you have lived, the ethnicity of your parents, or your place of birth.

The third and outer layer represents societal and experiential factors such as religion, marital status, income, and educational background. If you change these dimensions by converting to another religion, by getting married or divorced, or by enhancing your income and educational background, your "new" external dimensions will affect how you see yourself and how others see you.

Figure 4.1   Three Layers of Diversity

Obstacles to Understanding Others

Effective group members develop strategies and skills for interacting with others from diverse backgrounds. Yet simply *learning* about other cultures and the differences among group members will not make you a more effective group member. You must also avoid four obstacles that prevent group members from interacting productively and achieving their goals: ethnocentrism, stereotyping, prejudice, and discrimination (see Figure 4.2).

Ethnocentrism

Ethnocentrism is a belief that your culture is superior to others. Ethnocentrism is not the same as patriotism; it is a mistaken belief that your culture is a superior culture, with special rights and privileges that are or should be denied to others. An ethnocentric communicator believes the following:

- My culture should be the role model for other cultures.
- People would be happier if they lived like people in my culture.
- Most other cultures are backward when compared with my culture.

Ethnocentric group members offend others when they imply that they represent a superior culture with superior values. For example, have you ever been insulted by someone who implies that because her religious beliefs are "true," she can go to heaven whereas you cannot? Have you been disrespected by someone who believes that his traditions, language, or music preferences are "better" than yours? If so, you have seen ethnocentrism in action.

Figure 4.2 Obstacles to Working in Diverse Groups

Barrier	Definition	Example
Ethnocentrism	A **belief** that your culture is superior to others.	"We select the 'best production team member of the month' because that's the good ol' American way of motivating other workers!"
Stereotyping	A **generalization** about a group of people that oversimplifies their characteristics.	"Let's appoint Sharon to take minutes because women are so much better at secretarial tasks."
Prejudice	A negative **attitude** about other people based on faulty and inflexible stereotypes.	"What would it look like if we made William the public spokesperson of our organization? He never finished college."
Discrimination	The **act** of excluding people who are "different" from opportunities granted to others.	"If possible, let's not ask anyone older than 50 to join our technology work team."

Stereotyping

A **stereotype** is a generalization about a group of people that oversimplifies their characteristics. Depending on the observers, stereotypes about white (non-Hispanic) Americans can be silly (Whites can't dance or play basketball) or severe (Whites are cold, dishonest, greedy, and racist).[16]

When we stereotype others, we rely on exaggerated beliefs to make judgments about a group of people. Unfortunately, stereotyping usually attributes negative traits to an entire group when, in reality, only a few people in that group may possess those traits. A study of college students found that, even in the 1990s, African Americans were stereotyped as lazy and loud, and Jews were stereotyped as shrewd and intelligent.

In addition to negative stereotypes, we may hold positive ones, such as "Asian students excel in math and science" or "Females are more compassionate than males." While positive stereotypes may not seem harmful, they can lead to unfair judgments. Stereotyping other group members does more than derail progress; it prevents members from contributing their best skills and may create long-lasting resentment and anger.

Prejudice

Stereotyping leads to **prejudices**—"negative attitudes about other people that are based on faulty and inflexible stereotypes."[17] Prejudices often arise when we have little or no direct experience with a cultural group. The word *prejudice* has two parts: *pre* meaning "before," and *judice*, as in "judge." When you believe or express a prejudice, you are making a judgment about someone before you have taken time to get to know that person and see whether your opinions and feelings are justified.

Although some prejudices may seem positive—"He must be brilliant since he went to Yale"—the result can be negative for those who don't conform to the prejudice. Statements such as "He can't be brilliant because he only has a community college degree," "I don't want a person with disabilities working on our group project," and "I'm not voting for a pregnant woman to lead this group" are all examples of prejudices based on stereotypes. Such prejudices have several characteristics:

- They rarely are based on extensive direct experience and firsthand knowledge.
- They result in irrational feelings or dislike and even hatred for certain groups.
- They justify a readiness to behave in negative and unjust ways toward members of the group.[18]

Discrimination

Discrimination refers to the behaviors in which we act out and express prejudice. When we discriminate, we exclude groups of people from opportunities available to others in areas such as employment, promotion, housing, political expression, and equal rights.

Sadly, discrimination comes in many forms: racial, ethnic, religious, and gender discrimination; sexual harassment; discrimination based on sexual orientation, disability, or age; and discrimination against people from different social classes and political ideologies. Discrimination has no place in groups.

Figure 4.3   Obstacles to Understanding Others

	Ethnocentrism	Stereotyping	Prejudice	Discrimination
Race	Most important discoveries were made by white Europeans like us.	Latinos are very emotional.	I hate it when blacks demand welfare payments.	I won't hire someone of another race.
Nationality	The U.S. is the best country in the world.	Japanese people are very polite.	I dislike Oriental markets because they cheat their customers.	I won't go to Indian restaurants.
Gender Issues	My gender is more realistic and smarter than the other gender.	Men are good at home repairs; women are good at home decorating.	Most women are incapable of running a company as well as a man can.	I won't let a homosexual or lesbian babysit my kids.
Spiritual Beliefs	There is only one true religion and I am a faithful member of it.	Catholics are unquestioning in their obedience to the Pope.	If he's an atheist, he's not a decent or moral person.	I will vote against any proposal to build a Muslim mosque in our city.

Figure 4.3 above illustrates how these obstacles may apply with regard to race, nationality, gender issues, and spiritual beliefs.

Personality Dimensions

How would you answer the following question: Do members' personalities affect group productivity and member satisfaction? Anyone who has ever worked in a group knows the answer: Of course they do. Depending on the circumstances, these traits can help or hinder a group's interaction and progress toward a common goal.[19] Understanding personality theories helps a group balance its collection of diverse temperaments, traits, and talents.

The Big Five Personality Traits

Psychologists use the **Big Five Personality Traits** to describe five factors that, together, describe a personality. Like many of the group dimensions discussed in this textbook, personality traits have a dialectic perspective as well. Consider the five personality traits and their opposites in Figure 4.4 on the next page.[20]

Group researchers who study the Big Five Personality Traits conclude that high levels of agreeableness and emotional stability in groups are associated with group cohesiveness while conscientiousness is associated with task performance.[21] After all, who would choose or want to work with members who were unkind, neurotic, or careless?

Figure 4.4   The Big Five Personality Traits

Big Five Personality Traits	Characteristics Associated with the Big Five Personality Traits	Opposite Personality Trait
Extraversion	Outgoing, talkative, sociable, assertive, active	Introversion
Agreeableness	Cooperative, friendly, courteous, flexible, trusting, good-natured, tolerant	Disagreeableness
Conscientiousness	Self-disciplined, organized, thorough, responsible, hard-working, persevering	Carelessness
Emotional Stability	Calm, poised, secure	Neuroticism
Openness to Experience	Imaginative, curious, broadminded, intelligent, original, artistically sensitive	Closed to Experience

The Myers-Briggs Type Indicator®

In addition to the Big Five Personality Traits, a second personality theory demonstrates why and how group members react to group tasks and social interactions in different ways. The **Myers-Briggs Type Indicator (MBTI),** developed by Katharine C. Briggs and her daughter, Isabel Briggs Myers,[22] looks at the different ways in which "people *prefer* to use their minds, specifically, the way they perceive and the way they make judgments."[23] Thousands of corporations, including most Fortune 100 companies, use the Myers-Briggs Type Indicator "to identify job applicants whose skills match those of their top performers" and "to develop communication skills and promote teamwork among current employees."[24]

According to the MBTI, all of us have preferences of thought and behavior that fall into four categories, with two opposite preferences in each category. As you read about the following categories, ask yourself which preferences best describe your personality.[25]

Extrovert–Introvert.   These two traits describe where you like to focus your attention. An **extrovert**[26] focuses outward; an **introvert** focuses inward. The table below lists the characteristics of and differences between extroverts and introverts.

Whereas an extrovert usually likes working in groups and on committees, an introvert may prefer a solo assignment. Introverts need more time to think before they speak or act. A group may miss good ideas and needed analysis if it rushes into solutions proposed by enthusiastic extroverts.

Misunderstandings between extroverts and introverts are common in groups. "Extroverts complain that introverts don't speak up in meetings. Introverts criticize extroverts for talking too much and not listening well."[27] Effective groups balance the needs of both

Extrovert ◄──────►	Introvert
Outgoing, sociable, expressive	Reserved, private, contained
Enjoys groups and discussions	Prefers one-to-one interactions
Talks first, then thinks	Thinks first, then talks
Thinks out loud	Thinks to himself or herself
May dominate discussion	May speak less in discussion
Gets energy from being with others	Needs time alone to reenergize

Groups in Balance...

Value *Both* Introverts *and* Extroverts

In *The Introvert Advantage: How to Thrive in an Extrovert World*, psychologist Marti Olsen Laney writes that "introverts are often surprised when they are not valued for their considerable contributions" to a group, in part because they don't speak up. They also "find it hard to both absorb all the information and formulate an opinion about it. They need time away from meetings to sift and sort data." Some introverts can become "brainlocked" because they can't find the right words to express their meaning.[28] Yet introverts, rather than extroverts, are more likely to assume the important group roles such as monitor/evaluator, implementer, or observer/interpreter.

Laney offers several strategies for letting extroverts know that introverts are present, interested, and involved in a group and its work. If you are an introvert:

- Don't schedule too many meetings on the same day.
- Say hello and smile when you enter a meeting room.
- Take notes to help you focus your thoughts and avoid information overload.
- Nod your head, smile, and use eye contact to let others know you are listening.
- Say *something*. Ask a question, or restate what someone else has said.
- Let members know that you will continue to think about the topic and get back to them with a reaction.[29]

personality types by accommodating the differences in communication style and tapping the best ideas from all members.

Sensor–Intuitive. These two traits focus on how you look at the world around you. A **sensor** sees the trees; sensors like facts and details. An **intuitive** sees the forest; intuitives prefer the big picture. The table below lists the characteristics of and the differences between sensors and intuitives.

Sensors and intuitives often see things quite differently. Sensors like rules, systematic explanations, and detailed facts, whereas intuitives prefer theoretical models and often avoid rules and details.[30] Communication between sensors and intuitives can be difficult "because they see things so differently, and each believes that his or her information is more accurate, valid, and real."[31]

Groups need *both* kinds of members to function effectively and efficiently. Researchers Carl E. Larson and Frank M. J. LaFasto provide the following example: "In the construction business it's important to have the 'big picture' people who can see the conceptual side of a project and know when major changes are necessary. This viewpoint needs to be balanced by people who are at the job site supervising the very detail-oriented portions of the work. Both are necessary members of a good project team."[32]

Sensor ⟵	⟶ Intuitive
Focuses on details	Focuses on the big picture
Practical and realistic	Theoretical
Likes concrete information	Likes abstract information
Likes facts	Gets bored with facts and details
Trusts experience	Trusts inspiration and intuition
Values common sense	Values creativity and innovation
Likes rules	Likes to bend or break rules

Thinker	⟷	Feeler
Task oriented		People oriented
Objective, firm, analytical		Subjective, humane, appreciative
Prefers businesslike meetings		Prefers social interchange in meetings
Values competence, reason		Values relationships, harmony, and justice
Direct and firm minded		Tactful and tenderhearted
Thinks with the head		Thinks with the heart

Thinker–Feeler. These two traits explain how you make decisions. The **thinker** is task-oriented and logical. Thinkers take pride in their ability to think objectively. They often enjoy arguing and making difficult decisions; they want to get the job done, even if the cost is bad feelings among members. The **feeler** is people-oriented and seeks group harmony. Feelers want everyone to get along. They will spend time and effort helping others. The above table lists the characteristics of and the differences between thinkers and feelers.

When thinkers and feelers work together in groups, there is the potential for misunderstanding. Thinkers may appear unemotional and aggressive. Feelers may annoy others by "wasting" time with social chitchat. Thinkers should try to remember that what they intend as good advice may strike others as unkind. Feelers should learn not to take criticism too personally and to speak up if they feel they're being treated unfairly.[33] When thinkers and feelers appreciate their differences as decision makers, they can form an unbeatable team. While the thinkers make decisions and move the group forward, feelers make sure that the group is working harmoniously.

Judger–Perceiver. The last two traits focus on how you deal with the outer world and its problems. The **judger** is highly structured and well organized. Judgers plan ahead, follow lengthy to-do lists, and look for closure. They are very punctual and can become impatient with people who show up late or waste time. The **perceiver** likes open-endedness and sees being on time as less important than being flexible and adaptable. Perceivers are risk takers who are willing to try new options. However, they often procrastinate and end up in a frenzy to complete a task on time. The table below lists the characteristics of and differences between judgers and perceivers.

Judgers and perceivers often have difficulty working together. To a judger, a perceiver may appear "air-headed" or scatterbrained. To a perceiver, a judger may appear rigid and controlling. Whereas judgers come prepared to make decisions and solve problems, perceivers "aren't comfortable with things being 'decided'; [they] want to reopen, discuss, rework, argue for the sake of arguing."[34] As difficult as it is for them, judgers should try to stop "doing" and take time to relax with others. Perceivers should try to respect deadlines and keep the promises that they make to judgers.

Judger	⟷	Perceiver
Values organization and structure		Values flexibility and spontaneity
In control and definite		Goes with the flow
Likes deadlines and is usually punctual		Dislikes deadlines and is often late
Work now/play later		Play now/work later
Needs standards and expectations		Feels constrained by rules, takes risks
Adjusts schedules to complete work		Works at the last minute

Balancing Personality Types in Groups

Most groups benefit when there is an appropriate mix and balance of personality traits. A group without judgers or members who possess the conscientiousness trait may miss important deadlines and fail to achieve its goal. A group that lacks members who are open to experience will fail to develop innovative approaches or seek creative solutions. A group without a sensor can overlook important details or critical flaws in a proposal.

According to Otto Kroeger and Janet Thuesen, in an ideal group, "we would have a smattering of Extroverts, Introverts, Sensors, Intuitives, Thinkers, Feelers, Judgers, and Perceivers—and we would put them together in such a way that they would not only understand their differences but could also draw upon them."[35]

Remember This

Although it is tempting to choose members who are similar to you, your group will perform better with representatives of every personality type.

Motivating Personality Types in Groups

Chandra, an intuitive extrovert, is asked to edit and proofread a 50-page report analyzing her company's hiring procedures. She tries to do her best, but finds her eyes glazing over by the time she's on the second page. Jerome, an introverted sensor, is asked to answer impromptu questions about hiring problems at a staff meeting. He draws a blank because he needs time to think over the questions before answering. Instead of being motivated, Chandra and Jerome are frustrated. Fortunately, adapting to their personality types can motivate their productivity and personal satisfaction. Figure 4.5 offers a summary of the many ways in which different personality types call for different approaches to motivation.[36]

Figure 4.5 Personality Types and Member Motivation

Type-Based Motivational Strategies

Extrovert
- Encourage interaction.
- Allow time for "talking out" ideas.
- Provide frequent feedback.

Introvert
- Set clear and valued goals.
- Provide thinking time before and during discussions.
- Provide introverts more opportunities to speak.

Sensor
- Set realistic goals.
- Keep meetings short and relevant.
- Request real, practical information.

Intuitive
- Develop an engaging goal.
- Encourage visioning and creativity.
- Encourage brainstorming.

Thinker
- Focus on task dispassionately.
- Encourage debate on substantive issues.
- Encourage logical decision-making.

Feeler
- Discuss impact of decisions on people.
- Encourage cooperation and harmony.
- Recognize members' contributions.

Judger
- Encourage closure on issues.
- Provide an agenda and deadlines.
- Set standards and expectations.

Perceiver
- Focus on a variety of alternatives.
- Keep the time frame open.
- Let a decision gradually emerge from discussion.

Now reconsider Chandra's and Jerome's frustrations and their lack of motivation. One way to engage their unique talents more effectively is to let them switch tasks so that Chandra answers impromptu questions about hiring problems and Jerome edits the report. Understanding the personality types of group members helps you choose effective motivational strategies.

Cultural Dimensions

We owe a great deal to a social psychologist and an anthropologist for identifying several significant dimensions of culture. Dutch social psychologist Geert Hofstede's groundbreaking research on cultural dimensions has transformed our understanding of culture and diversity. He defines a **cultural dimension** as "an aspect of a culture that can be measured relative to other cultures."[37] Three of Hofstede's dimensions are individualism–collectivism, power distance, and masculine–feminine values. Anthropologist Edward T. Hall adds two more dimensions: high-context and low-context cultures and monochronic-polychronic time.[38] Figure 4.6 on the next page provides an overview of these six cultural dimensions and how they can be used to recognize and adapt to group member diversity.

Individualism–Collectivism

According to Hofstede and many contemporary researchers, most people in the United States accept **individualism** as a cultural value. As a whole, we believe that the individual is important, that independence is worth pursuing, that personal achievement should be rewarded, and that individual uniqueness is an important value.[39]

In the United States, an "I" orientation prevails. However, most cultures put less value on individualism: as much as 70 percent of the world's population regards *inter*dependence or **collectivism** as a more important value.[41] In these cultures, "we" is much more important than "I." The following behaviors are characteristic of collectivist cultures:

Remember This

The United States is the most individualistic culture in the world.

Geert Hofstede, *Culture's Consequences*[40]

- The views, needs, and goals of the group receive more emphasis than those of individual members.
- Group beliefs are more important than those of individuals.
- There is greater readiness to cooperate with group members.[42]

At first, a collectivist perspective may appear ideally suited for group work. Yet the opinions of individualistic members help a group recognize and adapt to a variety of useful perspectives.

Be careful not to stereotype *all* Americans as individualistic just because the United States ranks first among individualistic cultures. Many Americans are not highly individualistic; this is especially true of co-cultures in the United States. For example, African Americans often share the characteristics of collectivist societies, as do Mexican Americans and other Hispanic/Latino co-cultures. Even so, the predominant U.S. focus on individual achievement and personal

Figure 4.6 Cultural Dimensions of Group Members

Cultural Dimension	Definition and Example	Group Member Behavior	Recommended Adaptations
Individualist–Collectivist	Prefer to act independently or interdependently. **Individualism:** Value individual achievement and freedom. United States, Australia, Great Britain, Canada **Collectivism:** Emphasize group identity. Guatemala, Ecuador, Panama, Venezuela	**Individualistic members** tend to work alone and seek credit for their own work. **Collectivist members** like to work in groups and try to help each other.	Encourage collectivism. Help individualistic members understand that they are part of a larger group that needs their input and participation to achieve a shared goal.
Power Distance	Extent of equity or status among members. **High Power:** Inequity between high- and low-status members. Malaysia, Guatemala, Panama, Philippines **Low Power:** Equity and interdependence among group members. Austria, Israel, Denmark, New Zealand	**High-power-distance members** try to take charge and make decisions. **Low-power-distance members** seek consultation and consensus.	Establish clear norms for member behavior. To what extent will members participate in decision making? How willl specific tasks be assigned? How and by whom will members be evaluated? Who will serve as leader(s)?
Masculine–Feminine Values	Concern for self and success versus a focus on caring and sharing. **Masculine Values:** Assertive, decisive, dominant. Japan, Austria, Venezuela, Italy **Feminine Values:** Nurturing, cooperative. Sweden, Norway, Denmark, Costa Rica	**Masculine-value members** focus on the task and personal success. **Feminine-value members** focus on member relations and respect for others.	Balance masculine and feminine values in order to achieve task and social goals. Do not forgo action in order to achieve total cooperation and consensus.
High Context–Low Context	Directness of communication in specific circumstances. **High Context:** Messages are implied and context-sensitive. Japan, China Greece, Mexico **Low Context:** Messages are explicit, factual, and objective. Great Britain, United States, Germany	**High-context members** consider non-verbal cues and inter-personal history/background when communicating. **Low-context members** want facts and clear, direct, explicit communication.	Give high-context members time to review information and react; demonstrate the value of going beyond "just facts" to low-context members.
Monochronic–Polychronic	How people organize and value time. **Monochronic:** Adhere to plans, schedules, and deadlines; time is valuable. United States, Canada, Germany, Switzerland. **Polychronic:** Not obsessed with promptness or schedules. Kenya, Argentina, Saudi Arabia, Egypt, Mexico, Philippines	**Monochronic members** focus on one task at a time and work hard to meet deadlines. **Polychronic members** are frequently late, do many things at once, are easily distracted and tolerant of interruptions.	Encourage monochronic members to take responsibility for time-sensitive tasks while accepting that polychronic members will vary their promptness based on the nature and importance of a situation or relationship.

rewards can make interaction with group members from collectivist cultures quite challenging. Group members from these cultures may view a highly individualistic communication style and behavior as selfish, arrogant, ruthless, and impatient.

Power Distance

Can you walk into your boss's office unannounced, or do you have to run a gauntlet of administrative assistants and other gatekeepers? Is it easy to make a personal appointment with the president of your college or university? Does our society truly believe in the sentiments expressed in the U.S. Declaration of Independence that all people "are created equal"? These are the questions addressed in Hofstede's power distance dimension. **Power distance** refers to the physical and psychological distance between those who have power and those who do not have power in relationships, institutions, and organizations. It also represents "the extent to which the less powerful person in society accepts inequality in power and considers it normal."[43]

In cultures with **high power distance**, individuals accept major differences in power as normal, assuming that all people are *not* created equal. In a high-power-distance culture, you dare not challenge authority. Parents, for example, may have total control over their children, and men may have total control over the women in their family. The government, corporate officers, and religious or legal authorities dictate the rules of behavior and enforce them.

In cultures with **low power distance**, power distinctions are minimized: Supervisors work with subordinates; professors work with students; elected

Power distance refers to the physical and psychological distance between those who have power and those who do not have power in relationships, institutions, and organizations. How do the men in this photograph demonstrate the power distance dimension in the Japanese culture?

officials work with constituents. Despite the fact that the United States claims to be the greatest democracy on earth and an equal opportunity society, Hofstede ranks the United States sixteenth on the list of low-power-distance cultures—after countries such as Finland, Switzerland, Great Britain, Germany, Costa Rica, Australia, the Netherlands, and Canada.[44]

Power distance has enormous implications for groups, particularly given the strong correlation between collectivism and high power distance and between individualism and low power distance. If you are individualistic and are comfortable expressing your opinions, you are probably willing to challenge group members and leaders. If, on the other hand, your culture is collectivist and your personal opinion is subordinate to the welfare of others, you are less likely to challenge the collective authority of a group or its leader.

Masculine–Feminine Values

Hofstede uses the terms *masculine* and *feminine* to describe whether a culture *values* masculine or feminine traits. When first reading about this cultural dimension, many people mistakenly think we're describing cultures in which everyone is feminine (and even effeminate in behavior) or everyone is masculine (and even macho). Hofstede rates Japan as the society with the most masculine values. However, don't assume that all Japanese share masculine values. These traits describe a societal perspective, not individual men or women.

In **masculine value societies**, men are supposed to be assertive, tough, and focused on material success, whereas women are supposed to be more modest, tender, and concerned with the quality of life. In **feminine value societies**, gender roles overlap: *Both* men *and* women are more modest, tender, and concerned with the quality of life.[45]

Hofstede ranks the United States as fifteenth in terms of masculine values. Japan, as we noted, is first on the list, followed by Austria and Venezuela.[46] Masculine value societies esteem personal success, competition, assertiveness, and strength. Unselfishness and nurturing is often seen as a weakness or "women's work."

Think of the challenges groups face when there is a mix of masculine and feminine values. Members with masculine values may compete for leadership positions and exhibit highly assertive behavior. Members with more feminine values may be highly effective and supportive but never achieve a real voice or influence in the group. Later in this chapter, we take a closer look at the ways in which men and women view group work as well as how they communicate.

High Context–Low Context

All communication occurs in a **context**, a physical and psychosocial environment. Anthropologist Edward T. Hall sees context as the information that surrounds an event and clarifies its meaning.[47] He claims that context in and of itself may hold more meaning than the actual words in a message. As with Hofstede's dimensions, we can place cultures on a continuum from high context to low context.

In a **high-context culture**, people are *not* totally dependent on words to express their meaning. Gestures, silence, and facial expressions have meaning, as does the nature of relationships among communicators. In high-context cultures, meaning is also conveyed through status (age, gender, education, family background, title, and affiliations) and through an individual's informal network of friends and associates.[48]

In a **low-context culture**, people are more dependent on language to express what they mean. As members of a low-context culture, North Americans tend to speak more, speak louder, and speak more rapidly than people from a high-context culture. We "speak up," "spell it out," "tell it like it is," and "speak our mind."

High-context communication is a common characteristic in collectivist cultures where members share similar attitudes, beliefs, and values. As a result, spoken communication can be indirect and implied because everyone *gets* the meaning by understanding the context, the person's nonverbal behavior, and the significance of the communicator's relationships with others. Notice how the following sayings capture the nature of high-context communication:

Seeing is better than hearing. (Nigeria)

Once you preach, the point is gone. (Zen phrase)

Group members from high- and low-context cultures express and interpret messages differently. For example, suppose everyone knows that Allison and Philip have a close personal relationship. During a group discussion, Allison scowls every time Philip expresses his opinion or makes a suggestion. However, when asked whether she agrees with Philip, she says yes. Group members with high-context perspectives would pay more attention to Allison's nonverbal behavior and decide that she is angry with Philip and disapproves of his ideas, whereas members with low-context perspectives may only hear the "yes" and assume that Allison and Philip are in total agreement.

Monochronic Time–Polychronic Time

Edward Hall classifies time as a form of communication. He claims that cultures organize time in one of two ways: either monochronic or polychronic.[49] In **monochronic time (M time)**, events are scheduled as separate items—one thing at a time. M-time people like to concentrate on one job before moving to another and may become irritated when someone in a meeting brings up a personal topic unrelated to the purpose of the meeting.

In **polychronic time (P time)**, schedules are less important and are frequently broken. People in polychronic cultures are not slaves to time. If you are a P-time person, you probably like thinking about and doing several tasks at one time, and feel comfortable holding two or three conversations at the same time. In polychronic-time cultures—such as the Spanish-speaking cultures in Spain and Latin America—relationships are far more important than schedules. "Appointments will be quickly broken, schedules readily set aside, and deadlines unmet without guilt or apology when friends or family members require attention."[50]

When monochronic- and polychronic-time people interact in groups, the results can be frustrating. Hall notes that monochronic people become distressed by how polychronic people seem to disrespect deadlines and schedules. For P-time people, schedules and commitments, particularly plans for the future, are not firm, and even important plans may change right up to the last minute.[51]

If you are an M-time person, try to modify and relax your concern with time and scheduling when working with P-time members. If you are a P-time person, do your best to respect and adapt to monochronic members' need for careful scheduling and promptness.

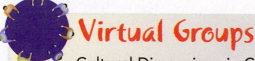

Virtual Groups

Cultural Dimensions in Cyberspace

Not surprisingly, cultural dimensions significantly affect the success of virtual groups. In their well-respected book *Mastering Virtual Teams*, Nancy Duarte and Deborah Snyder use Hofstede's dimensions and Hall's research on context to explain how culture affects the way we use communication technology.[52] We have added a brief discussion of how the monochronic–polychronic dimension affects virtual groups.

- *Individualism–collectivism.* Members from collectivist cultures prefer face-to-face interactions, whereas individualistic communicators like having the screen to themselves as they present their ideas and opinions.
- *Low power distance–high power distance.* Members from high-power-distance cultures communicate more freely when technologies are asynchronous (do *not* occur in real time) and when anonymous input is possible. In other words, when asynchronous technology conceals power relationships, subordinate members from high-power-distance cultures may be more willing to challenge authority.
- *Masculine–feminine values.* Members from cultures with more feminine values use technology as a way of encouraging, supporting, and motivating others, while members from cultures with more masculine values see such nurturing behavior as a waste of precious meeting time.
- *High context–low context.* People from high-context cultures prefer more information-rich technologies (such as videoconferences), as well as media that offer the feeling of social presence. People from low-context cultures prefer more asynchronous communication with the ability to "get it in writing" via email and other writing-only virtual media.
- *Monochronic–polychronic.* Monochronic members become frustrated by polychronic members who are late to join a teleconference. Polychronic members become distracted during an online meeting and interrupt the group to discuss unrelated issues.

Gender Dimensions

John Gray's popular (and misleading) book *Men Are from Mars, Women Are from Venus* describes stark psychological differences between men and women. His book has sold more than 30 million copies and has been translated into 40 languages.[53] Deborah Tannen's *You Just Don't Understand: Women and Men in Conversation* claims that boys and girls grow up in what are essentially different cultures, making talk between men and women a cross-cultural experience. Whereas men seek status and independence, women seek connection and interdependence.[54] Unfortunately, both books have perpetuated harmful stereotypes that negatively affect career opportunities and advancement, conflicts in male-female couples, and self-esteem problems among adolescents of both genders.[55] These stereotypes can also hamper groups working to achieve a common goal.

Researchers who scrutinize studies of male and female differences claim that men and women are alike on most—but not all—psychological variables.[56] In other words, males and females are much more similar than different.

Unfortunately, many people still believe there are major psychological differences between men and women. These beliefs are learned perceptions based on outdated assumptions, traditional family roles, and the influence of various media. (See the Muted

Remember This

Men are not from Mars; women are not from Venus. We are all from Earth.

Follow the Research

Who Talks More—Women or Men?

Who talks more: women or men? Many people believe that women talk more than men do. Yet most women experience just the opposite, particularly when they're working in groups. Social scientists Rodney Napier and Matti Gershenfeld explain that the opposite is true:

> Throughout history, women have been punished for talking too much or in the wrong way.… Yet study after study shows that it is men who talk more—at meetings, in mixed-group discussions held in classrooms where girls or young women sit next to boys or young men.… And not only did men speak for a longer time, but the women's longest turns were shorter than the men's shortest turns."[57]

A recent study of college students found that the number of words uttered by males and females were virtually the same. Men actually "yakked slightly more than women, especially when interacting with spouses or strangers and when the topic was non-personal." Women talked more with classmates, with parents and children, and in situations where the topic of conversation required disclosure of feelings.[58]

Group Theory feature below.) In cartoons, books, and films, knights in shining armor still save maidens in distress. And Mom knows best how to clean auto grease off Dad's pants.

Research in group communication finds that some female members feel undervalued or even invisible when working with male group members. William Sonnenschein, a diversity consultant and university professor, often hears working women complain that when they say something in a meeting, no one responds, yet a few minutes later a man makes the same suggestion and is praised for the quality of his input.[59]

Theory in Groups

Muted Group Theory

Cheris Kramarae's **Muted Group Theory**[60] examines "the ways that the communication practices of dominant groups suppress, mute, or devalue the words, ideas, and discourses of subordinate groups."[61] When Kramarae uses the term *dominant groups*, she refers to a dominant group and a subordinate group within a *single* group. For example, she often describes women and minorities as subordinate groups within a larger group in which white males are the dominant group.

Even though members of subordinate groups may speak *and* have a lot to say, their messages are "often disrespected, and their knowledge often not considered sufficient for decision or policy making."[62] Kramarae helps explain why and how women's voices, in particular, are subdued or silenced. "Women in most if not all cultures are not as free or as able as dominant men are to say what they want to say, when and where they wish to say it, without ridicule or punishment."[63] However, we urge you to avoid making hasty generalizations about the role of women and minorities in groups. For example, in a group composed primarily of influential African Americans, a less powerful white male may be muted. When black and white women work together in groups, the white women may criticize and try to mute the more outspoken speaking style of black women.[64]

Muted Group Theory has direct relevance to how we work in groups. Kramarae claims that subordinate groups (women and other minority groups) "do not control language and speech in the same way men do."[65] For example, Hofstede labels his dimension masculine–feminine values. Why not feminine–masculine values? What about the fact that most U.S. women take their husband's surname when they get married? And even when a married woman has kept her own surname, her children typically take their father's surname?

According to Muted Group Theory, groups with power in a society tend to mute the voices of less powerful groups. What can less powerful groups, such as women, do to counteract this tendency?

If you are a member of a less powerful subordinate group or (equally important) you are a member *with* power, you can use several strategies to counter the effects of Muted Group Theory and encourage interaction and contributions from *all* members:

- **Call attention to the silencing strategy.** If a member disrespects a subordinate group member, call out the person responsible for it. "Fred, you've interrupted Kara three times in the last few minutes. Please let her finish so I understand what she's saying."
- **Identify the value of differences.** "Of course, I'm emotional about this issue. Our decision could have negative consequences, so it's very important that we talk about how it affects others."
- **Be assertive.** Speak up and act in your own best interests without denying the rights and interests of others. "I realize you may not have known that my husband and I are Muslims. I think you owe me an apology, and I trust this won't happen again."
- **Resist stereotyping.** "Why are the women in this group always asked to take minutes? Let's practice an equal opportunity policy and ask the men do it, too."

Generational Dimensions

Once upon a time, we classified people based on their age by putting them into one of two categories: old and young. Today—probably because of marketing and advertising research—we catalogue, grade, and pigeonhole people of different ages based on their potential as buyers and voters. Labeling any group allows members to identify with their contemporaries and to view other generations with some level of suspicion and even disapproval. After all, how can "they" be as good and as smart as "we" are? What follows are brief descriptions of four generational dimensions:[66]

- *Traditionalists or the Builder Generation, born 1900 to 1945.* Two world wars and the Great Depression taught this generation how to live within limited means. Traditionalists are loyal, hardworking, financially conservative, and faithful to institutions.
- *Baby Boomers or the Boomer Generation, born 1946 to 1964.* This generation grew up with television and experienced the Vietnam War. Many of them bravely challenged the status quo and are responsible for many of the civil rights and opportunities we now take for granted. As a whole, this generation knows how to navigate political minefields in the workplace. Boomers often believe

they are always right and are willing to work hard to get what they want. The term *workaholic* was coined to describe Baby Boomers.

- *Generation Xers or the X Generation, born 1965 to 1980.* Generation Xers are technologically savvy in the era of video games and personal computers. Because they witnessed increasing employment layoffs and challenges to the presidency, organized religion, and big corporations, they are often skeptical and distrustful of institutions. Generation Xers believe that work isn't the most important thing in their lives.
- *Millennials, the Net Generation, Generation Yers, or Nexters, born 1981 to 1999.* Many Millennials are still in school or just graduating from college. This generation grew up with cell phones and personal computers. Generally, they're confident and have high self-esteem. They're collaborators and favor teamwork, having functioned in groups in school, organized sports, and extracurricular activities from a very young age. They take on many activities at once and like keeping their career options open.

The mixing of generations in families, communities, college classrooms, and work settings adds diversity *and* potential difficulties to the challenge of communicating in groups. Of all the generational mixes, the interaction of Baby Boomers with Generation Xers and Millennials may create problems. When a young worker says, "Why do you care what I wear if I do my job?" the Baby Boomer may explain that "Dressing appropriately is part of your job." When a Millennial says, "You're threatened by us because we know how to use technology better," the Baby Boomer may say, "Who do you think invented the technology?"[67]

Let's take a closer look at one set of intergenerational differences—how Baby Boomers and Generation Xers can learn to interact more effectively.[68] Many of these strategies also apply to the interaction of Baby Boomers and Millennials. If you belong to Generation X and work in groups with Baby Boomers, you should:

- Show respect to Baby Boomers and acknowledge that you have less experience and can learn from them.
- Communicate face to face rather than relying totally on email or text messages. Learn to play the political game. Baby Boomers are often diplomatic and can help Generation Xers navigate politically charged group environments.
- Learn the corporate history and culture. Nothing bothers Baby Boomers more than a new, young employee who wants to change things, with seemingly no thought given to what's gone on before.

As a Baby Boomer working with Generation Xers, you should:

- Get to the point. State your objectives clearly.
- Avoid micromanaging Generation Xers, who need autonomy.
- Don't expect them to be workaholics. Generation Xers—who value a healthy work–life balance—may not spend as many hours at work, and they're getting ahead anyway.
- Lighten up. Remind yourself that it's okay for work to be fun. Generation Xers tend to think that Baby Boomers are too intense and set in their ways.

Whereas many Baby Boomers see group work as being more like a football game in which all members act together according to a plan, the younger generations see group work as more like a relay race: "I'll give it all I've got—when and where I'm supposed to."[69]

Not surprisingly, the AARP, a nonprofit advocacy organization for people age 50 and over, enjoys pointing to research showing that older adults are better at solving problems, more flexible in their strategies, and better able to keep their cool during a crisis than are younger people. They also tend to bounce back from a bad mood more quickly. As one neurobiologist notes, in the old days, we called it wisdom.[70] Of course, in the not-too-distant future, today's younger generations will be older (and hopefully just as wise), and researchers will probably make the same claims about them.

Religious Dimensions

There are more than 4,000 religions in the world. Like most of us, you may be familiar only with the "big" religions and a few "obscure" faiths. Yet, as Stephen Prothero claims in his book *Religious Literacy*, many of us lack **religious literacy**, which he defines as "the ability to understand and use the religious terms, symbols, images, beliefs, practices, scripture, heroes, themes, and stories that are employed in American public life."[71]

Prothero, a professor of religion at Boston University, acknowledges that Americans are a very religious people: 90 percent of adults in the United States believe in God, 80 percent say that religion is important to them personally, and more than 70 percent report praying daily.[72] Yet many of these Americans know very little about their *own* religion, let alone the religions of others.

More recently, the independent Pew Forum on Religion and Public Life conducted a national survey of Americans asking questions about the Bible,

The power of religious respect and cooperation are evidence in this photo as Buddhist nuns join Catholic sisters and other religious leaders to mark a four-year ceasefire agreement between the Sri Lanka government and the Tamil rebels at an interreligious conference.

Christianity, and other world religions as well as famous religious figures. On average, people answered only half the questions correctly, and many flubbed questions about their own religions (e.g., 53 percent of Protestants could not identify Martin Luther as the person who started the Protestant Reformation). Interestingly, the groups with the highest scores were atheists and agnostics, followed by two religious minorities, Jews and Mormons.[73]

Test your own knowledge about a few of the world's major religions by taking the brief Religious Knowledge Quiz in Figure 4.7.[74] Prothero shares the following results from several of his own surveys:[75]

- Only 50 percent of survey respondents could name even one of the four Gospels.
- Most Americans could not name the first book of the Hebrew Bible.
- Ten percent of the surveyed Americans thought that Joan of Arc was Noah's wife.

Regardless of whether you are a Catholic, Mormon, Jew, Muslim, Buddhist, Baptist, Hindu, Sikh, Janist, or atheist, "you must remember that people feel

Figure 4.7   Religious Knowledge Quiz

Test Your Religious Literacy

T = True
F = False
? = I Don't Know

1. T F ? In Islam, Jesus, Abraham, and Mohammed are prophets.

2. T F ? Judaism is an older religion than Buddhism.

3. T F ? Islam is a monotheistic religion (belief in one God) just like Christianity and Judaism.

4. T F ? A Christian Scientist believes that disease is a delusion that can be cured by prayer.

5. T F ? Jews fast during Yom Kippur; Muslims fast during Ramadan.

6. T F ? Jesus Christ was a Jew.

7. T F ? Roman Catholics throughout the world outnumber all other Christians combined.

8. T F ? Sunni Muslims compose about 90 percent of all adherents to Islam.

9. T F ? Hindus believe in reincarnation.

10. T F ? The Ten Commandments are the basis of Jewish laws.

11. T F ? Mormonism is a Christian faith founded in the United States.[76]

12. T F ? Protestant reformer Martin Luther labeled the religious beliefs of Muslims, Jews, and Roman Catholics as false.

13. T F ? One-third of the world's population is Christian.

14. T F ? One-fifth of the world's population is Muslim.

15. T F ? Hinduism is the oldest of the world's major religions, dating back more than 3,000 years.

Answers: All the above statements are true.

strongly about their religion, and that differences between religious beliefs and practices do matter."[77] For example, the Oriya Brahmans of India consider it shameful and shocking if a husband and wife eat meals together. The French government has moved to ban religious attire in public schools, including headscarves for Muslim girls, Christian crosses, and the skullcaps worn by Jewish and Muslim men (as well as Catholic priests).[78]

Although a group's goal may have nothing to do with religion, members should be sensitive to the diverse religious beliefs of others. Lee Gardenswartz and Anita Rowe provide several examples. Seventh-day Adventists and observant Jews celebrate the Sabbath on Saturdays. These members may resent being asked or refuse to do group work on a Saturday. A Muslim group member who prays five times a day may want to be excused from meetings at worship times. Non-Christians and atheists may resent using group time for other members' religious holiday celebrations.[79] Groups can avoid such problems by asking and answering the following questions:

- How do the needs, attitudes, and practices of group members' religions affect our work?
- What adaptations should we make so we don't exclude members because of religious practices or beliefs?[80]

Ethics in Groups

The Golden Rule May *Not* Apply in Diverse Groups

The well-known Golden Rule—"Do unto others as you would have them do unto you"—may not work in groups with diverse members. Intercultural communication scholars Judith Martin and Thomas Nakayama note that "ethical principles are often culture-bound, and intercultural conflicts arise from varying notions of what constitutes ethical behavior."[81] For example, someone from an individualistic culture may see self-serving ambition as appropriate and ethical behavior—after all, that's how you get ahead and get things done. In collectivist cultures, however, the same behavior may be seen as unethical because the member is not putting group interests ahead of personal interests.

Ethical group members learn about cultural differences—the differences between their own culture and those of others. Martin and Nakayama recommend three strategies:[82]

1. **Practice self-reflection.**   When you learn about other cultures, you also learn more about your own beliefs—and your prejudices. For example, you may believe that arranged marriages are wrong because they deny individuals the right to choose a spouse. If, however, you meet someone in a successful arranged marriage, you may discover that there are some advantages, including a much lower divorce rate compared with traditional romantic marriages.

2. **Interact with others.**   Group members learn more about "others" by interacting with them and talking about differences. Although you can read about differences in racial perspectives or about European and Asian values, talking about such differences can help you understand group members as individuals rather than as stereotypical representatives of a different culture.

3. **Listen to others' voices.**   Listening to the experiences of others has the power to transform your understanding of cultures and realize how their voices may be stifled. Remember Muted Group Theory's claim that the communication practices of dominant groups mute or devalue the words and ideas of subordinate groups. Ethical group members should listen carefully to different voices as a way of integrating their contributions and perspectives into the group process.

Summary Study Guide

A Balanced Approach to Group Diversity

- Culture is a learned set of shared interpretations about beliefs, values, and norms which affect the behaviors of a relatively large group of people; the members of co-cultures coexist within a mainstream society yet remain connected to one another through their cultural heritage.
- A homogeneous group is composed of members who are the same or similar, and a heterogeneous group is composed of members who are not the same.
- Diversity exists in all groups and includes variables such as nationality, race, ethnicity, age, gender, occupation, physical ability, personality preferences, religion, marital and parental status, work experience, and much more.

Obstacles to Understanding Others

- Ethnocentric group members offend others by implying that they represent a superior culture with superior values.
- Stereotypes are generalizations about a group of people that oversimplify their characteristics.
- Prejudices are negative attitudes based on faulty or inflexible stereotypes rather than getting to know someone before drawing a conclusion.
- Discrimination wrongly excludes groups of people from opportunities granted to others.

Personality Dimensions

- In terms of the Big Five Personality Traits, high levels of agreeableness and emotional stability are associated with group cohesiveness while conscientiousness is associated with task performance.
- The Myers-Briggs Type Indicator® looks at the way we perceive the world around us and make judgments.
- Myers-Briggs categorizes personality traits in four categories with differing preferences: extrovert/introvert, sensor/intuitive, thinker/feeler, and judger/perceiver.

Cultural Dimensions

- As much as 70 percent of the world's population regards collectivism, or interdependence, as more important than individualism.
- High-power-distance cultures accept differences in power as normal, whereas low-power-distance cultures prefer to minimize power distinctions.
- In masculine value societies, men are supposed to be assertive and tough while women are expected to be more modest and tender. In feminine value societies, gender roles overlap.
- In high-context cultures, members are less dependent on words and rely on gestures, silence, and facial expressions because the relationships among communicators generate meaning. Low-context cultures depend more on language for meaning.
- In monochronic-time cultures, events are scheduled as separate items and deadlines are emphasized. In polychronic-time cultures, schedules are less important and many tasks are done at once.

Gender Dimensions

- Group members should monitor and, if necessary, adapt to differences in the ways that men and women interpret events and express their opinions.
- Muted Group Theory explains that those with power in a society "mute" the voices of less powerful groups.

Generational Dimensions

- Generational mixes of Traditionalists, Baby Boomers, Generation Xers, and Millennials present special challenges when working in groups.

Religious Dimensions

- Most people living in the United States know very little about their own religion and much less about other religions.
- Religious literacy is the ability to understand and use the religious terms, symbols, images, beliefs, practices, scripture, heroes, themes, and stories that are employed within a culture.

GroupWork
Personality Types in Groups

Directions: Read the two sets of descriptions for each pair of personality types. Put a check mark next to the individual phrases that *best* describe you. Note the personality type with the most check marks—extrovert or introvert, sensor or intuitive, thinker or feeler, judger or perceiver. Answer as you really are, not as you wish you were or wish you could be in the future.[83]

When you have finished the questionnaire and determined your personality type preferences, form a group of five members (or join a class group with whom you've been working) and share your results. Discuss the following questions and be prepared to share your conclusions with the entire class:

1. As a group, are we missing some personality traits? If so, how could this affect groupwork?

2. How can we adapt to the different personality traits? (For example, will perceiver and judgers be able to work collaboratively on projects with short deadlines?)

3. How can each of us improve our effectiveness as group members in light of our personality traits and preferences? (Example: As an extrovert, I need to remember and encourage introverts who may have difficulty joining and actively contributing group discussions.)

Identify Your Preferences

1. Are you an extrovert or an introvert?

Extrovert	Introvert
_____ I am outgoing, sociable, expressive.	_____ I am reserved, private, contained.
_____ I enjoy groups and discussions.	_____ I prefer one-to-one interactions.
_____ I talk first, think later.	_____ I think first, then talk.
_____ I can do many things at once.	_____ I focus on one thing at a time.
_____ I think out loud.	_____ I think to myself.
_____ Other people give me energy.	_____ Other people often exhaust me.
_____ I enjoy being the center of attention.	_____ I don't enjoy being the center of attention.
_____ Total	_____ Total

2. Are you a sensor or an intuitive?

Sensor	Intuitive
_____ I focus on details.	_____ I focus on the big picture.
_____ I am practical and realistic.	_____ I am theoretical.
_____ I like concrete information.	_____ I like abstract information.
_____ I like facts.	_____ I get bored with facts and details.
_____ I trust experience.	_____ I trust inspiration and intuition.
_____ I value common sense.	_____ I value creativity and innovation.
_____ I want clear, realistic goals.	_____ I want to pursue a vision.
_____ Total	_____ Total

3. Are you a thinker or a feeler?

Thinker	Feeler
_____ I am task-oriented.	_____ I am people-oriented.
_____ I am objective, firm, analytical.	_____ I am subjective, humane, caring.
_____ I enjoy arguing.	_____ I think arguing is disruptive.
_____ I prefer businesslike meetings.	_____ I prefer social interactions in meetings.
_____ I value competence, reason, and justice.	_____ I value relationships and harmony.
_____ I am direct and firm-minded.	_____ I am tactful and tenderhearted.
_____ I think with my head.	_____ I think with my heart.
_____ **Total**	_____ **Total**

4. Are you a judger or a perceiver?

Judger	Perceiver
_____ I value organization and structure.	_____ I value flexibility and spontaneity.
_____ I am in control and definite.	_____ I go with the flow.
_____ I like having deadlines.	_____ I dislike deadlines.
_____ I will work now, play later.	_____ I will play now, work later.
_____ I like standards and expectations.	_____ I feel constrained by rules.
_____ I adjust my schedule to complete work.	_____ I do work at the last minute.
_____ I plan ahead.	_____ I adapt as I go.
_____ **Total**	_____ **Total**

Summarize your scores by indicating the letter that best describes your personality traits and preferences:

_____	_____	_____	_____
E or I	S or N	T or F	J or P

Group Assessment

Identifying Cultural Dimensions

Directions: This chapter identifies five cultural dimensions. The 18 statements listed here represent a group member's attitude or behavior. Use the blank space before each statement and place the appropriate letter (A through E) in that space to indicate which dimension best explains the cultural perspective of the member. In some cases, more than one answer may be appropriate.

Cultural Dimensions

A. Individualism–Collectivism

B. High Power–Low Power Distance

C. Masculine–Feminine Values

D. High Context–Low Context

E. Polychronic–Monochronic

_____ 1. When a member of my group wins a prize, I feel proud.

_____ 2. I function best in a group when I can organize my responsibilities and put them on a schedule.

_____ 3. I prefer a leader who makes decisions, communicates them to the group, and expects us to carry out the task.

_____ 4. I rely on a member's nonverbal behavior to tell me what he or she is really thinking.

_____ 5. Groups don't function effectively if members are emotional and sensitive.

_____ 6. I am confident in my ability to predict how other group members will behave.

_____ 7. I enjoy "doing my own thing" in a group.

_____ 8. I prefer working in groups in which members are appreciative, curious, forgiving, kind, and understanding.

_____ 9. I become frustrated when someone in a meeting brings up a personal topic that is unrelated to the purpose of the meeting.

_____ 10. Groups don't function effectively when members are aggressive, hardheaded, and opinionated.

_____ 11. My satisfaction in a group depends very much on the feelings of other members.

_____ 12. I don't like to focus my attention on only one thing at a time because I may be missing something important or interesting.

_____ 13. I prefer a leader who calls a meeting when an important issue comes up, gives us the problem to discuss, and seeks group decision.

_____ 14. I can sit with another group member, not say anything, and still be comfortable.

_____ 15. I find silence awkward in conversations and group discussions.

_____ 16. I like to be clear and accurate when I speak to other group members.

_____ 17. I like doing several tasks at one time.

_____ 18. I like working in groups where I can compete with other members.

Group Leadership

Chapter Outline

Case Study

The Leader in Sheep's Clothing

The Peoples Project is a nonprofit organization with the mission of serving displaced families within their local communities. If a homeless family qualifies for help, the Peoples Project moves them into a local Peoples Project apartment. Every family receives job counseling, skills training, child care, and assistance in looking for a permanent home.

For 20 years, the Peoples Project was directed by Bill Blessing, one of its founders. When Blessing announced his retirement, the board of trustees hired an energetic and experienced nonprofit director named Will Dupree. From his first day at work, Dupree jumped right into the job. He met with residents of Peoples Project housing to listen to their needs and complaints. He scheduled meetings with community leaders and politicians to solidify their support. He delivered an eloquent speech at a local church that assists the Peoples Project. And when a fire left three families without shelter, he rolled up his sleeves and spent two days helping them move into Peoples Project housing. The board was thrilled. The community was delighted with the new charismatic leader.

Meanwhile, back at the Peoples Project headquarters, the mood was quite different. During his first week on the job, Dupree called a meeting of the senior staff, most of whom had been working for the Peoples Project for many years. He told them that to the outside community, he would always be responsive, caring, and empowering. Behind closed doors at the Peoples Project, he would be a tough, uncompromising director.

"I don't want to be your friend," he said. "You will meet all deadlines and give 110 percent without complaining." Within a few days, they learned that Dupree was a man of his word. One afternoon at 4:30, he marched into a senior staff member's office and said, "I need a report on how the proposed zoning legislation will affect our buildings and those we're trying to buy. I need it by noon tomorrow." The staff member worked past midnight to write the report. The next morning, she came in early to make revisions. By noon the report was sitting on the director's desk. A day later, she asked the director what he thought of the report. His response was "Oh, I've been busy—haven't read it yet."

As incidents like these increased, senior staff members became frustrated and wary of their new director. His popularity outside headquarters was high so they didn't think they could do anything. But when Dupree started to have "favorites" among the staff members, several veteran employees decided that retirement or looking for work elsewhere was a better and healthier option.

Even though the Peoples Project had never been more successful, staff members were at a breaking point. At the same time, their commitment and loyalty to the organization and its mission was strong. No one knew what to do or how to respond to the new leader.

When you finish reading this chapter, you should be able to answer the following critical thinking questions about this case study:

1   As a designated leader, how could Dupree have adapted his leadership style more effectively to accommodate the existing staff members?

2   According to Situational Leadership theories, is Dupree a task-motivated or relationship-motivated leader? How well does his leadership style match the group's situational dimensions?

3   Given that many staff members are currently unhappy working for Dupree, what strategies could they use to improve the group's situation?

4   How does Dupree measure up to the 5M Model of Leadership Effectiveness?

Planning a Playground

Virtual Miscommunication

Before you read any further, visit Pearson's MyCommunicationLab website and watch the short videos "Planning a Playground" and "Virtual Miscommunication," which illustrate Chapter 5 concepts. Each video comes with a set of study questions to keep in mind as you read this chapter.

What Is Leadership?

If you use the word *leadership* to search any major online bookseller's site, you will discover thousands of books on that subject. And if you review the first 300 offerings, you'll see that most of them are written by highly respected scholars and well-regarded business leaders. Some unusual titles, however, demonstrate the popularity of leadership books. Here are just a few:

- *Leadership Secrets of Attila the Hun*
- *Leadership Secrets of Colin Powell*
- *Leadership Secrets of Hillary Clinton*
- *Jesus on Leadership*
- *Lincoln on Leadership*
- *The Leadership Secrets of Billy Graham*
- *Robert E. Lee on Leadership*
- *Martin Luther King, Jr. on Leadership*
- *The Leadership Secrets of Santa Claus*

And before you chuckle too much over *The Leadership Secrets of Santa Claus*, consider how you could translate some of his "secrets" into useful leadership tips: Choose your reindeer wisely; make a list and check it twice; listen to the elves; find out who's naughty and nice; be good for goodness' sake.[1]

Apparently, everyone has something to say about leadership. You do, too. You have observed leaders at work, voted for leaders at school and in public elections, and probably led a group at some point in your life. That group could have been a sports team, a study group, a work team, or a group of children left in your care.

All groups need leadership. Without leadership, a group may be nothing more than a collection of individuals, lacking the coordination and motivation to achieve a common goal. Quite simply, "there are no successful groups without leaders.... Leaders lead because groups demand it and rely on leaders to satisfy needs."[2]

A leader and leadership are not the same thing. **Leadership** is the ability to make strategic decisions and use communication effectively to mobilize group members toward achieving a common goal. *Leader* is the title given to a person; *leadership* refers to the actions a leader takes to help group members achieve a common goal.

Another way to understand the nature of leadership is to contrast it with the functions of management. Whereas managers concentrate on getting an assigned job done, leaders focus on the ultimate direction and goal of the group. Note how the employee in the following situation describes the difference between a manager and a leader:

> Lee is the manager of our department, so he's technically our leader. He always follows procedures and meets deadlines for paperwork, so I guess he's a good manager. But we don't get much guidance from him. I think that managing and leading are somehow different. Allison supervises the other department. She inspires her workers. They're motivated and innovative, and they work closely with one another. We do our job, but they seem to be on a mission. I've always thought that working for Allison would be more rewarding and enjoyable.

As we see it, there is an obvious reason why some leaders succeed whereas others fail: Those who fail often lack effective and appropriate communication skills. In his book on leadership, Antony Bell describes communication as the mortar or glue that connects all leadership competencies. The ability to think and act, self-awareness, and self-discipline are critical leadership competencies, but it takes communication to bind these building blocks together.[3]

Ronald Heifetz, director of the Leadership Education Project at Harvard's School of Government, describes the dialectic tensions inherent in leadership. Leaders, he writes, must create a balance between the tensions required to motivate change and the need to avoid overwhelming followers.[4] Effective leaders walk a line between *both* fostering interdependence *and* encouraging self-reliance, between *both* building cohesion *and* welcoming disagreement, and between *both* imposing structure *and* promoting spontaneity.

 # Groups in Balance...

Value *Both* Leadership *and* Followership

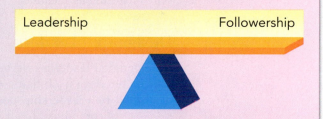

Who wants to be a follower? In the United States—the number one individualistic country in the world—we praise and value individual leaders. This admiration of leaders is not shared by all cultures. In collectivist cultures, standing out from the group is considered arrogant. Instead, loyal, hard-working followers are admired. In the United States, being a follower receives little praise. Garry Will captured this perception in his book, *Certain Trumpets: The Call of Leaders*:

> Talk about the nobility of leaders, the need for them, our reliance on them, raises the clear suspicion that followers are not so noble, not needed—that there is something demeaning about being a follower. In that view, leaders only rise by sinking others to subordinate roles.[5]

Of course, in an *effective* group, none of these suspicions make sense. Leaders and followers share ideas and opinions. They collaborate to achieve a common goal. Followers have a say about where they are being led. After all, without followers, there would be no one to lead.

In Chapter 1, we identified the leadership↔followership dialectic as significant to group success. We emphasized that effective leaders have the confidence to put their egos aside and bring out the leadership in others.[6] Think of how many "ordinary" people came forward to take leadership roles during the horrific events of September 11, 2001. Office workers in the World Trade Center organized coworkers to carry injured colleagues down thousands of stairs. Local businesses worked cooperatively to provide food to workers during the rescue and recovery operation.[7] Other businesses donated office space to companies whose operations had been destroyed when the towers collapsed.[8] Despite the fact that Mayor Rudy Giuliani was widely credited and praised for his leadership during the crisis, there were hundreds of extraordinary followers doing what was needed to help the stricken New York City community recover from the emotional, physical, logistical, and financial shocks it suffered.

Becoming a Leader

Anyone can become a leader. Abraham Lincoln, Harry S Truman, and Barack Obama rose from humble beginnings and hardship to become U.S. presidents. Corporate executives have worked their way up from the sales force and the secretarial pool to become chief executive officers.[9]

- Verizon CEO Ivan Seidenberg, the son of an electrical supply shop owner, started his business career as a telephone cable splicer's assistant.[10]
- Brenda C. Barnes, CEO of Sara Lee (now retired), the daughter of a maintenance man, worked as a waitress, post office mail sorter, and clothing salesperson before becoming a manager at a sporting goods store.[11]
- Oprah Winfrey, born to an unwed teenager and raised on her grandmother's farm in Kosciusko, Mississippi, became a CEO and the richest self-made woman in the United States.[12]

The path to a leadership position can be as easy as being in the right place at the right time or being the only person willing to take on a difficult job. Becoming the leader of a group primarily occurs in one of two ways: being chosen to lead or naturally emerging as a leader.

Designated Leaders

A **designated leader** is selected by group members or by an outside authority. You may be hired for a job that gives you authority over others. You may be promoted or elected to a leadership position. You may be assigned to chair a special work team or subcommittee. In all these cases, the selection of the leader depends on an election or an appointment.

Sometimes, less-than-deserving people are appointed or elected to powerful positions. Is it possible, then, for a designated leader to be an effective leader? Of course it is, particularly when a leader's abilities match the needs of the group and its goal.

Designated leaders face unique challenges. When a newly appointed leader enters a well-established group, there can be a long and difficult period of adjustment for everyone. One student described this difficult process as follows:

> For five summers, I worked as a counselor at a county day camp for underprivileged children. Anthony was our boss, and all of us liked him. We worked hard for Anthony because we knew he'd look the other way if we showed up late or left early on a Friday. As long as the kids were safe and supervised, he didn't bother us. But when Anthony was promoted into management at the county government office, we got Tyler. The first few weeks were awful. Tyler would dock us if we were late. No one could leave early. He demanded that we come up with more activities for the kids. Weekend pool parties were banned. He even made us attend a counselors' meeting every morning, rather than once every couple of weeks. But, in the end, most of us had to admit that Tyler was a better director. The camp did more for the kids, and that was the point.

When group members elect or appoint a leader from within a group, the problems can be as difficult as those faced by a leader from outside the group. If the person who once worked next to you becomes your boss, the adjustment can be problematic. Here, a business executive describes how difficult it was when she was promoted to vice president:

> When I was promoted, I became responsible for making decisions that affected my colleagues, many of whom were close friends. I was given the authority to approve projects, recommend salary increases, and grant promotions. Colleagues who had always been open and honest with me were more cautious and careful about what they said. I had to deny requests from people I cared about, while approving requests from colleagues with whom I often disagreed. Even though I was the same person, I was treated differently, and, as a result, I behaved differently.

Being plucked from a group in order to lead it can present problems because it changes the nature of your relationship with the other members of the group. Even though the members know you well, you still must earn their trust and respect as a leader. Here are three suggestions:

- Involve the group in decision making as much as possible.
- Discuss ground rules for interactions with friends while assuring them of your continued friendship.
- Openly and honestly address leadership concerns with group members and seek their help in resolving potential problems.[13]

Emergent Leaders

Very often, the most effective leadership occurs when a leader emerges from a group rather than being promoted, elected, or appointed. The leaders of many political, religious, and community organizations emerge. An **emergent leader** gradually achieves leadership by interacting with group members and contributing to the achievement of the group's goal. Leaders who emerge from within a group do not have to spend time learning about the group, its goals, and its norms. They also have some assurance that the group wants them to be its leader.

Strategies for Becoming a Leader

Although there is no method guaranteeing that you'll emerge or be designated as a group's leader, certain strategies can improve your chances. All of these strategies require a balanced approach that takes advantage of opportunities without abusing the privilege of leadership.

Talk Early and Often	Listen to Others
Know More	Share What You Know
Offer Your Opinion	Welcome Disagreement

How to Become a Leader

Talk Early and Often (and Listen to Others).   Research shows that the person who speaks first and most often is more likely to emerge as the group's leader.[14] The number of contributions is even more important than the quality of those contributions. The quality of your contributions becomes more significant *after* you become a leader.

The link between participation and leadership "is the most consistent finding in small group leadership research. Participation demonstrates both your motivation to lead and your commitment to the group."[15] Although talking early and often does not guarantee you a leadership position, failure to talk will keep you from being considered as a leader. Yet, don't overdo it. If you talk too much, members may think that you are

Ethics in Groups

Leadership Integrity

In his book on leadership, Andrew DuBrin makes the case that ethical leaders do "the *right* thing as perceived by a consensus of reasonable people."[16] Doing the right thing requires integrity.[17] Such leaders honor their commitments and their promises. They practice what they preach, regardless of emotional or social pressure. For example, if a good friend in your group asks to chair a committee, and you've promised the position to someone with better skills, you should keep your promise even if it upsets your friend.

Unethical leadership has enormous consequences, regardless of whether it affects a small study group or a global corporation. Unethical behavior has bankrupted companies, led to thousands of layoffs, exposed the unrestrained spending of self-centered corporate executives, and resulted in dangerous safety violations on off-shore oil-drilling rigs, at nuclear power plants, and in the contamination of the food we eat.

The Center for Business Ethics at Bentley College poses five questions to help you decide whether your (or someone else's) leadership behaviors are ethical or unethical:[18]

- *Is it right?* Do you conform to universally accepted principles of rightness and wrongness, such as "thou shalt not steal"?

- *Is it fair?* Would you overlook a competent person in order to promote a less competent relative or friend?

- *Who gets hurt?* Do you try to do the greatest good for the greatest number of people?

- *Would you be comfortable if the details of your decisions or actions were made public in the media or through email?* What would you tell your child or a young relative to do in similar circumstances?

- *How does it smell?* If a reasonable person with good common sense were to look at your decision or action, would it "smell" suspicious or bad to that person? Would it seem wrong?

Leadership can become an ego trip—or, even worse, a power trip. Warren Bennis and Joan Goldsmith use the metaphor of effective leadership as a stool with three legs—"ambition, competence, and integrity—[which] must remain in balance if the leader is to be a constructive force." If one of these leadership legs is missing, the group may fall apart. A leader with too much ambition and/or not enough competence or integrity risks becoming a destructive force, pursuing selfish goals rather than goals that benefit the group.[19]

not interested in or willing to listen to their contributions. While it is important to talk, it is just as important to demonstrate your willingness and ability to listen.

Know More (and Share What You Know).

Leaders often emerge or are appointed because they are seen as experts—people who know more about an important topic than others do. Even if a potential leader is simply able to explain ideas and information more clearly than other group members, that person may be perceived as knowing more.

Groups need well-informed leaders, but they do not need know-it-alls. Know-it-alls see their own comments as most important; leaders value everyone's contributions. Members who want to become leaders understand that they must demonstrate their expertise without intimidating other group members.

Offer Your Opinion (and Welcome Disagreement).

When groups have difficulty making decisions or solving problems, they appreciate someone who offers good ideas and informed opinions. Members often emerge as leaders when they help a group out of some difficulty. Offering ideas and opinions, however, is not the same as having those ideas accepted. Because your opinions may conflict with those of other group members, use caution when discussing these differences. Criticizing the ideas and opinions of others may cause resentment and defensiveness. Bullying your way into a leadership position can backfire. If you are unwilling to listen to alternatives or collaborate with members, the group may not want to follow you.

The strategies for *becoming* a leader are not necessarily the strategies needed for successful leadership. Although you may talk a lot, demonstrate superior knowledge, and assert your personal opinions in order to *become* a leader, you may find that the dialectic opposites—listening rather than talking, relying on the knowledge of others, and seeking a wide range of opinions—are equally necessary to *succeed* as a leader.

> ## Remember This
>
> Effective leaders welcome disagreement. They do not suppress conflict, they rise and face it.[20]
>
> —Jorge Correia Jesuino, in *Understanding Group Behavior*

Leadership and Power

You cannot fully understand the dynamics of leadership unless you also understand the dynamics of power. In the context of group communication, **power** is the ability or authority to influence and motivate others. Leadership experts Warren Bennis and Bruce Nanus claim that power is "the quality without which leaders cannot lead."[21] In the hands of a just and wise leader, power is a positive force; in the hands of an unjust or foolish leader, power can be a destructive and corrupting force.

Types of Leadership Power

Many researchers study power and its relationship to group leadership. Here, we combine the work of two sets of researchers. John French and Bertram Raven classify power into five categories: reward power, coercive power, legitimate power, expert power, and referent power. Psychologists Gary Yukl and Cecilia Fable add three additional types of power: informational power, persuasive power, and charisma. Yukl and Fable note that if you combine French and Raven's five categories with their three categories, you end up with two basic types of power,[22] which we've named *position power* and *personal power*. **Position power** depends on a member's job or status within an organization. **Personal power** stems from a member's individual character, competencies, and earned status. Figure 5.1 on the next page lists the four types of power in each of these two categories.

The Power of Power

What kind of power is best? The answer depends on many factors, including the type of group, the situation or organization, member characteristics, and the group's goal. For example, reward power works best in groups where the leader controls something members value. It is less effective when the so-called rewards are insignificant or trivial.

Research examining French and Raven's five categories of power concludes that reward power, legitimate power, and coercive power are the least effective. "They either have no influence or a negative influence both on how people act at work and on job satisfaction. Expert power and referent power tend to produce positive outcomes."[23]

In the extreme, highly coercive leaders can range from the "abusive tyrant, who bawls out and humiliates people, to the manipulative sociopath. Such leaders have an emotional impact a bit like the 'dementors' in the Harry Potter series, who 'drain peace,

Figure 5.1 Types of Power in Groups

Position Power: Comes with the Position		Personal Power: Comes from Personal Characteristics	
Legitimate Power: Relies on a job title, formal authorization, or assigned duty	"I have the authority and responsibility to lead."	**Referent Power:** Relies on members' opinion of and experience with the leader	"I've earned your respect and trust."
Informational Power: Controls and transmits needed information	"I have the information you need."	**Expert Power:** Relies on expertise and credentials	"I have the knowledge and skills you need."
Coercive Power: Controls and deals out sanctions and punishments	"I can reprimand, discipline, and punish you."	**Persuasive Power:** Relies on effective communication skills	"I know how to persuade and encourage others."
Reward Power: Controls and gives out resources valued by members	"I can recognize, promote, and reward you."	**Charismatic Power:** Relies on leader's vitality, character, and competence	"I have the energy, will, and passion to make things happen."

hope, and happiness out of the air around them.' At their worst, leaders who rely on coercive power have no idea how destructive they are—or they simply don't care."[24]

On the other hand, coercive power can be "effective when those subject to this form of power are aware of expectations and are warned in advance about the penalties for failure to comply. Leaders using coercive power must consistently carry out threatened punishments."[25]

Contrast coercive power with referent power. Referent power is the personal power or influence held by people we like, admire, and respect. Referent power, as a form of personal power, is influential because it is recognized and conferred by the group rather than by an outside source.

In most groups, a leader employs several kinds of power, depending on the needs of the group and the situation. Some leaders may have the power to reward, coerce, and persuade as well as having legitimate, expert, informational, referent, and charismatic power. In other groups, a leader may depend entirely on one type of power. The more power a leader has, the more carefully the use of power must be balanced with the needs of the group. If you exert too much power, your group may lose its energy and enthusiasm. If you don't exert enough power, your group may flounder and fail.

Leadership Theories

In *Leadership*, Warren Bennis and Bruce Nanus point out that "no clear and unequivocal understanding exists as to what distinguishes leaders from non-leaders, and perhaps more important, what distinguishes effective leaders from ineffective leaders."[26] Despite inconclusive results from thousands of research studies, there

Theory in Groups

The Evolution of Leadership Theory

Two early leadership theories have shaped the way many of us think about the people we elect, appoint, and look to as leaders. In 1841, Thomas Carlyle's book *On Heroes, Hero-Worship, and the Heroic History* led to what we now call Trait Leadership Theory.[27]

Trait Leadership Theory   Often referred to as "The Great Man" theory, this theory is based on an assumption many people now reject—that leaders are born, not made. **Trait Leadership Theory** identifies and prescribes individual characteristics and behaviors needed for effective leadership.

Think of the leaders you admire. What traits do they have? In his book *Leadership*, Andrew DuBrin identifies several personality traits that contribute to successful leadership: self-confidence, humility, trustworthiness, high tolerance of frustration, warmth, humor, enthusiasm, extroversion, assertiveness, emotional stability, adaptability, farsightedness, and openness to new experiences.[28] Although most of us would gladly follow a leader with the qualities described by DuBrin, many effective leaders only exhibit a few of these traits. For example, Harriet Tubman, an illiterate runaway slave, did little talking but led hundreds of people from bondage in the South to freedom in the North. Bill Gates, an introverted computer geek, became one of the richest men on earth as head of Microsoft, a company that all but dictates how we use personal computers.

At the same time and according to the Myers-Briggs Type Indicator®, a specific set of traits characterizes "life's natural leaders." These "extroverted thinkers" (the ENTJ types) use reasoning ability to control and direct those around them.[29] They are usually enthusiastic, decisive, confident, organized, logical, and argumentative. They love to lead and can be excellent communicators. And although they often assume or win leadership positions, extroverted thinkers may *not* necessarily be effective leaders because they may intimidate or overpower others. They also may be insensitive to the personal feelings and needs of group members. Although many extroverted thinkers become leaders, they may need a less intense, more balanced approach in order to be effective leaders.

Styles Leadership Theory   As a way of expanding the trait approach to the study of leadership, **Styles Leadership Theory** groups specific leadership traits into distinct styles. Actors work in different styles—tough or gentle, comic or tragic. Different styles are attributed to leaders, too. Early attempts to describe different leadership styles yielded three categories that stretch across a continuum of leadership control. As shown in the figure below, autocratic leaders exert a great deal of control, democratic leaders employ a moderate amount of control, and laissez-faire leaders give up control.[30]

Autocratic leaders seek power and authority by controlling the direction and outcome of group work. They make many of the group's decisions, expect followers to obey orders, take personal credit for group success, and tend to use reward power and coercive power. Dr. Sandy Faber, a world-renowned astronomer, wrote about her experience leading a group of six astronomers who developed a new theory about the expansion of the universe. An unfortunate back injury made her take a new look at her leadership style. Rather than directing and controlling the group process, she had to lie on a portable cot when she met with the research team. She discovered leading a group from a cot is almost impossible. But from that position, she also learned a valuable lesson about leadership:

The Leadership Style Continuum

| Autocratic | Democratic | Laissez-Faire |
| High Control | | Low Control |

(continued)

It was the best thing that could have happened to us. The resultant power vacuum allowed each of us to quietly find our own best way to contribute. I now think that in small groups of able and motivated individuals, giving orders or setting up a well-defined hierarchy may generate more friction than it is designed to cure.[31]

Although many people assume that democratic leadership is always best, an autocratic style may be more effective under certain circumstances. During a serious crisis, there may not be enough time to discuss issues or consider the wishes of all members. In such cases, a group may be thankful when a leader takes control of the situation.

Democratic leaders promote the interests of group members and practice social equality. As the name implies, democratic leaders behave quite differently than autocratic leaders. Democratic leaders share decision making with the group, promote collaboration, focus on *both* the task *and* group morale, give the group credit for success, and tend to rely on referent and expert power to motivate members.

There are potential costs, however, to democratic leadership. By failing to take charge in a crisis or to curb a discussion when decisions need to be finalized, democratic leaders may be perceived as weak or indecisive by their followers.

In groups with democratic leadership, members are often more satisfied with the group experience, more loyal to the leader, and more productive in the long run. Whereas members often fear or distrust an autocratic leader, they usually enjoy working with a democratic leader.[32]

Laissez-faire is a French phrase that roughly means "to let people do as they choose." A **laissez-faire leader** lets the group take charge of all decisions and actions. In mature and highly productive groups, a laissez-faire leader may be a perfect match for the group. Such a laid-back leadership style can generate a climate in which open communication is encouraged and rewarded. Unfortunately, laissez-faire leaders do little or nothing to help a group when it needs decisive leadership.

Although the Trait and Styles Leadership Theories are not as popular or accepted as they were in the past, they influenced the development of subsequent theories that advance our knowledge about and understanding of leadership.[33]

is something to learn from several leadership theories. This chapter examines four theoretical approaches to leadership (see Figure 5.2).

We now know that there isn't a single trait or style characteristic of effective leaders. Harvard University's Richard Hackman explains that effective leadership "involves inventing and competently executing whatever actions are most likely to create and sustain" an effective group.[34] Situational Leadership Theory and Functional Leadership Theory take on Hackman's challenge of describing the actions needed to achieve a group's common goal.

Figure 5.2 Leadership Theories

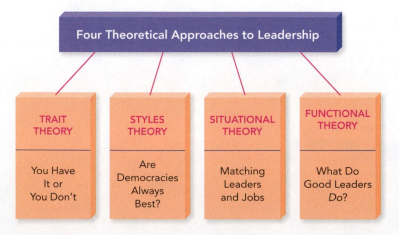

Situational Leadership Theory

Situational Leadership Theory claims that effective leaders use different leadership styles and strategies depending on the situation. Most of us do this in our daily interactions with other people. We may be extra patient with nervous colleagues on their first few days at a new job. We check up on some group members more than others because we know they'll forget meeting times and deadlines.[35] Situational Leadership Theory gives us the tools we need to become more effective leaders once we have carefully analyzed ourselves, our group, and the circumstances in which we work together.

Fiedler's Contingency Model of Leadership Effectiveness.   One of the most influential theories of situational leadership was developed by managerial expert Fred Fiedler. His **Contingency Model of Leadership Effectiveness** contends that effective leadership occurs only when there is an ideal match between the leader's style and the group's work situation.[36] Fiedler characterizes leaders as being either task motivated or relationship motivated. Notice the dialectic tensions between these two leadership styles in Figure 5.3.

Fiedler acknowledges that a small group of leaders are *both* task motivated *and* relationship motivated. Maintaining this delicate balance, however, is difficult given that most leaders are more motivated by one style than the other. At the same time, enlightened leaders recognize the leadership style they prefer and try to compensate by adopting the opposite style when it best serves the group and its members.

Once you have determined your leadership style, the next step is to analyze how your style matches the group's situation. According to Fiedler, every situation has three important dimensions: leader–member relations, task structure, and power.

- *Leader–member relations:* Because **leader–member relations** can be positive, neutral, or negative, they affect the way a leader mobilizes a group toward its goal. Are group members friendly and loyal to the leader and to the rest of the group? Are they cooperative and supportive? Do they accept or resist the leader?
- *Task structure:* The second situational factor requires leaders to analyze the structure of the task. **Task structure** ranges from disorganized and chaotic to highly organized and rule driven. Are the goals and the task clear? Is there an accepted procedure or set of steps for achieving the goal? Are there well-established standards for measuring success?
- *Power:* The third situational factor is power, the ability or authority to influence and motivate others. Is the source of that power an outside authority, or has the leader earned it from the group? What differences would the use of reward, coercive, legitimate, expert, referent, informational, persuasive, and charismatic power have on the group?

Figure 5.3   Task- and Relationship-Motivated Leaders

Type of Leader	Leader Motivation	Leader Behavior
Task-Motivated Leaders	Want the job done even if it results in not getting along with other members.	• May ignore group morale • May confront disruptive members • May appear efficient and strong • May do the work of other members because they're not satisfied with the quality or quantity
Relationship-Motivated Leaders	Want to get along with other members even if it results in not getting the job done.	• May ignore task requirements • May tolerate disruptive members • May appear inefficient and weak • May do the work of other members to avoid asking them to do more

Figure 5.4   Fiedler's Contingency Model of Leadership Effectiveness

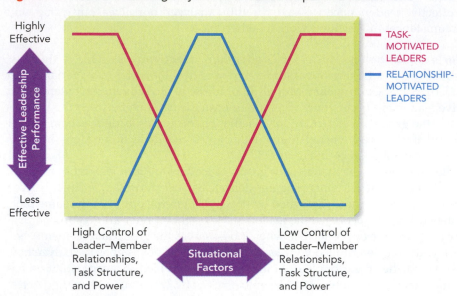

Fiedler's research suggests that there are ideal matches between leadership style and group situations. As depicted in Figure 5.4, a **task-motivated leader** performs best in extremes—such as when the situation is highly controlled or when it is almost out of control. These leaders shine when there are good leader–member relationships, a clear task, and a lot of power. They also do well in stressful leadership jobs where there may be poor leader–member relationships, an unclear and unstructured task, and little power. Task-motivated leaders do well in extreme situations because their primary motivation is to take charge and get the job done.

Relationship-motivated leaders are most effective when there is a mix of conditions. They may have a structured task but an uncooperative group of followers. Rather than taking charge and getting the job done at all costs, the relationship-motivated leader uses diplomacy and works with group members to improve leader–member relationships. If there are good leader–member relationships but an unstructured task, the relationship-motivated leader may rely on the resources of the group to develop a plan of action. Whereas a task-motivated leader might find these situations frustrating, a relationship-motivated leader will be quite comfortable in them.

According to Fiedler's Contingency Model of Leadership, when you know your leadership style and understand the situation in which you must lead, you can begin to predict how successful you will be as a leader. Of course, you cannot always choose when and where you will lead. You may find yourself assigned or elected to a leadership situation that does not match your leadership style. In such a case,

Fiedler proposed that effective leadership occurs only when there is an ideal match between the leader's style and the group's work situation. How might an athletic coach match his or her style to the situation of team competition?

rather than trying to change your leadership style, you may find it easier to change the situation in which you are leading. For example, if leader–member relationships are poor, you may decide that your first task is to gain the group's trust and support.

If your task is highly unstructured, you can exert your leadership by providing structure or by dividing the task into smaller, easier-to-achieve subunits. On the other hand, you may find yourself in a leadership situation where the task is highly structured and members know exactly what to do. Rather than accepting business as usual, ask for or introduce new and less structured tasks to challenge the group.

Finally, you may be able to modify the amount of power you have. If you are reluctant to use coercive power, or if you don't have enough legitimate power, you can earn referent and charismatic power by demonstrating your leadership ability. If you have a great deal of power and run the risk of intimidating group members, you may want to delegate some of your duties and power.

The Hersey-Blanchard Situational Leadership® Model.   The **Hersey-Blanchard Situational Leadership® Model** links leadership style to the readiness of group members.[37] **Member readiness** is the extent to which group members are willing (confident, committed, and motivated) and able (knowledgeable, expert, and skilled) to work together in order to achieve a common goal.

According to Paul Hersey and Ken Blanchard, as a group's readiness increases, leaders should rely more on relationship behaviors and less on task behavior. Here is a summary of guidelines for leaders based on the Hersey-Blanchard Situational Leadership Model, which is also illustrated in Figure 5.5:[38]

> *Situation 1. Low Readiness—The Telling Stage.*   When followers are unable, unwilling, or insecure, the leader should emphasize task-oriented behavior while being very directive and even autocratic. The leader *tells* the group what to do and closely supervises the work.

> *Situation 2. Moderate Readiness—The Selling Stage.*   When group members are unable but willing or confident, the leader should focus on being more relationship

Figure 5.5   The Hersey-Blanchard Situational Leadership® Model

High Supportive Leadership Behavior

2. The Selling Stage
(moderate member readiness)

3. The Participating Stage
(moderate to high member readiness)

High Guidance Leadership Behavior

Low Guidance Leadership Behavior

1. The Telling Stage
(low member readiness)

4. The Delegating Stage
(high member readiness)

Low Supportive Leadership Behavior

Follow the Research

The Two Sides of "Great" Leadership

In *Leadership without Easy Answers*, Ronald Heifetz describes effective leaders as people who walk a razor's edge (ouch!). He offers this example: If you challenge group members too quickly with too much, they will resist your leadership and resent the chaos your expectations create for them. If you challenge members too slowly with too little, they will blame you for their lack of motivation and progress. Heifetz claims that effective leaders stay balanced on the edge by adapting to the group, its members, and changing situations.[39]

Jim Collins, author of *Good to Great*, assembled a research team with the goal of comparing the attributes of "good" and "great" companies in similar industries, as well as those of companies that had tried to move from "good" to "great" status but failed. In terms of leadership, he found that the great leaders of great companies balanced two dimensions: professional will and personal humility.[40]

Collins contends that to lead your group to greatness, you must be willing to keep your ego in check for the sake of the group's goal and its well-being. Those who aren't willing to do this are not "made" for this kind of leadership. "For these people, work will always be first and foremost about what they *get*—fame, fortune, adulation, power, whatever—and not what they *build*, create, and contribute."[41] Notice how the "two sides" of leadership balance one another.[42]

Professional Will	Personal Humility
Creates superb results in achieving a clear goal	Acts modestly, never boastful; shuns public glorification
Does what needs to be done to achieve the goal	Acts with calm determination; relies on motivational strategies
Sets high standards for achieving the group's goal	Channels ambition into achieving the group's goal
Apportions responsibility for succeeding or failing objectively and fairly	Gives credit for success to other people, not to self

The Two Sides of Leadership

oriented. The leader *sells* by explaining the rationale for decisions and providing opportunities for member input.

Situation 3. Moderate to High Readiness—The Participating Stage. When group members are able but unwilling or insecure, the leader should provide a high degree of relationship-oriented behavior. The leader *participates* by sharing ideas, facilitating decision making, and motivating members.

Situation 4. High Readiness—The Delegating Stage. When group members are able as well as willing and confident, they are self-sufficient and competent. The leader *delegates* by granting group members independence and trust.

Functional Leadership Theory

Functional Leadership Theory claims that the leadership role is "to do, or get done, whatever is not being adequately handled for group needs."[43] Rather than focusing on who a leader *is*, the functional approach focuses on what a leader *does* to help the group achieve its common goal. According to this approach, leadership is not the sole responsibility of the leader; it is a job, not a person.

Functional Leadership Theory asks whether, and how well, group members assume critical leadership functions. Think back to the group roles in Chapter 3, "Group Membership," and how many of them assume leadership functions, such as coordinator, energizer, monitor–evaluator, information/opinion giver, implementer, and completer.

> **Remember This**
>
> Functional Leadership Theory focuses on how to lead instead of who is the leader.

Regardless of whether you are a leader or a follower, Functional Leadership Theory poses the following questions:[44]

- Do your behaviors and decisions help your group achieve its common goal?
- Do your personal traits and skills match the group's needs?
- Do your intelligence, creativity, knowledge, skills, and emotional maturity promote the common good?
- Do the members of your group assume essential leadership functions as needed?
- Do you have the courage to move toward and learn from difficult situations, rather than avoid them to reduce personal and group anxieties?

If you answer yes to most of these questions, you and your group have probably integrated essential leadership functions into the way you work toward achieving a common goal.

The 5M Model of Leadership Effectiveness

Given the millions of words about leadership published by scholars, management gurus, and popular press writers, you may have difficulty sorting out the dos and don'ts of effective leadership. To help you understand and apply the contributions made by these various approaches, we offer an integrated model of leadership effectiveness that focuses on specific *communication* strategies and skills that are appropriate for a particular group in a particular context.

The **5M Model of Leadership Effectiveness**, shown in Figure 5.6, divides leadership tasks into five interdependent leadership functions: (1) **m**odel leadership, (2) **m**otivate members, (3) **m**anage group process, (4) **m**ake decisions, and (5) **m**entor members. These strategies incorporate the features of several theories and provide a set of behaviors characteristic of effective leadership.[45]

Figure 5.6 The 5M Model of Leadership Effectiveness

Model Leadership

Model leaders project an image of confidence, competence, trustworthiness, and optimism. They provide a model of member effectiveness and build a climate of mutual trust between the leader and group members. Leadership expert Martin Chemers refers to this function as *image management* and notes that when "image management is particularly successful, the leader may be described as charismatic."[46] Yet no matter how much you may *want* to be a model leader, only your followers can grant you that honor. In *The Leadership Secrets of Colin Powell*, the author quotes Powell's view on modeling behavior:

> The leader sets an example. Whether in the Army or in civilian life, the other people in an organization take their cue from the leader—not from what the leader says but what the leader does.[47]

We recommend the following strategies for modeling effective leadership:

1. *Publicly champion your group and its goals.* In addition to praising group members directly, praise them to others outside the group.
2. *Speak and listen effectively and confidently.*
3. *Behave consistently and assertively.* Think about how you would want to be treated and make sure to follow your own golden rule.
4. *Demonstrate competence and trustworthiness.* Roll up your sleeves and take on difficult tasks. Stick with the task and the group until the goal is achieved.

Motivate Members

Motivation provides the inspiration, incentives, and reasons that move group members to work together to achieve a common goal. Without motivation, members may know what they need to do and even how to do it, but lack the will and energy to get it done. In Chapter 2, "Group Development," we introduced Kenneth Thomas's categories of intrinsic motivators—shared feelings of meaningfulness, choice, competence, and progress—all of which are available to leaders.

Mike Krzyzewski (Coach K), the highly successful men's basketball coach at Duke University, believes that motivating team members is the key to his success. "As a coach, leader, and teacher, my primary task is motivation. How do I get a group motivated, not only to be their individual best but also to become better as a team?"[48]

Motivating leaders guide, develop, support, defend, and inspire group members. They develop relationships that "match the personal needs and expectations of followers."[49] Four leadership skills are central to motivating members:

1. *Seek members' commitment to the group's common goal.* Even if it takes extra time and effort, make sure members genuinely support a clear and elevated goal.
2. *Appropriately reward the group and its members.* You can be firm as long as you are fair in recognizing and rewarding outstanding group work.

Remember This

Effective leaders use carrots, not sticks, to motivate members.

3. *Help solve interpersonal problems and conflicts.* Use the conflict resolution skills described in Chapter 8, "Conflict and Cohesion in Groups," to resolve conflicts constructively.
4. *Adapt tasks and assignments to members' abilities and expectations.* Don't try to fit the "square peg" member into a "round hole" role. Use group members' talents to enhance group productivity and members' satisfaction.

Manage Group Process

From the perspective of group survival, managing group process may be the most important function of leadership.[50] If a group is disorganized, lacks sufficient information to solve problems, or is unable to make important decisions, the group cannot be effective. Four leadership skills can enhance this important function:

1. *Organize and fully prepare for group meetings and work sessions.* In some cases, you may take more time to prepare for a meeting than to lead one.
2. *Understand and adapt to members' strengths and weaknesses.* Capitalize on member strengths and help compensate for weaknesses.
3. *Help solve task-related and procedural problems.* When group members are working productively, help them organize their tasks and adjust timetables. Secure necessary resources.
4. *Monitor and intervene to improve group performance.* If you see a problem developing, intervene and assist members before it becomes a crisis.

Make Decisions

A leader's willingness and ability to make appropriate, timely, and responsible decisions characterize effective leadership. Too often we hear disgruntled group members talk about their leader's inability to make critical decisions. A high school teacher described this fatal leadership flaw as follows:

> Everyone agrees that our principal is a "nice guy" who wants everyone to like him. He doesn't want to "rock the boat" or "make waves." As a result, he doesn't make decisions or take decisive action when it's most needed. He listens patiently to a request or to both sides of a dispute, but that's all he does. Our school comes to a standstill because he won't "bite the bullet." The teachers have lost respect for him, students and their parents know that they'll get what they want if they yell loudly enough or long enough, and the superintendent often intervenes to fix the problem.

When you assume a leadership role, you must accept the fact that some of your decisions will be unpopular, and some may even turn out to be wrong. But you still have to make them. In *The New Why Teams Don't Work*, Harvey Robbins and Michael Finley contend that it's often better for a group leader to make a bad decision than to make no decision at all: "For if you are seen as chronically indecisive, people won't let you lead them."[51] One company executive also noted that as much as you may value collaborative consensus, "sometimes you just need to make a decision."[52] The following strategies can help you determine when and how to intervene and make a decision:

1. *Make sure that everyone shares the information needed to make a quality decision.*
2. *If appropriate, discuss your pending decision and solicit feedback from members.* As long as members don't interpret your "out-loud" thinking as an order, you and your group will benefit by discussing proposed options.

3. *Listen to members' opinions, arguments, and suggestions.* When you listen effectively, you may discover that the group only needs a little help to make a decision or solve a problem on its own.

4. *Explain the rationale for the decision you intend to make.* When you are about to make a decision, let your group know. Not only will they be prepared for the outcome, they may help you make a better decision.

Mentor Members

Most successful people tell stories about significant mentors who helped them mature and move ahead. The word *mentor* comes from ancient Greece. In Homer's *Odyssey*, Mentor was the tutor and adviser to the hero Odysseus's son, Telemachus. Thus, the word *mentor* has come to mean a wise and trusted counselor who is usually older and more experienced than the *mentee*—that is, the person being mentored.

Good leaders are very busy people, particularly if they model leadership, motivate members, manage group process, and make decisions. Even so, great leaders find the time and energy to mentor others. They know that good mentoring does more than teach someone how to do a job—it also motivates that person to set high standards, seek advice when needed, and develop the skills characteristic of an excellent leader.

In his book *Great Leadership*, Anthony Bell urges would-be leaders to find a mentor because a good "mentor will challenge you to ask (and answer) the tough

Virtual Groups

Sharing Leadership Functions

Virtual groups need strong leadership. According to Jessica Lipnack and Jeffrey Stamps, the authors of *Virtual Groups*, "each member of a virtual team must adopt a leadership perspective."[53] Why? Consider the added responsibilities required of someone who leads a virtual group—be it a teleconference, an email discussion, or an intercontinental videoconference.

When participants live in different cities or time zones, arranging a virtual meeting can be more difficult than calling a regular meeting in a conference room down the hall. To prepare members for a virtual meeting:

- Someone must develop and send a detailed agenda to all members well in advance.
- Someone must make sure that the technology required for the conference is up and running.
- Someone must lead the discussion in which participants may neither see nor hear one another in real time.

Effective virtual groups manage these added tasks by *sharing* leadership roles rather than by assuming that one superhuman leader can handle all of these challenges.

The 5M Model of Leadership Effectiveness also applies to the unique responsibilities of a virtual group leader. When virtual groups first "meet," they often depend on a leader to model appropriate behavior for other virtual group members. Motivating a virtual group can be more difficult than motivating participants in a face-to-face discussion. Unmotivated members may ignore messages or respond infrequently. When this happens, a group is vulnerable to miscommunication, poor quality of work, missed deadlines, lack of cohesion, inefficiencies, and frustrated team members.

A virtual group leader also has additional managerial duties. For example, members may need training in the use of specialized software. In virtual groups, the leader may be responsible for determining when the virtual group will "meet," the rules of interaction, and the criteria for group decision making. Finally, leaders can mentor members who are apprehensive about interacting in a virtual environment or members who lack the technical skills needed to keep up with the group.

questions."[54] The following strategies can help a leader decide when and how to mentor group members:

1. *Be ready and willing to mentor every group member.* Although you cannot be a full-time mentor for everyone, you should be open to requests for advice. Eventually, you may develop a close relationship with a few mentees who share your vision.
2. *Encourage and invite others to lead.* Look for situations in which group members can assume leadership responsibilities. Ask them to chair a meeting, take responsibility for a group project, or implement a group's decision. And make sure they know you're there as backup.
3. *Inspire optimism.* When problems or setbacks occur, do not blame the group or its members. Instead, convert the situation into a teachable moment and make sure members learn to accept personal responsibility for a problem and its consequences.[55]

Effective mentors create appropriate balance and boundaries. They know when to intervene and when to back off. A mentor is neither a psychiatric counselor nor a group member's best friend. At some point, even the best mentors must let their mentees succeed or fail on their own.

Diversity and Leadership

In Chapter 4, "Diversity in Groups," we urged you to use appropriate communication strategies and skills to understand, respect, and adapt to member diversity. Here we issue a similar challenge at two levels. First, we tackle the negative stereotypes that often prevent women and culturally diverse members from becoming leaders. Second, we address the challenge of leading multicultural groups.

Gender and Leadership

In the early studies of leadership, there was an unwritten but additional prerequisite for becoming a leader: Be a man. Even today, despite the achievements of exceptional women leaders, some people still question the ability of women to serve in leadership positions.

In a summary of the research on leadership and gender, Susan Shimanoff and Mercilee Jenkins conclude that "women are still less likely to be preselected as leaders, and the same leadership behavior is often evaluated more positively when attributed to a male than a female."[56] In other words, even when women talk early and often, are well prepared and always present at meetings, and offer valuable ideas, a man who has done these same things is more likely to emerge as a leader. After examining the research on gender and leadership, Rodney Napier and Matti Gershenfeld conclude, "even though male and female leaders may act the same, there is a tendency for women to be perceived more negatively or to have to act differently to gain leadership."[57]

Unfortunately, such negative perceptions can make it difficult for women to assume and succeed in leadership positions. If their behavior is similar to that of male leaders, they are perceived as unfeminine. If they act "like a lady," they are viewed as weak or ineffective. One professional woman described this dilemma as follows:

I was thrilled when my boss evaluated me as "articulate, hard-working, mature in her judgment, and a skillful diplomat." What disturbed me were some of the evaluations from those I supervise or work with as colleagues. Although they had a lot of good things

Researchers conclude that women are less likely to be selected as leaders and that the same leadership behavior is often evaluated more positively when attributed to a male than a female. What, then, should female group members do to ensure their selection and success as leaders?

to say, a few of them described me as "pushy," "brusque," "impatient," "a disregard for social niceties," and "hard-driving." What am I supposed to do? My boss thinks I'm energetic and creative, while other people see the same behavior as pushy and aggressive.

Even though extensive research indicates that there are only slight differences between men and women leaders, stereotypical, negative expectations persist. These expectations make it more difficult for women to gain, hold, and succeed in leadership positions.[58] Our best advice is that instead of asking whether a female leader is different from a male leader, it is more important to ask whether she is an effective leader.

Culture and Leadership

The ways in which a leader models leadership, motivates members, manages group process, makes decisions, and mentors members may not match the cultural dimensions of all group members. According to management scholar Andrew Dubrin, a successful multicultural leader has "the skills and attitudes to relate effectively to and motivate people across race, gender, age, social attitudes, and lifestyles."[59]

A much-quoted academic program named Global Leadership and Organizational Behavior Effectiveness (GLOBE) studies leadership attributes in a variety of cultures to determine which ones are associated with outstanding leaders. Their results show that some attributes are universal regardless of the culture, whereas others are valued only in some cultures.[60] For example, which of the following two attributes is, in your opinion, universal and which attribute is valued in only some cultures: (1) ambition and (2) decisiveness? The answer: Ambition is not valued as a leadership attribute in some cultures, whereas decisiveness is valued universally.

If, as a leader, you model leadership by strongly and publicly advocating group goals, you may upset members from high-context cultures who would be less direct. Your way of modeling leadership behavior may not reflect *their* view of a model leader. For example, people from Western cultures (the United States,

Canada, and Europe) often assume that group members are motivated by personal achievement and status. However, when group members' cultural backgrounds are more collectivist, the same motivational strategies may not work. A collectivist member may act out of loyalty to the leader and the group rather than for personal achievement or material gain.[61]

Managing group process in a group composed of culturally diverse members can be difficult. If your leadership style reflects feminine values (nurturing, collaborative, caring), you may find yourself fighting a losing leadership battle with members who are more competitive, independent, and aggressive. Your feminine-value leadership style may be interpreted as weakness or indecision.

The decision-making style of a leader may not match that of a culturally diverse group. If members come from a low-power-distance culture, they will not welcome an authoritarian leader who takes control of all decision making. Conversely, a leader who prefers a more democratic approach to decision making may frustrate members who come from high-power-distance cultures, in which leaders make most decisions with little input from group members.

Before accepting any list of multicultural leadership attributes, remember that these findings are generalizations. Some members from collectivist cultures may seek public praise from a leader, while some members from an individualistic culture may shun or be embarrassed by being singled out for praise.

Negative stereotypes about leaders from minority groups are prevalent, and such members have more difficulty moving up the leadership ladder.[62] Balancing the needs of culturally diverse group members may be difficult but is essential for effective leadership.

The leader of this FEMA logistics team must understand, respect, and adapt to the diversity of his team members in order to model effective leadership, motivate his members, manage the group process, and appropriately mentor team members.

Summary Study Guide

What Is Leadership?

- Leadership is the ability to make strategic decisions and use communication effectively to mobilize group members toward achieving a common goal.
- Successful leaders effectively manage many dialectic tensions, especially the dialectics of individual goals ↔group goals, conflict↔cohesion, and structure↔ spontaneity.

Becoming a Leader

- Designated leaders are selected by group members or by an outside authority. Emergent leaders gradually achieve leadership by interacting with group members and contributing to the group's goal.
- Strategies for becoming a leader include talking early and often, knowing more, and offering opinions. At the same time, aspiring leaders should listen to others, share information, and welcome disagreement.

Leadership and Power

- Power associated with the *position* of leadership can be categorized into legitimate power, informational power, coercive power, and reward power.
- Power associated with the *personal* characteristics of the leader can be categorized into referent power, expert power, persuasive power, and charismatic power.

Leadership Theories

- Trait Leadership Theory identifies and prescribes individual characteristics and behaviors needed for effective leadership.
- Styles Leadership Theory describes a collection of specific behaviors that can be categorized into autocratic, democratic, or laissez-faire leadership styles.

- Fiedler's Contingency Model of Leadership Effectiveness seeks an ideal fit between a leader's style (task motivated or relationship motivated) and three dimensions of the group's situation (leader–member relations, task structure, and leadership power).
- The Hersey-Blanchard Situational Leadership® Model links leadership style to member readiness and ability. The more willing and able a group is to work together, the more a leader should rely on relationship behaviors and less on task behaviors.
- Functional Leadership Theory focuses on what a leader *does* rather than who a leader *is* by assuming that all group members can take on appropriate leadership functions when necessary.

The 5M Model of Leadership Effectiveness

- The 5M Model of Leadership Effectiveness divides leadership tasks into five interdependent functions: (1) **m**odel leadership, (2) **m**otivate members, (3) **m**anage group process, (4) **m**ake decisions, and (5) **m**entor members.

Diversity and Leadership

- In general, women are less likely to be selected as leaders, and the same leadership behavior is often evaluated more positively when attributed to a man rather than a woman.
- Multicultural leaders relate effectively to and motivate people across race, gender, age, social attitudes, and lifestyles.
- Negative stereotypes about leaders from minority groups make it more difficult for such members to gain leadership positions.

GroupWork

The Least-Preferred-Coworker Scale[63]

Directions: All of us have worked better with some people than with others. Think of the one person in your life with whom you have worked least well, a person who might have caused you difficulty in doing a job or completing a task. This person may be someone with whom you have worked recently or someone you have known in the past. This person must be the single individual with whom you have had the most difficulty getting a job done, the person with whom you would least want to work.

On the scale below, describe this person by circling the number that best represents your perception of this person. There are no right or wrong answers. Do not omit any items, and circle a number for each item only once.

Pleasant	8	7	6	5	4	3	2	1	Unpleasant
Friendly	8	7	6	5	4	3	2	1	Unfriendly
Rejecting	1	2	3	4	5	6	7	8	Accepting
Tense	1	2	3	4	5	6	7	8	Relaxed
Distant	1	2	3	4	5	6	7	8	Close
Cold	1	2	3	4	5	6	7	8	Warm
Supportive	8	7	6	5	4	3	2	1	Hostile
Boring	1	2	3	4	5	6	7	8	Interesting
Quarrelsome	1	2	3	4	5	6	7	8	Harmonious
Gloomy	1	2	3	4	5	6	7	8	Cheerful
Open	8	7	6	5	4	3	2	1	Guarded
Backbiting	1	2	3	4	5	6	7	8	Loyal
Untrustworthy	1	2	3	4	5	6	7	8	Trustworthy
Considerate	8	7	6	5	4	3	2	1	Inconsiderate
Nasty	1	2	3	4	5	6	7	8	Nice
Agreeable	8	7	6	5	4	3	2	1	Disagreeable
Insincere	1	2	3	4	5	6	7	8	Sincere
Kind	8	7	6	5	4	3	2	1	Unkind

Scoring: Obtain your Least-Preferred-Coworker (LPC) score by adding up the numbers you circled on the scale. Your score should be between 18 and 144.

Relationship-Motivated Leader. If your score is 73 or above, you derive satisfaction from good relationships with group members. You are most successful when a situation has just enough uncertainty to challenge you: moderate leader–member relationships, moderate task structure, and moderate power.

Task-Motivated Leader. If your score is 64 or below, you derive satisfaction from getting things done. You are most successful when a situation has clear guidelines or no guidelines at all: excellent or poor leader–member relationships, highly structured or unstructured tasks, and high or low power.

Relationship- and Task-Motivated Leader. If your score is between 65 and 72, you may be flexible enough to function in both leadership styles.

Group Assessment

Are You Ready to Lead?[64]

Directions: Indicate the extent to which you agree with each of the following statements, using the following scale: (1) strongly disagree, (2) disagree, (3) neutral or undecided, (4) agree, (5) strongly agree.

Leadership Readiness Statements					
1. I enjoy having people count on me for ideas and suggestions.	1	2	3	4	5
2. It would be accurate to say that I have inspired other people.	1	2	3	4	5
3. It's a good practice to ask people provocative questions about their work.	1	2	3	4	5
4. It's easy for me to compliment others.	1	2	3	4	5
5. I like to cheer people up even when my own spirits are down.	1	2	3	4	5
6. What my group accomplishes is more important than my personal glory.	1	2	3	4	5
7. Many people imitate my ideas.	1	2	3	4	5
8. Building team spirit is important to me.	1	2	3	4	5
9. I would enjoy coaching other members of the group.	1	2	3	4	5
10. It is important to me to recognize others for their accomplishments.	1	2	3	4	5
11. I would enjoy entertaining visitors to my group even if it interfered with my completing a report.	1	2	3	4	5
12. It would be fun to represent my group at an outside gathering.	1	2	3	4	5
13. The problems of my teammates are my problems.	1	2	3	4	5
14. Resolving conflict is an activity that I enjoy.	1	2	3	4	5
15. I would cooperate with another group with which my group works even if I disagreed with the position taken by its members.	1	2	3	4	5
16. I am an idea generator on the job.	1	2	3	4	5
17. It's fun for me to bargain whenever I have the opportunity.	1	2	3	4	5
18. Group members listen to me when I speak.	1	2	3	4	5
19. People have asked me to assume the leadership of an activity several times in my life.	1	2	3	4	5
20. I've always been a convincing person.	1	2	3	4	5

Scoring and Interpretation: Calculate your total score by adding the numbers circled. A general interpretation of the scoring follows:

90–100	high readiness for the leadership role
60–89	moderate readiness for the leadership role
40–59	some uneasiness with the leadership role
39 or less	low readiness for the leadership role

If you are already a successful leader and you scored low on this questionnaire, ignore your score. If you scored surprisingly low and you are not yet a leader or are currently performing poorly as a leader, study the statements carefully. Consider changing your attitude or your behavior so that you can legitimately answer more of the statements with a 4 or a 5.

chapter 6

Verbal and Nonverbal Communication in Groups

Chapter Outline

Case Study

How to Sink the Mayflower

The minute Joan Archer walked into the conference room, she knew she'd have a fight on her hands. Administrators from each state college were finding seats along the sides of a long conference table. Sitting at the far end of the table was Dr. Barton Mayflower III, a representative from the state Board of Higher Education and the person most likely to cause problems. He had the large picture windows at his back to make sure the sun was not shining in his eyes.

Joan looked at the table. There were empty seats along the sides, but no one had chosen the seat at the other end of the table. Realizing that she had to be seen and heard by everyone at this meeting, she planted herself in the unoccupied end seat.

The group was meeting to discuss and recommend a policy for accepting college credits from students transferring from one state college to another. As chair of the committee charged with drafting a policy, Joan had written most of the document herself. Given the difficulty of scheduling face-to-face meetings, the five-person committee had interacted only through conference calls and email. Two of the members made almost no contributions. The other two had faithfully read her draft and suggested changes. Fortunately, everyone on the committee had endorsed the draft policy and had asked Joan to present it at the statewide meeting.

Barton Mayflower called the meeting to order. As usual, he wore a well-cut dark suit with a starched white shirt and silk tie. His gray hair was meticulously groomed and his shoes shined. The delegates had always deferred to his leadership and guidance. Without looking at Joan or addressing her by name, he used his "I'm in charge" voice and asked that the chair of the policy committee present her report.

Joan stood. She put a stack of neatly stapled reports in front of her, made eye contact with group members around the table, and smiled. Although the sun was in her eyes, the group could see her quite well without straining their eyes. She began her presentation with these words:

"Beth, Aaron, Walter, Alicia, and I are pleased to share this report with you. If nothing else, we can now involve *all* of you in making this policy stronger and better. All of us fully endorse this policy—the vote was unanimous. The committee has asked me to present the report on their behalf. I think you'll see that we've addressed your concerns and come up with a plan that will help our students move from one college to another while ensuring that we maintain high academic standards. And please remember that if *we* don't come up with an acceptable policy, the state legislature will write it for us—and that's the last thing any of us want. Right? Right!"

As she spoke, Joan could see the four committee members basking in her praise. Barton Mayflower scowled. He could see that the rest of the delegates were buying into the policy even though Joan hadn't begun to describe its content. Much to his chagrin, no one saw his annoyance because they were looking at and listening to Joan.

When you finish reading this chapter, you should be able to answer the following critical thinking questions about this case study:

1   How did Joan use the seating arrangement to her advantage?

2   In what ways did Joan use the principles of team talk to address the group?

3   How did Joan's physical behavior enhance her credibility and competence?

4   What signs did Barton Mayflower notice that told him he had little hope of derailing Joan and her committee?

The Reunion   Virtual Miscommunication

Before you read any further, visit Pearson's MyCommunicationLab website and watch the short videos "The Reunion" and "Virtual Miscommunication," which illustrate Chapter 6 concepts. Each video comes with a set of study questions to keep in mind as you read this chapter.

Two Essential Tools

Every group member uses verbal and nonverbal communication to create messages that generate meaning. **Verbal communication** focuses on how you use words and language. Interaction may be "face to face, fax to fax, over the phone, or through electronic mail, but regardless of the channel used, groups do their work through language."[1] Without language, you cannot have a group discussion; you cannot follow an agenda, take minutes, read a report, or interact effectively with other group members. Linguists Victoria Fromkin and Robert Rodman note, "Whatever else people do when they come together—whether they play, fight, make love, or make automobiles, they talk. We live in a world of language."[2]

The other essential communication medium, nonverbal communication, is just as important as language. **Nonverbal communication** refers to message components other than words that generate meaning. Without the nonverbal component, it would be difficult to interpret the meaning of spoken language. Tone of voice, directness of eye contact, and physical proximity of group members can reveal at least as much about their thoughts and feelings as the words they speak. Some researchers claim that we convey as much as two-thirds of our meaning through nonverbal behavior.[3] Generally, verbal messages express the literal content of messages, while nonverbal messages express the emotional meaning.[4]

In dialectic terms, effective group members rely on *both* verbal *and* nonverbal communication to generate meaning. For example, as you know from Chapter 4, "Diversity in Groups," people in high-context cultures put more emphasis on nonverbal codes and interpersonal relationships to generate and interpret meaning. In low-context cultures, most people rely on words to generate and interpret the meaning of a message.

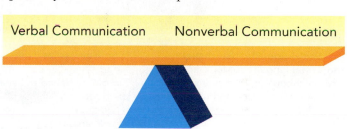

Team Talk

In her book *Team Talk,* sociologist Anne Donnellon examines the power of language in groups. Donnellon uses the term **team talk** to describe the language that group members should use as they work together. Not only does team talk enable group members to share information and express opinions, analysis of team talk also "reveals where the team is coming from and where it is headed. More importantly, talk is a tool for changing a team's destination" and achieving success.[5]

The Dimensions of Team Talk

Group members should listen carefully for words, sentences, and patterns of speech used repeatedly during discussions. By listening to and analyzing how the group uses language, group members can discover how the group's language fosters or inhibits success. Figure 6.1 on the next page illustrates six dimensions of team talk and provides examples of successful and unsuccessful language use. Use the blank space titled "Your Example" in each of the dimensions to add an additional illustration of team talk.

Remember This

The way a team talks reveals where the team is coming from and where it is headed.[6]

Figure 6.1 The Dimensions of Team Talk[7]

Team Talk Dimensions	Successful Examples	Unsuccessful Examples
1. *Identification:* **Use plural pronouns.** Members use plural pronouns rather than singular ones when talking about the group and its work.	"Let's keep working on this until we're ready for lunch." "We've finished this in record time." *Your Example:* "_____ _____ _____"	"I don't think you should quit until you've finished." "I'm pleased the discussion took so little time."
2. *Interdependence:* **Use collective language.** Members use language that acknowledges shared needs, solicits opinions, and expresses the need for cooperation.	"If we can develop a clear plan, our work will be much easier. What do you all think?" "What changes to the plan should we make?" *Your Example:* "_____ _____"	"Emilia and I can develop this plan without input from the group." "If there's no agreement here, the group must vote."
3. *Minimal Power Differentiation:* **Use considerate language.** Members talk to one another on equal terms.	"I'm sorry, my other meeting ran overtime. How can I catch up?" "Fred, would you tell me a bit more about that?" *Your Example:* "_____ _____"	"Stop and tell me what's happened so far in the process." "I don't like this. If Fred can't do it, we'll give it to someone else."
4. *Social Equality:* **Use casual, informal language.** Members use casual language, nicknames, slang. Members express empathy and liking avoid titles.	"Stephanie, what did that background report say?" "Jason, try to find out where Marie stands on this." "Hey, guys!" *Your Example:* "_____ _____"	"The secretary should review our report thus far." "Mr. Nunez, contact Dr. Ford after the meeting." "Ladies and gentlemen."
5. *Conflict Management:* **Use collaborative language.** Members express interest in solving problems, use a nonthreatening tone and nonjudgmental language, and paraphrase others.	"What do you need to know from us to do this?" "Could we back up and look at this from a different angle?" "Let me make sure I understand this . . ." *Your Example:* "_____ _____"	"How many of you think that Joshua is right?" "We're not getting anywhere, so I'll take it up with Dr. Lenski after the meeting."
6. *Negotiation:* **Use exploratory language.** Members ask "what if" questions, propose objective criteria for solutions, and summarize areas of agreement.	"What if we wrote up a justification for the cost?" "Does this meet our standard?" "What else can we do to make this work?" *Your Example:* "_____ _____"	"We've always done it this way." "Why not? Because I don't like it, that's why not." "You might as well change your mind; can't you see you're outnumbered?"

Always remember that language "creates thoughts, feelings, and behavior in team members which affect the way the team uses power, manages conflict, and negotiates."[8] Once group members analyze the nature of team talk, they can take steps to modify the way they interact and work with one another. The following recommendations can produce a stronger and more cooperative group that uses team talk effectively:

- Use the plural pronouns *we, us,* and *our* when referring to the group and its work.
- Express shared rather than individual needs: "We need to . . ." rather than "I want . . ."
- If you are in a position of power, don't talk more, interrupt more, or ask more questions than other members.
- Speak in a specific and active voice: "I haven't finished the report due next week" rather than an abstract and passive voice "The task hasn't been completed."
- Ask group members to address you by your first name or nickname.
- Encourage group members to express disagreement and listen patiently to dissenters.
- Ask more what-if questions and make fewer "we can't do it" statements.
- When in doubt, rephrase or ask questions about what someone else has said to ensure understanding.

Use "I," "You," and "We" Language Appropriately

When you use the word *I,* you take responsibility for your own feelings and actions: *I* feel great; *I* am a straight-A student; *I* am worried about the team's work on this project. Some people avoid using the word *I* because they think they're showing off, being selfish, or bragging. Other people use the word *I* too much and appear self-centered or oblivious to those around them.

Unfortunately, some people avoid "I" language when it is most important. Instead, they shift responsibility from themselves to others by using the word *you.* Sometimes, the word *you* is implied, as in "Stop telling me what to do" and "What a stupid thing to do." "You" language may express judgments about others. When the judgments are positive—"You did a great job" or "You look marvelous!"—there's rarely a problem. When *you* is used to accuse, blame, or criticize, it can arouse defensiveness and anger. Consider the following statements: "You make me angry" and "You drive too fast." Less accusatory approaches might include "I'm upset" or "I'd feel more comfortable if we drove slower."

Successful teams use the plural pronouns *we* and *you* when talking to one another.[9] Plural pronouns are inclusive. They announce that the group depends on everyone rather than on a single member. Plural pronouns also share credit for team achievements.[10] Members say *we, us,* and *our* when talking about the group and its work. When members say *you,* they are usually addressing the whole group.

Language Challenges

Although words have great power, they also pose challenges. As Mark Twain, the great American humorist, observed, "The difference between the almost right words and the right words is really a large matter—'tis the difference between the lightening bug and the lightening."[11] Mike Krzyzewski, Duke University's basketball coach, also recognizes the power of language: "I believe that my work is as much about words as it is about basketball. Choosing the right words is no less important to the outcome of a game than choosing the right players and strategies for the court."[12]

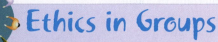

Ethics in Groups

Sticks and Stones May Break Your Bones, but Words Can Hurt Forever

When assaulted by abusive language, group members may become angry, discouraged, and withdrawn, or even be provoked into shouting matches with their attacker. Abusive language has the "immediate result of spoiling relationships (and productivity based on such relationships), and the long-term effect of ruining morale, teamwork, and loyalty."[13] Here are several characteristics of verbal abuse:

- *Tone of voice:* Harsh, sarcastic, angry, belittling
- *Content:* Sexual references, racial slurs, cruel comments about someone's appearance
- *Language choice:* Foul, obscene, or accusatory words
- *Nonverbal cues:* Insulting facial expressions, gross gestures, threatening movements
- *Speaking volume:* Loud, screaming voice or hissed messages[14]

Ethical communicators *both* take responsibility for what they say *and* take action when others use abusive language. Several techniques can help you avoid or confront verbal abuse:

1. *Express your objections.* At the first sign of verbal abuse, calmly explain that you feel abused but are willing to continue the discussion if the language becomes less inflammatory.

2. *Ask for repetition.* Ask the person to repeat what he or she has just said, as in "Please repeat that. I want to make sure I heard what you said."

3. *Step back.* When someone is verbally abusive, step back a few steps, as if to say that you will talk about the problem, but that you won't put up with yelling and insults. If the abuse continues, walk away.

4. *Quote the law.* When a discussion becomes abusive, quote the law or group norms: "That kind of language is inappropriate in this group" or "That word violates the company's civility policy."

5. *Take a time out.* Say "time out" when a discussion becomes uncomfortable or abusive. Follow that with "Let's take a minute to calm down before we continue."

6. *Practice what you preach.* If you take action against others, make sure that you avoid all forms of verbal abuse:
   - Do not raise your voice.
   - Do not swear.
   - Do not call members insulting names.
   - Do not use sarcasm to hurt others.

7. *Listen.* Listen more than you speak when you're upset, particularly if you're so mad that you're afraid of what you might say. As you listen, try to calm down physically and mentally.[15]

Group members can avoid many misunderstandings by overcoming language-based obstacles to communication. Among the most common language difficulties are abstract words, bypassing, offensive language, and jargon.

Abstract Words

You can minimize the misinterpretation of words by recognizing the ways in which different levels of meaning affect communication. The more abstract your language is, for instance, the more likely group members will interpret its meaning other than the way you intended. **Abstract words** refer to ideas or concepts you cannot see or touch. Words such as *fairness*, *freedom*, and *love* do not have the same meaning for everyone. Reliance on abstract words increases the chances of misunderstanding. **Concrete words** refer to specific things that you perceive with your senses—things you can see, hear, touch, smell, or taste. Concrete words narrow the number of possible meanings and decrease the likelihood of misinterpretation.

Figure 6.2 Common Language Difficulties

Abstract Words Abjure, Acumen, Adumbrate, Alacrity, Anathema, Ascetic, Aspersion, Assiduous	**Bypassing** Biweekly (twice a week or twice a month?) Next Wednesday (this week or next week?)
Offensive Language "?#@&*%!" Bitch, Ho, Wetback, Chink, Dago, Honky, Fag, Raghead, Sambo, Wop, Yid	**Jargon** Borking, POTUS, Trustafarian, TheoCon, Boll Weevil, Policy Wonk, NGO, Down-Ticket Race

Avoid using overly abstract words when working in groups. Use words that refer directly to observable objects, people, or behavior. For example, saying, "Greg's behavior was disruptive" could imply many things. Did he yell at a group member, use profanity, or refuse to participate? It is more concrete and descriptive to say, "Greg arrived 15 minutes late to the meeting" or "Greg interrupted the speaker three times during her presentation."

Bypassing

When group members use different meanings for the same words and phrases, they run the risk of **bypassing,** a form of miscommunication that occurs when people "miss each other with their meanings."[16] An entire group project may falter or fail if there are differences in the interpretation of a single word or phrase. Note the problems created by the following example of bypassing:

> At a routine staff meeting, a vice president tells her managers, "Survey the members of your department to find out whether they are satisfied with the new email system." During the following week, the vice president receives a copy of a memo from one manager requesting that everyone in his department fill out a two-page questionnaire about the email system. The vice president telephones the manager and asks, "What's this questionnaire all about?" The manager replies, "I thought you said I have to survey everyone in my department."

What the vice president had in mind was for the manager to informally ask staff members for their initial impressions rather than ask for a detailed analysis of the new system. Although the manager heard the vice president's words, the communicators "missed" each other's meaning.

Remember This

Meanings are in people, not in words.

"Communicators who habitually look for meanings in the people using words, rather than in the words themselves, are much less prone to bypass or to be bypassed."[17] In short, what's important is not what words mean to you, but what group members mean when they use or hear the same words.

Offensive Language

Offensive language demeans, inappropriately excludes, or stereotypes people. For example, sexist language may alienate and offend both male and female group members. Referring to women as "girls" implies that women are childlike and not capable of adult thought and responsibilities. Avoid words that specify the gender of individuals in particular roles or occupations. Instead, use words that refer to both men and women. For example, instead of referring to the *chairman,* use the term *chair* or *chairperson.*

Poorly chosen words can perpetuate discrimination. Avoid language that stereotypes people based on their culture, race, religion, or lifestyle.[18] Words such as *nigger, trailer trash,* and *faggot* are offensive and demeaning. Is it okay to use such words if none of your group members would be targeted by them? Absolutely not! This type of language can offend and alienate everyone in a group. A member of an insurance investigation team recounted the following experience:

> We were meeting to discuss ways to recognize fraudulent claims. At one point, another member said, "I'm working on a claim involving a carload of wetbacks." I couldn't believe he used that term. He obviously didn't know that my husband is Latino. I was insulted. Other group members were offended, too.

Jargon

Jargon is the specialized or technical language of a profession. Groups use jargon as "verbal shorthand that allows members to communicate with each other clearly, efficiently, and quickly."[19] In some groups, the ability to use jargon properly is a sign of team membership; it can also help the team to accomplish its work quickly and efficiently. For example, imagine how it would slow down a surgical team if every medical term and procedure had to be expressed in full Standard English instead of using short and concise jargon!

Even though jargon can be useful and efficient, it can also make ideas difficult to understand and, in some cases, can conceal the truth. Members who are unfamiliar with a group's jargon are easily intimidated and frustrated. Consider the experience of the vice president of a large corporation:

> When I first joined the company, I had to learn the lingo of the various groups in which I worked. I remember attending my first CMG meeting (I didn't even know what that meant at the time) and listening to people talk about red files and green files. Do we color-code files? No. Rather, the terms red file and green file refer to different pricing structures for our products. I also discovered that the same term might be used differently from one group to another. For instance, in some meetings IP refers to Internet provider. As an attorney, I use the term to refer to intellectual property. I'm now familiar with the language of our company, but I know how confusing it can be when you're new to the team.

Some people use jargon to impress others with their specialized knowledge. Such tactics usually fail to inform others and often result in misunderstandings and resentment. Use jargon only when you are sure that all the members of your group will understand it. If some of the jargon or technical terms of a field are important, take the time to explain those words to new members.

Language Differences

Group member diversity influences how we use and listen to language. Although there is nothing right or wrong about the different ways in which people use language, these differences can create misunderstandings among group members.

Language and Gender

Every group member should monitor and adapt to the different ways in which women and men may express their opinions. As we noted in Chapter 4, "Diversity in Groups," researchers claim that men and women may use language quite differently.[20] Rather than stereotyping men and women, we see these differences as tendencies rather than characteristics. For example, women *tend* to use language to maintain relationships and cooperate with others. Some women speak tentatively. Their speech is more likely to contain qualifiers and tag questions. A qualifier is a word that conveys uncertainty, such as *maybe* and *perhaps.* Tag questions are questions connected to a statement. For instance, "It may be time to move on to our next point, don't you think so?" is a tentative statement with a tag question. This style does not necessarily represent a lack of confidence. Instead, it can be a cooperative approach that encourages others to respond.

Men *tend* to use language to assert their ideas and compete with others. Men are less likely to express themselves tentatively. Male speech is generally more direct and forceful. One style of communication is no better than another. The two are simply different.

Language and Culture

For most groups, a single language is the medium of interaction, even though members from different backgrounds, generations, and geographic areas may speak the same language quite differently.

A **dialect** is a variation in vocabulary, pronunciation, syntax, and style that distinguishes speakers from different ethnic groups, geographic areas, and social classes. *All* of us have dialects depending on where we come from, where we live, the types of people and friends with whom we associate, and how we want to be perceived by others. In the United States, there are Southern dialects, New England dialects, and Brooklyn dialects, among others, and a whole range of foreign accents.

In the United States, Standard American English is the most commonly accepted dialect spoken by as much as 60 percent of the U.S. population. If, however, you enjoy "pizzer and beah" instead of pizza and beer, you may be from Massachusetts. If you say, "Ah nevah go theyuh," you could be from Alabama or parts of Texas. Unfortunately, studies repeatedly find that "accented speech and dialects provoke stereotyped reactions in listeners so that the speakers are usually perceived as having less status, prestige, and overall competence."[21] The implications of such research are clear: Group members who do not use Standard American English in business and academic settings may be viewed as less articulate or less competent. In other words, the dialect you speak at home may not be the best way to communicate in a business meeting.

Because dialects have the potential to influence the perceptions of group members, many speakers use codeswitching to avoid negative stereotypes related to language. **Codeswitching** refers to the ability to change from the dialect of your own cultural setting and adopt the language of the majority in particular situations.

African Americans often switch their linguistic codes depending on the context. They may speak one way among white people or in business settings (Standard English) and quite differently at home (Black English). Linguist John McWhorter notes that many middle-class African Americans typically speak both Black English and Standard English, switching constantly between the two, often in the same sentence.[22] As a result, many African Americans are competent in two sophisticated dialects of English.[23] The same is true in immigrant families whose members may use the "old country" language or a simplified version of English in private, while they use Standard English in public.

The ways in which you use language can also affect how others judge you and your ability to communicate. Communication scholar Carley Dodd concludes that: "(1) people judge others by their speech, (2) upward mobility and social aspirations influence whether people change their speech to the accepted norms, (3) general American speech is most accepted by the majority of the American culture, and (4) people should be aware of these prejudices and attempt to look beyond the surface."[24] Thus, you should try to understand, respect, and adapt to the dialects you hear in group communication contexts.

Theory in Groups

The Whorf Hypothesis

One of the most significant and controversial language theories attempts to explain why people from different cultures speak and interpret messages differently from one another. Linguist Edward Sapir and his student, Benjamin Whorf, spent decades studying the relationship among language, culture, and thought. Whorf's most controversial theory contends that the structure of a language *determines* how we see, experience, and interpret the world around us. For example, if we don't have a word for *red*, we won't be able to see red or separate it from other colors we do see.

Benjamin Whorf observed that the Hopi Indians of Arizona make no distinction in their language among past, present, and future tenses. In English, we understand the grammatical differences between "I saw the girl," "I see the girl," and "I will see the girl." The Hopi do not make such clear distinctions in their words. Whorf concluded that therefore they must perceive the world very differently. He also noted that the Hopi have a single word, *masa'ytaka*, for everything that flies, from insects to airplanes. Does that mean the Hopi cannot think about tomorrow and cannot see the differences between an airplane and a fly? Originally,

many linguists believed that the answer was yes. Now linguists understand that the Hopi do think about tomorrow but perceive it quite differently than those of us who have the word *tomorrow*. Language does not determine everything we think. At the same time, it does influence the way we perceive others and the world around us.[25]

Like many controversial theories, the Whorf Hypothesis (also referred to as the Sapir-Whorf Hypothesis) has been accepted, rejected, resurrected, and amended—several times. Today, most linguists accept a more moderate version of the **Whorf Hypothesis:** Language *reflects* cultural models of the world, which in turn influence how the speakers of a language come to think, act, and behave.[26] For example, in English, terms that end with *man*, such as *chairman*, *fireman*, and *policeman*, may lead us to view certain roles and jobs as only appropriate for men. Substituting words such as *chairperson*, *firefighter*, and *police officer* may change perceptions about who can work in these careers. Interestingly, in Finland there is only one pronoun for the words he and she, which avoids the tendency to link certain behaviors or jobs to either men or women.

The Importance of Nonverbal Communication

Nonverbal communication refers to the behavioral elements of messages other than spoken words. Your appearance, posture, and facial expressions send messages. Research suggests that nonverbal behavior accounts for between 60 and 70 percent of all meaning.[27] That is, people base their understanding of what you mean not only on what you say, but also on how you use nonverbal cues. Thus, nonverbal communication "is arguably one of the most powerful methods of communication."[28]

Group communication researcher Robert Cathcart and his colleagues note that "groups provide a rich source of nonverbal messages because so many behaviors occur simultaneously."[29] Unfortunately, we often put more thought into choosing the best words than into selecting the most appropriate behavior for conveying our ideas.

> ### Remember This
> Group members often rely more on your nonverbal behavior than your words to interpret your meaning.

Nonverbal Behavior

Group members send messages through their personal appearance as well as through their facial, vocal, and physical expression. When all of these nonverbal elements are combined, they add enormous complexity and subtlety to group interaction.

Personal Appearance

When group members meet for the first time, they know very little about one another beyond what they see. Physical appearance influences first impressions. Based on members' physical appearance, we draw conclusions about their education,

---

 ## Groups in Balance...

Speak "Silently"

The well-known phrase *Silence is golden* may be based on a Swiss saying, *Sprechen ist silbern, Schweigen ist golden*, which means "speech is silver; silence is golden." This metaphor suggests that while speech is important, silence may be even more significant. The power of silence is recognized and embraced in many cultures:

- Those who know do not speak. Those who speak do not know. (*Tao Te Ching*)
- Silence is also speech. (African proverb)
- Silence is a friend who will not betray. (Confucius)
- A loud voice shows an empty head. (Finnish proverb)

Understanding the communicative value of silence is important for several reasons. We use silence to communicate many things: to establish interpersonal distance, to put our thoughts together, to show respect for another person, or to modify others' behaviors.[30] When you work in groups, your silence may communicate a lot more than speech. If you are a talkative extrovert, silence gives you time to think and gives introverts a chance to speak. If someone's nasty tone during a heated discussion bothers you, silence can communicate your unwillingness to join the fray. Silence can also signal agreement, particularly when a group has talked an issue to death. Your silence might say, "We've said it all, now let's vote or move on to another issue." Finally, remember that members from collectivist cultures assign great meaning to silence. "Listening" to their silence can tell you more than any words.

Every group member relies on verbal and nonverbal messages to generate meaning. What messages might the facial expressions and body language of the two front-facing members be communicating to the third member?

success, moral character, social position, and trustworthiness.[31] For better or worse, we tend to see attractive people as friendlier and as more credible than those who are less attractive. One study found that good-looking people tend to make more money and get promoted more often than those with average looks.[32]

Even the clothes you wear send messages to other group members. Nonverbal communication scholar Peter Andersen maintains that "effective small group members should view clothes and hair styles as an important silent statement made to the group. Dress that is appropriate is perhaps most important."[33] Casual attire is more acceptable in informal groups, whereas a professional appearance is expected in business settings and important group presentations. Your appearance should communicate that you respect the group and take its work seriously.

Facial Expression and Eye Contact

Your face can produce more than a thousand different expressions.[34] The facial expressions of group members let you know if they are interested in, agree with, or understand what you have said. Facial expressions supplement and complement the verbal messages of group members.[35] Good listeners look at a speaker's facial expressions in order to comprehend the full message.

Of all your facial features, your eyes are the most revealing. Generally, North Americans perceive eye contact as an indicator of attitude. Lack of eye contact is frequently perceived as signifying inattentiveness, indifference, nervousness, or dishonesty. However, it is important to realize that perceptions about eye contact vary in different cultures; we will discuss these cultural variations later in this chapter.

Eye contact influences interaction in groups. A seating arrangement that allows group members to face one another and establish eye contact helps maintain interaction. Eye contact also tells others when you want to speak. Returning eye contact to a group leader indicates that you are ready to respond, whereas avoiding eye contact is typically perceived as an attempt to avoid interaction.

Vocal Expression

Vocal expression is the *way* you say a word by varying your pitch, volume, rate, and word stress. For example, a loud voice can imply anger, excitement, or dominance. Group members speaking quietly may signal that information is confidential. Also, a group may be bored by or stop listening to a member who speaks too slowly or in a monotone voice. A speaking rate that is too fast makes it difficult to understand the message. Adjust your volume and rate to the group setting and type of activity.

When pitch, volume, and rate are combined, they can be used to vary the stress you give to a word or phrase. **Word stress** refers to the "degree of prominence given to a syllable within a word or a word within a phrase or sentence."[36] Notice the differences in meaning as you stress the italicized words in the following three sentences: Is *that* the report you want me to read? Is that the report you want *me* to read? Is that the report you want me to *read*? Although the same words are used in all three sentences, the meaning of each question is quite different.

Physical Expression

Kinesics is the study of body movement and physical expression. Gestures are one of the most animated forms of kinesics. They can emphasize or stress parts of a message, reveal discomfort with the group situation, or convey a message without the use of words. For example, Jeff points to his watch to let the chairperson know that they will soon run out of time. At the end of a discussion, a thumbs-up gesture from group members signals that they are satisfied with the group's progress. Many people have difficulty expressing their thoughts without using gestures. Why else would we gesture when we are speaking on the phone? Research suggests that gesturing helps ease the mental effort when communication is difficult.[37]

Even your posture can convey moods and emotions. For example, if you slouch back in your chair, others may interpret your posture as lack of interest or dislike for the group. On the other hand, sitting upright and leaning forward communicate interest and are signs of attentive listening. Research links gestures and body movement to perceptions of leadership. Group members who lean forward, maintain eye contact, gesture often, smile, and assume a relaxed posture are more likely to emerge as group leaders and to be viewed as attractive by other group members.[38]

One of the most potent forms of physical expression is touch. Touch can convey a wide range of meanings. In groups, members often use brief touch to express encouragement, support, or happiness. Peter Andersen points out that "touch in a small group may establish greater teamwork, solidarity, or sharing."[39] Keep in mind that the use and meaning of touch may differ depending on the situation or type of group. For example, church group or support group members engage in more touch than do colleagues in a professional business meeting. Some work settings may even discourage touch among coworkers beyond a handshake.

Some group members are more comfortable with touch than others. At one end of a continuum are touch avoiders; at the other end are touch approachers. Misunderstandings can occur between these two kinds of people. Approachers may view avoiders as cold and unfriendly; avoiders may perceive approachers as invasive and rude. It is important to remember that gender and culture influence touch avoidance. Women are more likely to avoid opposite-sex touch, whereas men often avoid same-sex touch. In particular, Far Eastern women exhibit more touch avoidance than people from other cultures.[40] Make sure you know the members of your group very well before hugging them or putting your arm around their shoulder. A handshake is usually the safest option.

Virtual Groups

Expressing Emotions Online

When groups meet face to face, members can listen to other members' tone of voice and can observe their nonverbal behavior. However, most virtual groups rely on technologies that don't allow the members to hear or see one another. Participants can't see the facial expressions, head nods, gestures, or posture of other group members.

As a result, early users of computer-mediated communication developed emoticons to function in place of nonverbal cues. An **emoticon** is the use of ordinary typographical characters to convey a nonverbal expression. For example, ☺, :-), ;-), :-(, and :-D are commonly used emoticons that convey smiles, winks, frowns, and laughing.

In theory, emoticons serve as substitutes for nonverbal behavior. However, research suggests that emoticons have little or no effect on the interpretation of a typed message.[41] Thus, virtual group members are more likely to rely on your words than on your emoticons when interpreting the intention of your message.

In their book *Rules of the Net*, Thomas Mandel and Gerard Van der Leun offer the following suggestion: "Nothing—especially the symbols on the top row of your keyboard—can substitute for a clear idea simply expressed. Avoid :-) and all associated emoticons as you would avoid clichés—for example, like the plague."[42] Generally, we advise you to avoid emoticons. However, if using emoticons is a norm within your group, ☺ away.

Emoticons function as nonverbal cues in computer-mediated communication. However, research suggests that virtual group members are more likely to rely on words than on emoticons to determine meaning.

The Nonverbal Environment

Nonverbal communication extends beyond the behavior of group members; it also includes the group's environment. Two important aspects of a group's nonverbal environment are the arrangement of space and perceptions of personal space.

Arrangement of Space

Seating arrangements can affect group interaction in significant ways. Arrangements that physically separate group members make group interaction difficult. Arrangements that bring people closer together and permit direct eye contact among all members promote group interaction. Group members arranged in a circle or around a table can interact with one another more easily.

Your choice of seating position in groups has a direct effect on interaction and influence.[43] Several studies note that group members prefer corner-to-corner or side-by-side seating for cooperative activities. Such an arrangement allows them to be close enough to share materials. Members who anticipate competition or disagreement often choose seats across from each other.

A member's seating position often reflects the person's official position and amount of power. Group leaders are more likely to choose (or be assigned) a seat at the head of a table. Task-oriented leaders are attracted to the head of a table, while the middle position at the side of a table attracts more socially oriented leaders—members who are more concerned about group relationships and encouraging everyone to participate.[44] These two locations put the leader in a position to see and be seen by everyone in the group. Choosing one of the centrally located positions as depicted below in Figure 6.3 also makes it easier for a member to gain speaking opportunities.

Even the arrangement of a room or the shape of a conference table sends a message to group members. A long, rectangular table gives a group's leader a special place of prominence at its head. A round table allows all members to sit in equally important positions. The Paris peace talks that helped end the war in Vietnam bogged down for eight months until delegates from South Vietnam, the National Liberation Front, and the United States agreed to a round table as the setting for negotiation. When the leaders of Bosnia, Croatia, and Serbia met at Wright-Patterson Air Force Base in Ohio in 1995, the United States made sure that each party

Seating arrangements can affect group interaction in significant ways. For example, arrangements that bring people closer together and permit direct eye contact among all members promote group interaction. How does the seating arrangement in this photo enhance or inhibit member interaction?

Figure 6.3   Seating Arrangements

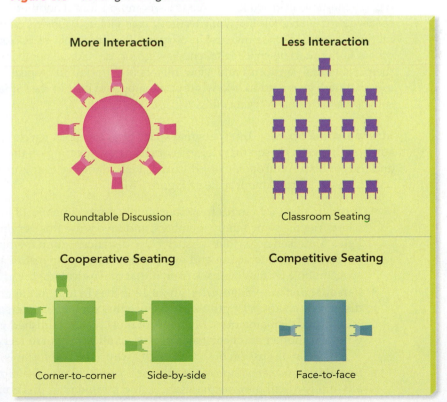

More Interaction

Roundtable Discussion

Less Interaction

Classroom Seating

Cooperative Seating

Corner-to-corner   Side-by-side

Competitive Seating

Face-to-face

had equal seating space around a modest but perfectly round table. The arrangement of space is not a trivial matter when the success of a group is so consequential.

In addition to seating arrangement, the décor of a room can have a direct influence on a group and its work. A New England advertising agency learned this lesson the hard way when heated arguments and even a fistfight broke out during meetings in which representative consumers were brought together to evaluate a new product or an advertising message.[45] Facilitators reported that regardless of the discussion topic, no one ever seemed happy in these meetings. Participants were grumpy, negative, and resistant to new ideas. Eventually, the company determined that the problem was the room itself: It was cramped, poorly ventilated, and forbidding—a cross between a hospital room and a police interrogation room. The solution: a total redesign and redecoration. The company expanded the room and gave it long, gently curved walls. Soft, indirect light filtered in through curved windows. Participants could choose to sit in armchairs or on small couches surrounding circular coffee tables. The results were better than expected. There were no more fistfights. Instead, group members became much more cooperative and positive.

Perceptions of Personal Space

Groups and their members may function quite differently depending on how they perceive the space and people around them. **Proxemics** refers to the study of how we perceive and use personal space. Within groups, two important proxemic variables are territoriality and interpersonal space.

Territoriality.   **Territoriality** is the sense of personal ownership we attach to a particular space. For instance, in most classrooms, students sit in the same place every day. If you have ever walked into a classroom and found another person in "your" seat, you may have felt that your territory was violated. Objects acting as territorial markers often designate ownership of space. Placing a coat or books on a chair lets others know that the space is taken. As a group develops, members often establish their individual territories and view members who fail to respect others' territory as violating a group norm. Many group members will sit in the same place near the same people during every meeting.

Interpersonal Space.   **Interpersonal space** is an invisible, psychological "bubble" surrounding each person that expands or shrinks depending on the communicators and the context. Anthropologist Edward T. Hall identifies four zones of interaction used by most North Americans (see Figure 6.4).[46]

- **Intimate distance** ranges from touching to approximately 18 inches apart. Close friends, some family members, and lovers use this very private zone. Peter Andersen notes that "at such close distances group members will feel inhibited from interacting and will make an attempt to restore their personal space bubble by moving back even if that means leaving the group."[47]
- **Personal distance** ranges from about 18 inches to four feet apart. The typical distance is an arm's length away. We use this zone for conversations with friends and acquaintances. Members of most well-established groups interact with one another at this distance because it allows them to feel close enough to engage in discussion but far enough away to be comfortable.
- **Social distance** encompasses a range of four to twelve feet apart. We usually interact with new acquaintances and strangers in this zone. Groups in

Figure 6.4 Zones of Personal Space

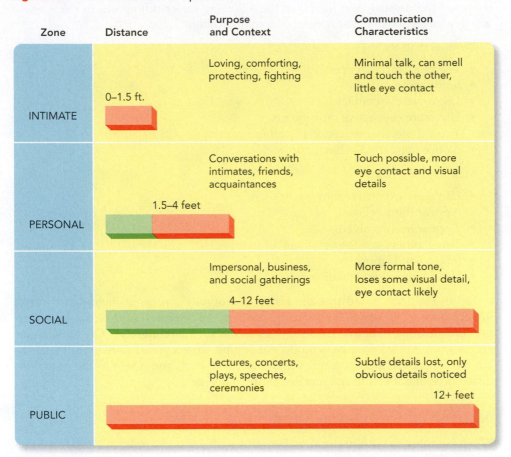

Zone	Distance	Purpose and Context	Communication Characteristics
INTIMATE	0–1.5 ft.	Loving, comforting, protecting, fighting	Minimal talk, can smell and touch the other, little eye contact
PERSONAL	1.5–4 feet	Conversations with intimates, friends, acquaintances	Touch possible, more eye contact and visual details
SOCIAL	4–12 feet	Impersonal, business, and social gatherings	More formal tone, loses some visual detail, eye contact likely
PUBLIC	12+ feet	Lectures, concerts, plays, speeches, ceremonies	Subtle details lost, only obvious details noticed

which members use the outer limits of this zone may find it difficult to interact with others.

- **Public distance** extends beyond twelve feet. Speakers use this distance for lectures and presentations. Groups are unlikely to use this zone unless they are making a presentation to a larger audience.

Nonverbal Differences

Earlier in this chapter, we noted that group member diversity affects the way we use and listen to language. The same is true for the way we use nonverbal communication. If you understand, respect, and adapt to the different ways in which members express themselves nonverbally, you and your group will be able to avoid misunderstandings and help one another achieve your group's common goal.

Nonverbal Communication and Gender

As with the use of verbal communication, there are differences in the ways that men and women use nonverbal communication. The stereotypical belief is that women are nonverbally more "expressive, involved, warm" and better at interpreting nonverbal messages.[48] But are these stereotypes accurate? Communication scholar Judith Hall surveyed the research and identified the following major differences in the ways in which women and men use nonverbal communication.[49]

Women tend to:

- Use more facial expression
- Smile more
- Use more eye contact
- Use more expressive movements
- Touch others more (especially other women)
- Notice nonverbal behavior more

Men tend to:

- Use more expansive movements
- Appear more relaxed
- Appear less involved
- Touch others less (especially other men)
- Shake hands more
- Use a larger personal distance

Judith Hall concluded that the above stereotypes "are overwhelmingly correct in substance."[50] Research continues to confirm that women more accurately interpret the meaning of nonverbal behaviors across various contexts.[51] Of course, there are many men and women who do not exhibit stereotypical nonverbal behavior. Ultimately, group members must understand, respect, and adapt to the nonverbal differences of both male and female group members.

Nonverbal Communication and Culture

When we interact with group members from different cultural backgrounds, interpreting their nonverbal behavior may be as difficult as translating an unfamiliar foreign language. The multiple meanings of nonverbal communication in other cultures can be illustrated by focusing on two elements: personal space and eye contact.

Research on personal space indicates that most Latin Americans, Arabs, and Greeks require less distance between people than North Americans do. Cultural differences also are evident when measuring the amount and directness of eye contact. For example, "direct eye contact is a taboo or an insult in many Asian cultures."[52] Similarly, African Americans may avoid direct eye contact as a sign of respect. As a result, if a white North American supervisor criticizes an employee who comes from one of these cultures, the employee may respond by looking downward rather than looking at the supervisor. In some cases, the employee's response may offend the supervisor, who interprets it as inattention or defiance.

There is a danger, however, of stereotyping people from different backgrounds and cultures on the basis of their nonverbal behavior. You may meet a Latino, Arab, or Greek group member who is not comfortable with less personal space than a North American. Asian or African American employees may look directly at a white supervisor with respect. When interpreting nonverbal behavior, then, it is important to try to understand, respect, and adapt to individual differences rather than assuming that all people from a particular culture behave alike.

Groups in Balance...

Survive

On August 5, 2010, the San José copper-gold mine in Chile collapsed, trapping 33 miners three miles below ground. When rescuers estimated it could take four months to dig them out, Chile's government asked NASA experts for advice on how to keep the miners physically and mentally healthy. The strategies they recommended come straight from group communication research.

Researcher Peter Suedfeld studies the health and well-being of groups in "extreme and unusual environments" (EUE) such as settlements in Antarctica and life in space capsules.[53] Communication researcher Irvin Altman's work with military and research groups in Antarctica have yielded similar results. Both of them advise groups on how to survive in confined spaces. As Altman found,

> [t]he epitome of a successful group was one in which the members, on the first or second day, laid out an eating, exercise, recreation schedule; constructed a deck of playing cards, a chess set, and a Monopoly game out of paper.[54]

Group members who adapted "decided how they would structure their lives over the expected lengthy period of isolation."[55] In his book *Group Dynamics*, Donelson R. Forsyth concludes that groups respond to stressful environments like these "by becoming better groups—more organized, more cohesive, and more efficient."[56]

Now consider the Chilean miners. They immediately organized themselves into work groups and took on appropriate roles. At first they rationed the little food they had: two spoonfuls of tuna, a sip of milk, and a morsel of peach each day. The shift foreman took

The San José miners were trapped underground for more than two months. What group processes contributed to their survival, as well as their physical and mental health, in these desperate conditions?

on the role of leader, another miner organized fitness exercises, and a third became the group's "doctor." Two miners became religious leaders and advisers, while two others maintained communication with the surface. Eventually, they were sent food and water, medical supplies, videos, board games, and messages from loved ones on the surface to keep them busy and hopeful. Thus, despite being trapped in what surely was an "extreme and unusual environment," the mining group adapted and balanced the contradictory tensions in a cooperative effort to survive.

All 33 miners were rescued on October 13, 2010. When they emerged from the capsule that brought them to the surface, they were joyous and, considering the conditions they'd lived in, a healthy group of brave men.[57]

Creating a Supportive Communication Climate

The way we use and react to language and nonverbal communication establishes a unique group atmosphere, or climate. Specifically, a group's **climate** is the degree to which group members feel comfortable interacting. In some groups, the climate is warm and supportive. Members like and trust one another as they work toward a common goal. In chillier group climates, defensiveness and tension pollute the atmosphere. Members may feel threatened by and suspicious of one another.

Figure 6.5 Gibb's Defensive and Supportive Group Behaviors

DEFENSIVE BEHAVIORS	SUPPORTIVE BEHAVIORS
EVALUATION: Judges another person's behavior. Makes critical statements. *Examples:* "Why did you insult Sharon like that? Explain yourself!" "What you did was terrible."	**DESCRIPTION:** Describes another person's behavior. Makes understanding statements. Uses more *I* and *we* language. *Examples:* "When we heard what you said to Sharon, we were really embarrassed for her." "I'm sorry you did that."
CONTROL: Imposes your solution on someone else. Seeks control of the situation. *Examples:* "Give me that report and I'll make it better." "Since I'm paying for the vacation, we're going to the resort I like rather than the spa you like."	**PROBLEM ORIENTATION:** Seeks a mutually agreeable solution. *Examples:* "Okay. Let's see what we can do to get that report finished to specifications." "Let's talk and figure out how both of us can enjoy our vacation."
STRATEGY: Manipulates others. Hides hidden agendas or personal motives. *Examples:* "Frankie's going to Florida over spring break." "Remember when I helped you rearrange your office?"	**SPONTANEITY:** Makes straightforward, direct, open, honest, and helpful comments. *Examples:* "I'd like to go to Florida with Frankie over spring break." "Would you help me move some heavy boxes?"
NEUTRALITY: Appears withdrawn, detached, and indifferent. Won't take sides. *Examples:* "You can't win them all." "Life's a gamble." "It doesn't matter to me." "Whatever."	**EMPATHY:** Accepts and understands another person's feelings. *Examples:* "I can't believe she did that. No wonder you're upset." "It sounds as though you're having a hard time deciding."
SUPERIORITY: Implies that you and your opinions are better than others. Promotes resentment and jealousy. *Examples:* "Hey—I've done this a million times—let me have it. I'll finish in no time." "Is this the best you could do?"	**EQUALITY:** Suggests that everyone can make a useful contribution. *Examples:* "If you don't mind, I'd like to explain how I've handled this before. It may help." "Let's tackle this problem together."
CERTAINTY: Believes that your opinion is the only correct one. Refuses to consider the ideas and opinions of others. Takes inflexible positions. *Examples:* "I can't see any other way of doing this that makes sense." "There's no point in discussing this any further."	**PROVISIONALISM:** Offers ideas and accepts suggestions from others. *Examples:* "We have a lot of options here—which one makes the most sense?" "I feel strongly about this, but I would like to hear what you think."

In 1961, sociologist Jack Gibb identified six pairs of communication behaviors that influence whether a group's climate is defensive or supportive.[58] A **defensive climate** triggers our instinct to protect ourselves when we are verbally criticized or physically threatened by someone. Even though such reactions are natural, they hinder productive group interaction. When the group climate is defensive, members devote attention to defending themselves and defeating perceived opponents. A **supportive climate** creates a setting in which members feel free to share their opinions and feelings. Synergy occurs only when a group functions in a supportive climate. Figure 6.5 on p. 142 shows the behaviors of each climate in pairs, one the opposite of the other, with defensive behaviors on the left and supportive behaviors on the right.

Evaluation	Description
Control	Problem Orientation
Strategy	Spontaneity
Neutrality	Empathy
Superiority	Equality
Certainty	Provisionalism

Try to avoid classifying Gibb's six pairs of supportive and defensive behaviors as "good" and "bad" behaviors. Rather, they represent dialectic tensions. There may be times when you *should* express yourself in evaluative, controlling, strategic, neutral, superior, or certain terms. For example, you may behave strategically when you have important and strong personal motives. You may behave with certainty when your expertise is well recognized and a critical decision must be made. And you may respond neutrally when the issue is of little consequence to you or others.

Take one more look at Gibb's six pairs of communication behaviors in Figure 6.5. Every one of these behaviors can be expressed verbally and nonverbally. Here are two sketches depicting the nonverbal differences between defensive and supportive behaviors:

- Defensive: She rolls her eyes or audibly sighs when other members make suggestions. She often intimidates others by standing and looking down at them or by interrupting them when they speak. If group members need help, she looks the other way or concentrates on her own work. Everything about her—the way she walks, dresses, stands, and speaks—conveys her conviction that she is right and better than other group members.

- Supportive: He always listens carefully to other members and speaks kindly even when he disagrees. He avoids bragging about his own accomplishments but is quick to praise the group and its efforts. When other members need help, he stops what he's doing to listen and, if possible, helps them. He smiles, leans forward, nods his head, maintains eye contact, and is physically close to others. Most members like and respect him, largely because he radiates honesty, warmth, and openness.

According to Martin Remland's review of nonverbal group behavior, nonverbal response styles are contagious.[59] He also notes that the more cohesive the group is, the more uniform their style of emotional expression.[60] Now ask yourself this question: Which kind of "contagion" is better for your group—nonverbal behavior that creates a supportive climate or behavior that leads to a defensive climate? Not surprisingly, defensive climates spread negative emotions and increase stress and burnout. On the other hand, supportive climates increase the expression of positive emotions and promote group productivity, member satisfaction, and genuine cooperation.[61]

Follow the Research

Immediacy in Groups

In general, we tend to avoid or are cautious around group members who are cold, unfriendly, or hostile. In contrast, we feel more comfortable with group members who are warm and friendly. Researchers have identified a concept called **immediacy**, the degree to which a person seems approachable and likable.[62]

Research by nonverbal communication scholar Albert Mehrabian identified several clusters of nonverbal behaviors that generate positive interactions:[63]

- More leaning forward
- More physical closeness to others
- More eye contact
- More openness of arms and body
- More direct body orientation
- More touching
- More relaxed posture
- More positive facial and vocal expressions
- More laughing and smiling

The concept of immediacy applies directly to group interaction. When group members are physically comfortable with one another, they work in a more supportive climate. Just think of the opposite behaviors and you'll see why members become more defensive in the absence of immediacy behaviors. Rather than leaning forward and closer in an open position, nonimmediate members lean back, sit farther away, and cross their arms or hunch over. Rather than facing members directly and establishing eye contact, nonimmediate members sit sideways and rarely make eye contact. Rather than smiling at others, nonimmediate members have no expression or even scowl. If you find yourself leaning back, sitting in a rigid posture, or looking at everything but the members of your group during a discussion, it may be time to change your nonverbal behavior to mannerisms and actions that communicate greater physical closeness to or liking of others. Once you take on a more relaxed posture and smile, you may even find yourself enjoying the group experience and the company of members.

Summary Study Guide

Two Essential Tools
- Whereas verbal communication focuses on how you use words and language, nonverbal communication refers to message components other than words that generate meaning.
- In dialectic terms, effective group members rely on *both* verbal *and* nonverbal communication to generate meaning. When verbal and nonverbal messages contradict one another, a group can become confused and defensive.

Team Talk
- Team talk is the means used to achieve group goals, the stimulus to build group relationships, and the evidence used to assess group work.
- Effective team talk uses plural pronouns as well as collective, considerate, casual, collaborative, and exploratory language.

Language Challenges
- Use specific, understandable concrete words rather than less tangible, abstract words.
- Avoiding bypassing and offensive language and minimizing jargon can improve group understanding.

Language Differences
- Some women tend to use a more tentative language style, whereas men's language tends to be more direct and to the point.
- Codeswitching refers to the ability to change from the dialect of your own cultural setting and adopt the language of the majority in particular situations.
- According to the Whorf Hypothesis, language *reflects* cultural models of the world, which in turn influence how the speakers of a language come to think, act, and behave.

The Importance of Nonverbal Communication
- Nonverbal communication can convey as much or more meaning than do words.
- As much as two-thirds of all meaning may be derived from nonverbal behavior.

Nonverbal Behavior
- Group members send messages through their personal appearance as well as through their facial, vocal, and physical expressions.
- The directness and length of eye contact significantly influence group interaction.
- Vocal characteristics include pitch, volume, rate, and word stress.
- Physical expression includes gestures, posture, and touch.

The Nonverbal Environment
- Group seating arrangements can promote or discourage communication. Leaders tend to sit in centrally located positions.
- Territoriality refers to a sense of ownership of a particular space.
- Proxemics refers to the study of how we perceive and use personal space, particularly in terms of the four zones of interaction: intimate, personal, social, and public.

Nonverbal Differences
- When interpreting nonverbal behavior, try to understand, respect, and adapt to individual differences rather than assuming that all people from a particular culture behave alike.
- Women tend to be more nonverbally expressive and are generally more accurate in interpreting nonverbal behavior.

Creating a Supportive Communication Climate
- Jack Gibb matches defensive and supportive characteristics: evaluation and description, control and problem orientation, strategy and spontaneity, neutrality and empathy, superiority and equality, certainty and provisionalism.
- Groups in supportive climates exhibit immediacy—behaviors that indicate greater physical closeness to or liking of others.

GroupWork

Getting Emotional about Nonverbal Cues

Directions: The following table lists seven types of nonverbal behavior in the left column. Four types of emotions you will encounter in groups are listed across the top row. As in the example for *warmth*, indicate the kind of nonverbal behavior you or others often use to express these feelings to one another. Be prepared to share your results with group members or the entire class in order to identify nonverbal cues that typically portray specific emotions.

NONVERBAL CUES AND EMOTIONS

Nonverbal Behavior	Warmth (Examples)	Happiness	Anger	Boredom
Facial Cues	Smiling, calm, interested			
Eye Contact	Direct			
Vocal Cues	Soft, expressive			
Touch	Gentle, reassuring			
Gestures and Body Movement	Open, slow, welcoming			
Distance	Close, intimate, personal			
Posture	Leaning in, relaxed			

Group Assessment

Auditing Team Talk

Directions: Circle the term that best describes the extent to which the members of your group engage in productive team talk.

When your group communicates . . .			
1. Do members use plural pronouns rather than singular ones?	Often	Sometimes	Rarely
2. Do members use language that acknowledges shared needs?	Often	Sometimes	Rarely
3. Do members solicit opinions and express the need for cooperation?	Often	Sometimes	Rarely
4. Do members talk to one another on equal terms?	Often	Sometimes	Rarely
5. Do members use casual language, nicknames, and/or slang?	Often	Sometimes	Rarely
6. Do members express empathy and liking?	Often	Sometimes	Rarely
7. Do members express interest in solving problems?	Often	Sometimes	Rarely
8. Do members use a nonthreatening tone and nonjudgmental language?	Often	Sometimes	Rarely
9. Do members paraphrase one another?	Often	Sometimes	Rarely
10. Do members ask what-if questions?	Often	Sometimes	Rarely
11. Do members propose objective criteria for solutions?	Often	Sometimes	Rarely
12. Do members summarize areas of agreement?	Often	Sometimes	Rarely

Scoring: Analyze your group's team talk by looking at the number of times you circled "Often," "Sometimes," and "Rarely." The more times you circled "Often," the more likely it is that your group engages in productive team talk. The more times you circled "Rarely," the more likely it is that talk inhibits the progress and success of your group.

For a more accurate assessment of team talk in your group, each member should complete the questionnaire and share their responses. Is there a consistent response to each question? Can members identify specific examples of team talk within the group? If there are significant disagreements on several questions, the members of your group may benefit from a discussion about the nature of their team talk.

Listening in Groups

Chapter Outline

Case Study

That's Not What I Said

A junior-level marketing class has been divided into four project teams. Each team must research and prepare a marketing proposal for a small business in the community. The members of Group 4 are Lilly, Wendy, Michael, John, and Peter.

Today, Group 4 is holding its eighth meeting at the usual time and place: 2:00 P.M. in Library Study Room 303B. Members are worried because they haven't finished the research portion of the project even though the due date for their marketing project and group presentation is three weeks away. It's now 2:15 and everyone is there except Lilly.

"Hi!" shouts a bright-eyed Lilly as she rushed into the room.

"Lilly," says John crisply, "before you get carried away with something else, please tell us that you brought the research we need in order to finish this part of the project report. At our last meeting, you said you'd have it done before today or, at the latest, would give it to us at today's meeting."

The other group members nod as John speaks. They are impressed with how well he addressed what had become an increasing group problem.

"Guess what?" Lilly throws her books down on the table and leans forward. "Jack is coming to visit this weekend! He didn't think he could get away until Thanksgiving break, but he just called—that's why I'm late—to say he got two days off. He's leaving in the morning to drive down!"

"That's great, Lilly," nods Peter, acknowledging Lilly's excitement and happiness. "But could we talk about your good news after the meeting? We have a lot to do today."

Lilly laughs. "Yeah, I know. Work, work, work and no play makes us dull boys and girls. You guys are worse task masters than our professor."

Michael looks up and takes out his earbuds. "What? Is there a problem here?"

Everyone rolls their eyes. "Go back to dreamland!" snaps Peter.

"Lilly," says Wendy in a hopeful tone, "we need to go through your research and see whether we're ready to move ahead with our marketing plan."

"I'm just so excited," says a grinning Lilly. "Just two more days 'til he's here."

"Excuse me," John interrupts, "but what about the research? I didn't get any email from you with it attached. Did anyone? You said you'd have it by today. Come on, Lilly, this is not the first time you've let us down."

Lilly is no longer smiling. "That's not what I said. What I said was that I'd *try* to get it done by today. Look, it's not that big a deal. We can go ahead and work on the marketing plan with or without this research because there's nothing in it we don't already know. I'm still tweaking the data and I didn't have time to finish the graphics. We can add the research later and adjust the report."

Michael, who's been paying attention now that he's turned off his iPod, can no longer sit still. "Damn it, Lilly, you haven't been part of this group since day one. We're always waiting for you to show up. And when you take on a task, you either don't do it or finish it late. What's up with you? Don't you care?"

"Of course I care," Lilly retorts.

"Now," reminds Peter, "We know Lilly had some health problems early in the semester and we agreed to make some allowances for her. Certainly everyone knows that Lilly often comes up with some great ideas."

John throws up his hands, "Does that mean we have to make allowances when Jack shows up for two days of sex?"

The rest of the members wince and fear that he may have gone too far. "Out of line. Out of line," murmurs Michael in an audible whisper.

Lilly stands glaring at the group. "Well," she says, "if that's how all of you feel, I guess you don't need my work. Oh—and thanks for ruining my day." With that, Lilly picks up her books and strides out of the room.

The remaining group members look at one another in frustration and begin talking about whether they should suck it up and do Lilly's work or ask the professor if they can "fire" Lilly.

(continued)

When you finish reading this chapter, you should be able to answer the following critical thinking questions about this case study:

1 What role did hearing play in the case study?

2 To what extent did members effectively understand, remember, interpret, evaluate, and respond to one another's statements and questions?

3 Which members, if any, demonstrated good listening skills?

4 What group roles and related listening skills could group members have used to resolve the problem and get their work done?

Helping Annie

Virtual Miscommunication

Before you read any further, visit Pearson's MySearchLab website and watch the short videos "Helping Annie" and "Virtual Miscommunication," which illustrate Chapter 7 concepts. Each video comes with a set of study questions to keep in mind as you read this chapter.

The Challenge of Listening in Groups

How well do you listen? Most students answer this question with a confident "Very well!" or "I always pay attention." Nevertheless, most students—like most people—overestimate how well they listen. Here are some questions to help you rethink your answer:

- Do you make yourself listen even when the topic or group member is boring?
- Do you listen respectfully and fairly when you don't agree with a group member?
- Do you ask questions if you don't understand what someone says?
- Can you summarize the main points of discussion after a meeting?

If you answered *yes* to these questions, you are probably an effective listener and valued group member. If you answered *no* or *sometimes*, you have a lot to learn about listening.

Effective listening in one-to-one situations is challenging. Now add this fact: Listening is more difficult in groups than in almost any other communication situation because there are multiple speakers, perspectives, and goals. In a group, you *both* listen *and* respond to unexpected news, unusual ideas, and conflicting points of view. Instead of concentrating on what *one* person says and does, you must pay attention to *everyone*. In a group discussion, a short daydream or a side conversation can result in missed information, misunderstood instructions, or inappropriate reactions. Complicating matters is the fact that the social pressure to listen is not as strong in groups as it would be in a two-person conversation. If one group member doesn't listen or respond, others usually will. Consequently, group members may not listen well because they count on others to listen for them.[1]

Listening   Speaking

The Nature of Listening

Listening is the ability to understand, analyze, respect, and appropriately respond to the meaning of another person's spoken and nonverbal messages. On the surface, listening may appear to be as easy and natural as breathing. But in fact nothing could be further from the truth. Although most of us can *hear*, we often fail to *listen* to what others say. Hearing requires only physical ability; listening requires complex thinking ability. People who are hearing impaired may be better listeners than those who have perfectly acute hearing.

Listening is our number-one communication activity. Studies of college students consistently find that listening occupies more than half of their communicating time.[2] In the corporate world, managers may devote more than 60 percent of their workday to listening to others.[3] Chief executives may spend as much as 75 percent of their communicating time listening.[4] Percentages vary from study to study, but Figure 7.1 shows how most of us divide up our daily communicating time.

Figure 7.1 Time Spent Communicating

- Listening 40–70%
- Speaking 20–35%
- Reading 10–20%
- Writing 5–10%

The Need for Better Listening

Despite the enormous amount of time we spend listening, most of us are not very good listeners. In fact, we tend to think we're better listeners than we really are. Several studies report that immediately after listening to a short talk, most of us cannot accurately report 50 percent of what was said. Without training, we listen at only 25 percent efficiency.[5] And, of that 25 percent, most of what we remember is a distorted or inaccurate recollection.[6]

Surveys of business leaders often point to listening as the communication skill most lacking in new employees. When asked how many high school graduates have good listening skills, the answer was only 19 percent.[7] A study of Fortune 500 company training managers concludes that "poor listening performance is ranked as a serious problem during meetings, performance appraisals, and superior-subordinate communication."[8]

As discussed in Chapter 5, "Group Leadership," the member who speaks first and most often is more likely to emerge as the group's leader.[9] On the other hand, when someone *becomes* a leader, listening is more important in determining that person's success.

In an interview with the co-founder and chief executive of a social networking company, an interviewer asked, "What do you think are the keys to effective leadership? Here is the answer: "It's really about listening to people." In the words of a successful aerospace leader: "The worst failing is a team leader who's a nonlistener. A guy who doesn't listen to his people—and that doesn't mean listening to them and doing whatever the hell he wants to do—can make a lot of mistakes."[10] Peter Nulty, an editor for *Fortune* magazine agrees: "Of all the skills of leadership, listening is the most valuable—and one of the least understood." He adds that great leaders "never stop listening. That's how they get word before anyone else of unseen problems and opportunities."[11]

> ### Remember This
>
> Effective leaders engage in listening more than talking and in asking more than telling.[12]
>
> —Fran Rees, *How to Lead Work Teams*

Virtual Groups

Listening Online

Effective listening in virtual groups requires adapting to a different medium. In a sophisticated videoconference, this adaptation is relatively easy—you can see and hear group members sitting at a conference table in another place almost as clearly as you can see and hear colleagues sitting next to you. In an email discussion, however, you can neither see nor hear participants, but you still must "listen" to their messages.

Ironically, it may be easier to "listen" to group members in some virtual meetings than in a face-to-face setting. In a face-to-face discussion, you hear what members say and respond immediately. Members can see you grimace, smile, or roll your eyes. In an email discussion—whether synchronous or asynchronous—you have more time to "listen" to others and can control the content and style of your responses.

For example, you can reread what someone has written to make sure that you comprehend the message.

In a virtual discussion you have more than a second or two to respond to a listener—more time than you would have in a face-to-face conversation. Use this time to enlist several listening styles as you analyze the message and choose the content and appropriate tone for your response.

The downside is that it is easier to fake attention in electronic meetings. You can pretend to participate online by occasionally typing a comment. During a teleconference, you can stop listening and work on other tasks, checking in and responding with an "I agree" or "Good job" to feign participation. Although it's also possible to fake listening in a face-to-face discussion, your physical presence makes it difficult to "be elsewhere."

The Habits of Listeners

You know what a habit is: It's something you do so frequently and have done for so long that you've stopped thinking about why and how you do it. Most people have a lot of good habits (brushing their teeth, exercising regularly, saying "please" and "thank you") and some bad habits (biting their nails, cracking knuckles, smoking). Many habits are difficult to break. People who exercise regularly may feel restless, anxious, or even ill if they stop exercising—as do people who try to stop smoking.

We believe that *effective* listening can become an enduring habit—something that becomes second nature to you. Stephen R. Covey, the author of *The Seven Habits of Highly Effective People*, states that habits require *knowledge, skills*, and *desire*. (See Figure 7.2 on the next page.) Given the many thousands of ways Covey could choose to explain the nature of a habit, he turns to the art of listening to illustrate how the three components of an effective habit interact with one another:[13]

1. *Knowledge.* I may be ineffective in my interaction with my work associates, my spouse, or my children because I constantly tell them what I think, but I never really listen to them. Unless I understand principles of human interaction, I may not even *know* I need to listen.
2. *Skills.* Even if I do know that to interact effectively with others, I really need to listen to them, I may not have the skill. I may not know how to really listen deeply to another human being.
3. *Desire.* But knowing I need to listen and knowing how to listen is not enough. Unless I *want* to listen, unless I have the desire, it won't be a habit in my life. The best listeners are motivated to listen; they let go of what's on their mind long enough to hear what's on the other person's mind. An appropriate listening attitude does not mean that you know exactly what another person thinks or feels. Instead, it is a genuine willingness and openness to listen and discover.[14]

In this chapter, we provide guiding principles of good listening (knowledge) and explain how to listen (skills). Yet we know that the *desire* to listen must come from you. Effective listening relies as much on your attitude and motivation as on your knowledge and skills.

Unfortunately—for lack of knowledge, skills, and/or desire—many group members have poor listening habits that prevent their group from achieving its common goal. Examine the list of poor listening habits in Figure 7.3 and ask yourself: Do I ever do this? Notice that the options do not include "always" and "never" because none of us is a perfect listener 100 percent of the time.

If you answered with an honest *rarely* to all of the questions, you are probably a good listener and valued group member. If you answered *often* or *sometimes,* you have a lot to learn about listening. Accordingly, we devote this entire chapter to the challenge of improving listening in groups.[15]

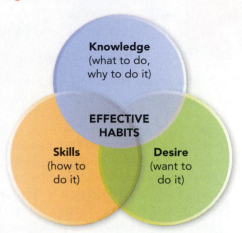

Figure 7.2   Effective Habits

Figure 7.3   Poor Listening Habits[16]

Poor Listening Habits	How frequently do you use this poor listening habit?		
Pseudolistening. Do you fake attention or pretend to listen when your mind is elsewhere, you're bored, or you think it pleases the speaker? Do you nod or smile even though your response has nothing to do with the message?	Often	Sometimes	Rarely
Selective Listening. If you don't like or agree with a member, do you avoid listening or look for faults in what the speaker says? Do you tune out when listening to complex or highly technical information?	Often	Sometimes	Rarely
Superficial Listening. Do you pay more attention to the way members look or how they speak rather than to what they say? Do you evaluate what members say before they've finished talking?	Often	Sometimes	Rarely
Defensive Listening. Do you interpret critical remarks by group members as personal attacks? Do you focus on how to respond to or challenge members' questions and criticisms rather than listening objectively?	Often	Sometimes	Rarely
Disruptive Listening. Do you interrupt members while they're speaking? Do you exaggerate your responses by sighing audibly, rolling your eyes, shaking your head in a *no*, or obviously withholding your attention?	Often	Sometimes	Rarely

Theory in Groups

The HURIER Listening Model

Communication researchers, cognitive scientists, and neurologists describe listening as a complex process. As a way of grasping the complexity of listening, Judi Brownell, a well-respected listening researcher, presents a six-component **HURIER Listening Model**. The letters in HURIER represent six interrelated listening processes: **H**earing, **U**nderstanding, **R**emembering, **I**nterpreting, **E**valuating, **R**esponding. Brownell links each of these six components to appropriate listening attitudes, relevant listening principles, and methods for improving your listening skills.[17]

Notice how Brownell's HURIER Model "recognizes that you are constantly influenced by both internal and external factors that color your perceptions and subsequent interpretations." These listening filters include your role in the group; your attitudes; and your values, biases, and previous experiences.[18] For example, a group leader may listen quite differently than a member who assumes the role of innovator in order to advance new ideas and provide insights on courses of action. If you frequently argue with a particular member or dislike his or her opinions, you are more likely to listen to the person quite differently than you would to a member you like and agree with.

The HURIER Model also recognizes that different listening skills become more or less important depending on both your purpose and the nature of the communication context.[19] For example, when you're listening to a member who's a topic expert, you may listen to learn. In contrast, you may listen more critically when a less informed member presents a questionable proposal for solving a problem. If your group is working in a hot, noisy room at a late hour of the day, these contextual factors may make it difficult for members to devote their attention and energy to listening.

We use the HURIER model as a guide for understanding listening in groups because it takes into account the group's goal, the interdependence of group members, and the task and social dimensions in which group members work with one another.

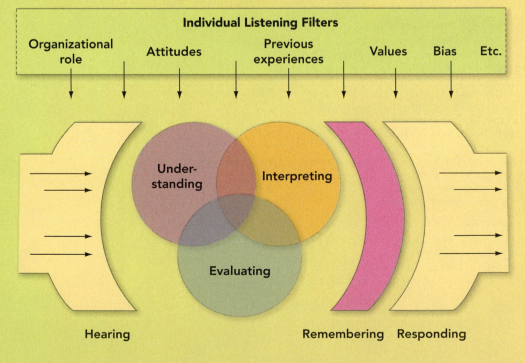

The HURIER Listening Model

Individual Listening Filters

Organizational role · Attitudes · Previous experiences · Values · Bias · Etc.

Understanding · Interpreting · Evaluating

Hearing · Remembering · Responding

Types of Listening

Brownell's HURIER Listening Model emphasizes that listening is a complex process and skill. Moreover there are six different types of listening you can call on to meet the challenge of working in groups. In this section, we take a more detailed look at the different kinds of listening in the HURIER Model to help you decide which ones best meet your own communication needs and those of group members.

Listening to Hear

Listening to hear is the ability to make clear, aural distinctions among the sounds and words in a language. Judi Brownell explains, "Hearing is a prerequisite to all listening, regardless of its purpose."[20] Answering the following questions can help you understand why hearing is the gateway to effective listening.

- Can you make clear, aural distinctions among the sounds and words in your language?
- Do you often ask group members to repeat what they've said or misunderstand what they've said because you did not hear them accurately?
- Do you notice nonverbal messages expressed in members' facial expressions, gestures, posture, movement, and vocal sounds (sighs, groans, laughter, gasps)?

Listening to Understand

Listening to understand, also known as **comprehensive listening**, focuses on accurately grasping the meaning of group members' spoken and nonverbal messages. After all, if you don't understand what someone means, how can you respond in a reasonable way? For example, an after-class discussion might begin as follows: "Let's have a party on the last day of class," says Geneva. A comprehensive listener may wonder whether Geneva means that (1) we should have a party instead of an exam, (2) we should ask the instructor whether we can have a party, or (3) we should have a party after the exam. Misinterpreting the meaning of Geneva's comment could result in an inappropriate response.

Answering the following questions can help you focus on several characteristics of effective comprehensive listening.

- Do you understand the meaning of words spoken by others?
- Do you generally interpret nonverbal behavior accurately?
- Can you accurately identify the main ideas and evidence used to support a group member's claim?

Listening to Remember

Listening to remember is the ability to accurately recall what you hear. How good is your memory? How well do you store, retain, and recall information? Do you ever forget what you're talking about during a discussion? Can you remember a person's name or a phone number even before you have a chance to write it down? Occasionally, everyone experiences memory problems. As we noted earlier in this chapter, most people cannot recall 50 percent of what they

Groups in Balance ...

Ask Questions to Enhance Comprehension

Asking good questions can enhance listening comprehension.[21] Here are several listening strategies that can help you ask productive questions in a group discussion.

1. *Have a plan.* Make sure you have a clear and appropriate goal. If you don't know your purpose, your question may be misunderstood or worthless.
2. *Keep the questions simple.* Ask one question at a time and make sure it's relevant to the discussion.
3. *Ask nonthreatening questions.* Avoid questions that begin with "Why didn't you...?" or "How could you...?" because they can create a defensive climate in responders.

4. *Ask permission.* If a topic is sensitive, explain why you are asking the question and ask permission before continuing. "You say you're fearful about sharing this report with Tom. Would you mind helping me understand why you're so apprehensive?"
5. *Avoid biased or manipulative questions.* Tricking someone into giving you the answer you want can destroy trust. There's a big difference between "Why did we miss the deadline?" and "Who screwed up?"
6. *Wait for the answer.* In addition to asking good questions, respond appropriately. After you ask a question, give other members time to think and then wait for the answer.

Follow the Research

Listening and Working Memory Theory

Early studies of listening focused on understanding **short-term memory**, the content you remember immediately after listening to a series of numbers, words, or sentences. Psychologist Samuel Wood and colleagues note that this kind of "short-term memory has a very limited capacity—about seven (plus or minus two) different items or bits of information at one time. This is just enough for phone numbers and ordinary zip codes."[22] We use something much more complex than short-term memory to engage in effective listening.

Working Memory Theory recognizes that listening involves more than the ability to tap your short-term memory. Effective listening engages your working memory. Psychologists define **working memory** as the memory subsystem we use to comprehend, remember, and form a mental image of what is going on around us; we use working memory to learn new things, solve problems, and form and act upon goals.[23] Listening researcher Laura Janusik describes working memory as "a dual-task system involving processing and storage functions. The processing function is synonymous with attention, and the storage function is synonymous with memory. Attention is allocated, and resources not used for attention are

available for storage."[24] Your working memory does more than store what you've heard; it allows you to shift what you've heard and understood "from and into long-term memory" as a way to create new meanings.[25]

Peter Desberg, author of *Speaking Scared Sounding Good*, describes working memory as a clearinghouse where you have fewer than 30 seconds to decide if the information is worth keeping and storing in your long-term memory. If your brain is preoccupied or doesn't take the time to process the information, it disappears.[26]

Group members with more working memory capacity are more likely to understand what other members mean, to analyze complex issues and discussion threads as they develop, to track relevant and irrelevant interactions, and to develop appropriate responses. As we note in the opening of this chapter, listening is more difficult in groups than in almost any other communication situation. Engaging your working memory is a complex process when talking to one person. It becomes a huge challenge when communicating with several group members because you must both listen and be able to respond, on the spot, to multiple ideas and views you can't anticipate.

hear immediately after hearing it. At the same time, your ability to remember directly affects how well you listen.

How good is *your* working memory? Often, the answer is "It depends." For example, if you're very interested in what someone's saying, you're more likely to remember the conversation, discussion, or presentation. However, if you're under a lot of stress or preoccupied with personal problems, you may not remember anything. Here are just a few suggestions that, with practice, can improve your memory.

- *Repeat.* Repeat important ideas or information after you hear it; say it aloud if you can. For example, if you've just learned that your group report is due on the 22nd, use this date in a sentence several times ("Let's see how many meetings we need to have before the 22nd"; "We'll need to have our first draft done a week ahead of time—22 minus 7 is 15"). If you're in a situation where it's not appropriate to do this aloud, repeat the information in your mind several times.
- *Associate.* Associate a word, phrase, or idea with something that describes it. For example, when you meet someone whose name you want to remember, associate the name with the context in which you met the person (Steve in biology class) or with a word beginning with the same letter that describes the person (Blonde Brenda).
- *Visualize.* Visualize a word, phrase, or idea. For example, when a patient was told she might need to take calcium channel blockers, she visualized a swimmer trying to cross the English Channel filled with floating calcium pills.
- *Use mnemonics.* A **mnemonic** is a memory aid that is based on something simple like a pattern or rhyme. For example, the HURIER in Brownell's Model of Listening is an acronym (the first letters for the six types of listening). Many people remember which months of the year have 30 days with the poem that begins "Thirty days hath September...." In fact, by rearranging these memory suggestions, you might be able to remember MARV (mnemonics, associate, repeat, visualize).

Listening to Interpret

Judi Brownell writes that **listening to interpret** is "a primary factor in empathic listening, where your ability to recognize and respond appropriately to emotional meanings is critical."[27] Empathic listening in a group discussion answers this question: How do group members feel? **Empathic listening** goes beyond comprehending what a person means; it focuses on understanding a member's situation, feelings, or motives. Can you see the situation through the other member's eyes? How would you feel in a similar situation?

By not listening for feelings, you may overlook the most important part of a message. Even if you understand every word a person says, you can still miss anger, enthusiasm, or frustration in a group member's voice. As an empathic listener, you don't have to agree with or feel the same way as other group members, but you do have to try to understand the type and intensity of feelings that those members are experiencing. For example, during an after-class discussion about having a party on the last day of class, Kim exclaims: "A class party would be a waste of time!" An empathic listener may wonder whether Kim means that

(1) she has more important things to do during exam week, (2) she doesn't think the class or the instructor deserves a party, or (3) she doesn't want to attend such a party. Empathic listening is difficult, but it also is "the pinnacle of listening" because it demands "fine skill and exquisite tuning into another's mood and feeling."[28]

Answering the following questions can help you understand the scope of empathic listening.

- Do you show interest and concern about other group members?
- Does your nonverbal behavior communicate friendliness and trust?
- Do you avoid highly critical reactions to others?
- Do you avoid talking about your own experiences and feelings when someone else is describing theirs?[29]

Listening to Evaluate

Listening to evaluate, also known as **analytical listening**, requires critical thinking skills to analyze what you hear, as in a group discussion. Once you are sure you've comprehended the meaning of a message, ask yourself whether the reasoning is sound and the conclusion is justified. Analytical listeners understand why they accept or reject another member's ideas and suggestions.

Russell makes the following proposal: "Suppose we chip in and give Professor Hawkins a gift at the party?" An analytical listener might think that (1) the instructor could misinterpret the gift, (2) some class members won't want to contribute, or (3) there isn't enough time to collect money and buy an appropriate gift.

Recognizing that another group member is trying to persuade—rather than merely inform—is the first step in improving your evaluative listening. Answering the following questions can help you assess your ability to listen analytically.[30]

- Do you recognize persuasive strategies?
- Can you tell when a group member appeals to your emotions and/or to your critical thinking ability?
- Do you know how to assess the quality and validity of arguments and evidence?

Listening to Respond

When you **listen to respond**, you are likely to react verbally and nonverbally. You may ask a question, provide support, offer advice, or share your opinion. You may frown, smile, laugh, shrug, or look confused. In the best of groups, members will listen to hear, understand, remember, interpret, and evaluate your response and "listen" to your nonverbal behaviors. Fortunately, there is a critical responding skill that can help you make sure you fully understand someone else's meaning. That skill is called paraphrasing and is vital to becoming a highly effective listener.

The Nature of Paraphrasing. **Paraphrasing** is the ability to restate what people say in a way that indicates you understand them. When you paraphrase, you go beyond the words you hear to understand the feelings and underlying meanings that accompany the words. Too often, we jump to conclusions and incorrectly assume that we know what a speaker means and feels.

Paraphrasing is a form of feedback—a listening check—that asks, "Am I right—is this what you mean?" Paraphrasing is not repeating what a person says; it requires finding *new* words to describe what you have heard. If you want to clarify someone's meaning, you might say, "When you said you were not going to the conference, did you mean that you want one of us to go instead?" If you want to make sure that you understand a person's feelings, you might say, "I know you said you approve, but I sense that you're not happy with the outcome—am I way off?" If you are summarizing someone's comments, you might say, "What you seem to be saying is that it's not the best time to change this policy, right?"

The Complexities of Paraphrasing.   Paraphrasing is difficult. Not only are you putting aside your own interests and opinions, but you are also finding *new* words that best match someone else's meaning. Figure 7.4 shows how a paraphrase can vary in four critical ways: content, depth, meaning, and language.[31]

Paraphrasing says, "I want to hear what you have to say, and I want to understand what you mean." If you paraphrase accurately, the other person will appreciate your understanding and support. And if you don't get the paraphrase right, your feedback provides another opportunity for the speaker to explain.[32]

Figure 7.4 Types of Paraphrasing

Type of Paraphrase	Ineffective Paraphrase Examples	Effective Paraphrase Technique and Example
Paraphrase Content	Susan: "I never seem to get anywhere on time, and I don't know why." You: "Ah, so you don't know why you never seem to get anywhere on time?" Susan: "Yeah, that's what I just said."	Find new words to express the same meaning. Paraphrase, don't parrot. *Example:* "What I'm hearing is that you've tried to figure out why you're often late but can't. Is that what you're saying?"
Paraphrase Depth	Susan: "People, including my boss, bug me about being late, and sometimes I can tell that they're pretty angry." You: "In other words, you worry that other people are upset by your lateness."	Match the emotions to the speaker's meaning. Avoid responding lightly to a serious problem and vice versa. *Example:* "When you say that people are angry, you sound as though it's become serious enough to put your job at risk or damage your relationships with your boss and coworkers; is that right?"
Paraphrase Meaning	Susan: "I really don't know . . ." You: ". . . how to manage your time?" (Susan would have finished with "what to do.")	Do not add unintended meaning or complete the person's sentence. *Example:* "Let me make sure I understand what you're saying. Is it that you don't know why you're always late, or that you wish you had a better idea of how to manage your time?"
Paraphrase Language	Susan: "I never seem to get anywhere on time, and I don't know why." You: "Ahh, your importunate perplexities about punctuality are inextricably linked." Susan: "Huh?"	Use simple language to ensure accuracy. *Example:* "It sounds as though being late has become a big problem at work and you're looking for ways to fix it. Right?"

Key Listening Strategies and Skills

You will spend the vast majority of your time in groups listening to others. Even during a half-hour meeting of five people, it is unlikely that any member will talk more than a total of ten minutes—unless that member wants to be accused of monopolizing the discussion. Unfortunately, many of us place more emphasis on the roles and responsibilities of group members who talk rather than on those who listen. "This unbalanced emphasis, especially as it actually affects persons in real discussions, could be an important cause of the problems that speaking is supposed to cure."[33] In other words, if you only focus on what *you* intend to say in a group discussion, you can't give your full attention to what others say.

Several key listening strategies and skills can help you more effectively listen to hear, understand, remember, and interpret what is said by other group members. They can also help you frame an appropriate response to what you hear.

You, however, are the only one who can provide the desire. You must want to listen.

Use Your Extra Thought Speed

Most people talk at about 125 to 150 words per minute. There is good evidence that if thoughts were measured in words per minute, we'd find that most of us can think at three to four times the rate at which we speak.[34] Thus, we have about four hundred extra words of spare thinking time during every minute a person is talking to us.

Thought speed is the speed (in words per minute) at which most people can think compared to the speed at which others can speak. Listening researcher Ralph Nichols asks the obvious question: "What do we do with our excess thinking time while someone is speaking?"[35] Poor listeners use their extra thought speed to day-dream, to plan how to confront the speaker, to take unnecessary notes, or to engage in side conversations (which is increasingly being done through electronic texting or email). Most people do not use their extra thought speed efficiently or productively. When listening, use your thought speed intentionally and methodically to:

- make sure you can *hear* what other members are saying.
- determine the *meaning* of a member's comments and contributions.
- identify and summarize *key ideas*.
- identify how members are responding *emotionally*.
- enlist strategies to help you *remember* what is said.
- interpret the meaning of *nonverbal behavior*.
- *analyze* and *evaluate* arguments.

Apply the Golden Listening Rule

The **golden listening rule** is easy to remember: Listen to others as you would have them listen to you. Unfortunately, this rule can be difficult to follow. It asks you to suspend your own needs in order to listen to someone else's.

The golden listening rule is not so much a "rule" as it is a positive listening attitude. If you aren't motivated to listen, you won't listen. The best listeners let go of what's on their minds long enough to hear what's on someone else's mind. They make listening into an enduring habit by understanding the importance

Remember This
If you aren't willing to stop talking, you won't listen.

of good listening, learning effective listening skills, and—perhaps most important of all—*wanting* to listen. An appropriate listening attitude does not mean that you know exactly what another person thinks or feels. Rather, it requires a strong motivation to listen and discover.[36] The six positive listening attitudes in Figure 7.5 have six negative counterparts:[37]

Figure 7.5   Positive and Negative Listening Attitudes

How Positive Is Your Listening Attitude?	
Positive Listening Attitudes	**Negative Listening Attitudes**
Interested	Uninterested
Responsible	Irresponsible
Group-centered	Self-centered
Patient	Impatient
Equal	Superior
Open-minded	Closed-minded

Minimize Distractions

Distractions can take many forms in a group discussion.[38] Loud and annoying noises, uncomfortable room temperature and seating, frequent interruptions, or distracting décor and outside activities are environmental distractions. Distractions also occur when members speak too softly, too rapidly, or too slowly; when someone speaks in a monotone or with an unfamiliar accent; or when a member has unusual or annoying mannerisms. It is difficult to listen when someone is fidgeting, doodling, tapping a pencil, or openly reading or writing something unrelated to the discussion.

When a distraction is environmental, you can get up and shut the door, open the window, or turn on more lights. When another member's behavior is distracting, you can try to minimize or stop the disruption. If members speak too softly, have side conversations, or use unreadable visual aids, a conscientious listener will ask a member to speak up, postpone their side conversations, or move closer to a visual.

"Listen" to Nonverbal Behavior

Speakers do not communicate all their meaning through words. Often you can understand others by observing their nonverbal behavior. A change in vocal tone or volume may be another way of saying, "Listen up—this is very important." A person's sustained eye contact may be a way of saying, "I'm talking to you!" Facial expressions can reveal whether a thought is painful, joyous, exciting, serious, or boring. Even gestures can express an excitement that words cannot convey.

It is easy, however, to misinterpret nonverbal behavior. Effective listeners verbally confirm their interpretation of someone's nonverbal communication. A question as simple as "Do your nods indicate a *yes* vote?" can ensure that everyone is on the same nonverbal wavelength. If, as research indicates, more than half of a speaker's meaning is conveyed nonverbally,[39] we miss a lot of important information if we fail to "listen" to nonverbal behavior.

Correctly interpreting nonverbal responses can tell you as much as or more than spoken words. The nonverbal reactions of listeners (head nods, smiles, frowns, eye contact, and gestures) can also help you adjust what you say when you are speaking.

Ask WIIFM

Wouldn't it be great if every speaker and topic were interesting and worth listening to? Unfortunately, this is rarely the case. As a result, it's easy to stop listening if you are bored, if you think you've heard it all before, or if you don't like what you're hearing. Ralph Nichols has written that when you're "trapped" in this kind of situation, try to figure out "if anything being said can be put to use."[40]

In the lingo of sales literature, ask yourself WIIFM (**What's In It For Me**?). This is what potential customers are thinking as they listen to a sales pitch. WIIFM also applies to any listening situation. Ask yourself this version of WIIFM: "How can I use what I'm hearing?" For example, you might hear a fact you mistrust and that you'll look up to see if it's true or prepare a question to ask the speaker about it. If you stop listening because something is "boring," you may miss important and useful information. A colleague of ours told us that she listens attentively to all of her minister's sermons even when they're not very interesting because he always asks her what she thinks after the service.

Listen Before You Leap

One of the most-often-quoted pieces of listening advice from Ralph Nichols's writings is, "We must always withhold evaluation until our comprehension is complete."[41] This counsels listeners to make sure that they understand a speaker before they respond.

When we become angry, friends may tell us to count to ten before reacting. This is also good advice when we listen. Counting to ten, however, implies more than withholding evaluation until comprehension is complete. You may comprehend a speaker perfectly but be infuriated or offended by what you hear. If an insensitive leader opens a meeting by demanding, "One of you girls take minutes," it may take a count to 20 to collect your thoughts before you can respond to this sexist comment in a professional manner ("Dave, did you mean to ask for a volunteer to take minutes today?"). If a group member tells an offensive joke, you may have a double reaction—anger at the speaker and disappointment with those who laughed. Listening before you leap gives you time to adjust your reaction in a way that will help rather than disrupt a group discussion.

Take Relevant Notes

If most of us listen at only 25 percent efficiency, why not take notes during a discussion to make sure we remember? Why not write down the important ideas and facts? Taking notes makes a great deal of sense, but only when it is done correctly.

The inclination to take notes is understandable. After all, that's what we do in a classroom when an instructor lectures. However, there are several reasons why this method of note taking is less than ideal in a group. For one thing, even if it were possible to copy down every word uttered in a group discussion, your notes would be missing the nonverbal cues that often tell you more about what a person means and feels. And if you spend all your time taking notes, when will you put aside your pen and participate? Perhaps most important, trying to "robotically" write down every word defeats the purpose of active listening in note taking, which is to mentally process what is being said and restate its main points in your own words. Thus, striving to "get it all down" may interfere with your ability to accurately hear, understand, remember, interpret, evaluate, and respond to what you hear. Ralph Nichols summarized the dilemma of balancing note taking and listening when he concluded that "there is some evidence to indicate that the volume of notes taken and their value to the taker are inversely related."[42]

Remember This

Flexibility is the key to taking useful and personalized meeting notes.

The ability to take useful notes depends on how well you listen and how wisely you decide which ideas and information should go in your notes.

Thus, the challenge for a group member is this: How do I obtain brief, meaningful records of a group discussion? If you are like most listeners, about 25 percent of what you hear will end up in your notes, so it is vital to develop the skill of deciding quickly, while the discussion is in progress, whether a given piece of information belongs in your notes.

If a group member takes minutes in a meeting, you can rely on those minutes as the official record of what took place. But here, too, there are potential problems. What if the recorder is a poor listener? What if you need the notes immediately and can't wait for the official minutes to be distributed and approved? Suppose you want more personalized meeting notes that also record your assignments? In such cases, minutes may not be enough.

Good listeners adjust their note-taking system to a group's agenda or impose a note-taking pattern on a disorganized discussion. In some cases, margin notes on an agenda may be sufficient. If you attend a lot of meetings, you may find it helpful to use a brief notetaking form—such as the one in Figure 7.6—to record key details, information, and actions.

Figure 7.6 Sample Form for Meeting Notes

Meeting Notes

Group: Goal/Topic:

Date and Time: Place:

Members Attending:

Members Absent:

Vital Information

1.

2.

3.

Decisions Reached

1.

2.

3.

Personal To-Do List   Date Due

1.

2.

3.

Date/Time/Place of Next Meeting:

Listening to Differences

Just as group members differ in their backgrounds, perceptions, and values, people differ in the ways they listen. In a group setting, different listening abilities and styles can be an asset. For instance, if you have difficulty analyzing an argument, another group member can take on the role of analytical listener. If members focus only on words rather than the emotions expressed nonverbally, appoint yourself as the group's empathic listener.

Gender Differences

As you've seen elsewhere in this book, listening behavior may differ between male and female members. Men, for example, may put more focus on the content of a message when they listen, whereas women may focus on the relationships among speakers.[43] In other words, men tend to listen comprehensively and analytically, whereas women are more likely to listen empathically. If "males tend to hear the facts while females are more aware of the mood of the communication," a group is fortunate to have both kinds of listeners contributing to the group process.[44]

Personality Differences

Differences in personalities may also affect the way members listen. The Myers-Briggs Type Indicator® predicts that introverts will be better comprehensive listeners than extroverts, who are eager to speak—even when they haven't understood what others have said. Sensing members may listen for facts and figures, while intuitives listen for key ideas and overarching themes. Thinking members are often effective analytical listeners, whereas feeling members are more likely to be effective empathic listeners. Judging listeners may drive the group to reach a decision, while perceivers take the time to appreciate what they hear without leaping to immediate conclusions.[45]

Cultural Differences

Cultural differences have significant effects on the ways in which group members listen and respond to one another. One study concludes that international students see U.S. students as less willing and less patient listeners than students from African, Asian, South American, or European cultures.[46] Intercultural communication scholars Myron Lustig and Jolene Koester explain these differences in perceived listening behavior by noting that English is a speaker-responsible language in which the speaker structures the message and relies primarily on words to provide meaning. In contrast, Japanese is a listener-responsible language in which speakers indirectly indicate what they want the listener to know. The listener must rely on nonverbal communication and an understanding of the relationship between the speaker and the listener to interpret meaning.[47] Thus, English-speaking listeners may believe that Japanese speakers are leaving out important information or being evasive; Japanese listeners may think that English speakers are overexplaining or talking down to them. Such misunderstandings and perceived discourtesies are the result of speaking and listening differences rather than of substantive disagreement.

Groups in Balance ...

Learn the Art of High-Context Listening

In Chapter 4, "Diversity in Groups," we explore the high-context–low-context cultural dimension and note that someone from a high-context culture goes well beyond a person's words to interpret meaning. High-context communicators also pay close attention to nonverbal cues when they listen. For example, the Chinese symbol for listening includes characters for eyes, ears, and heart as well as full attention.

For the Chinese, "it is impossible to listen…without using the eyes because you need to look for nonverbal communication. You certainly must listen with ears" because Chinese is a tonal language in which intonation determines meaning. "Finally, you listen with your heart because" you must sense the "emotional undertones expressed by the speaker." In Korean, *nunchi* means "communicating through your eyes." "Koreans believe that the environment supplies most of the information that we seek, so there is little need to speak."[48]

Hearing Ability Differences

According to the National Institute on Deafness and Other Communication Disorders, about 36 million U.S. adults report some degree of hearing loss. Given that hearing loss is usually gradual and cumulative throughout your life, older adults have greater hearing losses than children and young adults. However, "approximately 15 percent (26 million) of Americans between the ages of 20 and 69 have high frequency hearing loss due to exposure to loud sounds or noise at work or in leisure activities."[49] Researchers at Gallaudet University claim that about 2 to 4 of every 1,000 people in the United States are "functionally deaf," though more than half became deaf relatively late in life.[50]

Adapting to members who have difficulty hearing requires a lot more than speaking louder. In addition to using an appropriate volume, articulate your words clearly. Reduce background noise by closing doors to hallway sounds or turning off noisy equipment. Make eye contact and begin your message by speaking the person's name so that he or she knows to pay attention to you. And while you are speaking, make sure you are facing the person who has difficulty hearing; in this way, your facial expressions, gestures, and other body language will help convey your message.[51]

If a member of your group is deaf, keep in mind that not all deaf people are alike. Most, but not all, deaf people are skilled lipreaders. Jamie Berke, a deaf contributor to *About.com* writes: "Lipreading (speechreading) is a skill that I could not live without. However, it does not replace written or visual communication. Even the best lipreaders can miss a good bit because only about 30–40 percent of speech is visible. Many letters and words look the same on the lips, which can cause misunderstanding. For example, p(all), b(all), and m(all) all look the same."[52] Here are some recommendations for speaking to someone who lipreads:

- Remember that the deaf person needs to *see* you to read your lips—don't turn your back to the person or put yourself in a setting where it's difficult to see you.
- Do not exaggerate your speech or talk too loudly. Exaggeration makes it harder to lipread.
- It can be difficult or impossible to read the lips of a man with a mustache.
- Using appropriate facial expressions and gestures can help the deaf person make sense of what you're trying to say.[53]

If a deaf member of a group attends meetings with an interpreter who can translate your words into sign language, do not talk to the interpreter. Look directly at the member of your group when you speak. If you only look at the interpreter, the deaf member may not be able to read your lips or see your facial expressions and gestures. Even worse, looking at the interpreter ignores the deaf person and implies she or he is not even visible.

Ethics in Groups

Self-Centered Roles and Listening

As you know from Chapter 3, "Group Membership," self-centered roles emerge when members put their own needs ahead of the group's goal and other members' needs. Although members who assume self-centered roles may be excellent comprehensive and analytical listeners, their goals may be counterproductive and unethical. For example, aggressors and dominators may only listen to evaluate and expose the weaknesses in others' comments in order to get their own way. Blockers may be good listeners who purposely ignore what they hear or poor listeners who are incapable of comprehending or appreciating the comments of others. Recognition seekers, confessors, and special interest pleaders may be so preoccupied with their own needs hat they are unable to listen to anyone else in the group.

Unethical listening can take other forms that serve self-centered goals:

- Listening behavior that shows no respect for the opinions of others
- Listening for the purpose of criticizing the ideas of others
- Listening for personal information that can be used to humiliate or criticize others

- Faking listening in order to gain the favor of high-status members

Ethical listening is as important as ethical speaking, particularly because we spend most of our communicating time listening. Alexander Solzhenitsyn, a winner of the Nobel Prize in literature, lamented that "many hasty, immature, superficial, and misleading judgments are expressed every day...without any verification."[54] Ethical listeners have a responsibility to hear, understand, remember, interpret, evaluate and respond appropriately to messages that have personal, professional, political, and moral consequences for themselves and others.

Judi Brownell, creator of the HURIER Listening Model, contends that ethical listening "is not a passive activity; as a listener, you choose what to listen to and what to do with what your hear." Ethical listeners "ask themselves, would I want this done to me." In this sense, self-centered listening is unethical because it prevents a group from achieving its goals and from building member "relationships that are healthy and productive."[55]

Summary Study Guide

The Challenge of Listening in Groups

- Listening is the ability to understand, analyze, respect, and respond appropriately to the meaning of another person's spoken and nonverbal messages.
- Although listening is our number-one communication activity, most people cannot accurately report 50 percent of what they hear after listening to a short talk.
- Most highly effective leaders are also effective listeners.
- Poor listening habits include pseudolistening, selective listening, superficial listening, defensive listening, and disruptive listening. Good listening habits require knowledge, skills, and desire.

Types of Listening

- There are many types of listening, each of which calls on unique listening skills, beginning with listening to hear, understand, remember, interpret, evaluate, and respond as represented in Brownell's HURIER Listening Model.

- Effective listeners engage their working memory to process, store, and retrieve information they have heard.
- Paraphrasing is the ability to restate what people say in a way that indicates that you understand them and the feelings that underlie their meaning.

Key Listening Strategies and Skills

- Several key strategies can improve how well you listen in groups: (1) use your extra thought speed, (2) apply the golden listening rule, (3) minimize distractions, (4) "listen" to nonverbal behavior, (5) ask WIIFM, (6) listen before you leap, and (7) take notes.

Listening Differences

- Differences in gender, personality, culture, and hearing ability can significantly affect how well group members listen to one another.
- When members assume self-centered roles that prevent a group from achieve its goals and harm member relationships, their behavior is unethical.

GroupWork

Practice Paraphrasing[56]

Directions: Read the four statements made by group members and write the response you would make that best paraphrases their meaning. As a guide, we recommend that you include at least three components in your paraphrase:

- State your interest in understanding the other person, such as "I sense that…" or "If I understand you correctly, you…" or "It sounds as if you…."
- Identify the other person's emotion or feeling, but make sure you find alternatives to the words the person uses. For example, if a person says, "I'm angry," you will need to decide whether this means that the person is annoyed, irritated, disgusted, or furious. Try to find a word that matches the person's meaning and emotion.
- Describe the situation, event, or facts in your own words.

Sample Situation and Paraphrase:

Group Member: I get really frustrated when André yells at one of us during a meeting.

Paraphrase: <u>You're saying that André shouts at you or another group member, and that this upsets you a great deal. Am I right?</u>

1. **Group Member:** I have the worst luck with laptops. Every single one I've ever used has problems. Just when the warranty runs out, something goes wrong and I have to spend a lot of money to get it fixed. The laptop I have now has crashed twice, and each time I lost all of my documents. I've tried to find out if I'm doing something wrong, but I've never been able to get an answer. Why me? I must be cursed or something.

    Paraphrase: _____

    _____

    _____

    _____

2. **Group Member:** I hope Anita doesn't react too strongly to Chris and Manuel's concerns about the scope of our project at today's meeting. She can be very emotional when she feels strongly about something she really believes in.

    Paraphrase: _____

    _____

    _____

    _____

3. **Group Member:** I dislike saying no to anyone in our group who asks for help, but if I agree to help everyone who asks me then I have to rush or stay up late to get my own work done. I want to help, but I also want to do my own job—and do it well.

    Paraphrase: _____

    _____

    _____

    _____

4. **Group Member:** How on earth are we going to get an A on this assignment if we can't even find time to meet?

    Paraphrase: _____

    _____

    _____

    _____

Group Assessment

Student Listening Inventory[57]

Directions: This inventory should help identify your listening strengths and weaknesses within the context of a college classroom. The word *speaker* can mean the instructor or another student. Also remember that most of us overestimate how well we listen. Give some serious and realistic thought to each statement before responding. Use the following numbers to indicate how often you engage in these listening behaviors: 1 = almost never, 2 = not often, 3 = sometimes, 4 = more often than not, 5 = almost always.

LISTENING BEHAVIOR	1	2	3	4	5
1. When someone is speaking to me, I purposely block out distractions such as side conversations and personal problems.	1	2	3	4	5
2. I am comfortable asking questions when I don't understand something a speaker has said.	1	2	3	4	5
3. When a speaker uses words I don't know, I jot them down and look them up later.	1	2	3	4	5
4. I assess a speaker's credibility while listening.	1	2	3	4	5
5. I paraphrase and/or summarize a speaker's main ideas in my head as I listen.	1	2	3	4	5
6. I concentrate on a speaker's main ideas rather than the specific details.	1	2	3	4	5
7. I try to understand people who speak indirectly as well as I understand those who speak directly.	1	2	3	4	5
8. Before reaching a conclusion, I try to confirm with the speaker my understanding of his or her message.	1	2	3	4	5
9. I concentrate on understanding a speaker's message when she or he is explaining a complex idea.	1	2	3	4	5
10. When listening, I devote my full attention to a speaker's message.	1	2	3	4	5
11. When listening to someone from another culture, I factor in my knowledge of cultural differences to interpret meaning.	1	2	3	4	5
12. I watch a speaker's facial expressions and body language for additional information about the speaker's meaning.	1	2	3	4	5
13. I encourage speakers by providing positive nonverbal feedback—nods, eye contact, vocalized agreement.	1	2	3	4	5
14. When others are speaking to me, I establish eye contact and stop doing other nonrelated tasks.	1	2	3	4	5
15. I avoid tuning out speakers when I disagree with or dislike their message.	1	2	3	4	5
16. When I have an emotional response to a speaker or the message, I try to set aside my feelings and continue listening to the message.	1	2	3	4	5
17. I try to match my nonverbal responses to my verbal responses.	1	2	3	4	5

(continued)

18. When someone begins speaking, I focus my attention on the message.	1	2	3	4	5
19. I try to understand how past experiences influence the ways in which I interpret a message.	1	2	3	4	5
20. I attempt to eliminate outside interruptions and distractions.	1	2	3	4	5
21. When I listen, I look at the speaker, maintain some eye contact, and focus on the message.	1	2	3	4	5
22. I avoid tuning out messages that are complex, complicated, and challenging.	1	2	3	4	5
23. I try to understand the other person's point of view when it is different from mine.	1	2	3	4	5
24. I try to be nonjudgmental and noncritical when I listen.	1	2	3	4	5
25. As appropriate, I self-disclose a similar amount of personal information as the other person shares with me.	1	2	3	4	5

Scoring: Add up your scores for all of the questions. Use the following general guidelines to assess how well you think you listen. Please note that your score only represents your personal *perceptions* about your listening behavior and skills.

Score	Interpretation
0–62	You perceive yourself to be a poor classroom listener. Attention to all of the items on the inventory could improve your listening effectiveness.
63–86	You perceive yourself to be an adequate listener in the classroom. Learning more about listening and listening skills could improve your overall listening effectiveness.
87–111	You perceive yourself to be a good listener in the classroom, but you could still improve your listening skills.
112–125	You perceive yourself to be an outstanding listener in the classroom.

chapter 8

Conflict and Cohesion in Groups

Chapter Outline

Case Study

Sociology in Trouble

Five faculty members in a college's sociology department meet to discuss the course offerings for the next semester.

Steve, the department chair, thanks everyone for the brainstorming session they just completed. He then asks the tired faculty members to address an important issue: Which courses should they eliminate and which new courses should they add to the curriculum? "We need," he says, "to balance the integrity of our department and our offerings with the need to bring in more students and the need to have a strong curriculum." Although faculty members nod their heads, they don't seem to have much enthusiasm for the task.

Trevor declares, "We don't want enrollment to dictate—you know—what our offerings …." Before he finishes his sentence, Helen interrupts. "Here we go, here we go. Trevor, you need to look at the enrollment numbers!" The group senses that Trevor seems more interested in preserving his own low-enrollment courses than developing new ones that attract more students. The faculty has dealt with this issue before. Should they allow professors to protect their smaller courses or should they cut these courses? Should they offer more popular courses to improve their numbers even if it means cutting time-honored sociology courses?

Art interrupts the interaction by telling everyone that he has an exciting idea for a new course, the Sociology of Time. He explains that the course would look at time as a commodity that people use for various sociological purposes. The group has mixed reactions. Trevor questions whether the course is rigorous enough and worthy of a separate course on its own. Georgia just nods her head at everything group members say. Helen supports Art's proposed new course. Steve reminds everyone they have to eliminate, not just add, courses. Group members suggest cutting Trevor's Culture of Consumerism course. He strongly opposes this move. Helen raises her voice and declares that the enrollment numbers speak for themselves. Finally Georgia says, "We can do this without an argument happening." Helen accuses Trevor of living in the past. At this point, the chair intervenes again and tells his colleagues that they need to look at the bigger goal, not individual courses.

The lines of conflict are drawn. Art wants his course on the Sociology of Time approved; Trevor opposes it on academic grounds. He also doesn't want the department to cut his Culture of Consumerism course. The chair again reminds everyone that if they add new courses to attract more students, they must cut existing courses. Helen seems very aggravated—maybe she's heard all these arguments before, maybe she has a grudge against Trevor for something he did in the past, maybe she wants to stay in the department chair's favor, or maybe she's just tired. Georgia seems drained by all the agitation and only wants it to stop.

When you finish reading this chapter, you should be able to answer the following critical thinking questions about this case study:

1   What are the individual conflict styles of Steve, Trevor, Helen, Georgia, and Art? How could the group move toward a more collaborative group conflict style?

2   To what extent do group members' responses to conflict reflect diversity factors such as gender, culture, ethnicity, seniority, age, and personality traits?

3   Which conflict management strategy or strategies have the potential to resolve the sociology department's conflict in this situation?

4   Based on this meeting, how cohesive does the sociology department appear? What strategies could the group use to enhance group cohesiveness?

5   Which dialectic tensions are most evident in this group, and what could be done to achieve a *both/and* resolution to these tensions?

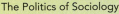
The Politics of Sociology

The Reunion

Before you read any further, visit Pearson's MySearchLab website and watch this case study's video, "The Politics of Sociology." You may also want to watch the short video "The Reunion," which illustrates Chapter 8 concepts. Each video comes with a set of study questions to keep in mind as you read this chapter.

Conflict in Groups

Effective groups balance the conflict↔cohesion dialectic. Whereas group members with different perspectives and opinions can promote critical thinking and creative problem solving, "too many differences, or one difference that is so strong it dominates group resources, can overwhelm the group" and its ability to achieve the group's goal.[1]

In a summary of research examining the links between conflict and cohesion, communication researcher John Gastil observes that cohesive groups gain a boost in effectiveness, whereas conflict—particularly when it is personal—can have the opposite effect.[2] In terms of resolving this dialectic tension, groups must find ways to balance constructive conflict with the need for unity and cohesiveness. In short, highly effective groups are cohesive *and* also willing to engage in conflict.

Many people believe that good groups never have conflicts. Quite the reverse is true: Conflict in groups is inevitable. Unfortunately, some groups try to avoid or suppress conflict because they believe that effective groups are conflict-free. Here, too, researchers claim the opposite. "Many effective teams look more like battlegrounds.... Teams with vastly competent members embrace conflict as the price of synergy and set good idea against good idea to arrive at the best idea."[3]

The word *conflict* is frequently associated with fighting, anger, and hostility. Conflict does not have to involve negative emotions. When treated as an expression of legitimate differences, conflict can improve group problem solving, promote cohesiveness, increase group knowledge, enhance creativity, and promote the group's goal.[5]

We define **conflict** as the disagreement and disharmony that occur in groups when members express differences regarding group goals; member ideas, behavior, and roles; or group procedures and norms. This definition reflects three types of conflict: substantive, affective, and procedural.[6]

Conflict   Cohesion

Remember This

Conflict management requires "a delicate balancing act, like that of a tightrope walker, or a rock climber who must find just the right handholds."[4]

—William Wilmot and Joyce Hocker, *Interpersonal Conflict*

Substantive Conflict

Substantive conflict occurs when members disagree about issues, ideas, decisions, actions, or goals. For example, when members of a student government council try to answer the question, "Should student activities fees be raised?" their conflict is substantive because it focuses on the group's goal of serving students' cocurricular needs.

When a group cannot negotiate a *both/and* approach to the individual goal↔group goal dialectic, hidden agendas emerge. As we noted in Chapter 2, "Group Development," when members' hidden agendas become more important than

Figure 8.1   Sources of Group Conflict

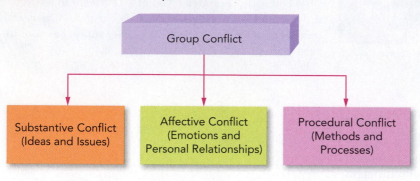

a group's stated goal, the result can be group frustration, unresolved conflict, and failure. Dean Barnlund and Franklyn Haiman, two pioneers in the study of group communication, described hidden agendas as arising when "there are a significant number of private motives, either conscious or unconscious, lurking beneath the surface and influencing the course of the discussion in subtle, indirect ways."[7] Conflicts become serious problems when the members' hidden goals conflict and interfere with the group's goal.

Affective Conflict

Affective conflict is the result of interpersonal disagreements, differences in personalities and communication styles, and members' conflicting core values and beliefs. Affective conflict also occurs when members do not feel appreciated, feel threatened by the group, or struggle for power. Affective conflict is more difficult to resolve than substantive conflict because it involves people's feelings and the way members relate to one another.

In *The Group in Society*, John Gastil notes that when a personal relationship between two group members turns sour, the entire group may suffer, particularly if the conflict is characterized by insults, acts of revenge, or loss of time on task. "This often leads to avoidance. The parties in the conflict begin to seek ways to do their work without having to interact—a serious problem for groups undertaking collaborative tasks. From there, the conflict can spread quickly and change a two-member rift into a groupwide faultline, with members taking sides in the conflict."[8]

Substantive and affective conflict may occur at the same time. For example, imagine that students Dee and Charles are members of the student activities budget committee. Dee advocates an increase in student fees to fund more activities. Charles disagrees; he suggests using existing funds more efficiently rather than placing a larger financial burden on students. At this point, the conflict is substantive; it focuses on issues. However, when Charles rolls his eyes and says to Dee, "Only a fool believes higher fees are the answer," not only does Dee disagree with Charles on the issues, she is also hurt and angry. The conflict has gone beyond substance; it has also become personal (affective).

Procedural Conflict

Procedural conflict is disagreement among group members about the method or process the group uses in its attempt to accomplish a goal. For example, some group members may want to begin a discussion by suggesting solutions to a problem, whereas others may want to gather information first. Some members may want to vote using secret ballots; others may want a show of hands.

Procedural conflicts sometimes arise when groups have difficulty resolving substantive or affective conflict. Rather than facing the issues, they rely on procedures such as moving to the next topic or taking a vote to get them through.[9]

Theory in Groups

Attribution Theory and Member Motives

When you make an attribution about a group member's behavior, you are speculating about the causes of that behavior—attributing the behavior to one or more causes. For example, suppose Tyree says, "I propose we meet Thursday at 3:30 P.M. rather than Monday at 10:00 A.M." You may attribute his statement to one of several motives:

1. He proposed this because he knows only Melinda can't attend at that hour. What's he got against Melinda? That's mean, self-centered, and heartless.
2. He proposed this because he knows only Melinda can't attend at that hour. That was an ingenious way of getting rid of a highly disruptive member who causes most of our problems. He's very clever, group centered, and goal focused.
3. He proposed this because he knows only Melinda can't attend at the hour. That's certainly better than the 10 A.M. hour when three other members can't attend. He's found the best option for the most members.

Attribution theory claims that we make judgments about people's motives and characteristics that go beyond what we see and hear. Even though we know that we shouldn't make snap judgments about others, we often attribute negative motives or blame others rather than considering alternative explanations. "It's Melinda's fault we didn't finish the project on time" or "How could we expect to finish when three members couldn't attend the 10 A.M. meetings?"

Attribution theory is the brainchild of psychologist Fritz Heider, who applied it to all kinds of human interaction.[10] Subsequent research used attribution theory to examine group conflict. Here, for example, are three attributions that could prompt anger among group members:

- What other members do seems to constrain what I want to do.
- What other members do seems intended to harm me or others.
- What other members do seems abnormal or illegitimate.[11]

All these attributions may be erroneous when, in fact, members are not trying to restrain a member, do harm, or behave illegitimately. One of the most significant types of attribution error is the "self-serving bias," a tendency to blame negative consequences on external forces and attribute positive consequences to our own behavior.[12] According to the self-serving bias, if your group has problems, it's *their* fault, not yours, but if your group succeeds, it is because of the great contributions you made.

At the same time, other group members may be thinking the same thing: "It's not my fault we're having problems; it's *everyone else's* fault" or "If I hadn't stepped in and done such-and-such, we never would have reached our goal." Because attribution errors occur all the time, group members should watch out for and openly discuss them when they arise.

Constructive and Destructive Conflict

All groups, no matter how conscientious or well mannered, experience conflict. In and of itself, conflict is neither good nor bad. However, the way in which a group expresses and deals with conflict can be either constructive or destructive.

Constructive conflict occurs when group members express disagreement in ways that value everyone's contributions and promote the group's goal. Kenneth Cloke and Joan Goldsmith of the Center for Dispute Resolution explain that all of us have a choice about how to deal with conflict. We can treat conflict as dialectic experiences "that imprison us or lead us on a journey, as a battle that embitters us or as an opportunity for learning. Our choices between these contrasting attitudes and approaches will shape the way the conflict unfolds."[13]

Figure 8.2 Constructive and Destructive Conflict

Constructive Conflict	Destructive Conflict
Focus on issues	Focus on personalities; makes personal attacks
Respect for others	Disrespectful tone of voice or body language; insults
Supportiveness	Defensiveness
Flexibility	Inflexibility
Cooperation; seeking win-win solutions	Competition; seeking "I win" solutions
Commitment to conflict management	Conflict avoidance

Destructive conflict results when members engage in behaviors that create hostility and prevent the group from achieving its goals. Complaining, personal insults, conflict avoidance, and loud arguments or threats contribute to destructive conflict.[14] The quality of group decision making deteriorates when members are inflexible and not open to other views. Destructive conflict has the potential to disable a group permanently. Figure 8.2 characterizes the differences between destructive and constructive conflict.

Groups that promote constructive conflict abide by the following principles:[15]

- Disagreement does not result in punishment. "I'm not afraid of being fired if I disagree with powerful members."
- Members work with one another to achieve a mutually satisfying resolution of conflict. "We can work this out. After all, we're all after the same thing."
- Lower-status group members are free to disagree with higher-status members. "I know she's the CEO, but I think there are some disadvantages to the approach she suggests."
- The group has an agreed-upon approach for conflict resolution and decision making. "Our group lets every member speak, so I know my ideas will be heard."
- Members can disagree and still respect one another. "The group may not like my idea, but members would never personally attack me for expressing my opinion."

Conflict Styles

A significant body of research indicates that all of us have individual conflict styles we tend to use regardless of the situation.[16] Whereas some people will move heaven and earth to avoid conflict of any kind, others enjoy the competitive atmosphere and the exultation of "winning."

There are five traditional conflict styles: avoidance, accommodation, competition, compromise, and collaboration.[17] These styles reflect the tension between seeking *personal* goals and working cooperatively to achieve the *group's* goal. For example, if you are motivated to achieve your own goals, you may use a more competitive conflict style. If you are dedicated to achieving the group's goals, you may use a more accommodating or collaborative conflict style. Kenneth Thomas, whose research with Ralph Kilmann identified the five conflict styles illustrated in Figure 8.3, acknowledges the dialectic nature of these dimensions. "They are *not* opposites," he writes. Collaborating, for example, is *both* assertive *and* cooperative.[18]

Avoidance Conflict Style

Members use an **avoidance conflict style** when they are unable or unwilling to accomplish their own goals or contribute to achieving the group's goal. In some cases, members who care about the group and its goals may adopt the avoidance style because they are uncomfortable with or unskilled at asserting themselves. Group members who use this style may change the subject, avoid bringing up a controversial issue, and even deny that a conflict exists. Avoiding conflict in groups is usually counterproductive because it fails to address a problem and can increase group tensions. Ignoring or avoiding conflict does not make it go away.

Figure 8.3   Conflict Styles

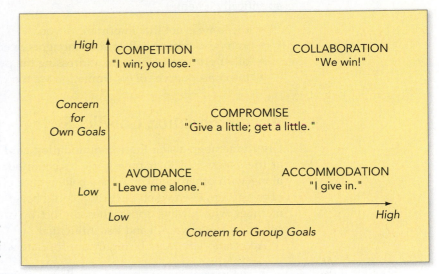

Groups in Balance...

Know When and How to Apologize

An apology can go a long way toward defusing tension and opening the door to constructive conflict resolution. It may even deter lawsuits. Studies indicate that 73 percent of legal complainants will accept a settlement offer when a full apology is given. When there is no apology, only 52 percent are willing to accept a settlement and avoid going to court.[19]

In spite of the importance and simplicity of an apology, we often find it difficult to say, "I'm sorry." When you apologize, you take responsibility for your behavior and the consequences of your actions. Although you may feel you've lost some pride, a willingness to own up to your actions can earn the respect of other group members and help build trust. Here are some suggestions for making an effective apology:[20]

- *Take responsibility for your actions with "I" statements.* "I failed to put all the group members' names on the final report."
- *Clearly identify the behavior that was wrong.* "Everyone provided valuable input and should have been acknowledged."
- *Acknowledge how others might feel.* "I understand that most of you are probably annoyed with me."
- *Acknowledge that you could have acted differently.* "I should have asked the group about this first."
- *Express regret.* "I'm angry with myself for not thinking ahead."
- *Follow through on any promises to correct the situation.* "I'll send an email out tomorrow acknowledging that your names should have been included on the report."
- *Request, but don't demand, forgiveness.* "This group is important to me. I hope you will forgive me."

In some circumstances, however, avoiding conflict can be appropriate, specifically when:

- the issue is not that important to you.
- you need time to collect your thoughts or control your emotions.
- other group members are addressing the problem effectively.
- the consequences of confrontation are too risky.

Accommodation Conflict Style

Group members using the **accommodation conflict style** give in to other members at the expense of their own goals. Accommodators have a genuine desire to get along with other members. They believe that giving in to others serves the needs of the group, even when the group could benefit from further discussion. A group member who always approaches conflict by accommodating others may be perceived as less powerful and less influential.

Accommodation can be highly appropriate when:

- the issue is very important to others but is not very important to you.
- it is more important to preserve group harmony than to resolve the issue.
- you realize you are wrong or you have changed your mind.
- you are unlikely to succeed in persuading the group to adopt your position.

Competition Conflict Style

The **competition conflict style** occurs when group members are more concerned with their own goals than with those of the group. Competitive members want to win; they argue that their ideas are superior to alternatives suggested by others.

Elected officials in Amsterdam, New York, negotiate with other municipalities to bring water service from one town to another. Successful groups use various conflict styles. Which style or styles does this group seem to be using: avoidance, accommodation, competition, compromise, and/or collaboration?

When used inappropriately, the competitive style generates hostility, ridicule, and personal attacks against group members. Approaching conflict competitively tends to divide group members into winners and losers. Ultimately, this may damage the relationships among group members and prevent a group from achieving its common goal.

In certain group situations, however, the competitive approach may be appropriate, such as when:

- you have strong beliefs about an important issue.
- the group must act immediately on an urgent issue or in an emergency.
- the consequences of the group's decision may be very serious or harmful.
- you believe that the group may be acting unethically or illegally.

Compromise Conflict Style

The **compromise conflict style** is a middle ground approach to conflict in which group members give in on some goals in order to achieve other goals they want more strongly. Group members who approach conflict through compromise argue that it is a fair method of resolving problems because everyone loses equally. "However, when each person gives up something in order to meet the others halfway, the result is only partial satisfaction for all concerned. Commitment to solutions will be questionable."[21]

The compromise approach works best when:

- other methods of resolving the conflict are not working.
- the members have reached an impasse and are no longer progressing toward a reasonable solution.
- the group does not have enough time to explore more creative solutions.

Collaboration Conflict Style

The **collaboration conflict style** searches for new solutions that will achieve *both* the individual goals of group members *and* the goals of the group. Instead of arguing over who is right or wrong, the collaborative group seeks creative solutions that satisfy everyone's interests and needs.[22] Collaboration promotes synergy and resolves the dialectic tension between competition and cooperation. It also involves trying to find a win-win solution that enables the group to make progress toward achieving its common goal.[23]

There are, however, two drawbacks to the collaborative approach. First, collaboration requires a lot of the group's time and energy, and some issues may not be important enough to justify this investment. Second, for collaboration to be successful, all group members must participate fully. Avoiders and accommodators can prevent a group from truly collaborating.

Groups should approach conflict resolution collaboratively when:

- they want a solution that will satisfy all group members.
- they need new and creative ideas.
- they need a commitment to the final decision from every group member.
- they have enough time to commit to creative problem solving.

> **Remember This**
>
> Successful groups use various conflict styles to respond to different types and levels of conflict.

Choosing a Conflict Style

While individuals may be predisposed to a particular conflict style, effective group members choose the style that is most appropriate for a particular group in a particular situation. As situations change, so may the approach. Consider the following example of a jury:

> During the first hour of deliberation, the jury engaged in a heated debate over a controversial, yet central, issue in the case. Tony was conspicuously silent throughout this discussion. Jury members asked his opinion several times. Each time, he indicated that he agreed with the arguments that Pam presented. On a later issue, Tony became a central participant. He argued vehemently that one of the defendants was not guilty. He said, "I'm just not going to give in here. It's not right for the man to go to jail over this." Eventually, one of the jurors suggested that Tony reexamine a key document presented as evidence of the defendant's guilt. Tony was quiet for a few minutes and carefully reviewed the document. He then looked up at the group and said, "Well, this changes everything for me. I guess he really was a part of the conspiracy."

Tony used several approaches to deal with conflict in the group. First, he avoided it altogether. He simply had nothing to add to the discussion. Tony then became competitive when he thought that a person might be unjustly imprisoned. He became accommodating, however, when a review of the evidence convinced him that he had been wrong.

When selecting a conflict style, consider the following questions:

- How important is the issue to you?
- How important is the issue to other members?
- How important is it to maintain positive relationships with group members?
- How much time does the group have to address the issue?
- How fully do group members trust one another?[24]

Virtual Groups

Conflict in Cyberspace

Have you ever received emails that were not intended for you and that you found disturbing to read? Have you ever fired off an angry email, only to regret it later? The efficiency of email makes it easy to forward messages without reading them carefully, reply while you're still angry, and send a message to many people without knowing if each will interpret it the same way.

The time, distance, and possible anonymity that separate members of virtual groups may increase conflict. Unfortunately, some group members feel less obligated to behave politely when the interaction isn't face to face. As a result, virtual groups tend to communicate more negative and insulting messages than face-to-face groups do.[25] However, just because someone can't challenge or reprimand you in person

is no reason to abandon civil behavior. Susan Barnes, author of *Online Connections,* notes that "challenging comments can quickly turn professional working adults into 'textual mud slingers.' Curt email messages are rapidly thrown back and forth."[26]

Not responding properly to conflict in a virtual team significantly interferes with the group's ability to solve problems.[27] Some technologies are better suited for dealing with conflict than others. Audio-only (e.g., telephone) and data-only (e.g., email) technologies are less effective for resolving conflict than videoconferencing, which in turn is less effective than face-to-face interaction. Virtual group members need to be extra vigilant when conflict threatens to derail group progress and damage group morale.

Selecting an appropriate conflict styles requires an understanding and analysis of the group's goal, member characteristics and perspectives, and the nature of the conflict situation. For instance, if group members do not trust one another, the compromising style would be less appropriate. If the issue is very important to everyone, and the group has plenty of time to discuss it, collaboration is ideal. Effective groups do not rely on one conflict style. Rather, they balance their choice of conflict style with the needs of the group.

Conflict Management Strategies

Appropriate conflict styles help resolve disagreements. Sometimes, however, a group must set aside the substantive, affective, or procedural issues under discussion and address the causes of the conflict directly. In short, groups need effective strategies for analyzing and resolving conflicts (see Figure 8.4).

Figure 8.4   Conflict Management Strategies

The A-E-I-O-U Model

Jerry Wisinski's **A-E-I-O-U Model** focuses on collaboration and what he calls *positive intentionality*, the assumption that other people are not trying to cause conflict.[28] In other words, every group member must want to resolve the conflict. If you sense that some members are not willing to cooperate or have hidden agendas, the method may not work. If your group is working on an important project that is behind schedule and group members are blaming one another for the problem, ask them to put aside the *blame game* in order to objectively analyze why the group is behind schedule. The five steps in the A-E-I-O-U model (illustrated in Figure 8.5 on the next page) can give you a constructive approach to managing this conflict.[29]

Figure 8.5 A-E-I-O-U Model

	Description	Example
A	**A**ssume that the other person means well.	"I know that all of us want this project to succeed."
E	**E**xpress your feelings.	"Like most of you, I'm frustrated because it seems we're not putting in the work that's needed."
I	**I**dentify what you would like to have happen	"I'd like to be assured that all of you are as concerned about the success of this project as I am, and that you've been thinking about how we can make sure the work gets done on time."
O	**O**utcomes you expect are made clear.	"I sincerely believe that if we don't work late for the next couple of days, we won't finish this project on time."
U	**U**nderstanding on a mutual basis is achieved.	"Could we try staying late tonight and tomorrow and then evaluate our progress? What do you think?"

Negotiation in Groups

Negotiation is a process of bargaining in order to settle differences or solve a problem. Normally, negotiation takes the form of compromise, with group members conceding some issues in order to achieve agreement on other points. Group members may be more willing to bargain if they believe that they will be no worse off and might even be better off by the end of the negotiation process.

Roger Fisher, William Ury, and Bruce Patton of the Harvard Negotiation Project offer a process for resolving conflict known as **principled negotiation**.[30] Four elements characterize this negotiation process: people, interests, options, and criteria (see Figure 8.6 on the next page). Keep in mind that principled negotiation is not a set of skills but a process for resolving conflict.[31]

When group members only focus on defending their positions, the result is winners and losers. When the members focus on group interests, options, and fair criteria, the entire group wins. However, even principled negotiation can become deadlocked when members fail to recognize or appreciate the needs of others and are unwilling to make concessions. The following strategies can help break a deadlock:[32]

- Limit the scope of the problem by dividing it into manageable parts.
- Minimize defensive behavior by having members explain or paraphrase the other side's position.
- Summarize areas of agreement to promote cooperation.
- Take a break to relieve group tensions.
- Ask for more information to avoid inaccurate assumptions.

Clearly, group members must balance a variety of needs during negotiation.[33] They must be willing to cooperate with others while attempting to meet as many of their own needs as possible. They must openly communicate what they are willing to concede yet not sacrifice more than is necessary. And members must balance the need to gain their own short-term goals against the benefits of mutually desirable long-term conflict resolution.

Figure 8.6 Elements of Principled Negotiation

Elements	Principles
People	**Separate the people from the problem.** Do not blame or accuse members. Rather, find a way of working together to resolve the problem and restore balance. You won't eliminate conflicts by ignoring or expelling members who disagree, but you can resolve or reduce the conflicts among them.
Interests	**Focus on interests, not positions.** Look for common needs and interests, not a position or specific point of disagreement. When members stake out positions, they feel obligated to defend them. Understanding common interests allows members to focus on solutions rather than personal success.
Options	**Generate a variety of possible solutions for mutual gain.** Consider multiple options before deciding what to do. Be creative, flexible, and open to alternatives. Make sure that the group's common goal is specific, realistic, and achievable as well as clear and elevated.
Criteria	**Establish fair and objective criteria for evaluating and choosing a solution or course of action.** When a group seeks and adopts fair standards for resolving a conflict or choosing an option, they have an agreed-upon basis for making decisions.

Third-Party Intervention

Sometimes group conflicts are so intense and potentially destructive that members turn to a third party for help. **Third-party intervention** occurs when a group seeks the services of an impartial outsider who has no direct connections to the group but has the skills needed to analyze the conflict and help resolve it. Here, we focus on two kinds of third-party interventions: mediation and arbitration.

Mediation. Mediation is "facilitated negotiation [that] employs the services of impartial third parties only for the purpose of guiding, coaching, and encouraging the disputants through negotiation to successful resolution and agreement."[34] Mediation is an appropriate approach to conflict resolution when group members cannot resolve the conflict by themselves and when everyone concerned is willing to participate in the process and abide by the final settlement. If members cannot agree to these terms, mediation is not a good option.

Effective mediation has two basic requirements: an impartial mediator and a well-planned mediation session. The group must choose an impartial mediator who is *not* involved in the conflict and will not take sides in the dispute. The mediator guides the group through the process and facilitates negotiation. For a mediation session to be well planned, all group members must be prepared to tell their side of the story and express the reasons they believe a given outcome is fair.

Effective mediators establish rapport with disputing group members through empathic listening.[35] They explain the goals of the mediation sessions, list the issues that need to be negotiated, and then guide the group toward possible solutions. When a workable solution is found, they articulate what the parties have agreed upon. Finally, they make sure everyone understands the specifics of the solution and what each group member needs to do to implement it.

Ethics in Groups

The Group and the Golden Mean

The ancient Greek philosopher Aristotle equates *ethics* with *virtue* (such as goodness, moral excellence, righteousness, and integrity). Aristotle explains that virtue can be destroyed by too little or too much of certain behaviors. For example, someone who runs away is a coward while someone who fears nothing is reckless. The virtue bravery is the mean between two extremes. Aristotle offered his "doctrine of the mean," also known as the "golden mean," as a practical way of looking at ethical behavior.[36] Ethical behavior is based on moderation and appropriateness. If, for example, you face an ethical decision, you should select an *appropriate* response somewhere between the two extremes of expressing mild annoyance and uncontrolled rage. Thus, if a group member says something that angers you, according to the golden mean, you should find an appropriate response somewhere between screaming back at the other person in anger or simply giving in. It may be much more appropriate and productive to state in a strong, but reasoned tone that you disagree. Aristotle maintained that anyone can become angry—that is easy. But to be angry at the right things, with the right people, to the right degree, at the right time, for the right purpose, and in the right way—is worthy of praise.[37] For Aristotle, being "brutally honest" in all situations is not an ethical virtue because your honesty may do more harm than good.[38]

In examining the nature and consequences of group conflict, Aristotle's golden mean represents a desirable balance of two dialectic extremes. Consider how the following table illustrates dialectic tensions and the golden mean for three of Aristotle's virtues.[39]

Dialectic Tension	Golden Mean
Cowardice ↔ Rashness	Courage
Shyness ↔ Shamelessness	Humbleness
Boastfulness ↔ Understatement	Truthfulness

Arbitration. If mediation does not work, a group may seek arbitration. **Arbitration,** like mediation, involves a third party. After considering all sides, the agreed-upon arbitrator decides how to resolve the conflict. The arbitrator may choose one person's solution or may develop a solution the group has not considered. Whatever the final decision, group members are obligated to accept and implement the solution, no matter what they think about it.

When turning to an arbitrator, group members "have acknowledged that their own decision-making powers are insufficient to resolve the dispute. Their function, therefore, is to present their side of the case as fully and as capably as possible so that fairness and justice can prevail."[40] Despite the hope for a just outcome, professional arbitrators understand that their decisions may not please everyone in a group. However, for groups that cannot solve problems on their own or with the help of a mediator, arbitration may be the only way to resolve a conflict.

Conflict and Member Diversity

Conflict becomes more complex in diverse groups. Differences in cultural and gender perspectives may result in misunderstandings, prejudices, and unintentionally offensive behavior. Organizations and companies that fail to understand, respect, and adapt to such differences are likely to have more strikes and lawsuits, low morale among workers, less productivity, and a higher turnover of employees.[41]

Cultural Responses to Conflict

The cultural values of individual members greatly influence the degree to which they feel comfortable with conflict and how it is resolved. Members from collectivist cultures that value cooperation are less likely to express disagreement than are members from cultures that place a higher value on individualism. While people from Japanese, German, Mexican, and Brazilian cultures tend to value group cooperation, people from U.S., British, Swedish, and French cultures are generally more comfortable expressing differences.[42] As another example, Chinese group members may feel uncomfortable with adversarial approaches to conflict.[43] Also remember that cultural differences may be regional rather than international. For example, Franco-Canadians are often more cooperative in negotiating a conflict, while Anglo-Canadians are slower to agree to a resolution.[44]

Gender Responses to Conflict

Researchers have devoted a great deal of attention to the impact of gender on conflict styles. Their conclusion is that—at least for conflict styles—there is less difference than you might think between the way women and men respond to conflict.

 ## Groups in Balance...

Let Members Save Face

Collectivist cultures place a high value on face, or the ability to avoid embarrassment. From a cultural perspective, **face** is the positive image you wish to create or preserve. Cultures that place a great deal of value on "saving face" discourage personal attacks and outcomes in which one person "loses." Here are some collectivist perspectives about conflict and face to keep in mind:[45]

- Conflict operates within the context of relationships and the need to preserve "face."
- Conflict resolution requires that "face" issues be mutually managed before discussing other issues.
- Conflict resolution succeeds when both parties save "face" and claim that they have "won."

In Chapter 4, "Diversity in Groups," we note that the individualism–collectivism cultural dimension strongly influences how group members communicate. Not surprisingly, this dialectic also explains how members define and respond to conflict. For example, collectivist members may merge substantive and affective concerns, making conflict more personal. As Myron Lustig and Jolene Koester write in their book *Intercultural Competence*, "To shout and scream publicly, thus displaying the conflict to others, threatens everyone's face to such an extreme degree that such behavior is usually avoided at all costs [in collectivist cultures]." In individualistic cultures, group members may express their anger about an issue and then joke and socialize with others once the disagreement is over. "It is almost as if once the conflict is resolved, it is completely forgotten."[46]

Studies in the late 1990s claimed that women were more likely to avoid conflict or to leave a group when there is continuous conflict.[47] Deborah Tannen claimed that women are more likely to address conflict privately rather than in front of the entire group.[48] But as Ann Nicotera and Laura Dorsey conclude in their 2006 study, "conflict style is not driven by biological sex, regardless of how many studies try to find the effect; it's simply not there."[49]

However, there *are* differences in how people may *expect* women to think and behave in a conflict situation. Women are often expected to value relationships, to be nice and supportive when they encounter conflict, whereas men are expected to be more assertive and focus on the task. And when women use competitive conflict styles, "there is some evidence that they are viewed more negatively than men who compete."[50] At the same time, women may compete more forcefully in reaction to what they perceive as betrayal or underhanded behavior by others.[51]

Group Cohesion

Working in groups requires group **cohesion**, the mutual attraction that holds the members of a group together. Cohesion is a shorthand term for strongly bonded groups; it encompasses group members' attraction to one another, commitment to the group's tasks, and pride in the group itself.[52] A cohesive group has:

Remember This

Cohesive groups feel committed and unified; members develop a sense of teamwork and pride in the group.

- high levels of interaction.
- a friendly and supportive communication climate.
- a desire to conform to group expectations.
- the use of creative and productive approaches to achieving goals.
- satisfied members.[53]

Enhancing Group Cohesion

Four general strategies for developing group cohesion are to establish a group identity and group traditions, to emphasize teamwork, to recognize and reward participation, and to respect group members.[54]

- **Establish a group identity and traditions.** Refer to the group by using terms such as *we* and *our* instead of *I* and *my*. Some groups create more obvious signs of identity, such as a group name, logo, or motto. Many groups develop rituals and ceremonies to reinforce their traditions.
- **Emphasize teamwork.** Cohesive group members believe that their combined contributions are essential to group success. Group members feel responsibility for and take pride in both the work that they do and the work of other members. Rather than individual members taking credit for success, a cohesive group will emphasize the group's accomplishments.
- **Recognize and reward contributions.** Some group members become so involved in their own work, they don't praise others for their contributions. Other members are quick to criticize others. Cohesive groups establish a supportive climate in which members continually thank others for their efforts.

Groups may also reward member contributions more formally with celebrations, letters of appreciation, certificates, and gifts.

- **Respect group members.** When there are strong interpersonal relationships in a group, members become more sensitive to one another's needs. Treating members with respect, showing concern for their personal needs, and appreciating diversity promote a feeling of acceptance.

Groupthink

Although promoting group cohesiveness benefits groups in many ways, too much of it can result in a phenomenon that Yale University psychologist Irving Janis identified as **groupthink**. He defines groupthink as "a mode of thinking that people engage in when they are deeply involved in a cohesive in-group, when the members' strivings for unanimity override their motivation to realistically appraise alternative courses of action.... Groupthink refers to a deterioration of mental efficiency, reality testing, and moral judgment that results from in-group pressure."[58]

Janis identified three preconditions or causes of groupthink.

- *The group is highly cohesive.* As a result, members may overestimate their competence and perceptions of rightness. To maintain cohesiveness and total consensus, members may discourage disagreement.
- *There are structural flaws.* Such flaws "inhibit the flow of information and promote carelessness in the application of decision-making procedures."[59] For example, the leader or a few members may have too much power and influence, or the group's procedures may limit access to outside or contrary information.
- *The situation is volatile.* When a group must make a high-stakes decision, stress levels are high. Members may rush to make a decision (that turns out to be flawed) and they may close ranks and shut out other reasonable options.[60]

The homogeneous↔heterogeneous dialectic discussed in Chapter 1, "Introduction to Group Communication," and Chapter 4, "Diversity in Groups," is particularly important when dealing with groupthink. The more members have in common, the more cohesive they may become. However, they also run the risk of being "more insulated from outside opinions, and therefore more convinced that the group's judgment on important issues must be right."[61]

Symptoms of Groupthink.   Irving Janis developed the theory of groupthink after recognizing patterns in what he called "policymaking fiascoes." He suggested that groupthink was a significant factor in several major political policy decisions with adverse consequences, including the 1961 Bay of Pigs invasion of Cuba, the escalation of the Vietnam War in the 1960s, and the 1972 Watergate burglary and subsequent cover-up.[62] Groupthink may also have contributed to the explosion of the space shuttle *Challenger*[63] in 1986 and the U.S. decision to invade Iraq in 2003. After analyzing many of these policy decisions, Janis identified eight symptoms of groupthink (see Figure 8.7).[64]

Figure 8.7   Groupthink

Groupthink Symptoms	Expressions of Groupthink
Invulnerability: Is overly confident; willing to take big risks.	"We're right. We've done this many times, and nothing's gone wrong."
Rationalization: Makes excuses; discounts warnings.	"What does Lewis know? He's been here only three weeks."
Morality: Ignores ethical and moral consequences.	"Sometimes the end justifies the means."
Stereotyping Outsiders: Considers opposition too weak and stupid to make real trouble.	"Let's not worry about the subcommittee—they can't even get their own act together."
Self-Censorship: Doubts his or her own reservations; unwilling to disagree or dissent.	"I guess there's no harm in going along with the group—I'm the only one who disagrees."
Pressure on Dissent: Pressures members to agree.	"Why are you trying to hold this up? You'll ruin the project."
Illusion of Unanimity: Believes everyone agrees.	"Hearing no objections, the motion passes."
Mindguarding: Shields members from adverse information or opposition.	"Rhea wanted to come to this meeting, but I told her that wasn't necessary."

Preventing Groupthink.   The best way to deal with groupthink is to prevent it from happening in the first place. For example, when commenting on the raid of Osama bin Laden's compound in May 2011, President Barack Obama told a reporter that he encourages all White House team members to speak their minds and express any doubts they may have when a decision is to be made.[65]

This now famous photo shows President Obama with his national security team in the White House Situation Room as they watched live video of the mission to capture and kill Osama bin Laden. The president met with senior intelligence, military, and diplomatic teams in the Situation Room days before the raid to review several options. His advisers were divided about which option to choose. Obama encouraged them to speak their minds openly and freely express their doubts (a strategy for avoiding groupthink). In the end, it was the President who made the decision.

The following list provides practical ways to minimize the potential of group-think.[66] Choose the methods that are most appropriate for your group.

- Ask each member to serve in the role of critical evaluator. Consider having members take turns serving as *devil's advocate*, someone who will argue against a proposal or take an opposite side in an argument in order to provoke discussion, test the quality of an argument, or subject a plan to thorough examination.
- If possible, have more than one group member work on the same problem independently.
- Discuss the group's progress with someone outside the group. Report that feedback to the entire group.
- Periodically invite an expert to join your meeting and encourage constructive criticism.
- Discuss the potential negative consequences of any decision or action.
- Follow a formal decision-making procedure that encourages expression of disagreement and evaluation of ideas.
- Ask questions, offer reasons for positions, and demand justifications from others.
- Before finalizing the decision, give members a second chance to express doubts.

In the short term, groupthink decisions are easier. The group finishes early and doesn't have to deal with conflict. However, such decisions are often misguided and may result in serious harm. Spending the time and energy to work through differences will result in better decisions without sacrificing group cohesiveness.

Summary Study Guide

Conflict in Groups
- Conflict is the disagreement and disharmony that occurs in groups when members express differences regarding group goals, member behavior and roles, and group procedures.
- There are three types of conflict: substantive (disagreement over issues), affective (interpersonal disagreement), and procedural (disagreement over processes).

Constructive and Destructive Conflict
- Constructive conflict results when group members express disagreements in ways that value everyone's contributions and promote the group's goals.
- Destructive conflict results when group members engage in behaviors that create hostility and prevent the group from achieving its goals.

Conflict Styles
- All of the five conflict styles—avoidance, accommodation, competition, compromise, and collaboration—reflect the individual goals↔group goals dialectic tension.
- Effective groups choose conflict styles appropriate for their members and the particular situation. As the situation changes, so may a group's conflict style.

Conflict Management Strategies
- The A-E-I-O-U Model is a five-step technique for expressing your concerns and proposing alternatives in a supportive and constructive manner.

- Principled negotiation involves separating the problem from attitudes about members, focusing on common issues, generating a variety of options, and establishing fair criteria.
- Mediation and arbitration are methods of conflict resolution that rely on a third party who is not involved in the conflict.
- Mediation uses an impartial third party to guide a group in identifying possible solutions and coming to agreement.
- Arbitration empowers an impartial third-party to dictate a final decision to the group.

Conflict and Member Diversity
- The cultural values of individual group members influence the degree to which they feel comfortable with conflict and how it is resolved.
- Men and women from similar cultures do not differ significantly in terms of conflict strategies and styles. However, men and women may differ in terms of their expectations of one another in conflict situations.

Group Cohesion
- Groups can promote cohesion by establishing a group identity and group traditions, stressing teamwork, recognizing and rewarding contributions, and respecting individual members' needs.
- Groupthink occurs when group members value consensus so highly that they fail to think critically about their decisions. Highly cohesive groups have a greater risk of succumbing to groupthink.

GroupWork

Conflict Awareness Log

Directions: Recall two memorable conflict situations in which you did *not* behave in a way that helped minimize or resolve the conflict. Fill out the following Conflict Awareness Log to help you identify effective strategies to use in the future when you are called on to help resolve conflict in groups.

- In column 1, briefly describe the incident.
- In column 2, explain your actions or the reason(s) for your unhelpful behavior.
- In column 3, describe what you wish you had said or done to help resolve the situation.

Conflict Awareness Log

Incident Example	Unhelpful Behavior	Helpful Behavior
Example: Our group was preparing a customer service training presentation. I agreed to take the lead on preparing the team's PowerPoint slides, but Jim submitted an entire PowerPoint show to the group two days before my deadline for getting a draft of the slides to the group.	I was angry with Jim for hijacking my portion of the group project. His PowerPoint slides were no better than mine. I said nothing and let Jim take over that part of the task. I felt unappreciated and didn't want to contribute to any other group projects.	I wish I had spoken up and suggested that Jim work with me on the PowerPoint slides. I think I could have made a real contribution to the group if I hadn't given in to the situation or become so angry.
Incident #1	**Unhelpful Behavior**	**Helpful Behavior**
Incident #2	**Unhelpful Behavior**	**Helpful Behavior**

Group Assessment

How Do *You* Respond to Conflict?[68]

The following 20 statements represent how people respond to conflict situations. Consider each message separately and decide how closely it resembles your attitudes and behavior in a conflict situation, even if the language is not exactly the way you would express yourself. Use the following numerical scale to select the rating that best matches your approach to conflict. Choose only one rating for each message.

5 = I always do this.
4 = I usually do this.
3 = I sometimes do this.
2 = I rarely do this.
1 = I never do this.

When I'm involved in a conflict …

_____ 1. I try to change the subject.
_____ 2. I play down the differences so the conflict doesn't become too serious.
_____ 3. I don't hold back in a conflict, particularly when I have something I really want to say.
_____ 4. I try to find a trade-off that everyone can agree to.
_____ 5. I try to look at a conflict objectively rather than taking it personally.
_____ 6. I avoid contact with the people when I know there's a serious conflict brewing.

_____ 7. I'm willing to change my position to resolve a conflict and let others have what they want.
_____ 8. I fight hard when an issue is very important to me and others are unlikely to agree.
_____ 9. I understand that you can't get everything you want when resolving a conflict.
_____ 10. I try to minimize status differences and defensiveness in order to resolve a conflict.
_____ 11. I put off or delay dealing with the conflict.
_____ 12. I rarely disclose much about how I feel during a conflict, particularly if it's negative.
_____ 13. I like having enough power to control a conflict situation.
_____ 14. I like to work on hammering out a deal among conflicting parties.
_____ 15. I believe that all conflicts have potential for positive resolution.
_____ 16. I give in to the other person's demands in most cases.
_____ 17. I'd rather keep a friend than win an argument.
_____ 18. I don't like wasting time in arguments when I know what we should do.
_____ 19. I'm willing to give in on some issues but not on others.
_____ 20. I look for solutions that meet everyone's needs.

Conflict Style	Avoid	Accommodate	Compete	Compromise	Collaborate
Item Scores	1 =	2 =	3 =	4 =	5 =
	6 =	7 =	8 =	9 =	10 =
	11 =	12 =	13 =	14 =	15 =
	16 =	17 =	18 =	19 =	20 =
Total Scores					

Your scores identify which conflict style or styles you use most often. There are no right or wrong responses. Depending on the issues, the others involved, and the situation's context, you may use different conflict styles. The conflict style or styles with the highest total scores reflect your behavioral preferences in conflict situations.

chapter 9

Structured and Creative Problem Solving in Groups

Case Study

No More Horsing Around

Horseback-riding stable owners in the county meet to develop a joint plan for attracting more customers, particularly in light of the recent economic downturn. Three group members own prestigious private stables that board and train horses for their owners. Four members own open-to-the public stables that rent horses by the hour and offer riding lessons. Sally—who owns one of the public stables—agrees to chair the group's meetings.

All seven group members are competent, hardworking, and interested in increasing business at their stables. At the first meeting, they agree to seek consensus when making decisions; *all* members have to be satisfied with the final group decisions. They also talk about the need for a promotional campaign to increase their business.

At the second meeting, Sally works diligently to encourage equal participation by everyone in the group. Within a short time, however, things are not going well. Tension runs high because the private and public stable owners see the problem quite differently. The three members who own private stables are very forceful and insistent. Perhaps because these members are wealthy and highly respected among horse professionals, the rest of the group lets them do most of the talking. The private owners want to place full-color ads in specialized horse publications, while the public owners are more interested in getting free publicity about their stables and in funding a few small ads in public outlets. Even though they constitute a majority, the public stable owners feel powerless; they resent the unspoken power and influence of the other three members.

In an attempt to broaden the scope of the discussion, Sally distributes a list of questions she believes the group should talk about and answer:

- How serious is our decline in business?
- Why do we have fewer customers?
- How have stables in other counties responded to the problem?
- What limitations do we face in addressing this problem (lack of finances, lack of public relations expertise)?
- What should we do?

The three private stable owners jump to the last question. One of them says, "We know the answers to these questions. We need a good PR campaign. So let's stop talking about other things and decide how to do this—as soon as possible." Rhett, the owner of a public stable, responds quickly with, "Whoa, there. The last thing I want to do is spend a lot of money on fancy-pants ads that none of my customers will see."

Sally interrupts and beseeches the group to slow down before deciding what to do. She tries to include everyone in the discussion by turning the meeting into a brainstorming session. Sally explains brainstorming "rules" and asks the group to think creatively about ways to increase business. If nothing else, the brainstorming session succeeds in reducing tensions between the two factions.

When you finish reading this chapter, you should be able to answer the following critical thinking questions about this case study:

1   How would you word the questions this group should try to answer?

2   Was choosing consensus as the decision-making method appropriate for this group? Why or why not?

3   Which dialectic tensions are likely to affect the group's ability to achieve its goal?

4   How well did the group select and use a structured, problem-solving procedure or a creative, problem-solving method?

5   How did politics, preexisting preferences, and/or power affect the group's ability to make decisions and solve problems?

Planning the Playground

The Politics of Sociology

Before you read any further, visit Pearson's MyCommunicationLab website and watch the short videos "Planning a Playground" and "The Politics of Sociology," which illustrate Chapter 9 concepts. Each video comes with a set of study questions to keep in mind as you read this chapter.

Group Decision Making

What do you do when you have to make an important decision? Do you consider several options and select the most reasonable one? Do you rely on your instincts and do what *feels* right? Do you ask other people's advice and go with the majority? Or do you just ignore it and hope it will go away?

Now think about what groups must do when they make *collective* decisions. Should they use logic, trust their instincts, rely on majority rule, or pass it on to a higher authority? As hard as it is to make a *personal* decision, the difficulties of *group* decision making are multiplied many times. At the same time, groups often make better decisions than individuals working alone. In this chapter, we examine the many ways in which groups address the challenge of making decisions and solving problems.

Decision Making and Problem Solving

Decision making and *problem solving* are not the same. **Decision making** involves making a judgment, choosing an option, and making up your mind about something. Group decision making results in a position, opinion, judgment, or action. Most groups make decisions but may not solve problems. For example, hiring committees, juries, and families make decisions. Which applicant is best? Is the accused guilty? Whom should we invite to the wedding? Management expert Peter Drucker explains, "A decision is a judgment. It is a choice between alternatives."[1] (See Figure 9.1 for a comparison of decision making and problem solving.)

Figure 9.1   Decision Making and Problem Solving

Decision Making	A judgment: The group chooses an alternative.	Asks who, what, where, and when.
	• Guilty or not guilty	• Whom should we invite?
	• Hire or not hire	• What should we discuss?
	• Spend or save	• Where should we meet?
	• Voting or consensus seeking	• When should we meet?
Problem Solving	A process: The group develops a plan.	Asks why and how.
	• Analyze the problem	• Why don't more students vote in student government elections?
	• Develop options	• How should we publicize and persuade students to vote?
	• Debate the pros and cons	
	• Select and implement a solution	

Problem solving is a more complex process in which groups analyze a problem and develop a plan of action for solving the problem or reducing its harmful effects. For example, if student enrollment has declined significantly, a college faces a serious problem that can jeopardize its future. Problem solving requires many decisions. Fortunately, there are decision-making and problem-solving procedures that can help a group make up its mind.

There are many reasons to trust group decision making and problem solving. Sheer numbers enable a group to generate more ideas than a single person working alone. Even more important, a group is better equipped to find rational and workable solutions to complex problems. As a rule, group decision making generates more ideas and information, tests and validates more arguments, and produces better solutions to complex problems.[3]

In Chapter 1, "Introduction to Group Communication," we introduce the structure↔spontaneity dialectic by noting that structured procedures help groups balance participation, resolve conflicts, organize discussions, and empower members. They also help groups solve problems. If a group becomes obsessed with procedures, however, it loses the benefits of spontaneity and creativity. Group communication scholar Marshall Scott Poole notes:

> Too much independence may shatter group cohesion and encourage members to sacrifice group goals to their individual needs.... Too much structured work...is likely to regiment group thinking and stifle novel ideas.[4]

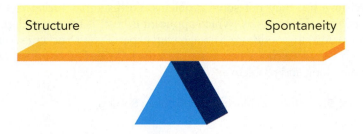

Decision-Making Methods

There are many ways to make group decisions. A group can let the majority have its way, reach a decision that everyone can live with, or leave the final decision to someone else. Effective groups match the virtues of each method to the needs and purpose of the group and its task.

Voting.   Voting is the easiest and most obvious way to make a group decision. No other method is more efficient and decisive. Nevertheless, voting may not be the best way to make important decisions. When a group votes, some members win, but others lose.

A **majority vote** requires that more than half the members vote in favor of a proposal. When a group makes a major decision, there may not be enough support to implement the decision if only 51 percent of the members agree on it. The 49 percent who lose may resent working on a project they dislike. Some groups use a two-thirds vote rather than majority rule. In a **two-thirds vote,** at least twice as many group members must vote for a proposal as vote against it. A two-thirds vote ensures that a significant number of group members support the decision.

Voting works best when:

- a group is pressed for time.
- the issue is not highly controversial.
- a group is too large to use any other decision-making method.
- there is no other way to break a deadlock.
- a group's constitution or rules require voting on certain types of decisions.

Consensus. Because voting has built-in disadvantages, many groups rely on consensus to make decisions. A **consensus** decision is one "that all members have a part in shaping and that all find at least minimally acceptable as a means of accomplishing some mutual goal."[5] Consensus does not mean 100% agreement. Rather, it reflects a sincere effort and willingness to make an acceptable decision that will help the group achieve its common goal.

When reached, consensus can unite and energize a group. Not only does consensus avoid a disruptive win/lose vote, but it also presents a united front to outsiders. Figure 9.2 lists guidelines for seeking consensus.

Figure 9.2 Consensus Guidelines and Strategies

Guidelines	Strategies
• Listen carefully to other members and consider their information and points of view.	• Try to be logical rather than emotional. • Be open to the opinions of others rather than stubbornly argue for your own position.
• Don't change your mind in order to avoid conflict or reach a quick decision.	• Hold out rather than giving in, especially if you have a crucial piece of information or new argument to share. • Remind members that they don't have to agree to a decision or solution they can't possibly support.
• Avoid "easy" ways of reaching a decision.	• Avoid techniques such as flipping a coin, letting the majority rule, or trading one decision for another.
• If the group is deadlocked, work hard to find the next best alternative that is acceptable to everyone.	• Make sure that members not only agree but also will be committed to the final decision.
• Get everyone involved in the discussion.	• Engage even the quietest member, who may have key information or suggestions that can help the group make a better decision.
• Welcome differences of opinion.	• Remind the group that disagreement is natural and can expose the group to a wide range of information and opinions.

Groups in Balance...

Avoid False Consensus

Many groups fall short of achieving their common goal because they believe the group *must* reach consensus on *all* decisions. The problem of false consensus haunts every decision-making group. **False consensus** occurs when members reluctantly give in to group pressures or an external authority. Rather than achieving consensus, the group has agreed to a decision masquerading as consensus.[6]

In addition, the all-or-nothing approach to consensus "gives each member veto power over the progress of the whole group." To avoid an impasse, members may "give up and give in" or seek a flawed compromise. When this happens, the group will fall short of success as "it mindlessly pursues 100% agreement."[7]

In *The Discipline of Teams,* John Katzenbach and Douglas Smith observe that members who pursue complete consensus often act as though disagreement and conflict are bad for the group. Nothing, they claim, could be further from the reality of effective group performance. "Without disagreement, teams rarely generate the best, most creative solutions to the challenges at hand. They compromise...rather than developing a solution that incorporates the best of two or more opposing views.... The challenge for teams is to learn from disagreement and find energy in constructive conflict, not get ruined by it."[8]

Consensus does not work well for all groups. Imagine how difficult it would be to achieve genuine consensus if a leader had so much power that group members were unwilling to disagree or express their honest opinions. Consensus works best when members have equal status or where there is a supportive climate in which everyone feels comfortable expressing their views.

Authority Rule. Sometimes groups use **authority rule,** in which a single person or an executive group within or outside the group makes the final decision. For this method, groups gather information and recommend decisions to another person or a larger group. For example, an association's nominating committee may consider potential candidates and recommend a slate of officers to the association. A hiring committee may screen dozens of job applications and submit the top three to the person making the hiring decision.

Authority rule can have detrimental effects on a group. If a leader or an outside authority ignores or reverses group recommendations, members may become demoralized, resentful, or nonproductive on future assignments. Even within a group, a strong leader or authority figure may use the group and its members to give the appearance of collaborative decision making. The group thus becomes a rubber stamp and surrenders its will to authority rule.

Decision-Making Questions

As is the case with all groups, decision-making and problem-solving groups need a clear goal. We strongly recommend wording the group's goal as a question for the group to answer. A question focuses group members on seeking a specific and realistic answer. Choosing a question of fact, conjecture, value, or policy can help your group clarify what members need to know and do in order to make a good decision or solve a problem.

Questions of Fact.   A **question of fact** asks whether something is true or false, whether an event did or did not happen, or whether something caused this or that. Did product sales decrease last year? The answer to this question is either yes or no. A question such as "What was the decrease in sales?" requires a more detailed answer, with possible subquestions about the sales of particular products or product sales in different regions. When a group confronts a question of fact, it must seek and scrutinize the best information available.

Questions of Conjecture.   A **question of conjecture** asks whether something will or will not happen. Will the economy generate more jobs next year? Will the unemployment rate go up or down? Unlike a question of fact, only the future holds the answer to this type of question. Instead of focusing on what *is*, the group does its best to predict the future. If a group waits until the future arrives, it may be too late to make a good decision or solve a problem. Groups should use reputable facts, expert opinions, and valid data to answer questions of conjecture.[9]

Questions of Value.   A **question of value** asks whether something is worthwhile: Is it good or bad; right or wrong; moral or immoral; best, average, or worst? Questions of value are difficult to discuss because the answers depend on the attitudes, beliefs, and values of group members. In many cases, the answer to a question of value may be, "It depends." Is a community college a better place to begin higher education than a prestigious university? The answer to this question depends on a student's finances, professional goals, academic achievement record, work and family situation, and beliefs about the quality of education at each type of institution.

Questions of Policy.   A **question of policy** asks whether a specific course of action should be implemented to address a problem. Questions of policy ask: What should we do about a particular problem? Here are some examples: What changes, if any, should we make to improve customer service? Which candidate should we support as president of the student government association? What can we do to ensure that our school system maintains a culturally diverse teaching staff? Policy questions often require answers to subquestions of fact, conjecture, and value.

Use All Four Types of Questions.   Problem-solving groups rarely focus on one type of question. Dennis Gouran, a pioneer in group communication research, notes: "A fascinating aspect of many policy discussions is that in trying to determine the most suitable course of action, group members must deal with the other three kinds of questions."[10] For example, if your family were trying to make a decision about where to go for a summer vacation while saving money for a new car, you might start with questions of fact and conjecture: "How much do we usually spend on a summer vacation?" "How much money will we have in savings for a new car next year?" Then the discussion could move to questions of value: "How much do we value the time and place where our family vacations?" "How important is it that we buy a new car this year?" Finally, you would conclude with a question of policy: "How can we both take a summer vacation and save money for a new car?" In many cases, a group must address all four types of questions to make a rational decision or solve a complex problem. When preparing for a group meeting or discussion, make sure you are prepared to share accurate and relevant facts, make informed projections, support your opinions with strong arguments, and offer logical and realistic solutions to a problem.

Decision-Making Styles

The way you make decisions may be very different from other group members. In Chapter 4, "Diversity in Groups," we identify two Myers-Briggs traits—thinking and feeling—that focus on how we make decisions. Thinkers, for example, are task-oriented members who use logic when making decisions. Feelers are people-oriented members who want everyone to get along, even if it means compromising to avoid interpersonal problems. When thinkers and feelers work together, misunderstandings often occur. However, when thinkers and feelers appreciate their differences as decision makers, they become an unbeatable team. Thinkers make decisions and move the group forward, while feelers make sure the group is working harmoniously.

In *Decision Making Style,* Suzanne Scott and Reginald Bruce take a detailed look at various decision-making styles.[11] They describe five styles, all of which have the potential to improve or impair group decision making:

- **Rational Decision Maker.** "I've carefully considered all the issues." Rational decision makers carefully weigh information and options before making a decision. They use logical reasoning to reach and justify their conclusions. However, they must be careful not to analyze a problem so long that they never make a decision.
- **Intuitive Decision Maker.** "It just feels like it's the right thing to do." Intuitive decision makers make decisions based on instincts and feelings. They may not always be able to articulate specific reasons for decisions but know that their decisions "feel" right.
- **Dependent Decision Maker.** "If you think it's okay, then I'll do it." Dependent decision makers seek the advice and opinions of others before making a decision. They feel uncomfortable making decisions that others may disapprove of or oppose. They may even make a decision they aren't happy with just to please others.
- **Avoidant Decision Maker.** "I just can't deal with this right now." Avoidant decision makers feel uncomfortable making decisions. As a result, they may not think about a problem at all, or they delay making a final decision until the very last minute.
- **Spontaneous Decision Maker.** "Let's do it now and worry about the consequences later." Spontaneous decision makers are impulsive and make quick decisions on the spur of the moment. They often make decisions they later regret.

Consider the ways in which different decision-making styles could improve or impair group decision making. For example, what would happen if half of the group were rational decision makers and the other half were intuitive decision makers? Also consider the potential pitfalls of having only one type of decision-making style in a group, such as dependent or avoidant decision makers. Effective groups respect, adapt to, and benefit from members' different decision-making styles.

Structured Problem Solving

Group communication scholar Marshall Scott Poole identifies structured procedures as "the heart of group work [and] the most powerful tools we have" for improving the quality of group work.[12] Even a simple procedure such as constructing and following a short agenda enhances meeting productivity. Time and effort spent on developing and using a well-planned, structured procedure can produce the following benefits:

- *Balanced participation.* Procedures can minimize the impact of powerful leaders or members by making it difficult for them to dominate a group's discussion.
- *Conflict resolution.* Procedures often incorporate guidelines for managing conflict, resolving disagreements, and building genuine consensus.
- *Organization.* Procedures require members to follow a clear organizational pattern and focus on the same thing at the same time. Procedures also ensure that group members do not skip or ignore major discussion items.
- *Group empowerment.* Procedures provide a sense of control. "This happens when members know they have followed a procedure well, managed conflict successfully, given all members an equal opportunity to participate, and as a result have made a good decision."[13]

There is no "best" structured procedure to ensure effective problem solving in groups. As a group gains experience and successfully solves problems, members learn that some methods work better than others and some need modification to suit the group's needs. In this chapter, we present two well-established methods: the Standard Agenda and the Single Question Format. (See Figure 9.3.)

To appreciate the similarities and differences between these two procedures, let's follow a hypothetical example that illustrates how the various steps apply to group problem solving.

Fallingstar State College

For three consecutive years, Fallingstar State College has experienced declining enrollment and no increase in funding from the state. To balance the budget, the college has had to raise tuition every year. There are no prospects for more state funding in the near future. Even with significant tuition increases, overall college revenue is down. The college's planning council, composed of representative vice presidents, deans, faculty members, staff employees, and students, has been charged with answering the following question: Given the severe budget constraints and declining enrollment, how can the college preserve high-quality instruction and student services?

Although the Fallingstar example does not offer many details, it can help demonstrate the ways in which a group may use structured procedures to solve problems.

Figure 9.3 Structured Problem-Solving Procedures

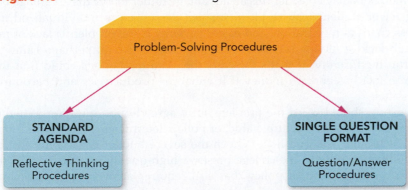

Figure 9.4 Steps in the Standard Agenda

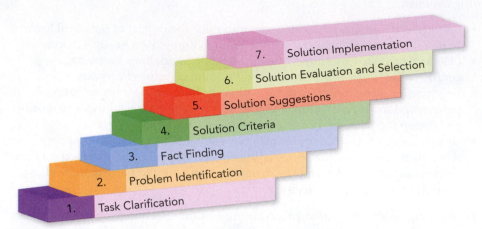

7. Solution Implementation

6. Solution Evaluation and Selection

5. Solution Suggestions

4. Solution Criteria

3. Fact Finding

2. Problem Identification

1. Task Clarification

The Standard Agenda

The founding father of problem-solving procedures is John Dewey, a U.S. philosopher and educator. In 1910, Dewey wrote *How We Think,* in which he described a set of practical steps that a rational person should follow when solving a problem.[14] These guidelines are known as the **Reflective Thinking Process.** Dewey's approach begins with a focus on understanding the problem and then moves to a systematic consideration of possible solutions. The **Standard Agenda** incorporates the seven major steps in Dewey's process[15] (see Figure 9.4).

Task Clarification. During this initial phase, a group makes sure that everyone understands the task or assignment. For example, the planning council at Fallingstar State College could dedicate the beginning of its first meeting to reviewing the council's goal and deadlines as well as the need to produce written recommendations. During this phase, group members ask questions about their roles and responsibilities in the problem-solving process.

Problem Identification. Overlooking this second step can send a group in the wrong direction. In the case of Fallingstar State College, there may be several different ways to define the college's problem. Is declining enrollment a problem? Some group members may consider this an advantage rather than a disadvantage because having fewer students can result in smaller classes, more individualized instruction, less chaos at registration, and easier parking. Is the problem a lack of money? Although lack of money seems to be a universal problem, perhaps Fallingstar is being run inefficiently. If that's the case, the planning council could find that the college in fact has enough money if it enhances productivity and becomes more businesslike.

The group should word the problem as an agreed-upon question. Whether this is a question of fact, conjecture, value, or policy determines the focus and direction of the discussion. The question, "Given the severe budget constraints and declining enrollment, how can the college preserve high-quality instruction and student services?" is a question of policy that also requires answering questions of fact, value, and conjecture.

Fact Finding. During the fact-finding step, group members have several obligations reflected in the following questions of fact and value: What are the facts of the situation? What additional information or expert opinions do we need? How serious is the problem? What are the causes of the problem? What prevents us from solving the problem? These questions require investigations of facts, conclusions about causes and effects, and value judgments about the seriousness of the problem.

Fallingstar State College's planning council could look at many factors: the rate of enrollment decline and future enrollment projections, the anticipated budgets for future years, the efficiency of existing services, the projected impact of a slow economy, estimated salary increases, predictable maintenance costs, the likely causes of declining enrollment, and so on. It could take months to investigate these questions, and even then it may be impossible to find clear answers to all of them. Failure to search for such answers, however, is much more hazardous than not searching at all.

> ## Remember this
>
> A group's "ability to gather, share, and retain a wide range of relevant information is the single most important determinant of high-quality decision making."[16]
>
> —Randy Hirokawa, *Small Group Communication: Theory and Practice*

Solution Criteria. In a review of group procedures, Susan Jarboe describes solution criteria as member ideas about what a solution should accomplish.[17] For example, the Fallingstar planning council recognizes the need for an *affordable* method for *both* increasing enrollment *and* preserving high-quality instruction and student services. Here are some general criteria to consider:

- Will the solution work—is it reasonable and realistic?
- Do we have the resources (money, equipment, personnel) to implement the solution?
- Do we have enough time to implement the solution?
- Does the solution reflect and protect our values?[18]

Criteria should reflect a realistic understanding of *solution limitations,* which may include financial, political, and legal restrictions. For the college planning council, criteria could include affordability, acceptance of the solution by all subgroups (administrators, faculty members, staff members, and students), a commitment to using fair and open procedures to assess existing programs, and considerations of the political and legal consequences of proposed actions.

Solution Suggestions. At this point in a group's deliberations, some solutions may be obvious. Even so, the group should concentrate on suggesting as many solutions as possible. Having spent time understanding the task, identifying the problem, analyzing its consequences and causes, and establishing solution criteria, members should be able to offer numerous solutions. Later in this chapter, we describe a technique called *brainstorming* that can help a group generate creative options.

Suggestions from the college's planning council could include a wide range of options: raise tuition, embark on a new promotional campaign, seek additional grants and corporate donations, freeze raises and promotions, require additional teaching by faculty members, increase class size, reduce the number of administrators and staff members, eliminate expensive programs and services, lobby the state for more funds, and charge student fees for special services. This list could double or triple, depending on the creativity and resourcefulness of the group.

Solution Evaluation and Selection. This stage of the Standard Agenda may be the most difficult and controversial. Here, group members discuss the pros and cons of each suggestion in light of their agreed-upon solution criteria. Questions of conjecture arise as the group considers the possible consequences of each option. Discussion may become heated, and disagreements may grow fierce. In some groups, members may be so tired or frustrated by the time they get to this phase that they have a tendency to jump to conclusions. If group members have been conscientious in analyzing the problem and establishing criteria for solutions, however, they will reject some solutions quickly, while others will swiftly rise to the top of the list.

The college's planning council may hear students argue against increased tuition, whereas faculty members predict a decline in instructional quality if they are required to teach more or larger classes. Administrators and staff members may cringe at freezing salaries, whereas faculty members may support reductions in administrative staff. In this phase, group members should remember their solution criteria and use them to evaluate the strengths and weaknesses of each suggested solution. At the end of this stage, a group selects one or more solutions.

Solution Implementation. Having made a difficult decision, a group faces one more challenge: How should we implement our solution? Is our group responsible for implementation or do we delegate implementation to someone else? For all the

Theory in Groups

The Functional Perspective and Group Problem Solving

Group communication scholars Dennis Gouran and Randy Hirokawa have identified a set of critical functions that help predict the success of decision-making and problem-solving groups.[19] Their **Functional Perspective** claims that "communication is the instrument by which members or groups, with varying degrees of success, reach decisions and generate solutions to problems."[20]

Effective communication, they contend, is more important than the order in which groups perform these functions. As was the case with the Standard Agenda, the origin of the Functional Perspective is John Dewey's Reflective Thinking Process. A second major source is sociologist Robert Bales's study of problem-solving groups. Bales claimed that groups strive for equilibrium (or balance) in satisfying the demands of both task and social dimensions that enable members to perform as a unit.[21]

Unlike the Standard Agenda (and the Single Question Format in the next section), the Functional Perspective is not a set of steps or rules but a call for effective critical thinking and communication skills.

Task Dimensions   Social Dimensions

Three functions stand out as essential for effective group problem solving:

1. Members must be well-prepared and skilled critical thinkers, and effective communicators who know how to generate strong arguments and how to analyze the validity of arguments made by other members.
2. Members with leadership skills must cultivate a supportive communication environment and push the group toward making a high-quality decision.[22]
3. Members must make sure they have identified the sources of information they will need.

time a group spends trying to solve a problem, it may take even more time to organize and implement the solution. If the planning council wants a new promotional campaign to attract students, the campaign must be well planned and affordable to achieve its goal. If the college wants to enhance fundraising efforts, a group or office must have the authority and resources to seek such funds.

The Single Question Format

The **Single Question Format** is a seemingly simple problem-solving procedure that, according to researchers Frank LaFasto and Carl Larson, approximates the way successful problem solvers and decision makers naturally think.[23] Its five steps, shown in Figure 9.5, provide a sharp focus on an agreed-upon question that, if thoroughly analyzed and responsibly answered, should provide the solution to a problem.[24]

Identify the Problem.   What is the *single* question, the answer to which is all that the group needs to know in order to accomplish its agreed-upon goal? Although reaching agreement on the single question may take many hours, the investment is essential.[25] For example, the planning council at Fallingstar State College decides to address this question: How can we increase enrollment and preserve high-quality instruction and student services? In a business setting, a single question might be: How should we eliminate $4 million of annual expenses without damaging the company or its customer relationships? At home, you could ask: Given limited funds, how can we take a vacation and purchase another car?

Create a Collaborative Setting.   This second step is absent from most other problem-solving procedures. Here, you ask group members to agree on a set of norms by generating a list of "we will" statements designed to foster open discussion and participation. For example:

- We will listen to *all* points of view.
- We will ask for facts as well as opinions.
- We will be tough on issues but not on one another.
- We will put aside personal agendas.

In addition to the "we will" list, identify assumptions and biases that may influence the discussion. Ask the group the following questions: Have past approaches worked, or do we need a new approach? Do we *really* understand the problem, or do we need to take a fresh look at the situation? Are we ignoring some approaches because of personal or political biases?

In the case of the Fallingstar planning council, members may decide not to use the names of specific administrators when describing failed programs. Rather than assuming that the college recruitment office "ain't broke, so why fix it?" they may decide that there is room for improvement

Figure 9.5 The Single Question Format

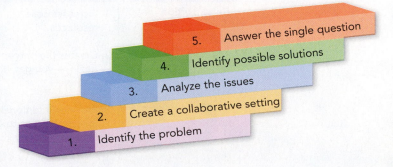

5. Answer the single question
4. Identify possible solutions
3. Analyze the issues
2. Create a collaborative setting
1. Identify the problem

in all offices. When a group such as the Fallingstar planning council examines volatile issues such as tuition increases, staff reductions, and increased workloads, members will understandably want to protect their personal interests. If the group fails to create a collaborative setting for such discussion, the process could deteriorate into destructive conflict and flawed decision making.

Analyze the Issues. The third step requires a group to identify and analyze relevant subquestions such as these:

- What issues should we address in order to answer our single question?
- Do we have accurate and relevant facts about each issue?
- Given what we know, what is the best or most reasonable response to each issue?

Completing this step helps a group "avoid arriving at a solution too early, before understanding the critical components of the problem."[26] This step is similar to the second and third steps in the Standard Agenda (problem identification and fact finding).

Analyzing issues differs by focusing on critical thinking rather describing. Fallingstar council members must do more than share facts about the rate of enrollment decline and future enrollment projections or anticipated budgets. They must determine whether the facts and suggested causes are valid.

Identify Possible Solutions. This step asks a group to suggest two or three reasonable solutions to the overall single question *and* to discuss the advantages and disadvantages of each solution, much like similar steps in the Standard Agenda. This is a crucial step in which strong opinions and disagreements may arise. By listing advantages and disadvantages, however, a group may be able to *see* that the advantages for one solution far outweigh the disadvantages.

A Fallingstar vice president might suggest efficiency moves such as increasing class size as well as a more aggressive marketing plan. A student might recommend an organized protest at the state capitol in support of more funding. In the Single Question Format, the group would consider the advantages and disadvantages of every reasonable solution and determine the extent to which each suggestion could or should be part of an *ideal* solution that answers its single question. A simple table as shown in Figure 9.6 could help group members generate the pros and cons for each option.

Figure 9.6   Identifying Possible Solutions

Possible Solution	Advantages	Disadvantages
Raise Tuition	1. Increases college resources.	1. Spurs protests by angry students.
	2. Creates the perception of quality—you get what you pay for.	2. Causes students to leave for less expensive colleges.
	3. Provides additional funds for scholarships to financially needy students.	3. Leads to erroneous beliefs that the college can now fund expensive new projects.

Your textbook describes three structured procedures to solve problems: the Standard Agenda, the Functional Perspective, and the Single Question Format. Which procedure would you recommend to this group as it makes critical decisions about what to include in the next edition of the school newspaper?

Answer the Single Question.   After analyzing the pros and cons of each potential solution, the group selects "the best solution to the problem based on a clear, shared understanding of all the relevant issues. This clarity, in turn, allows a group to proceed with sufficient confidence to their final decision and commit to it."[27]

Although the Single Question Format shares many characteristics with the Standard Agenda, two features make it both different and highly effective. First, it focuses sharply on goal clarity (a prerequisite for any work group) and issue analysis. Second, it cultivates a supportive group climate that helps members identify, raise, and resolve many interpersonal and procedural problems that can affect group success.

Creative Problem Solving

Curiosity and creativity fuel all *great* groups. These two qualities allow groups to "identify significant problems and find creative, boundary-bursting solutions rather than simplistic ones."[28] When Walt Disney "asked his artists to push the envelope of animation, he told them 'If you can dream it, you can do it.' He believed that, and, as a result, they did too."[29]

Creativity has two components: (1) the nonjudgmental process of seeking, separating, and connecting unrelated ideas and elements, and (2) combining these elements into new ideas.[30] Encouraging and rewarding creativity can be as important to problem solving as following any of the structured procedures described in this chapter. For example, one of us once chaired a meeting in which the injection of creativity broke through a problem-solving logjam:

> I was chairing a meeting of graphic artists, copywriters, and public relations staff members at the college. Our assignment was to write and design a commemorative booklet for the college's fortieth anniversary. On the conference table sat a dozen such booklets from other colleges. The group had reviewed all the samples and come up with a list

Remember This

Effective group leaders understand the near-magical quality that creativity can inject into the group process.

of common features. The problem was this: We had limited funds to print the booklet, so we had to confine ourselves to twenty-four pages. Very quickly, the process bogged down. An uncomfortable silence settled over the group. At this point, I asked, "If you hadn't seen any of these model booklets, what would you write and design to commemorate our anniversary?" The response was immediate and energizing: "You mean we can come up with something new and different?" The answer was yes. The result: A new sense of excitement and eagerness permeated the group. The "model" booklets were swept off the table. Highly creative, outside-the-box alternatives materialized.

When groups engage in creative problem solving, members share imaginative ideas and unusual possibilities. Although it is impossible to describe the creative process in precise terms (it wouldn't be all that creative if we could), we can outline the basic stages of the process in groups. Usually, there are four stages:

- *Investigation.* Group members gather information and attempt to understand the nature and cause(s) of a problem.
- *Imagination.* Group members engage in free thinking by removing procedural and mental roadblocks. The group generates and discusses new and unusual ideas.
- *Incubation.* The group allows a period of time in which imaginative ideas can percolate and recombine in new ways. During this stage, the group may take a break or focus on another topic or issue.
- *Insight.* The "aha!" moment occurs and new approaches or solutions emerge. Group members recognize the "breakthrough moment" and may build on or improve the idea.

Fortunately, group members can learn to use creativity in effective ways when solving problems. In fact, when members receive training in creative problem solving, they participate more, criticize one another less, support new ideas more, exhibit more humor, and produce ideas that are more worthwhile.[31] John Kao, the academic director of the Managing Innovations program at Stanford University, compares balancing creativity and structured group process to tending the flames of a fire. "The spark needs air, breathing room, and freedom to ignite. But let the air blow too freely, and the spark will go out. Close all the doors and windows, and you will stifle it."[32]

As is the case with structured problem solving, there are many creative problem-solving methods. Again, there is no best technique. Fortunately, there are procedures for making decisions and solving problems more effectively by harnessing group ingenuity and creativity (see Figure 9.7).

Figure 9.7 Creative Problem-Solving Methods

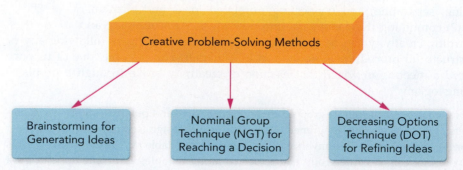

Brainstorming

In 1953, Alex Osborn introduced the concept of brainstorming in his book *Applied Imagination*.[33] **Brainstorming** is a technique for generating as many ideas as possible in a short period of time. When a group wants to identify the causes of or solutions to a problem, brainstorming can increase the number and creativity of responses. Brainstorming is fairly simple and widely used. In fact, more than 70 percent of businesspeople use brainstorming in their organizations.[34] Unfortunately, many groups do not use brainstorming effectively.

Brainstorming is based on two key principles: (1) Deferring judgment improves the quality of input, and (2) the quantity of ideas and output breeds quality. The idea that quantity breeds quality comes from the notions that the first ideas we come up with are usually the most obvious and that truly creative ideas will come only after we have gotten the obvious suggestions out.[35] The guidelines in Figure 9.8 present six strategies and related skills for an effective brainstorming session.

Figure 9.8   Brainstorming Strategies and Skills

1. Sharpen the Focus
   - Start with a clear statement of the problem.
   - Give members a few minutes to think about possible ideas before brainstorming begins.

2. For All to See
   - Assign someone to write down the group's ideas.
   - Post the ideas where everyone can see them.

3. Number the Ideas
   - Numbering can motivate a group, e.g., "Let's try to get 50 ideas."
   - Numbering makes it easier to jump back and forth among ideas.

4. Encourage Creativity
   - Wild and crazy ideas are welcome.
   - Quantity is more important than quality.

5. All Input, No Putdown
   - Don't analyze, oppose, or praise another member's ideas.
   - Don't discuss, defend, clarify, or comment on your own suggestions.
   - Keep the ideas coming.
   - Ideas are evaluated only after brainstorming is over.

6. Build and Jump
   - Build on or modify ideas offered by others.
   - Combine two or more ideas into a new idea.
   - It's okay to jump back to an earlier idea or forward to a completely different line of thinking.

Brainstorming is based on two key principles: (1) Deferring judgment improves the quality of input, and (2) the quantity of ideas and output breeds quality. How does this photograph illustrate a group's use of these principles?

However, brainstorming may be counterproductive under certain circumstances.[36] For example, the comments of a powerful member or "the boss" may influence and limit the direction of ideas. In some cases, group members may not participate in group brainstorming if they experience high levels of communication apprehension, become distracted by member comments, or leave it to others to come up with good ideas.[37]

In an effort to be more democratic, some groups have members speak in turn. But this approach prevents the group from building momentum and results in fewer ideas. Finally, some members try to write down all the group's ideas. Those members end up being so focused on note taking that they rarely contribute ideas. Instead, one person should record and post all the ideas contributed by the group members.

Although brainstorming is popular, its effectiveness depends on the nature of the group and its members. If a group is self-conscious and sensitive to implied criticism, brainstorming can fail. If a group is comfortable with such a freewheeling process, brainstorming can enhance creativity and produce many worthwhile ideas.

Nominal Group Technique (NGT)

Andre L. Delbecq and Andrew H. Van de Ven developed the **Nominal Group Technique (NGT)** as a way of maximizing participation in problem-solving and program-planning groups while minimizing some of the interpersonal problems associated with group interaction.[38] The term *nominal* means "existing in name only." Thus, a nominal group is a collection of people who, at first, work individually rather than collectively. NGT combines aspects of silent voting with limited discussion to help a group build consensus and arrive at a decision.[39]

There are two separate phases in a Nominal Group Technique session: an idea generation phase and an evaluation/voting phase. During the idea generation phase, group members sit around a table in full view of one another.

Phase 1: Idea Generation

1. Each member writes his or her ideas on a piece of paper.
2. At the end of five to ten minutes, a structured sharing of ideas takes place. Each member, in turn, presents one idea from his or her private list.
3. A recorder writes the ideas on a flip chart (or posts ideas using computer projections) in full view of other members. There is no discussion at this point—only the recording of members' ideas.
4. Round-robin listing continues until all members have no further ideas to share.[40]

Returning to the case of the college planning council, members could use the Nominal Group Technique to generate a list of possible causes of declining enrollment or a list of possible solutions. The listing of ideas in an NGT session is different from brainstorming because each member works alone to generate ideas.

During the second, evaluative phase of a Nominal Group Technique session, the group discusses each recorded idea and then votes to create a rank order of items.

Phase 2: Idea Evaluation and Voting

1. Members discuss each idea before independent voting.
2. Members may clarify or state their support or nonsupport for each listed item.

Follow the Research

Which Is Better—Brainstorming or the Nominal Group Technique?

Several researchers comparing the usefulness of brainstorming and the Nominal Group Technique conclude that the Nominal Group Technique often works better than brainstorming for generating ideas that are both numerous and creative. An article in the *Encyclopedia of Creativity* claims that the number of ideas generated in a period of time using the Nominal Group Technique almost always exceeded those from group brainstorming, and that brainstorming usually fails to match the Nominal Group Technique in terms of the quality of ideas.[41] There are several possible reasons for this conclusion.[42]

- Waiting for a turn to speak in a brainstorming group (rather than writing down ideas in advance) may disrupt the thinking of group members and slow the production of ideas.

- Group members who fear negative evaluation from others may withhold good ideas even though the brainstorming group has been told to defer judgment.

- Some members may loaf, or "free-ride," and let others do all the thinking and talking.

- Members who make more contributions to a brainstorming session often earn higher status, which may discourage others from speaking.

The Nominal Group Technique avoids most of these problems because members have time to think and write during the idea-generating process. Brainstorming can avoid these problems when group members use networked computers programmed to generate a master list of ideas simultaneously *and* anonymously.[43]

Even though the Nominal Group Technique may be more effective in generating both the quantity and quality of ideas, brainstorming does have advantages. It can benefit a group by improving morale and by giving members time to have fun in a supportive communication climate as they generate creative ideas.

3. Members vote by ranking or rating ideas privately, in writing.
4. The group decision is the mathematically pooled outcome of the individual votes.[44]

The Nominal Group Technique works particularly well when individual judgments and expertise are valued. Groups use NGT to rank job applicants, determine which of many possible solutions receives the most support, establish budget priorities, and reach consensus on the causes of a problem. The highly structured NGT process guarantees equal participation during the idea generation phase and provides opportunities for discussion and critical evaluation in the second phase. NGT can also be useful when dealing with a sensitive or controversial topic on which contrary opinions or a myriad of details could paralyze the discussion.[45]

An NGT session requires a great deal of time and a skilled moderator to make it work efficiently and effectively. Given NGT's highly structured format, it is difficult to adjust or modify suggested items, and this may frustrate group members who prefer spontaneous interaction. At the same time, NGT can curb members who dominate or block the ideas and comments of others.

Decreasing Options Technique (DOT)

When a group generates dozens of ideas, the number of topics to be reviewed can overwhelm a group and discourage members from participating. Valuable meeting time can be consumed by discussing every idea, regardless of its merit or relevance. The **Decreasing Options Technique (DOT)** is a decision-making tool that helps groups reduce and refine a large number of suggestions into a manageable number of ideas[46]

Generate Individual Ideas. At the beginning of the DOT process, group members generate ideas or suggestions related to a specific topic. Ideas can be single words or full-sentence suggestions. Groups can generate and submit ideas before the group meets or at the beginning of a meeting. Group members should follow the guidelines for effective brainstorming to generate ideas.

Post Ideas for All to See. Each idea should be written on a separate sheet of paper in large, easy-to-read letters—only one idea per page. These pages are posted on the walls of the group's meeting room for all to see and consider. When members submit their ideas in advance, the postings can be completed before the meeting begins.

Figure 9.9 Criteria for Using the DOT Approach

Use the DOT Approach when...

- the group is so large that open discussion of individual ideas is unworkable

- a significant number of competing ideas has been generated

- members want equal opportunities for input

- dominant members exert too much influence

- there is not enough time to discuss multiple or controversial ideas

Sort Ideas.   Not surprisingly, many group members will contribute similar or overlapping ideas. When this happens, sort the ideas and post similar ideas close to one another. For example, when facilitating the development of a college's vision statement, phrases such as *academic excellence, quality education,* and *high-quality instruction* were posted near one another. After everyone is comfortable with how the postings are sorted, give a title to each grouping of ideas. In the vision statement session, for instance, the term *quality education* was used as an umbrella phrase for nearly a dozen similar concepts.

Prioritize Ideas.   At this point, individual members decide which of the displayed ideas are most important. To prioritize ideas efficiently, every member receives a limited number of colored sticky dots. They use their stickers to "dot" the most important ideas or options. For example, each member of a group developing an organization's vision statement receives ten dots; then the members are told to "dot" the most important concepts from among 25 phrases posted on the walls. After everyone has finished posting their dots, the most important ideas are usually very apparent. Some ideas will be covered with dots; others will be speckled with only three or four; some will remain blank. After a brief review of the outcome, the group can eliminate some ideas, decide whether marginal ideas should be included, and end up with a limited and manageable number of options to consider and discuss. Figure 9.10 summarizes the four steps of DOT.

Perhaps the greatest advantage of DOT is its most obvious feature: It is visual. In his book, *Visual Meetings*, David Sibbet notes that adding a visual component to group decision making and problem solving enhances both the efficiency and effectiveness of group work. Two of the factors that support his claim are directly applicable to the reason the DOT Method succeeds:

Figure 9.10   Steps in the DOT Method

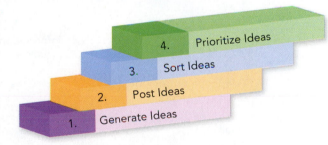

1. Participation and engagement explode when group members' contributions are posted for all to see.
2. Groups get smarter when they can see the big picture that allows for comparisons and pattern finding.[47]

Although the examples described focus on face-to-face interaction, the DOT strategy also works very well in virtual settings. A virtual group can follow the same steps by using email or networked software designed for interactive group work.

Enhancing Group Creativity

Given the benefits of creative problem solving, we recommend four strategies for enhancing group creativity, regardless of the chosen method: (1) control judgment, (2) encourage innovation, (3) ask "what-if" questions, and (4) use metaphors.

Control Judgment.   It's hard to think of anything that inhibits group creativity more than negative responses to new ideas and innovative solutions. "That won't work." "We've tried that." "That's bizarre." Sometimes a bizarre idea can evolve into a creative solution. "Keeping the process open and avoiding premature closure are crucially important. Because creative work is exploratory in nature, it deserves suspension of belief in the early stages."[48]

Virtual Groups

Adapting Decision-Making and Problem-Solving Methods

The group decision-making and problem-solving methods in this chapter were designed for face-to-face meetings. These methods also work well in virtual groups using commonly available technology. Specialized computer software can facilitate group collaboration, decision making, and problem solving.

Different types of technology, however, are not equally well suited to all types of virtual groups. In *Mastering Virtual Teams*, Deborah Duarte and Nancy Tennant Snyder offer a matrix (see below) that rates the effectiveness of different types of technology to the goals of a meeting.[49] In this matrix, *product production* refers to a meeting in which group members work on a collaborative project such as analyzing complex data, developing a design, or drafting a policy. Electronic meeting systems are used in face-to-face settings and range from electronic voting systems to computer-aided systems in which members use a laptop computer to provide input into a central display screen.[50]

Group experts John Katzenbach and Douglas Smith remind us that "whenever teams gather through groupware to advance, they need to recognize and adjust to key differences between face-to-face and groupware interactions."[51] They also caution against approaching every virtual meeting in the same way. Group problem-solving and decision-making tasks require more opportunity for interaction than, for example, does information sharing or presentations. A virtual group should select the technology that is best suited to its problem-solving method.

Interestingly, virtual groups have the potential to stimulate more ideas and overall productivity

Meeting Selection Matrix for Virtual Groups

Type of Technology	Information Sharing	Discussion & Brainstorming	Decision Making	Product Production
Telephone or Computer Audioconference	Effective	Somewhat effective	Somewhat effective	Not effective
Email	Effective	Somewhat effective	Not effective	Not effective
Bulletin Board, Restricted Blog	Somewhat effective	Somewhat effective	Not effective	Not effective
Videoconference without shared documents	Effective	Somewhat effective	Effective	Not effective
Videoconference with text and graphics	Effective	Effective	Effective	Effective
Electronic Meeting System with audio, video, and graphics	Effective	Highly effective	Highly effective	Effective
Collaborative Writing with audio and video	Effective	Effective	Somewhat effective	Highly effective

with fewer blocking behaviors. Some studies have found that idea generation and consolidation using computers are more productive and satisfying than if done face-to-face.[52] However, computer groups require more time for task completion, and group members may become frustrated or bored.

In light of the advantages *and* cautions associated with virtual group problem solving, we offer several strategies to help your group meet the various challenges that arise in such meetings:[53]

1. Ask members to send in their opinions or recommendations prior to the meeting. Appoint someone to collect and summarize these contributions and share them with members so they have time to process the information.
2. Make sure that all members receive the agenda and any other documents they need in time to review them before the meeting begins.
3. Depending on the topic and type of technology, use anonymous features for functions such as brainstorming, voting, and reaching consensus.
4. When possible, use technology such as group editing and collaborative writing to obtain "buy in" on the final recommendations or product from everyone.

Encourage Innovation. In his book on creativity in the workplace, Lee Towe presents four approaches that affect how we solve problems (see Figure 9.11).[54] These approaches also apply to group problem solving. Remember the group trying to design the commemorative booklet for the college's anniversary? Until their creativity was released, they were bogged down in inertia, instruction, and imitation. Encouraging group members to be innovative and imaginative sparked the group's creative powers.

Figure 9.11 Problem Solving Approaches

Four Sources of Action	
Inertia	We've done it before.
Instruction	Someone showed us how to do it.
Imitation	We've seen how it's done
Innovation	We've developed a new way to do it!

Ask What-If Questions. Group members are often reluctant to think creatively because they have preconceived notions about what to do. Asking what-if questions can set aside these constraints. John Kao suggests that there are two types of knowledge. The first is raw knowledge—facts, information, and data. The second type of knowledge is insight, or the "aha!" It is "a response to the *what ifs* and *if only we coulds*."[55]

Here are some questions that the commemorative booklet committee could have asked: What if we had a million dollars to design and print the commemorative booklet; what would we do? What if we had one hundred pages to work with? What if we created an online only brochure? What if we could hire a famous author or designer to do this—what would they do? Group members could consider one more "what-if" scenario: What if we do nothing?[56] What are the consequences, if any, if we don't produce a commemorative booklet?

Ethics in Groups

The Morality of Creative Outcomes

In *Organizing Genius: The Secrets of Creative Collaboration*, Warren Bennis and Patricia Ward Biederman warn that "creative collaboration is so powerful a phenomenon that it inevitably raises moral issues."[57] John Rawls, a contemporary ethicist, urges us to examine the consequences of group creativity. He believes fairness is an important consideration in creative problem solving.[58] For example, creative groups need to ask if their creative innovations have the potential to help or hurt others. Should political consulting firms help the wealthiest or the worthiest candidates? What are the consequences when corporate executives find creative ways to "cook the books" and collect millions of unearned dollars?

Many of the creative geniuses who collaborated to create and test the atomic bomb during World War II subsequently struggled to deal with the consequences of their work. Dr. Richard Feynman, who later won a Nobel Prize in physics, was one of those scientists. He recalled that the group became so caught up in the frenzy and excitement of creating the bomb that they didn't stop to think about the consequences. However, when a colleague of Feynman's said, "It's a terrible thing that we made," he realized that they had unleashed the greatest terror on earth.[59]

Use Metaphors.   The answers to many problems already exist. It's just that they are hiding in other areas of our lives.[60] You can find these hiding places in common metaphors. Metaphors can help group members explain, understand, guide, and direct their creative thinking in ways they would not have thought of otherwise.[61] For example, the metaphor of an emergency room could help redesign the registration process at some colleges. Students who don't need help can register online. Those who need help meet a kind of "triage nurse," a college advisor who can answer simple questions, direct them to a clerk for processing, or send them to a private room where they can receive "intensive care" from a "specialist" counselor. The beauty of metaphors is that they force group members to look at a problem in new and creative ways.

Problem-Solving Realities

Although procedures may be the most powerful tool available to improve the conduct of meetings, several other factors affect the outcome of group decision making and problem solving. We would be remiss if we did not acknowledge that politics, preexisting preferences, and power often infiltrate the group process. Group "decision making in the real world is often messy."[62]

Politics

In organizational settings, almost all decisions have a political component. Regardless of the procedures, many group members come to meetings with hidden agendas and political interests. For example, a member who wants to get ahead may be reluctant to oppose an idea supported by the boss. Another member who knows why a plan won't work may remain silent in order to make sure that the person responsible for implementing the plan fails. Although most conscientious and ethical group members do not engage in such deceptive behavior, it would be naïve to assume that all members care equally about achieving the group's common goal. In some groups, meetings are political arenas in which individuals and special-interest groups are only dedicated to meeting their own needs. Fortunately, the use of clear procedures can minimize the influence of such members.

> **Remember This**
>
> Meetings can become a political arena in which individuals and special-interest groups are dedicated to fulfilling their own needs.

Preexisting Preferences

An intelligent group member is rarely a blank slate who walks into a meeting uninformed or unconcerned about the topic or issue to be discussed. Well before it's time for a decision, most of us have powerful preexisting preferences that affect how we vote.

Psychologists report that we often resist or dismiss information that doesn't mesh with our preconceived beliefs, and that when we hear or read something that supports our preferences, we view it as valid and persuasive—a phenomenon known as **confirmation bias**.[63] When we encounter something that challenges our beliefs, we often view it as flawed.[64] In his book *True Enough*, Farhad Manjoo writes that in addition to holding different opinions, "we're also holding different facts," a tendency that distorts our "perceptions about what is 'real' and what isn't."[65] For example, in a 2004 survey of 928 studies about climate change published in prestigious scientific journals, not a single one disagreed with the view that humans contribute significantly to global warming.[66] Why, then, do polls continue to show that less than half of Americans believe there is strong evidence that human actions are changing the Earth's climate?[67] Preconceived beliefs take a long time to change.

Fortunately, a combination of open discussions, clear goals, and the use of procedures can moderate these preferences, particularly when members analyze them logically and fairly. Even when members have preexisting preferences, procedures that require a pro-and-con discussion of each option help members understand the nature and causes of a problem.

Power

The power of individual group members can have a significant effect on whether a group achieves its goals. It is no secret that powerful people influence group decisions. They affect how and whether other members participate as well as whose ideas and suggestions get serious consideration. Highly influential members can convince a group "to accept invalid facts and assumptions, introduce poor ideas and suggestions, lead the group to misinterpret information presented to them, or lead the group off on tangents and irrelevant discussion."[68] In short, one powerful but misguided member can be responsible for the poor quality of a group's decision.

Summary Study Guide

Group Decision Making

- Decision making results in a judgment or a choice from among alternatives. Problem solving is a complex process in which groups analyze a problem and agree to a plan that will solve it or reduce its negative effects.
- Groups make decisions by voting, seeking consensus, and/or relying on authority rule.
- Groups should be wary of false consensus, which occurs when members reluctantly give in to group pressures or an external authority.
- There are four types of decision-making questions: questions of fact, questions of conjecture, questions of value, and questions of policy. Some discussions require answers to all four types of questions.
- Differences in rational, intuitive, dependent, avoidant, and spontaneous decision-making styles can cause conflict and tension in groups.

Structured Problem Solving

- The Standard Agenda includes the following steps: task clarification, problem identification, fact finding, solution criteria, solution suggestions, solution evaluation and selection, and solution implementation.
- The Single Question Format differs from the Standard Agenda in that it focuses on goal clarity and issue analysis and recommends cultivating a supportive group climate.
- The Functional Perspective emphasizes the importance of seeking the best possible information and having members with effective critical thinking and communication skills.

Creative Problem Solving

- Creative problem solving in groups includes four stages: investigation, imagination, incubation, and insight.
- Brainstorming asks group members to generate as many ideas as possible in a short period of time without criticism or analysis.
- The Nominal Group Technique (NGT) is a two-phase process in which individual members engage in fact finding and idea generation on their own, followed by an analytical discussion of ideas and, as a result, decision making.
- The Decreased Options Technique (DOT) helps groups reduce and refine a large number of ideas into more manageable categories.
- Virtual groups must carefully match the decision-making or problem-solving method to the appropriate technology.
- Regardless of the method, groups can enhance creativity by controlling judgment, encouraging innovation, asking "what-if" questions, and using creative metaphors.

Problem-Solving Realities

- Politics in a group manifests itself in hidden agendas and special interests.
- Open discussion and clear procedures can diminish the impact of preexisting preferences.
- Differences in power affect how and whether group members participate, whose ideas are accepted, how decisions are made, and which solutions are chosen.

GroupWork

What Is Your Decision-Making Style?[69]

Directions: For each of the following statements, indicate the degree to which you agree or disagree by circling a number based on the following scale:

1 = Strongly disagree
2 = Disagree
3 = Undecided
4 = Agree
5 = Strongly agree

There are no right or wrong answers. Respond to the statements as honestly as you can. Think carefully before choosing option 3 (Undecided)—it may suggest you cannot make decisions.

Scoring: To determine your score in each category, add the total of your responses to specific items for each type of decision making. Your higher scores identify your preferred decision-making style(s).

DECISION-MAKING STATEMENTS	1	2	3	4	5
1. When I have to make an important decision, I usually seek the opinions of others.	1	2	3	4	5
2. I tend to put off decisions on issues that make me uncomfortable or that are unpleasant.	1	2	3	4	5
3. I make decisions in a logical and systematic way.	1	2	3	4	5
4. When making a decision, I usually trust my feelings or gut instincts.	1	2	3	4	5
5. When making a decision, I generally consider the advantages and disadvantages of many alternatives.	1	2	3	4	5
6. I often avoid making important decisions until I absolutely have to.	1	2	3	4	5
7. I often make impulsive decisions.	1	2	3	4	5
8. When making a decision, I rely on my instincts.	1	2	3	4	5
9. It is easier for me to make important decisions when I know others approve or support them.	1	2	3	4	5
10. I make decisions very quickly.	1	2	3	4	5

Answers to items 3 and 5   = _____ Rational Decision Maker
Answers to items 4 and 8   = _____ Intuitive Decision Maker
Answers to items 1 and 9   = _____ Dependent Decision Maker
Answers to items 2 and 6   = _____ Avoidant Decision Maker
Answers to items 7 and 10 = _____ Spontaneous Decision Maker

Group Assessment

Problem-Solving Competencies

Directions: Use this instrument to evaluate your communication behavior in group problem-solving discussions. There are five competencies related to accomplishing the group's task and three competencies dealing with conflict, climate, and interaction. Rate yourself on each item in order to assess how well you help your group solve problems and make important decisions.

1 = Superior   2 = Satisfactory   3 = Needs improvement

PROBLEM-SOLVING COMPETENCIES	1	2	3
Defining and analyzing the problem. I help clarify, define, and analyze the problem confronting the group.	1	2	3
Identifying solution criteria. I actively participate in identifying criteria for assessing the quality of the group's outcome.	1	2	3
Generating solutions. I suggest and explain potential solutions or options.	1	2	3
Evaluating solutions. I participate in evaluating potential solutions and options.	1	2	3
Focusing on the task. I stay focused on the task, issue, or agenda item under discussion.	1	2	3
Managing conflict. I encourage constructive disagreements and do my best to resolve nonproductive conflict.	1	2	3
Maintaining a collaborative climate. I support other group members.	1	2	3
Communicating effectively. I interact with others and encourage other members to participate.	1	2	3

1. What are my strengths and communication competencies as the member of a problem-solving group:

_____
_____
_____

2. What and how can I improve my communication competencies as the member of a problem-solving group:

_____
_____
_____

chapter 10

Critical Thinking and Argumentation in Groups

Chapter Outline

Case Study

Slicing the Pie

At Gorgias College, the Student Finance Board is responsible for distributing funds to campus clubs and organizations. Board members include the president, vice president, and treasurer of student government, four members from active student groups, two faculty members, and the college's comptroller. The director of student activities chairs the meeting but has no voting power. He does, however, provide data and background information about how previous boards made these decisions.

The board meets twice a year to consider funding requests. Clubs usually request more money than is available. Board members read funding requests and listen to presentations by club members who argue that their organization should receive the funding they requested. Then the board discusses the requests and argues for or against funding amounts for particular organizations. Finally, the group makes its decision—even though it knows that some clubs and advisors will argue that the decision was unfair or unjust.

This year, the student members on the Finance Board come from the Philosophy Club, the Latino Heritage Club, the Intramural Sports Council, and the Drama Society. The group has $500,000 to distribute and has received requests for $875,000. Clearly, many groups will receive less than they requested.

Patrice, president of the student government, proposes that the board should begin with a blank slate. That is, they won't guarantee clubs the same budgets received in past years. Instead, they should use four criteria to decide how much each club should get: (1) the number of members, (2) the quality of their written funding request, (3) the value of their activities to students and others, and (4) their cost-effectiveness.

Several board members respond immediately. Wendell, a faculty member who is also the Nursing Club advisor, objects by saying, "Many clubs depend on getting what they've had in the past. Their numbers, as well as the quality and quantity of their activities, have not changed—so why should their funding change?"

Patrice responds, "Well, their funding may not change at all. It might even go up." Charlie, a member of the Philosophy Club, answers, "But that doesn't

respond to Wendell's argument. For example, the Debating Society doesn't have many members, but their activities boost the college's academic reputation. So should we give them less?"

"The answer to your question, Charlie, is yes," says Mark, a member of the Intramural Sports Council. "Thirty times as many students participate in intramurals and we get only ten times as much as the debate team."

Charlie quickly adds, "And the intercollegiate sports teams get more money than all the other clubs combined. Let's look at the quality of each program, its value to the college, and how much it costs. Remember when college Republicans invited Rush Limbaugh to speak on campus? Remember how much that cost?"

The director of college activities gently interrupts and suggests that the group pause and listen to a couple of stories about how previous boards dealt with such problems in the past.

Patrice—who's been silent as long as she can stand it—interrupts the director: "The past is the problem. Some groups got more than they deserved and others got much less than they needed to survive."

Caesar, from the Latino Heritage Club, sighs audibly and shakes his head. "Look, that's fine for clubs that have been around for years. But the Latino Heritage Club is new. We don't have many members right now—but we will if we have the funds to get the word out to potential members. We don't have a track record—but we will if we have the funds to sponsor activities. We're not even sure we wrote the funding proposal correctly. As I see it, Patrice's criteria will only make sure we get nothing."

The Drama Society member nods her head, "And then there are the thousands of people who come to our theatre productions—how do you count them?"

Charlie concedes and says, "I never thought about it that way."

Finally the college's comptroller calls for order. "I'm appointed to this board by the college to make sure that our decisions are justifiable and legal. Let's stop bickering about the clubs we do and don't support. Instead, we need an orderly way of letting everyone make their arguments clearly and fairly. Okay?"

When you finish reading this chapter, you should be able to answer the following critical thinking questions about this case study:

1. To what extent did the Student Finance Board benefit from argumentation? Did it enhance understanding and critical thinking, avoid groupthink, and improve decision making?

2. What types of evidence did Student Finance Board members use to support their arguments? Was the evidence valid? Why or why not?

3. Which fallacies of reasoning were evident in some of the board members' arguments?

4. How can the Student Finance Board improve the quality of their arguments in order to reach final budget decisions that are fair and justifiable?

Helping Annie

The Politics of Sociology

Before you read any further, visit Pearson's MySearchLab website and watch the short videos "Helping Annie" and "The Politics of Sociology," which illustrate Chapter 10 concepts. Each video comes with a set of study questions to keep in mind as you read this chapter.

Critical Thinking and Argumentation

Do you *like* being criticized by others? Do you *enjoy* arguing? Do you get a kick out of a lively and thought-provoking debate? Our guess is that many people would answer no to these questions. Yet, as you learned in Chapter 8, "Conflict and Cohesion in Groups," it's quite normal for disagreement and conflict to occur when group members work together to make decisions and complete tasks.

Highly effective group members excel as critical thinkers. They know how to engage in constructive argumentation and recognize the value of an open exchange of ideas. Members who disagree are resources, not rivals. Although effective arguers want to win arguments, they do not want to do so at the expense of the group goal and member relationships.

Critical thinking is not about criticizing, belittling, or attacking someone's ideas. Rather, **critical thinking** is the kind of thinking you use when you analyze and evaluate what you read, see, or hear in order to arrive at a justified conclusion or decision. Critical thinking is the conscious process of assessing the validity of facts, evidence, and claims for the purpose of reaching an outcome—a personal or group decision. Effective critical thinking promotes reasoned, productive argumentation among group members working to achieve a common goal. In a review of research on critical thinking in groups, D. Christopher Kayes concludes that critical thinking is more important than ever for groups dealing with a complex and changing world as they coordinate a diverse set of goals, roles, and intellectual challenges.[1]

Like critical thinking, the function of argumentation in groups is often misunderstood. Argumentation is not about fighting, condemning, or bickering. Rather,

argumentation is the way in which group members use critical thinking to advocate proposals, examine competing ideas, and influence one another. Effective argumentation helps group members develop, present, and defend their own viewpoints as well as objectively listen to and analyze the views of others.

Cooperative Group Argumentation

Many people view an argument as a hostile confrontation between two or more combatants. In effective group communication, however, arguments are something much less threatening. An **argument** is a claim supported by evidence and reasons for accepting it. As you will see later in this chapter, emotions can play a significant role in many group arguments.[3]

An argument is more than an opinion, such as "I think the Latino Heritage Club should be given more funds next year." An argument is an idea or opinion *supported* by evidence and reasoning: "The Latino Heritage Club should be given more funds next year because it has doubled in size and cannot provide the same number or quality of programs without more funds." When viewed this way, an argument does not necessarily involve conflict or disagreement. An argument is a way of demonstrating that an idea, proposal, or decision is reasonable and worthwhile.

Unlike what happens when two people argue, groups engage in unique kinds of argumentation. For example, once a group makes a decision based on listening to and analyzing arguments from its members, the argument is over. A decision signals the end of argumentation and the beginning of implementation or the discussion of a different issue. In addition, when an entire group argues—rather than only two people—there are more questions and challenges, which force "the group's argument into more complex realms of reasoning, challenging members to reevaluate" arguments "in light of new evidence."[4]

Effective arguers balance their personal desire to win an argument with the group's need to solve a problem or make a decision. As communication scholars Josina Makau and Debian Marty put it, argumentation in groups should be cooperative rather than competitive. They define **cooperative argumentation** as "a process of reasoned interaction…intended to help participants…make the best assessments or the best decisions in any given situation."[5] Cooperative arguers focus on the group's shared goal of solving a problem or making the best decision. This approach is very similar to the collaboration conflict style discussed in Chapter 8, "Conflict and Cohesion in Groups." Thus, a cooperative approach to argumentation in groups recognizes that:

- others' ideas and arguments are as important as your own.
- it is important for ideas to be discussed and understood by all members.
- argumentation is a way to effectively solve problems.[6]

Cooperative Argumentation   Competitive Argumentation

The Value of Argumentation in Groups

Effective argumentation helps groups understand and analyze ideas, influence members, and make informed decisions. Thus, the quantity and quality of argumentation is a significant factor in determining whether a group achieves its goal. Figure 10.1 illustrates the benefits of argumentation in groups.

Promotes Understanding.   In most groups, members use argumentation to express opinions in various ways. Some group members argue logically; others, emotionally. A few use a both/and approach that combines logical and emotional arguments into a powerful, persuasive message. Some group members argue on behalf of what's best for the group; others argue for personal gain. A few use a both/and approach that uses arguments to demonstrate how their position benefits the group *and* its individual members. For example, as a member of the Student Finance Board, Charlie argues in favor of funding the Philosophy Club because he is a club member. A faculty member may support the Philosophy Club request because it visibly highlights the academic goals of the college's humanities department. Both members support the same position but for different reasons. Understanding how other group members reason and feel about issues can help you strengthen and adapt your arguments.

Figure 10.1   Benefits of Argumentation

Promotes Critical Thinking.   Effective argumentation helps group members analyze issues and critically examine ideas. When you present an argument, another member may challenge your claim and ask you to justify your position. Your response requires skilled argumentation supported by strong evidence, sound reasoning, and an understanding of how other group members think and feel about an issue. The process of argumentation may even cause you to rethink your own positions and beliefs. Argumentation in groups goes hand-in-hand with critical thinking.

Decreases the Risk of Groupthink.   As you learned in Chapter 8, "Conflict and Cohesion in Groups," groupthink occurs when efforts to discourage conflict and maintain cohesion go overboard, leading a group to make flawed decisions. Argumentation decreases this risk because "groups trained to employ cooperative argumentation are able to form constructive forms of cohesion."[7] Constructive and cooperative argumentation encourages the critical examination of opposing ideas without impairing group cohesion. Groups can avoid groupthink when members think critically, ask questions, offer reasons for their positions, and appropriately seek justifications from others.

Improves Group Decision Making.   Argumentation helps group members examine the consequences of a potential action before making a final decision. Errors in reasoning are exposed, and weaknesses in evidence are uncovered. Argumentation can also improve group decision making because, unlike one-on-one argumentation, it enables several members to work together to develop the same argument. In this "tag team" situation, like-minded members build on the arguments presented by others by providing additional evidence or reasons to support a particular position. The result is a single comprehensive argument constructed cooperatively by a subgroup. Although there is strong evidence that argumentation improves group decision making,[8] it is based on the assumption that group members know how to develop and use arguments effectively.

Values Minority Opinions. When groups value constructive argumentation and welcome arguments from both sides in a dispute, the majority generally wins. However, minority viewpoints can succeed when the arguments that support them are forceful and consistent.[9] For example, during the college Student Finance Board discussion of "slicing the pie" of available funds for student activities, the members of two smaller clubs (the Latino Heritage Club and the Drama Society) argue that Patrice's proposal is not fair to new clubs or those that serve a wider student and public audience. A third member changes his mind. These kinds of shifts "can cascade relatively quickly in the minority's favor."[10]

Structuring Arguments

Stephen Toulmin, an English philosopher, compares an argument to a living organism, with its own anatomical structure and specific physiological functions.[11] The **Toulmin Model of Argument** provides a way of building sound arguments and refuting the arguments of others.

Before you can build or refute an argument, you need to understand the components of a complete argument. In his layout of an argument, Toulmin identifies six components: claim, evidence, warrant, backing, reservation, and qualifier.[15] The first three are essential in all arguments; the second three help clarify the nature and power of an argument.

Theory in Groups

Argumentative and Aggressive Communication

Chapter 3, "Group Membership," introduces the concept of communication apprehension to explain why some group members are reluctant and lack confidence in their ability to interact with others in a group. Similarly, we also vary in how comfortable we feel arguing—a characteristic called **argumentativeness**, or the willingness to debate controversial issues with others.[13] At the end of this chapter is a self-test called the Argumentativeness Scale, which will help identify your level of argumentativeness. You might want to pause and complete the questionnaire now and calculate your results before continuing.

A group member's level of argumentativeness provides some insight into how that member will approach a discussion or debate. Group members with lower levels of argumentativeness generally avoid conflict. As a result, other group members may see them as not only unskilled in argumentation, but less influential in group decision making.

Argumentative members like defending a point of view and perceive argumentation as a practical and enjoyable form of communication.[14] Highly argumentative group members defend their positions confidently and challenge the arguments of others with skill. Groups usually view their most argumentative members as skilled communicators with high credibility and influence. Argumentative members often become group leaders. Argumentativeness benefits a group as long as it does not lead to aggression and hostility. The responsible argumentative member focuses on issues and avoids personal attacks.

Argumentative members are highly influential in group decision making. In fact, argumentative group members create more arguments on *both* sides of a position.[15] When the number of choices a group must consider expands, the group is less likely to reach a biased decision or succumb to groupthink.

Claim, Evidence, and Warrant

The **claim** is the conclusion or position you advocate—a statement you wish others to believe. **Evidence** describes the facts, statistics, opinions, examples, and other materials you use to support your claim. For example, the statement "My group will do well on our class project" is a claim. The evidence for this claim might be the fact that during the first meeting, all members of the group said that they would work hard on the project. Evidence answers a challenger's questions: "What makes you say that?" or "What do you have to go on?"

A **warrant** answers the questions "How did you get there?" and "Why does that evidence lead you to that conclusion?"[16] Although the word *warrant* has several different meanings (e.g., arrest warrant), it also means a way to justify our beliefs and actions as in "Given the way she behaved, his angry reaction was warranted." In argumentation, warrants explain how the evidence supports and proves a claim. For example, a warrant might state that when group members are willing to work hard, a successful outcome is usually the result.

Warrants authorize or confirm the validity of a conclusion and give you the right to make your claim. Here's an example of an unwarranted argument: Patrice says to Mark: "Are you saying that because you saw me talking to the president of the Young Democrats before the meeting, you jumped to the conclusion that we were making a funding deal? That inference is unwarranted!" The evidence (Patrice spoke to the president of the Young Democrats) is insufficient to make the claim (Patrice and the club president were making a deal for more funding) because the warrant is unreasonable (If the president of student government talks to the president of a club before a funding meeting, it must be because they're making a deal.)

Figure 10.2 illustrates the relationship among these three components of the Toulmin Model. The argument in Figure 10.2 would sound like this: "All group members say they will work hard. Because hard work usually results in success, the group will do well on the class project." The combined evidence, claim, and warrant make up the "basic T" of the Toulmin Model.

Figure 10.2   "Basic T" of the Toulmin Model

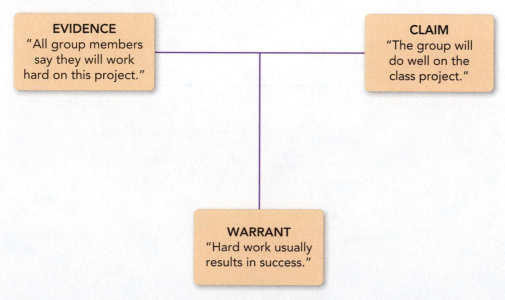

Backing, Reservation, and Qualifier

Beyond the "basic T" of the Toulmin Model, there are three additional components: backing, reservation, and qualifier. The **backing** provides support for the argument's warrant. In the class project example, backing for the warrant might be the fact that the group that worked the hardest on the last assignment received the best grade. If you believe that members may doubt the validity of your evidence, make sure you have backing to support it.

Not all claims are true all the time. The **reservation** component of the Toulmin Model recognizes exceptions to an argument or indicates that a claim may not be true under certain circumstances. At the first meeting, group members said they would work hard. If, however, some members do not attend the planning meetings, the group is less likely to do well. You now have reason to doubt your claim about group success.

The final component of the model is the qualifier. The **qualifier** states the degree to which the claim appears to be true. Qualifiers are usually words or phrases such as *likely, possibly, certainly, unlikely,* or *probably.* A claim with a qualifier might be "The group will *probably* do well on the class project." Figure 10.3 illustrates the relationship among all six components of this argument.

The Toulmin Model provides a blueprint for creating and evaluating arguments. In most cases, you don't need to state every component of the argument. However, understanding the model lets you know what questions to ask about your own and other members' arguments. If someone only states an argument's claim, you may ask for evidence to support that claim. If the warrant is questionable, you may ask for backing to support it. Recognizing that situations may alter the certainty of your claim, you may ask for qualifiers that recognize exceptions. When you develop your own arguments, the Toulmin Model can help you test the strength of every component. When you are analyzing someone else's argument, the model helps reveal

Figure 10.3   The Toulmin Model of an Argument

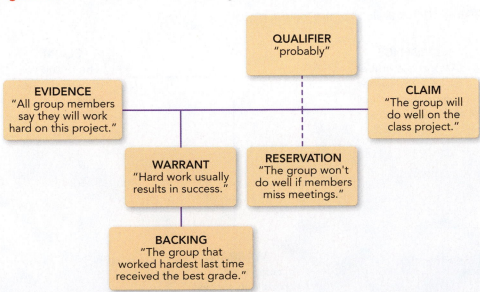

Elected officials, such as Florida State Senator Eleanor Sobel, must present and refute claims in both private and public group settings. Even in a small group, the Toulmin Model of an Argument can help you ask critical questions about other members' claims and can make sure that your claims are appropriate, reasonable, and persuasive.

the strengths and weaknesses of the claims. The following example illustrates how you can use the Toulmin Model to ask critical questions about your own or others' arguments:

- **Initial Claim:** The Ravens will win the Super Bowl this year. *Question: What makes you say that?*
- **Evidence:** They have the best defense in the league. *Question: Why does that evidence lead you to believe that they'll win the Super Bowl?*
- **Warrant:** A good defensive team is the key to winning a Super Bowl. *Question: How sure are you that this is the factor that matters?*
- **Backing:** The team with the best defense has won the Super Bowl each of the last five years. *Question: But aren't there other factors that also affect who wins?*
- **Reservation:** I guess it's possible that the Ravens' defense might have a lot of injuries or that the other team's quarterback might improve significantly. *Question: How confident are you in your prediction?*
- **Qualifier:** I believe that the Ravens have the best chance. *Question: So how does that affect your original claim?*
- **Revised Claim:** The Ravens will probably win the Super Bowl this year.[17]

Supporting Arguments

All arguments gain strength when you research your position and use appropriate evidence to make your case. **Research** is a systematic search or investigation designed to find useful and appropriate evidence. Even if you already know something about the topic area, good research can make you look and sound even better. For example, you may know that Americans watch a lot of television; research lets you know that the average American watches approximately 153 hours of TV every month at home.[18] That's an average of about 5 hours a day!

A researcher with a good research strategy becomes an effective investigator with a systematic plan for searching sources of information—in the same way a detective searches for clues. The information you need is out there; you just have to find it. As you do your research, make sure you choose appropriate types of evidence and test the validity of your evidence.

Types of Evidence

Toulmin lists evidence as an essential component in his model of an argument. Evidence takes many forms: (1) facts and opinions, (2) definitions and descriptions, (3) examples and illustrations, and (4) statistics.

Facts and Opinions. A **fact** is a verifiable observation, experience, or event, something known to be true. An **opinion** is a personal conclusion regarding the meaning or implications of facts. Here is a fact: In 1876, Colonel Henry M. Robert used the British Parliament's procedures and Thomas Jefferson's code of congressional rules as a basis for *Robert's Rules of Order*. Here are two contrasting opinions:

- *Robert's Rules of Order* is outdated and makes a meeting more complicated than necessary.
- *Robert's Rules of Order* is time tested and ensures fair and objective decision making.

Unlike opinions, facts can usually be proved true or false. Group members should not mistake their opinions for facts. As Daniel Patrick Moynihan (sociologist, U.S. Senator, and ambassador) is quoted as saying: "Everyone is entitled to his own opinion, but not to his own facts."[19]

When used as evidence, opinions usually express an authority's judgment or interpretation of facts. Keep in mind that different experts may not reach the same conclusions even when relying on the same facts. Look for a variety of opinions rather than relying on claims that represent only one perspective.

Definitions and Descriptions. A **definition** clarifies the meaning of a word, phrase, or concept. A definition can be as simple as explaining what *you* mean by a word or as complex as an encyclopedia entry. Here is an example:

> According to Warren Bennis and Bruce Nanus, "There is a profound difference between management and leadership, and both are important. 'To manage' means 'to bring about, to accomplish, to have charge of or responsibility for, to conduct.' 'Leading' is 'influencing, guiding in direction, course, action, opinion.'"[20]

During an initial meeting, a group should define key terms. For example, a group dealing with sexual harassment policies should gather several definitions of sexual harassment.

Descriptions are more detailed than definitions. Rather than clarifying the meaning of a word or concept, a **description** creates a mental image of a person, event, place, or object. Causes, effects, historical contexts, characteristics, and operations can all be included in a description. Here is a description of *feelers*, one of the Myers-Briggs personality types: Feelers are people-oriented members who seek group harmony. They want everyone to get along. Feelers will spend time and effort helping other members.

Examples and Illustrations.   An **example** refers to a specific case or instance. Examples are usually brief. An **illustration** is a longer, extended example that can take up an entire paragraph or tell a lengthy story. Here's a series of examples from Chapter 1, "Introduction to Group Communication," of this textbook: "We work in groups at school and on the job; with family members, friends, and colleagues; in diverse locations from sports fields and battlefields to courtrooms and classrooms." The case studies that appear at the beginning of each chapter in this textbook are illustrations. For example, the case of the Student Finance Board at the beginning of this chapter illustrates the challenge of group argumentation.

Statistics.   Information presented in a numerical form is the basis for **statistics.** There are various types of statistics, including averages, percentages, rates, rankings, and so on. For example, in Chapter 4, "Diversity in Groups," the U.S. Census Bureau reported that "in 2010, there were 50.5 million Hispanics in the United States, composing 16 percent of the total population."

Many of us believe statistics, particularly when published by reputable sources. However, you should examine all statistical findings carefully. The source and form of a statistic can result in different interpretations of the same numbers. Misinterpreting statistical information can jeopardize a group's effectiveness and success. For example, in 2005, the number of miles driven by Americans grew by just 1 percent, the smallest increase since the 1991 recession.[21] Here are some interpretations of that statistic: (1) health-conscious Americans were walking more and driving less, (2) Americans concerned about the environmental effects of automobile exhaust decreased their driving, and (3) record-high gas prices encouraged people to cut down on optional trips and use mass transit. Expert analysts identify the third reason as the correct interpretation.

 ## Groups in Balance...

Document Sources of Evidence

Documentation is the practice of citing the sources of evidence. All group members should document their evidence, including information from Internet sources and interviews, in writing and then orally in discussions. Documentation enhances your credibility and the validity of your arguments.

Unlike writers, you will rarely display footnotes during a discussion, unless perhaps a PowerPoint presentation gives you that opportunity. Rather, you provide an **oral citation**, a comment that includes enough information to let members find the original source you're citing. It's a good idea to provide the name of the person (or people) whose work you are using, say a word or two about their credentials, and mention the source (e.g., publication, website, television program) and its date. For example, if you claim that the United States puts a greater proportion of its citizens in jail than any other country, you could say, "According to a 2008 report by the International Center for Prison Studies in England, the United States has 2.3 million criminals behind bars, more than any other nation. Even China, which has four times the population of the United States, is a distant second."[22]

Tests of Evidence

Evaluate every piece of evidence before using it in an argument or sharing it with group members. Make sure your information is **valid,** that the ideas, opinions, and information you include are accurate, reasonable, and justified.[23] Test your evidence by asking the following questions:

- *Is the Source Identified and Credible?* How credible are your information sources? Who are the author(s) and publisher(s)? Are they reputable?
- *Is the Source Unbiased?* Do their opinions seem one-sided, self-serving, unreasonable, or unfair?
- *Is the Information Recent?* When was the information collected? When was it published? Is the information no longer true?
- *Is the Information Consistent?* Is the information similar to information reported in other sources on the same subject? Does the information make sense based on what you know about the topic?
- *Are the Statistics Valid?* Do the statistics accurately measure what they claim to measure? How are the statistics reported?

Virtual Groups

Think Critically About the Internet

Although our ability to do research electronically has enormous benefits, it also has significant disadvantages. William Miller, a former president of the Association of College and Research Libraries, notes, "Much of what purports to be serious information [on the Web] is simply junk—neither current, objective, nor trustworthy.[24]

The Internet does not cover all the possible sources of information. What you find can be difficult to test for validity. The most trustworthy websites include information from major newspapers and magazines, professional associations, government agencies, libraries, institutions of higher education, legitimate media outlets, and well-known experts. Here are four related criteria to consider when you find and want to use an Internet source:

Criterion 1: Authority

1. Are the sponsor's identity and purpose clear?
2. Are the author's identity and qualifications evident?
3. Can you verify the legitimacy of the page's sponsor (e.g., a phone number or postal address to contact for more information)?

Criterion 2: Accuracy

1. Are the sources of information available so you can verify their claims?
2. Has the sponsor provided links you can use to verify claims?
3. Is statistical data well labeled and easy to read?
4. Is the information free of grammatical, spelling, and typographical errors that could indicate poor quality control?

Criterion 3: Objectivity

1. Is it evident why the sponsor is providing the information?
2. Is the sponsor's point of view presented clearly with well-supported arguments?
3. Does the sponsor account for opposing points of view?

Criterion 4: Currency

1. Is the material recent enough to be accurate and relevant?
2. Are there any indications that the material is revised and kept up to date?
3. Do you see statements indicating when data for charts and graphs were gathered?

Presenting Arguments

If you want your ideas taken seriously by your group, you must present your arguments skillfully.[25] Figure 10.4 shows a four-step process for presenting arguments.

In some cases, you may not need to include every step when you present an argument. If the evidence is strong and clear, you don't need to provide the warrant. If your argument is very brief, a summary may not be necessary. However, you should be prepared to include all the steps if group members challenge your arguments.

State Your Claim

The first step in presenting an argument is to state your claim clearly. Chapter 9, "Structured and Creative Problem Solving in Groups," identifies four types of discussion questions—fact, conjecture, value, and policy. Claims for arguments fit into similar categories. When presenting arguments, however, group members rarely state claims in the form of questions. A *claim* is a declarative statement that identifies your position on a particular issue.

- A **claim of fact** attempts to prove that something is true, that an event occurred, or that a cause did have an effect. For example, "Sex education in schools promotes teenage promiscuity" is a claim of fact. Whether this claim is true or not depends on further analysis of the evidence and the warrant.
- A **claim of conjecture** suggests that something will or will not happen. For example, you could say, "Enrollment at the college will increase by 5 percent by next year." Although your group cannot foresee the future, it can make reasonable predictions based on the best information available.
- A **claim of value** asserts that something is worthwhile—good or bad; right or wrong; best, average, or worst. "My instructor is the best professor at the college" is a claim that places a value on someone. Arguments involving claims of value are often difficult to prove because each group member brings personal opinions and beliefs to the discussion.
- A **claim of policy** recommends a particular course of action. "We should oppose next year's 9 percent tuition increase" is a claim of policy.

Support Your Claim

The fact that a claim is stated does not mean that it is true. To be convincing, you must support your claim with strong and valid evidence. Regardless of whether that evidence takes the form of facts, opinions, definitions, descriptions, examples, illustrations, or statistics, groups should continuously evaluate the quality of any evidence.

Provide Reasons

If it isn't clear to others why a particular piece of evidence proves your claim, demonstrate the link between your evidence and your claim. In the Toulmin Model, this

Figure 10.4 Procedure for Presenting Arguments

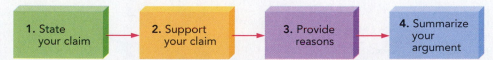

1. State your claim → 2. Support your claim → 3. Provide reasons → 4. Summarize your argument

link is the warrant and the backing—statements that explain why the evidence is sufficient to prove the claim.

Suppose a friend tells you that drinking one glass of red wine daily can prevent heart disease and reduce your chances of a life-threatening heart attack. Your friend cites the conclusions of several scientific studies as evidence. You may wonder: How can this be? Isn't alcohol dangerous—doesn't it do more harm than good? When you question the claim, your friend provides the argument's warrant: The alcohol in a glass of red wine suppresses the accumulation of fatty plaques in the blood vessels, particularly the coronary arteries that supply the heart. Now the argument makes sense because you understand the reason for the claim.[26]

Summarize Your Argument

A good summary restates the original claim and summarizes the supporting evidence. Be brief. Don't repeat all your evidence and reasons. When the presentation of the claim and the evidence has been brief and clear, you can omit the summary. However, lengthy and complicated arguments often need a summary to ensure that all members understand your argument.

Refuting Arguments

Refutation is the process of proving that an argument is false or lacks sufficient support. Refutation can question, minimize, and deny the validity or strength of someone else's argument. Group members should be willing and able to refute claims that are unsupported or untrue. A group unwilling to evaluate arguments risks the dangers of groupthink. Figure 10.5 shows six steps that can help you refute another member's argument.

Listen to the Argument

First, listen for comprehension. You must fully understand an argument before you can refute it effectively. Ask questions and take notes. Once you comprehend the meaning of an argument, you can shift to critical listening. What type of claim is it? Is there evidence to support the claim? How well does the evidence support the claim? What is the implied or stated warrant? Is the claim qualified in any way? Analyzing the argument as you listen will help you formulate an appropriate response.

> *Remember This*
>
> You must fully understand an argument before you can refute it effectively.

State the Opposing Claim

Group members may offer several claims during an argumentative discussion. Don't try to respond to all of them at once. When you are ready, state the claim you

Figure 10.5 Procedure for Refuting Arguments

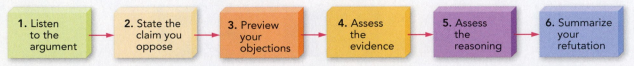

1. Listen to the argument → 2. State the claim you oppose → 3. Preview your objections → 4. Assess the evidence → 5. Assess the reasoning → 6. Summarize your refutation

oppose. Clearly stating the claim gives you the opportunity to make sure that you understand the argument. You may think the claim was "Employees are stealing supplies from the company." Instead, the claim was "The company should identify ways to use supplies more efficiently." If you have misunderstood a claim, other group members can clarify their arguments for you.

Preview Your Objections

Provide a brief overview of your objections or concerns. Let other group members know the general direction of your argument, particularly when your refutation will be lengthy or complicated, such as "I don't believe we should raise funds for a carnival for three reasons: the high cost, the unpredictable weather, and the undesirable location." If they have a general idea of the reasons for your refutation, group members will be better prepared to listen to and understand your objections and concerns.

Assess the Evidence

When refuting a claim, you may be able to show that the evidence supporting the claim is faulty. You can do this by presenting contradictory evidence. For example, if a group member contends that the college's tuition is high, you may present evidence from a survey showing that the college's tuition is one of the lowest in the state. You can also question the quality of evidence. For example, an outdated statistic or a quotation by a discredited source can be reason enough to reject an arguer's evidence—and claim. Proving that the evidence is of poor quality does not mean that the claim is untrue but does highlight potential weaknesses.

Assess the Reasoning

Assess reasoning by identifying fallacies. A **fallacy** is an argument based on false or invalid reasoning. It is not always necessary to identify the fallacy by name, particularly if group members are not familiar with the different types of fallacies. It is much more important to explain why the reasoning in the argument is flawed. Figure 10.6 on the next page lists and briefly describes some of the most common fallacies of argument.

Summarize Your Refutation

The final step is to summarize your response. If your refutation has been lengthy or complex, it is helpful to restate the major points of your response. It is not necessary to review all your arguments in detail because doing so wastes valuable group discussion time. If your refutation has been short and to the point, it may not be necessary to summarize your argument.

Adapting to Argumentation Styles

Research suggests that men and women argue differently, as do group members from different cultures. Moreover, group members' emotional intelligence also affects how they develop and refute arguments. These differences appear to be a function of how we learn to argue and what values we believe are important. Effective group members recognize and try to adapt to other members' ways of arguing.

Figure 10.6 Fallacies of Argument

Fallacy	Description	Example
Ad Hominem Attack	Attacks the person rather than the argument made by that person.	"What would you know about the benefits of a year-round school schedule? You don't even have kids!"
Appeal to Authority	Relies on biased or unqualified expert opinion to support a claim.	"According to a popular television talk show host, most men cheat on their wives."
Appeal to Popularity	Justifies an action because many others do the same thing or share the same opinion.	"Almost everyone I know has cheated on an exam. It's really no big deal."
Appeal to Tradition	Resists changes to traditional behavior and opinions.	"The group should continue to meet on Monday afternoons because that's when we've always met."
Faulty Analogy	Compares two items that are not similar or comparable.	"The war in Afghanistan is just like the Vietnam war. Thus, the U.S. war in Afghanistan is doomed to fail."
Faulty Cause	Claims that an effect is caused by something that has little or no relationship to the effect.	"Since the college's basketball team began doing poorly two years ago, overall enrollment at the college has declined."
Hasty Generalization	Uses isolated or too few examples to draw a conclusion.	"A Volvo is an unreliable car. The one I used to own was always breaking down."

Gender Differences

Researchers have devoted a great deal of attention to the impact of gender on critical thinking and argumentation. Their conclusion is that—in general—there are fewer differences than you might think between the way women and men argue. Studies in the late 1990s claimed that men tend to be competitive arguers, whereas women are more likely to seek consensus within a group. The same research found that men tend to view issues as only two-sided (for or against, right or wrong), whereas women are more likely to search out many different perspectives on a subject as well as ask questions.[27] As was the case with conflict research in Chapter 8, "Conflict and Cohesion in Groups," there may be differences in how people *expect* women to think and argue. Women are often expected to be nice whereas men are expected to be more aggressive when arguing.

Generally there are *no* differences in men's and women's use of facts, opinions, statistics, or other types of evidence. In addition, men and women were relatively equal in voicing objections to others' statements.

Ethics in Groups

Ethical Argumentation

Regardless of how persuasively you present an argument, you should also argue ethically. In *Advocacy and Opposition*, Karyn and Donald Rybacki describe four ethical responsibilities in argumentation: research responsibility, common good responsibility, reasoning responsibility, and social code responsibility.[28]

1. *The Research Responsibility.* Group members should be well informed and prepared to discuss the issues.
   - Do not distort or suppress important information and evidence.
   - Never fabricate or make up information.
   - Reveal the sources of information so others can evaluate them.

2. *The Common Good Responsibility.* Ethical arguers look beyond their own needs and consider the circumstances of others.
   - Consider the interests of those affected by the decision.
   - Promote the group's goal as more important than winning an argument.

3. *The Reasoning Responsibility.* Group members understand the structure of an argument and apply that knowledge to presenting arguments and recognizing fallacies.
   - Do not misrepresent the views of others.
   - Use sound reasoning supported by evidence.
   - Avoid making or accepting fallacious arguments.

4. *The Social Code Responsibility.* Group members promote an open and supportive climate for argumentation.
   - Treat other group members as equals.
   - Give everyone, including those who disagree, the opportunity to respond to an argument.
   - Do not insult or attack the character of a group member.
   - Give the group an opportunity to review the evidence.

We caution you against stereotyping the way men and women argue. Don't assume that the women in your group are more submissive and emotional and the men are more assertive and objective. Instead, we prefer a dialectic approach: Groups benefit when members value *both* competition *and* cooperation. A study by Renee Meyers and her colleagues found that when group members argue, they must balance "the tension between the need to agree and disagree, to challenge and reach convergence, to ask questions and make statements." Although these "tasks may be divided along gender lines...there is nothing inherently superior or inferior about either men's or women's communication. They may be different, but they are both necessary and equally important to the group's success in argument."[29]

Cultural Differences

Cultures often dictate who should and should not argue. In some cultures, a young person would not challenge or argue with an older adult. Among several American Indian and African cultures, the elderly rightfully claim more wisdom and knowledge than do younger members.

In Neah Bay, Washington, a Makah elder teaches children about a sea star they have found on the beach. In many American Indian and African cultures, young people rarely challenge or argue with an older adult. Do you believe that older people in a community can rightfully claim more wisdom and knowledge than younger members?

One of the most significant cultural differences in argumentation is the way in which people use evidence to support a claim:

> There are no universally accepted standards about what constitutes evidence. Among many devout Muslims and Christians, for instance, parables or stories—particularly from the Koran or Bible—are a powerful form of evidence.... The European American culture prefers physical evidence and eyewitness testimony, and members of that culture see "facts" as the supreme kind of evidence...[whereas] in certain portions of Chinese culture...physical evidence is discounted because no connection is seen between...the physical world and human actions.... In certain African cultures, the words of a witness would be discounted and even totally disregarded because the people believe that if you speak up about seeing something, you must have a particular agenda in mind; in other words, no one is regarded as objective.[30]

Given such different perspectives about the value of evidence, the data used to support a claim in one culture may seem irrational in another.

Argumentation and Emotional Intelligence

When group members argue about the wisdom of adopting a controversial proposal, whether to hire an unconventional job applicant, or how to break bad news to colleagues, they may need emotional intelligence to help them achieve their goal. In some cases, members must restrain their emotions. In other circumstances, they can exert influence by heating up a discussion and by expressing strong emotions.

Remember This

"Feelings are indispensable for rational decision making."

—Dr. Antonio Damasio

The role of emotions in critical thinking and argumentation can take two forms: (1) curbing inappropriate emotions and (2) expressing appropriate emotions. Effective group members understand the need for both and learn how to balance their use.[31] The following five skills can help you and the members of your group to improve your emotional intelligence and your group's ability to think critically and argue reasonably:

- *Self-awareness:* Tune in to your own feelings, calm down, and be willing to share your feelings with group members.
- *Self-regulation:* Handle your emotions responsibly. Delay personal gratification and, instead, focus on achieving group goals.
- *Self-confidence:* Show that you are willing to work things out by talking over the issue rather than escalating the controversy.
- *Self-control:* State your own point of view in neutral language rather than using an antagonistic tone or combative words.
- *Empathy:* Look for an equitable way to resolve the dispute by working with those who disagree to find a resolution that both sides can embrace.[32]

If you care about your group and its goal, express your emotions openly to emphasize what you say. Emotions capture attention and operate as warnings, alarms, and motivators. They generate powerful nonverbal messages by conveying crucial information without using words.[33]

Follow the Research

Emotional Intelligence in Groups

Psychologist Antonio Damasio was one of the first researchers to link emotions to communication, critical thinking, and decision-making ability.[34] While studying patients with damage to the emotional center of their brains, he noted that his patients make terrible decisions. Despite having high IQs, they "make disastrous choices in business and their personal lives, and can even obsess endlessly over a decision so simple as when to make an appointment." Dr. Damasio contends that feelings are *indispensable* for rational decision making.[35]

Daniel Goleman, author of *Emotional Intelligence*, has taken Damasio's findings a step further and extended the concepts of emotional intelligence well beyond the behavior of brain-damaged patients. Goleman defines **emotional intelligence** as the "capacity for recognizing our own feelings and those of others, for motivating ourselves, and for managing emotions well in ourselves and in our relationships."[36]

In an article on approaches to argumentation in groups, Renee Meyers and Dale Brashers note that we need to take a closer look at emotional arguments. As they see it, emotions play a significant role in arguments. "The more committed group members are to a cause, the more familiar arguers are with one another, and the more the topic is recurrent, the more likely emotional arguments will surface."[37]

Summary Study Guide

Critical Thinking and Argumentation

- Argumentation is the way in which group members use critical thinking to advocate proposals, examine competing ideas, and influence one another.
- Effective argumentation promotes understanding of others' views, helps avoid groupthink, promotes critical thinking about ideas, improves group decision making, and values minority opinions.
- Argumentativeness describes the extent to which a member feels comfortable and willing to debate controversial issues with others.

Structuring Arguments

- The Toulmin Model of Argument represents the structure of an argument and provides a way to develop and evaluate arguments. The components of the model include a claim, evidence, warrant, backing, reservation, and qualifier.

Supporting Arguments

- Evidence takes many forms, including facts, opinions, definitions, descriptions, examples, illustrations, and statistics.
- Valid evidence must meet several criteria. It should come from an identified, credible, unbiased, and recent source, and the information should be consistent with other evidence.
- Determining the validity of statistical evidence requires answering two questions: (1) Are the statistics accurate? and (2) How are the statistics reported?
- Use the following criteria when evaluating evidence from a website: authority, accuracy, objectivity, and currency.

Presenting Arguments

- When presenting an argument, state your claim, support your claim, provide reasons, and summarize your argument.

- Argument claims generally fit into four categories—claims of fact, claims of conjecture, claims of value, and/or claims of policy.

Refuting Arguments

- Six guidelines can help you refute an argument: (1) listen to the argument, (2) state the opposing claim, (3) preview your objections, (4) assess the evidence, (5) assess the reasoning, and (6) summarize your refutation.
- A fallacy is an argument based on false or invalid reasoning. Common fallacies include *ad hominem* attack, appeal to authority, appeal to popularity, appeal to tradition, faulty analogy, faulty cause, and hasty generalization.

Adapting to Argumentation Styles

- Women and men may argue differently. Men tend to be competitive arguers, whereas women may prefer to seek consensus. However, there is no significant difference in men's and women's use of evidence.
- Cultures often dictate who should and should not argue. Culture also influences the way in which people use evidence to support a claim.
- Four ethical responsibilities in every argument focus on research, common good, reasoning, and social code.
- Emotional intelligence refers to the capacity to recognize our own and others' feelings and to manage our emotions. The role of emotions in argumentation can take two forms: (1) curbing inappropriate emotions and (2) expressing appropriate emotions.

GroupWork

Analyze the Argument

Read the following example in which each of Toulmin's six components is identified. Then read the second argument and see if you can identify the six components.[38]

> Want whiter teeth? Want to stand out in photographs with a sparkling white smile? Then get yourself a tube of White Up, our tooth-whitening dental paste. Independent laboratories have confirmed that White Up will make your teeth 50 percent whiter after using it for two weeks. Of course, if you drink a lot of coffee—the most significant cause of stained teeth—we can't guarantee such good results. So put down that coffee cup and pick up a tube of White Up.

Initial Claim	Buy White Up, the tooth-whitening dental paste.
Evidence	Independent laboratories have confirmed that your teeth will become 50 percent whiter after using White Up for only two weeks.
Warrant	Most people want whiter teeth.
Backing	People want whiter teeth in order to look better in photographs, to mask ugly stains, and to impress others with a sparkling smile.
Reservation	Coffee drinking is the most significant cause of stained teeth and may negate the effects of a tooth whitener.
Qualifier	Coffee drinkers should not expect their teeth to become 50 percent whiter.
Qualified Claim	If you want whiter teeth and a bright smile, put down that coffee and pick up a tube of White Up.

Now it's your turn. Read the following argument. Identify the six components of the Toulmin Model of Argument. Then write the final qualified claim:

> The U.S. Congress should ban animal research because animals are tortured in experiments that have no necessary benefits for humans, such as testing cosmetics. The well-being of animals is more important than the profits of the cosmetics industry. Only Congress has the authority to make such a law because corporations can simply move from state to state to avoid legal penalties. On the other hand, a law to ban all animal research could go too far, such as banning critical medical research. So the law would probably have to be written carefully to define the kinds of animal research that should be banned.

Initial Claim	: _____
Evidence	: _____ _____
Warrant	: _____
Backing	: _____ _____
Reservation	: _____ _____
Qualifier	: _____
Qualified Claim	: _____

Group Assessment

Argumentativeness Scale[39]

Directions: This questionnaire contains statements about arguing over controversial issues. Indicate how often each statement is true for you personally by placing the appropriate number in the blank. Use the following ratings to respond to each statement:

1 = Almost never true
2 = Rarely true
3 = Occasionally true
4 = Often true
5 = Almost always true

_____ 1. While in an argument, I worry that the person I am arguing with will form a negative impression of me.

_____ 2. Arguing over controversial issues improves my intelligence.

_____ 3. I enjoy avoiding arguments.

_____ 4. I am energetic and enthusiastic when I argue.

_____ 5. Once I finish an argument, I promise myself that I will not get into another.

_____ 6. Arguing with a person creates more problems for me than it solves.

_____ 7. I have a pleasant, good feeling when I win a point in an argument.

_____ 8. When I finish arguing with someone, I feel nervous and upset.

_____ 9. I enjoy a good argument over a controversial issue.

_____ 10. I get an unpleasant feeling when I realize I am about to get into an argument.

_____ 11. I enjoy defending my point of view on an issue.

_____ 12. I am happy when I keep an argument from happening.

_____ 13. I do not like to miss the opportunity to argue about a controversial issue.

_____ 14. I prefer being with people who rarely disagree with me.

_____ 15. I consider an argument an exciting intellectual exchange.

_____ 16. I find myself unable to think of effective points during an argument.

_____ 17. I feel refreshed after an argument on a controversial issue.

_____ 18. I have the ability to do well in an argument.

_____ 19. I try to avoid getting into arguments.

_____ 20. I feel excitement when I expect that a conversation I am in is leading to an argument.

Scoring Instructions

1. Add your scores on items 2, 4, 7, 9, 11, 13, 15, 17, 18, and 20.
2. Add 60 to the sum obtained in step 1.
3. Add your scores on items 1, 3, 5, 6, 8, 10, 12, 14, 16, and 19.
4. To compute your argumentativeness score, subtract the total obtained in step 3 from the total obtained in step 2.

Interpretation of Scores

73–100 = High in argumentativeness
56–72 = Moderate in argumentativeness
20–55 = Low in argumentativeness

chapter 11

Planning and Conducting Meetings

Chapter Outline

Case Study

Monday Morning Blues

At 1:30 P.M. on the second Monday of every month, the full-time employees of the Foxglove Athletic Club get together for a staff meeting. During the early afternoons, very few club members are in the gym. Four part-time staff members share reception duties and assist members.

Promptly at 1:30, seven staff members assemble in the aerobics studio sitting on floor mats or bouncing on large exercise balls. Darrell, the club director, rushes in at 1:40, looks around, and asks, "Where's Maggie and Guy?" Everyone shrugs; Maggie and Guy are late for everything. Then Darrell addresses Eli, "I think it's your turn to take minutes. Kim did it last month." Eli groans, resigns himself to this bothersome task, leaves to get paper and a pen, and returns a few minutes after the meeting has begun.

Darrell takes his usual seat on a short stool in front of the full-wall mirror. "Okay," he begins, "we have a lot to cover today, but I promise we'll be done by 3:00." Darrell lifts his clipboard on which he's written a list of topics on the back of an exercise workout form. The first two items are announcements about new treadmills and plans to redesign the layout of the small shop in which they sell athletic equipment, athletic wear, energy bars, and fortified beverages.

As Darrell talks, the two aerobics instructors begin a whispered conversation about their aerobics group. Meanwhile, Chris, the shop manager, interrupts Darrell and describes, in detail, how great the redesigned shop will be and how he's ordered the latest designs in athletic wear. Darrell tries to interrupt him, but Chris chatters on and on. It's now 2:00 and in walks Maggie. "Where's Guy?" asks Darrell. "He's busy doing something," answers Maggie. The rest of the group members shake their heads as though they're thinking, "Typical."

Since the meeting began, Rob has been sitting in his usual corner, stewing. Finally he can't stand it anymore. "We've been here for half an hour and accomplished nothing. This is a joke!"

"Robert!" exclaims Darrell in his I'm-in-charge voice. "I know *you* may not be interested in all this, but others are. Let's give it a rest and jump ahead to the fifth item on my list."

"It's time," announces Darrell, "to decide whether we should expand our aerobics classes to meet growing demand." The preoccupied aerobics instructors look up in confusion, hoping they haven't missed anything important. This discussion drags on…2:30…2:45…3:00…3:15. A few members have begun doing barely-concealed stretching exercises. Others nod at Darrell—no matter what he says—in faked attention. Finally, Rob breaks in saying that it's almost 3:30 and the gym is beginning to fill up. Darrell looks out the glass door of the aerobics studio to see a line of people on the treadmills. "Well, we didn't get through everything but there's always next month's meeting. So let's get out there with lots of energy, excitement, and enthusiasm!"

When you finish reading this chapter, you should be able to answer the following critical thinking questions about this case study:

1   How well was this meeting planned and structured?

2   Would the meeting have been more productive if everyone had seen Darrell's agenda in advance? Why or why not?

3   To what extent did group members behave productively and responsibly during the meeting?

4   Did these staff meetings need someone to take minutes? Why or why not?

5   Which dialectic tensions were most evident in the way the staff meeting was conducted and in its outcome?

Planning a Playground

The Reunion

Before you read any further, visit Pearson's MySearchLab website and watch the short videos "Planning a Playground" and "The Reunion," which illustrate Chapter 11 concepts. Each video comes with a set of study questions to keep in mind as you read this chapter.

Meetings, Meetings, Meetings

More than 11 million business meetings take place in the United States every day. The typical employee spends almost 15 hours a week in meetings and may attend 60 formal or informal meetings a month.[1] Odds are that you've spent your share of time in meetings. Certainly you will attend them in the future. Unfortunately, many of these meetings will not be productive or rewarding group experiences. Humorist Dave Barry has nothing nice to say about meetings. He compares them to funerals—people sit around in uncomfortable clothes and would rather be somewhere else. At least, he notes, funerals have a purpose and a definite conclusion. Unfortunately, many meetings don't.[2]

Figure 11.1 Three Essential Elements of a Meeting

Tyler Cowen, an economist at George Mason University, has a very different view of meetings. He preaches "good news for the legions of meeting haters: Most meetings aren't as wasteful as they seem." When meetings are well planned and conducted, they build strong alliances and confer a sense of control. Members are more motivated to implement group ideas and actions when they have a real voice in the decision-making process.[3] We hope that by the conclusion of this chapter you'll side with Tyler Cowen about the value and necessity of effective group meetings.

If people get together in the same room at the same time, you have a meeting, right? Wrong. You merely have a gathering of people in one place. A **meeting** is a scheduled gathering of group members for a structured discussion guided by a designated chairperson. Let's take a closer look at the three elements in this definition: schedule, structure, and chairperson (see Figure 11.1).

First, most meetings are scheduled in advance for a particular time and place; a coincidental gathering of group members does not constitute a meeting. Second, meetings can be formal and highly structured or informal and loosely structured. A meeting using parliamentary procedure is an example of a formally structured meeting, whereas an emergency staff meeting relies on an event to structure the discussion. Effective groups balance the need for *both* structure *and* spontaneity appropriate for the meeting's goal and the group's norms. The third element of a meeting is a designated **chair** or **chairperson**, an appointed or elected member who conducts the meeting.

Structure   Spontaneity

Follow the Research

Why Do Many Meetings Fail?

Odds are that over the course of your career you will spend a significant amount of time in meetings. Research shows that meetings can take up 25 to 80 percent of many workers' time. Is this time well spent? More than 70 percent of executives report that most of the meetings they attend are a waste of time.[4] In another study, workers rated 69 percent of the meetings that they attended as "ineffective."[5] All this wasted meeting time comes at a cost. The estimated annual cost of unnecessary and ineffective meetings in the United States ranges from $54 million to $3.7 billion annually.[6]

Time wasted in meetings also has significant negative effects on employee attitudes. Research reveals that workers' feelings of fatigue, perceptions of workload, and overall job satisfaction are directly related to perceptions of meeting effectiveness.[7] The result, as one study reports, "is a direct correlation between time spent each week in meetings and an employee's desire to find another job."[8] Studies and our own observations suggest several explanations for why so many people dread meetings:[9]

- The meeting was unnecessary.
- Members arrived late or left early.
- The meeting was too long and wasted time.
- The meeting's goal was unclear.
- The meeting failed to use or follow an agenda.
- The meeting used an agenda that had too many items on it.
- There was not enough prior notice or time to prepare.
- There were too many people at the meeting.
- The right people did not attend or were not invited.
- The meeting was held at the wrong time or place.
- The chairperson was ineffective.

- There was too much political pressure to conform or take sides.
- The meeting ended without accomplishing anything.
- Members failed to follow up on tasks after the meeting.

Meetings also fail because we take them for granted. Too often, we resign ourselves to attending unproductive meetings rather than trying to improve them. A survey conducted by Donald Kirkpatrick, professor emeritus at the University of Wisconsin, revealed that effective meetings exhibit several critical characteristics:[10]

- The chairperson has a clear goal and prepares an agenda.
- The chairperson effectively controls the meeting.
- Group members actively participate in the meeting.
- The chairperson provides sufficient advance notice of a meeting.
- Group members prepare for the meeting.

You should not dread the inevitable bad meeting. Rather, you and your group can and should take responsibility for contributing to a positive and productive meeting experience. Organizational psychology researcher Steven Rogelberg and his colleagues point out the importance of learning how to lead effective meetings:

Leaders are stewards of their employees' time. Given the sheer amount of time spent in meetings compounded by the number of attendees, it is imperative that future leaders become highly aware of and sensitive to how well they leverage, manage, and participate in meetings.[11]

Planning and Chairing Meetings

The success or failure of a meeting largely depends on good planning. One study found that careful planning can prevent at least 20 minutes of wasted time for each hour of a group's meeting.[12] Planning a meeting is not something you do a few minutes before the meeting takes place. In some cases, a critical meeting requires weeks of preparation and planning to make sure that it achieves its goal.

Questions About Meetings

Of all the reasons so many people criticize and dread meetings, "The meeting was unnecessary" topped the list. Before spending hours preparing for a meeting, make sure your group needs to meet. Use the answers to the following questions to guide the planning process.

- Why are we meeting?
- Who should attend the meeting?
- When should we meet?
- Where should we meet?
- What materials do we need?

Why Are We Meeting?   The best way to avoid wasting time or frustrating group members is to be sure you need a meeting. Is an immediate decision or response needed? Are group input and interaction critical? Are members prepared to discuss the topic? What is the purpose of the meeting?

In addition to making sure you need a meeting, make sure everyone understands whether the meeting's specific purpose is to share information, provide training, and/or solve problems.[13]

- **Information-Giving Meeting**—provides the chairperson or a member the opportunity to present important information to everyone else.
- **Information-Getting Meeting**—provides an opportunity for members to provide reports or briefings to the chairperson and other members.
- **Instructional Meeting**—provides members with training in a specific skill or knowledge area.
- **Problem-Solving Meeting**—provides an opportunity for all members to participate in solving a problem and/or making a decision.

In many situations, a memo, fax, email, voicemail message, or one-to-one conversation may accomplish the goal more effectively than a meeting. A survey of senior and middle managers reported "that phone calls, memos, emails, or voicemails could have replaced 25% of the meetings" they attend.[14] In other situations, however, a meeting is the most effective and efficient way to inform and interact with a group of people.

The most important step in planning a meeting is defining its goal as clearly as possible. A meeting's goal is not the same as its subject. The subject is the topic of the discussion. The goal identifies the desired outcome. For example, if an executive calls her assistant and says, "Call a staff meeting next Thursday at 2:00 P.M.," the assistant may ask, "What will the meeting be about?" "Employer-provided day care," the executive replies. Has the

Remember This

"A clear purpose is the first step in an effective and successful meeting."[15]

executive revealed the goal of the meeting? No. We only know that the subject of the meeting is employer-provided day care. If the executive had said, "We need to determine whether our employer-provided day-care system needs expansion," we would know the purpose or goal of the meeting.

Who Should Attend the Meeting? The membership of many groups is predetermined. However, if a task does not require input from everyone or if it needs the expertise of only certain people, you should select participants who can make a significant contribution and who have a stake in the outcome of the meeting. Consider the following criteria when determining who should attend a meeting:[16]

- Will the member contribute useful information or insights during the discussion?
- Will the member be an active participant in the meeting?
- Is the member committed to finding effective solutions?
- Is the member available at the designated meeting time?
- Do members represent diverse points of view?
- Are important decision makers and implementers represented?

Make sure that your group is a manageable size. Try to limit meetings to fewer than 12 participants; a group of five to seven members is ideal for problem-solving sessions. In many situations, the size of the group is predetermined. For instance, an organization's bylaws may require that a majority of the board members attend in order to conduct a vote.

When Should We Meet? The next step is deciding what day and time are best for the meeting. Should the meeting be in the morning, in the afternoon, after work hours, or during lunch? Generally, the best time to schedule a meeting is between 9:00 and 11:00 A.M. and between 1:30 and 3:30 P.M. The following considerations will help you determine an ideal meeting time for your group:[17]

- Avoid Friday afternoon meetings when energy and enthusiasm may be low.
- Avoid meetings immediately after lunch when members may be sluggish.
- Avoid early morning meetings that are difficult for members to arrive to on time.
- Avoid scheduling group meetings near holidays or at the beginning or end of the week.

Meeting before lunch may be convenient and allows for some members to continue a discussion informally during their lunch.

Determine what time the meeting should begin *and* end. The optimal meeting length is 1 hour. If your meeting must run longer, schedule breaks every hour or hour and a half to give members a chance to stretch, get food or drinks, or visit the restroom.[18] When they return, they should be relaxed and ready to work when the meeting reconvenes.[19] If the task is complex, time-consuming, and difficult, you may need to schedule a series of meetings to achieve the group goal.

Contact group members to find out when they are available, and schedule the meeting at a time when the most essential and productive participants are free. If only a few can attend, the meeting will not be very productive and will waste the time of those who do show up.

Where Should We Meet?   Choose an appropriate location and room size for group meetings. The room should be large enough, clean, well lit, not too hot or cold, and furnished with comfortable chairs. In addition, look for a quiet meeting room where members cannot hear ringing phones and hall conversations. You may want to consider a "no cell phone or texting" rule as well. Although you may have little control over such features, do your best to provide a comfortable setting. Working in an attractive meeting room can make a group feel more important and valued.

What Materials Do We Need?   The most important item to prepare and distribute to a group prior to a meeting is an agenda, outlining what topics will be discussed and in what order. The chairperson should also distribute essential reading materials to every member and make sure that needed supplies and equipment, such as markers, paper, flip charts, projectors, or computers, are available to the participants.

Groups in Balance...

Choose Good Meeting Places

The location and quality of a meeting's setting can mean the difference between comfortable, attentive members who participate fully in a discussion and distracted members who must contend with disruptions or an uncomfortable room. For instance, business meetings typically occur in four types of locations, each with its own advantages and disadvantages.[20]

Business consultants Robert Heller and Tim Hindle point out that "the choice of location is vitally important to the success of a meeting. It is not only a question of comfort; participants must feel that the place is appropriate for the occasion."[21]

Types of Location	Advantages	Disadvantages
Leader's Office	Convenient; access to materials and resources; enhances the meeting's importance	Members may feel like "guests" rather than equals; subject to distractions
Member's Office	Convenient; access to materials and resources; boosts the member's status	Subject to distractions; may be a small cubicle with cramped seating
On-site Meeting Room	Avoids distractions of a working office; more spacious and comfortable than an office	Subject to interruptions; distant from materials and resources; may be time limits on use
Off-site Meeting Room	Eliminates most distractions; provides neutral territory; more attractive and comfortable	Costly in terms of room rental and travel time; distant from materials and resources

Preparing the Agenda

An **agenda** is an outline of the items for discussion at a meeting. A well-prepared agenda is an organizational tool—a road map that helps group members focus on a progression of tasks. When distributed ahead of time, it helps participants prepare for a meeting by telling them what to expect and what they will need to contribute. An agenda also provides a sense of continuity for a group—it tracks members' assignments and provides status checks for work in progress. After a meeting, you can use the agenda to assess the meeting's success by looking at how the group addressed each item.

When you are very busy or when a meeting is routine and predictable, preparing an agenda may seem like a waste of time. Just the opposite is true. Failure to plan and prepare an agenda denies a chairperson and a group one of the most powerful tools in meeting management.

Remember This

"A meeting without an agenda is like a search party without a map."[22]

Elements of an Agenda. Although the chairperson is responsible for preparing and distributing an agenda in advance of the meeting, member input can ensure that the agenda covers the topics that are important to the entire group. Figure 11.2 summarizes the elements of a traditional business meeting agenda.

Figure 11.2 Elements of a Business Agenda

Purpose of the Meeting	A clear statement of the meeting's objective and topic for discussion helps members prepare.
Names of Group Members	A list of all participants lets members know who will be attending.
Date, Time, and Place	The agenda clearly indicates the date, time, duration, and precise location of the meeting.
Call to Order	This is the point at which the chairperson officially begins the meeting.
Approval of the Agenda	This gives members an opportunity to correct or modify the agenda.
Approval of the Minutes	The minutes of the previous meeting are reviewed, revised if necessary, and approved by the group as an accurate representation of the last meeting's discussion.
Reports	Officers, individuals, or subcommittees report on the progress of their activities.
Unfinished Business	The agenda lists topics that require ongoing discussion or issues that the group was unable to resolve during the last meeting.
New Business	New discussion items are outlined and discussed in this section.
Announcements	Any items of information that the group needs to know but that do not require any discussion are announced.
Adjournment	The chairperson officially dismisses the participants and ends the meeting.

Many meetings do not follow the traditional sequence of business agenda items. The norms of a group and the goals of a meeting should determine the agenda's format. For example, if you schedule a meeting to address or solve a specific issue or problem, the agenda items may be in the form of questions (see Figure 11.3) rather than the key-word format of a more formal agenda.

Agenda questions should follow the problem-solving method the group decides to use. In addition to identifying the discussion topics, agenda items should include any information that will help group members prepare for the meeting. The following guidelines can improve meeting productivity:

- Note the amount of time it should take to complete a discussion item or action. This will let the group know the relative importance of the item and help to manage the time available for discussion.
- Identify how the group will deal with each item. Will the group share information, discuss an issue, and/or make a decision? Consider putting the phrases *For Information*, *For Discussion*, *For Decision*, and *For Implementation* next to appropriate agenda items.
- Include the name of members responsible for reporting information on a particular item or facilitating a portion of the discussion. Such assignments remind members to prepare for a specific topic or action item.

Figure 11.3   Sample Discussion Meeting Agenda

Recycling Task Force
November 6, 2012, 1:00 P.M. – 3:00 P.M.
Conference Room 4

Purpose: To recommend ways to increase the effectiveness of and participation in the company's recycling program.

I.   What is the goal of this meeting? What have we been asked to do?

II.   How effective is the company's current recycling effort?

III.   Why has the program lacked effectiveness and full participation?

IV.   What are the requirements or standards for an ideal program?
A. Level of Participation
B. Reasonable Cost
C. Physical Requirements
D. Legal Requirements

V.   What are the possible ways in which we could improve the recycling program?

VI.   What specific methods do we recommend for increasing the recycling program's effectiveness and level of participation?

VII.   How should the recommendations be implemented? Who or what groups should be charged with implementation?

Determine the Order of Items.   After selecting the agenda items, carefully consider the order for discussing each topic. When a group must discuss several different topics during a single meeting, put them in an order that will maximize productivity and group satisfaction:

- Begin the meeting with simple business items and easy-to-discuss issues.
- Reserve important and difficult items for the middle portion of the meeting.
- Use the last third of the meeting for easy discussion items that do not require difficult decisions.

This sequence provides the group with a sense of accomplishment before it launches into more complex, controversial issues. If a difficult but important decision takes more time than anticipated, the group may be able to deal with the remaining, less important items at the next meeting or via email. For example, when preparing an agenda for the monthly School Library Resources Committee meeting, Ron anticipates a lengthy and controversial discussion about purchasing new sex education books. He decides to begin the meeting by reviewing the schedule for library tours and then to devote a significant amount of meeting time to discussing the sex education books. The last item on the agenda is a discussion of plans to purchase foreign-language books, which the group can address at another meeting if time runs out.

Groups in Balance...

Avoid Meetingthink

In Chapter 8, "Conflict and Cohesion in Groups," we introduced the concept of *groupthink* which is the deterioration of group effectiveness as a consequence of in-group pressure.[23] After observing the negative outcomes of groupthink, communication professors and consultants Kelly Quintanilla and Shawn Wahl noticed that some groups make equally poor or disastrous decisions even though they have none of the preconditions or causes of groupthink: a volatile situation, high cohesiveness, or a structural flaw that inhibits progress. Quintanilla and Wahl identify what they call **meetingthink** to explain why group members often fail to think critically in meetings and, as a result, make faulty decisions.[24] Recognizing and trying to avoid the conditions that lead to meetingthink can help you and your group avoid its destructive consequences. Quintanilla and Wahl describe three contributory reasons why group members suspend critical thinking in meetings:

- *Deceitful Leadership.* The leader falsely claims he or she will involve members in the decision-making process. Group members soon realize "that their opinions, ideas, and thoughts are not valued, so they remain silent during meetings."[25]

- *Information Overload.* Too much information burdens the group and prevents members from concentrating on or understanding the issues in the meeting. "Overloaded group members may withhold valuable input because they fear it will somehow lead to more work."[26]

- *Poorly Run Meetings.* There may be no agenda to guide the group and member participation. The meeting may go too long; the leader or influential members may be doing all the talking.[27]

What can you and your group do to avoid meetingthink? The answer only *appears* simple: Run a good meeting. Plan the meeting and notify members well in advance so they can be well prepared, too. Prepare, use, and stick to a clear and realistic agenda. Seek an appropriate balance between conflict and cohesion, between leadership and followership, and between structure and spontaneity. If you are the group leader, facilitate the discussion; don't dominate it. Encourage participation and constructive disagreement. Welcome new or competing ideas but also question them, challenge them, and insist on evidence to back them up.

Chairing the Meeting

If you are chairing a meeting, you have tremendous influence over, and responsibility for, the success of the meeting. In addition to conducting the meeting, you may also create the agenda, schedule the meeting, distribute the minutes, and follow up or implement decisions after the meeting is over. Effective chairpersons facilitate productive discussions by making sure that they have fulfilled their responsibilities prior to, during, and after the meeting (see Figure 11.4).

Prior to a meeting, the chairperson should notify every group member, preferably in writing. The announcement should include a clear statement of the meeting's goal; a list of pre-meeting

Figure 11.4   Chairperson's Tasks

Pre-Meeting	During Meeting	Post-Meeting
• Notify members	• Begin on time	• Evaluate the meeting
• Distribute the agenda	• Delegate minutes	• Distribute minutes
• Distribute materials	• Follow the agenda	• Monitor assigned tasks
• Remind members	• Facilitate discussion	
• Prepare for discussion	• Provide closure	

responsibilities (such as reading a report in advance or preparing recommendations); and the time, location, and duration of the meeting. In addition, send group members all materials needed for the discussion, including a preliminary agenda, in advance. Check with all members to confirm that they plan to attend and send a brief reminder before the meeting.

During meetings, effective chairpersons "balance strength with sensitivity; they balance knowing where they want the meeting to go with allowing the group to sometimes take it way off course; they balance having something to say with the restraint to say nothing; they assume the role of traffic cop in discussions without coming across with stifling authority."[28]

The agenda is your guide for conducting the discussion in an orderly manner. Begin on time, distribute an up-to-date agenda, and determine who will record the minutes. Take attendance and make sure the recorder includes the results in the minutes. Ask the group to review the agenda and make any needed revisions. Then take up each of the agenda items in order. Refrain from dominating the meeting. Your first priority is facilitating the group's discussion.

At the end of a meeting, the chairperson should briefly summarize meeting accomplishments and identify items that still need attention and action. Delegate assignments with deadlines to specific members. All group members should clearly understand the follow-up tasks for which they are responsible. If the group plans to schedule another meeting, ask for agenda suggestions and, if possible, set the date, time, and place of the next meeting.

The 3M Meeting Management Team describes the critical role of the chairperson as "a delicate balancing act" in which chairpersons must

> ...influence the group's thinking—not dictate it. They must encourage participation but discourage domination of the discussion by any single member. They must welcome ideas but also question them, challenge them, and insist on evidence to back them up. They must control the meeting but take care not to overcontrol it.[29]

 ## Groups in Balance...

Pace the Meeting

There may be nothing worse than sitting through a meeting that moves too slowly, strays from the agenda, or lasts too long. A good chairperson allows enough time for everyone to participate but still ends the meeting on time. Management consultant Barbara Streibel points out that "one of the key characteristics of a successful meeting is productivity or, at least, progress."[30] The following strategies can help keep your meetings moving at a comfortable pace:[31]

- Start the meeting on time and stick to the agenda.
- Don't waste time reviewing the earlier discussion for latecomers.

- Place a time limit on each agenda item.
- Stay focused on the meeting's goal.
- End the meeting on time or schedule another meeting to discuss unfinished business.

One study found more than 90 percent of attendees admit to daydreaming in meetings, 73 percent have brought other work, and 39 percent have fallen asleep.[32] However, in a well-planned and skillfully chaired meeting, group members are so involved, they focus their attention and energy on the discussion.

Adapting to Member Behavior

A well-planned meeting, clear agenda, and skilled chairperson are prerequisites for a productive meeting. However, none of these elements prepares a group for the challenging mix of member behaviors. In previous chapters, we address how member needs, personalities, and communication styles affect group interaction. Here, we examine specific behaviors that can distract members, disrupt a meeting, or lead to misunderstandings.

Dealing with Disruptive Behavior

A carefully planned meeting can fail if members' behavior disrupts the group process. Group members should address such behavior rather than assuming that the chairperson can or will resolve the problem. In *How to Make Meetings Work,* Michael Doyle and David Straus write that "dealing with these problem people is like walking a tightrope. You must maintain a delicate balance between protecting the group from the dominance of individual members while protecting individuals from being attacked by the group."[33] Here, we examine a few common types of disruptive behavior.

Nonparticipants.　You don't need full participation from all members all the time; the goal is a balanced group discussion over the course of a meeting. However, you should be concerned about **nonparticipants**, members who never or rarely contribute. Take some time to analyze why such members are not participating. Are they anxious or intimidated by group members with more experience or seniority? Are they unprepared, uninterested, or annoyed?

Do not put apprehensive or introverted members on the spot by forcing them to contribute before they are ready to do so. At the same time, provide opportunities for reluctant members to become involved in the discussion. When nonparticipants

Successful groups deal effectively with behaviors that distract members, disrupt a meeting, or lead to misunderstandings.

do contribute, respond positively to their input to demonstrate that you see the value in their ideas.

Texters.   Texting during meetings became a problem almost as quickly as texting technology became generally available. Although **texters** may believe they're not being disruptive, the fact is that group members preoccupied with checking and responding to their messages are not listening effectively, nor are they fully engaged in the meeting. In addition to distracting other members, texting is rude because it sends an implied message that whatever a member is texting about is more important than the meeting. Groups can establish ground rules at the beginning of a meeting that include no texting, talking on cell phones, or checking email during a meeting unless there is a true emergency. After the meeting, the chairperson should talk to members who violate these rules.

Loudmouths.   A member who talks more than others is not necessarily a problem. However, when a person talks so much that no one else gets a chance to speak, the group has a **loudmouth** problem and must respond appropriately. At first, allow loudmouths to state their ideas, and acknowledge that you understand their positions. It may be necessary to interrupt them to do so. Then shift your focus to other members or other issues by asking for alternative viewpoints. If a loudmouth continues to dominate, remind this person of the importance of getting input from everyone. The next time the group meets, you may want to assign the loudmouth the task of taking minutes as a way of shifting focus from talking to listening and writing.

Interrupters.   Sometimes group members are so preoccupied with their own thoughts and goals that they interrupt others whenever they have something to say. Although most **interrupters** are not trying to be rude, their impatience and excitement cause them to speak out while other members are still talking. When a group member continually interrupts others, it is time to interrupt the interrupter. Invite the interrupted member to finish speaking. A more assertive option is to intervene and say, "Let Mary finish her point first, and then we'll hear other viewpoints."

Whisperers.   A **whisperer** carries on confidential conversations with another group member during a meeting. The interference caused by whispering or snickering makes it hard for other members to listen and concentrate. It can also be very unnerving when members are unsure whether they are the target of the whispered comments. Directing eye contact toward such sideline conversations can make the offenders more aware of their disruptive behavior. If the behavior persists, ask the talkers to share their ideas with the group. This usually stops the behavior; it may also uncover issues that deserve discussion by the group as a whole.

Latecomers and Early Leavers.   **Latecomers** and **early leavers** disrupt meetings and annoy group members who have managed their time well enough to arrive on schedule and stay through the entire meeting. If you are the chairperson, start the meeting at the scheduled time. Do not waste meeting time by summarizing meeting business for the benefit of latecomers. Let them sit without participating until they have observed enough to contribute to the discussion. Rather than publicly reprimanding or embarrassing latecomers or early leavers, talk to them after the meeting about the importance of attending the entire meeting.

Remember This

"The more you make a practice of waiting for people, the more likely people will continue to arrive to meetings late."[34]

When you have to confront disruptive members, be sensitive and focus on the behavior rather than making personal attacks. Describe the behavior, suggest alternative behaviors, and indicate the consequences if the behavior continues. Don't overreact; your intervention can be more disruptive than the problem member's behavior. It is best to begin with the least confrontational approach and then work toward more direct methods as necessary.

Adapting to Differences

Very often, group members from different cultural, ethnic, and age groups do not share similar expectations about group roles and individual behavior in meetings. In some cultures, a young group member would never interrupt an older member; a new group member would not challenge a veteran member. In such cases, it is easy to interpret lack of participation as inattention or lack of interest, when, in fact, the group member is demonstrating a high degree of respect for its members.

At one college, the president appointed an advisory council to coordinate activities designed to improve the racial climate on campus. A member of the group reported the following observation:

> One council member was a former diplomat from a West African country. He rarely spoke, but when he did, he always began with a very formal "Madam Chairman." After that, he would deliver a three- to five-minute speech in which he would summarize the discussion and offer his opinion and recommendations. When he was finished, he would thank everyone for listening. At first, we didn't know how to respond. It was

Virtual Groups

Meeting in Cyberspace

In virtual groups, write Deborah Duarte and Nancy Snyder, "The right technical tools enhance our ability to share concepts, merge ideas, and use synergy to accomplish our group goals." At the same time, they emphasize, "Technology cannot make up for poor planning or ill-conceived meetings. In fact, it can make the situation worse."[35] Fortunately, many of the same principles that apply to planning a productive face-to-face meeting apply equally well to planning virtual meetings. Test your group's readiness to meet in cyberspace by checking off items on the following "to-do" list:

_____ 1. Does everyone know the meeting's goal?

_____ 2. Did all members get the agenda in advance, including notes on which discussion items will use any specialized technology?

_____ 3. Are only the members who need to participate invited?

_____ 4. Is the group small enough to allow everyone a chance to contribute actively?

_____ 5. Is the group meeting at the most convenient time for the most members?

_____ 6. Is the group using the most appropriate technology for achieving the meeting's goal?

_____ 7. Does the group have access to the technology or facilities that support audioconferences, videoconferences, and text conferences?

_____ 8. Do all the members have compatible technology?

_____ 9. Are all members trained adequately on the chosen technologies?

_____ 10. Does someone always test the technology prior to the meeting?

so formal, so complex. Eventually we learned to expect at least one "speech" from this member. We learned to listen and respond to a very different style of participation. This member defined his role very formally and acted accordingly. Patience on the part of other participants helped the group understand, respect, and adapt to his style of participation.

Group members may represent different ages, genders, educational and work backgrounds, religions, political viewpoints, and cultures. All these elements can affect how well a meeting accomplishes its goals. Adapting to the diversity of group members involves understanding and accommodating differences while pursuing shared goals.

Preparing the Minutes

The **minutes** of a meeting are the written record of a group's discussion and actions during a meeting. The minutes record a group's discussions and decisions for those who attend a meeting and provide a way to communicate with those who did not attend. By looking through a group's minutes over a period of time, you can learn about the group's activities, measure how productive the group has been, learn about individual members' contributions to the group, and know whether group meetings tend to be formal or informal. Most important, minutes help prevent disagreement over what was decided in a previous meeting and what tasks individual members agreed to do.

Selecting a Recorder

The chairperson is ultimately responsible for the accuracy and distribution of the minutes. During the meeting, however, the chairperson must be free to conduct the meeting. It makes more sense to assign the task of taking minutes to another group member. The group may designate a **recorder** or secretary to take minutes at every meeting, or members can take turns. Remember that, regardless of who takes the minutes, the chairperson is responsible for checking, editing, and distributing copies to all group members.

Determining What Information to Include

For the most part, the minutes should follow the format of the agenda and include the following:

- Name of the group
- Date and place of the meeting
- Names of those attending
- Name of the person who chaired the meeting
- Names of absent members

CLOSE TO HOME   JOHN McPHERSON

As soon as Mrs. Felster began to read the minutes of the last meeting, the board members knew she was not going to work out as the new secretary.

- The exact time the meeting was called to order
- The exact time the meeting was adjourned
- Name of the person preparing the minutes
- Summary of the group's discussion and decisions, using agenda items as headings
- Specific action items

An **action item** is a task assigned to individual members for completion after the meeting. An action item includes the person's name, the assignment, and the deadline. For example, an action item might look like this: "Action: Mark Smith will review and bring samples of good website designs to the next meeting." Underline or italicize action items in the minutes to make it easier to refer back to them when reviewing the group's progress.

Taking Minutes

Well-prepared minutes are brief and accurate. They are not a word-for-word record of everything that every member said. To be useful, they must briefly summarize the discussion. These guidelines can help you take useful minutes:

- Write clear statements that briefly and accurately summarize the main ideas and actions.
- Word decisions, motions, action items, and deadlines exactly as the group makes them in order to avoid future disagreements and misunderstandings.

Ethics in Groups

Use Discretion When Taking Minutes

The person charged with taking minutes has an ethical obligation to exercise good judgment when deciding what to include in the minutes and what to omit. Everything included in the minutes must accurately reflect the discussion of major issues and group decisions. At the same time, a recorder must balance the need for accuracy with discretion.

There are times when a group does not want the details of its discussion recorded in the minutes. For instance, groups discussing sensitive legal or personnel issues often keep information confidential. If the agenda includes confidential items, the chairperson should remind members that some information should not leave the group and the recorder should not include details of some the discussion in the minutes.[36]

During a meeting, group members may make comments that should not appear in the minutes. For example, a group that vents its frustration with a boss will not want to read the following in the minutes: "The

group agreed that Dan is unreasonable and insensitive." Groups often express complaints in a meeting. Including such comments in the minutes can stifle open communication and is not necessary for making the meeting minutes useful.

These guidelines can help you determine when to include information and when to leave it out:

- Report the facts and all sides of a discussion accurately.
- Never insert your own personal opinions.
- Be discreet. If the group determines that a portion of the discussion should be "off the record," you should honor that decision.
- When in doubt, ask the group if an issue should be included or how to word it for the minutes.
- Always keep in mind that the minutes are often the only record of the meeting and that individuals outside the group may read them.

- If you are not sure about what to include in the minutes, ask the group for clarification. Many workplaces, teams, and organizations have examples in their files of past minutes that can be used as a model.
- Obtain a copy of the agenda and any reports that were presented to attach to the final copy of the minutes. These documents become part of the group record along with the minutes. The minutes may also include links to electronic formats of important documents and reports.

Immediately after the meeting—or as soon as possible—prepare the minutes for distribution. The longer you delay, the more difficult it will be to remember the details of the meeting. After preparing the minutes, give them to the chairperson for review. When a group officially approves the minutes, they are final and become the official record of the meeting. Figure 11.5 shows a sample of informal minutes.

Figure 11.5   Sample of Informal Minutes

Domestic Violence Class Discussion Group Meeting
February 10, 2012, in Library Conference Room 215

Present: Gabriella Hernandez (chairperson), Eric Beck,
Terri Harrison, Will Mabry, Tracey Tibbs

Absent: Lance Nickens

Meeting began at 2:00 P.M.
Group Topic: The group discussed whether emotional and verbal abuse should be included in the project. Since we don't have much time to do our presentation, we decided to limit the topic to physical abuse only.

Research Assignments: Since the assignment is due in two weeks, we decided to divide the issue into different topics and research them on our own.

    Action: Eric will research why people stay in abusive relationships.
    Action: Gabriella will research the effects on the children.
    Action: Terri will find statistics and examples of the seriousness of the problem.
    Action: Will is going to find out why and how the abuse happens.
    Action: Tracey will find out what resources are available in the area for victims.

Members will report on their research at the next meeting.

Absent Members: Lance has not been to the last two class meetings. We don't know if he is still going to participate in the group. *Action: Gabriella will call Lance.*

Class Presentation: We need to think of creative ways to make a presentation to the class. The group decided to think about this and discuss it at the next meeting.

Next Meeting: Our next meeting will be at 2:30 on Tuesday, February 14th, in the same place. *Action: Terri will reserve the room.*

The meeting ended at 3:15 P.M.
(Meeting notes taken by Tracey Tibbs)

Using Parliamentary Procedure

A detailed guide to parliamentary procedure is provided in the Web chapter accompanying this text, available at www.pearsonhighered.com/engleberg. In this chapter, we describe the basic principles behind parliamentary procedure.

Parliamentary procedure is a set of formal rules used to determine the will of the majority through fair and orderly discussion and debate. Today's parliamentary procedure has evolved from the rules of order used for centuries in Britain's parliament, which is where the name originated. For group members who are new to parliamentary procedure, learning and following the rules can be confusing and intimidating. Not only are there hundreds of rules, but the language of parliamentary procedure also has a unique vocabulary, including statements such as "Mr. Chairman, I call the previous question" or "Madam President, I rise to a point of order."

Many organizations and associations specify in their constitution or bylaws that parliamentary procedure must be used to conduct meetings. *Robert's Rules of Order* is considered the "parliamentary procedure bible" by many organizations. First published in the 1870s and updated periodically, this book provides rules that ensure reasonable and civil debate as well as timely group decisions that are accepted by supporters and opponents alike. This time-honored system ensures that group decisions express the will of the majority while also protecting the rights of minority members.[37]

When groups use parliamentary procedure, only official group members may participate and vote. For example, when a neighborhood association meets, each residential unit (each home, apartment, or condo) has only one vote, regardless of how many people live in that unit. On a corporate board, however, every member has a vote unless the company's constitution or bylaws specify different categories of membership. In addition, there are rules governing the number of members needed to hold a meeting as well as the responsibilities of key players.

Many organizations and associations specify that parliamentary procedure must be used to conduct meetings. Here, the newly elected mayor of a small city in New York state presides over the organizational meeting for the city council. How does parliamentary procedure help groups make decisions that express the will of the majority while also protecting the rights of minority members?

Most groups that use parliamentary procedure require a specific percent of members to attend a meeting in order to conduct business as well as certain "players" to help run the meeting: a chairperson, a clerk, and, in some cases, an official parliamentarian.

Before learning the rules of parliamentary procedure, you should understand its guiding principles. In this way, you can appreciate why this procedure continues as "the law of the land" in many meetings. *Robert's Rules of Order, Newly Revised* claims that the rules of parliamentary procedure are "constructed upon a careful balance of the rights of persons or subgroups within an organization's...total membership."[38] These guiding principles form the basis for all parliamentary rules:

- *Majority Will.* The group accepts the will of the majority. In the case of critical or controversial issues, decisions may require a two-thirds vote rather than a simple majority.
- *Minority Rights.* The group protects the rights of all members by guaranteeing everyone the right to speak. At the same time, parliamentary rules ensure that, in the end, the majority prevails.
- *Balanced Discussion.* The group guarantees the rights of all members to speak on different sides of an issue by balancing participation between frequent and infrequent contributors as well as between members who support and those who oppose a proposal.
- *Orderly Progress.* The group follows an approved agenda that promotes orderly business while also allowing flexibility to make decisions.

Many groups do not use formal parliamentary procedure to conduct business or achieve their goals. At the same time, there is great value in borrowing the basic principles of parliamentary procedure to guide the deliberations of a group and balance majority and minority interests. When everyone has an equal opportunity to speak, and discussion follows an orderly progression, a sense of fairness is more likely to prevail.

Evaluating the Meeting

To determine the effectiveness of meetings and identify areas for improvement, groups should evaluate their meetings. There are a number of ways to do so:

- Throughout the meeting, the chairperson may ask for comments and suggestions before moving on to the next item. This feedback allows the group to modify its behavior and improve its interaction when discussing the next item.
- At the end of the meeting, the chairperson can briefly summarize his or her perceptions of the meeting and ask for comments and suggestions from the group before adjourning.
- After the meeting, the chairperson should ask members for their comments and suggestions for improving the group's next meeting.
- Before adjourning a meeting, the chairperson may distribute a Post-Meeting Reaction form to all members.

A **Post-Meeting Reaction (PMR) form** is a questionnaire designed to assess the success of a meeting by collecting written reactions from participants. The chairperson should prepare the form in advance of the meeting, distribute it at the end of a meeting, and collect it before participants leave. A PMR form should ask questions about the discussion, the quantity and quality of group interactions, and the effectiveness of meeting procedures. Use group feedback to improve subsequent meetings. The sample PMR form in the assessment section at the end of this chapter contains typical questions for evaluating a meeting.

Theory in Groups

Chaos and Complexity Theories

Group meetings can be boring and/or exciting, simplistic and/or complex, orderly and/or chaotic. Watching a well-planned meeting underscores the role of group dialectics as members strive to find a *both/and* approach to accomplishing a variety of group goals. Chaos and complexity theories give us valuable scientific tools for analyzing group dynamics, particularly as applied to meetings.

Chaos Theory claims "that although certain behaviors in natural systems are not predictable, there is a pattern to their randomness" that emerges over time.[39] In other words, you can never predict exactly what will happen in a meeting, but you can assume that most meetings will eventually share similar properties and processes.

Complexity Theory goes even further than a search for patterns; it examines three characteristics of complex systems—order, complexity, and chaos. Mitchell Waldrop, author of *Complexity: The Emerging Science at the Edge of Order and Chaos,* explains Complexity Theory with an analogy that contrasts and compares order, complexity, and chaos to different states of water: ice, liquid, and steam. Order is like ice—frozen and solid. Chaos is like steam—in constant motion and insubstantial. Complexity, however, has the properties of liquid—fluid and relatively controllable. Waldrop also uses the example of national economies

to illustrate order (economic stagnation), chaos (economic collapse), and a complex economy (strong *and* flexible).[40]

What, you may ask, does this have to do with planning and conducting meetings? Throughout this textbook and particularly in this chapter, we emphasize the need for groups to balance dialectic tensions such as group goals↔individual goals, structure↔spontaneity, and conflict↔cohesion. Meetings require a judicious mix of such opposites. McClure's analysis of leadership gives us an example of this *both/and* approach: "You can either contain a group or perturb [agitate and arouse] it."[41] Consider what happens in meetings. Group members work best when they have a clear goal for the meeting, but they also need the freedom to change that goal if needed. Group agendas provide a clear structure for group work, but they also constrict groups if they prohibit or restrict spontaneity. Genuine cohesiveness relies on conflict to settle differences and find common solutions. The seeming rigidity of parliamentary procedures may obscure rules designed to guarantee minority rights and opinions.

Effective meetings walk a fine line that balances order and chaos. Enlightened group members understand that too much order or too much chaos stifles group progress. A *both/and* approach allows a group to make first-rate decisions and progress toward its common goal.

Summary Study Guide

Meetings, Meetings, Meetings
- The primary characteristics of a meeting are a schedule, a structure, and a designated chairperson.
- When meetings are well planned and well conducted, they build strong alliances, confer a sense of control, and give members a voice in decision making.

Planning and Chairing Meetings
- For an effective meeting, decide the meeting's purpose, who should attend, where and when to meet, and what materials members need in order to be prepared and productive.
- An agenda is an outline of the items to be discussed and the tasks to be accomplished at a meeting.
- The chairperson is responsible for planning, preparing for, conducting, and following up a meeting.

Adapting to Member Behavior
- Common types of disruptive group behavior include member labels such as nonparticipants, texters, loudmouths, interrupters, whisperers, latecomers, and early leavers.

- Meetings should be adapted to the diverse needs and expectations of members.
- Virtual meetings require agendas and minutes as well as special adaptation to group size, member availability, and choice of technology.

Preparing the Minutes
- The minutes of a meeting are the written record of the group's discussion, decisions, and actions.

Using Parliamentary Procedure
- Parliamentary procedure equips groups with a set of formal rules to determine the will of the majority through fair and orderly discussion and debate.

Evaluating the Meeting
- Groups can learn from experience by evaluating meetings and using such feedback to improve future meetings.
- A Post-Meeting Reaction (PMR) form can help a group analyze the quality of a discussion, the quantity and quality of group interactions, and the effectiveness of meeting procedures.

Group Work

Disrupting Disruptive Behavior

Directions: Read the following descriptions of disruptive meeting behaviors. In the space provided, describe two strategies you could use to deal effectively with each behavioral problem before, during, *or* after a meeting.

The Broken Record: Brings up the same point or idea again and again. Regardless of what other members say, the broken record keeps "singing the same song."

1. _____

   _____

   _____

2. _____

   _____

   _____

The Grenade: Sits quietly and rarely participates but becomes more and more annoyed or angry as the meeting continues. Finally, the grenade cannot hold it in any more and explodes into a tirade of harsh criticism.

1. _____

   _____

   _____

2. _____

   _____

   _____

The Know-It-All: Uses age, seniority, credentials, and experience to argue a point. Know-It-Alls declare, "I've been here for 20 years and I know this won't work," or "I'm the only one here with an accounting degree, so you'd better listen to me."

1. _____

   _____

   _____

2. _____

   _____

   _____

The Backseat Driver: Keeps telling everyone what they should do or should have done. "If we'd met earlier this week, we could have avoided this problem," or "I would have let everyone read the report rather than summarizing it."

1. _____

   _____

   _____

2. _____

   _____

   _____

The Attacker: Launches personal attacks on other group members or the chairperson. Purposely zeros in on and criticizes the ideas and opinions of others.

1. _____

   _____

   _____

2. _____

   _____

   _____

The Headshaker: Nonverbally disagrees or disapproves in a dramatic and disruptive manner. Shakes head, rolls eyes, groans and sighs, taps on the table, or madly scribbles notes after someone has said something.

1. _____

   _____

   _____

2. _____

   _____

   _____

Group Assessment

Post-Meeting Reaction (PMR) Form

Directions: After a selected meeting, complete the following PMR form by circling the number that best represents your answer to each question. After compiling the answers from all participants, including the chairperson, use the results as a basis for improving future meetings.

1. How clear was the goal of the meeting?

   Unclear   1   2   3   4   5   Clear

2. How useful was the agenda?

   Useless   1   2   3   4   5   Useful

3. Was the meeting room comfortable?

   Uncomfortable   1   2   3   4   5   Comfortable

4. How prepared were group members for the meeting?

   Unprepared   1   2   3   4   5   Well prepared

5. Did everyone have an equal opportunity to participate in the discussion?

   Limited opportunity   1   2   3   4   5   Ample opportunity

6. Did members listen effectively and consider different points of view?

   Ineffective listening   1   2   3   4   5   Effective listening

7. How would you describe the overall climate of the meeting?

   Hostile   1   2   3   4   5   Friendly

8. Were assignments and deadlines made clear by the end of the meeting?

   Unclear   1   2   3   4   5   Clear

9. Did the meeting begin and end on time? Did the group use its meeting time efficiently?

   Unproductive   1   2   3   4   5   Productive

10. How would you rate this meeting overall?

    Unsuccessful   1   2   3   4   5   Successful

Additional Comments:

chapter **12**

Technology and Virtual Groups

Chapter Outline

The Nature of Virtual Groups
FTF Versus CMC
Synchronous and Asynchronous Communication

Synchronous Groupware
Audioconferences
Videoconferences
Textconferences
Group Decision Support Systems

Asynchronous Groupware
Email
Bulletin Boards

Group Diversity and the Digital Divide
Age
Geography
Income

Case Study

Virtual Misunderstanding

A project manager has organized a conference call with a writer and designer to discuss a missed deadline for a sales brochure. Ellen, the writer, is listening on speakerphone at her desk. She is also doing unrelated work on her laptop as she participates in the audioconference. Charlie, the designer, is speaking on a phone line. A partial transcript of the audioconference follows:

Manager: Listen, how're you guys doing?

Ellen: Ah, okay.

Manager: Listen, you guys. We have got to get that brochure finished by next Friday for the sales meeting. I did not get final graphics from you, Charlie, and I did not get the final edited copy from you, Ellen.

Ellen: I have the edited copy. I left you a voice mail that I had it ready. I was waiting for graphics from Charlie, so there is nothing I could do.

Manager: Did you contact Charlie?

Ellen: Yes, I left him emails and voice mail—and he never got back to me.

Manager: Charlie?

Charlie: Yeah…ah…uh…no…ah, I, uh…What'd you do? Change some more stuff?

Manager: No, Charlie. Did you get the communication from Ellen?

Charlie: No, ah, I'm sorry. I haven't looked at my email. What did you change…I thought we were done. I thought we had finished.

Ellen: Why don't you check your email?

Charlie: Because the last email I did check said we were done. You were finishing up the copy that you…and the graphics were fine.

Manager: Okay, there must have been a misunderstanding.

Charlie: I guess.

Manager: We had a slight change in direction for the concept for the brochure. We talked about this at our last conference call. I need to go ahead and get the final graphics from you, and I need to get the final copy from Ellen.

Ellen: I have the final copy.

Charlie: Did you send me the final copy?

Ellen: Yes, I did!

Charlie: Is it more copy than there was before?

Ellen: No, it's the same amount.

Manager: What I need you to do, Charlie, is send off a draft to me by 9 o'clock tomorrow.

Charlie: By 9 A.M. tomorrow.

Manager: Yes.

Charlie: Ah…I…

Ellen: Don't count on it.

Charlie: I heard that.

After listening to more sniping between the writer and designer, the manager interrupts.

Manager: We set up this project in this fashion because you guys wanted the flexibility of working from home. This is the concern that we had—that we were going to have communication difficulties. If you guys cannot sort this out, then you're either going to have to come in for a face-to-face or I'm going to have to find another designer and another editor—and I don't want to do that because you guys are the best I've got.

The manager's message gets both Ellen's and Charlie's attention rather quickly. They come up with a plan for getting the design and copy to the manager by 9 A.M. the next day. The audioconference concludes as follows.

Manager: Do both of you have each other's cell phone numbers, so if there are any questions you can get them resolved?

Ellen: I have Charlie's.

Charlie: Yeah, yeah. I've got hers.

Manager: I expect that brochure tomorrow at 9 o'clock. We'll have a conference call at 9:30 tomorrow morning!

Charlie: Oh? You mean 9 A.M.? In the morning? Nah, I'm just kidding you.

Manager: Yeah, that's why we love you. Okay, thanks guys. 'Bye.

Virtual Miscommunication

The Group Project

Before you read any further, visit Pearson's MySearchLab website and watch this case study's video, "Virtual Miscommunication." You may also want to watch the short video "The Group Project," which illustrates Chapter 12 concepts. Each video comes with a set of study questions to keep in mind as you read this chapter.

The Nature of Virtual Groups

Whether you love it or hate it, we live in a wired society. You can connect to the world electronically at home, at work, or in your favorite Wi-Fi–enabled coffee shop using your cell phone, laptop computer, and a host of other devices. You can communicate with friends, family, shopping outlets, and colleagues by text, photo, video, or voice throughout the day—and night. You also can use these same technologies to work in groups.[1] But before claiming bragging rights about the wonders of U.S. technology, let's consider where we stand compared to other countries. In terms of the number of online subscribers per 100 inhabitants, Denmark, the Netherlands, Norway, Switzerland, Iceland, and South Korea are more wired than the United States, and so is our northern neighbor Canada.[2] The United States can no longer claim high status as an influential leader in a wired world.

As we've noted in other chapters, **virtual groups** rely on technology to communicate, often across time, distance, and organizational boundaries. Thousands of miles and several time zones may separate virtual group members, while others may work in the same room using technology to do groupwork.

Virtual teams are everywhere. Approximately 75 percent of U.S. companies allow employees to work remotely—and that number is expected to increase significantly in the next few years.[3] A 2010 survey of employees of multinational corporations found that 64 percent were part of a virtual team. Eighty percent of these virtual groups included members in different locations, and 63 percent had group members in other countries.[4] Diverse and geographically distributed teams have become the norm for businesses and governments around the world.[5] In fact, research concludes that "with rare exceptions all organizational teams are virtual to some extent."[6]

In the preface to *CyberMeeting: How to Link People and Technology in Your Organization*, James Creighton and James Adams emphasize the need to balance the advantages and disadvantages of using technology for working in groups. On the one hand, they note that organizations spend billions of dollars "connecting their employees through technology that will permit collaboration and electronic participation in meetings." On the other hand, "hundreds of millions of those dollars will be wasted chasing fads and installing technology that people will use to work the same way they worked before the technology was installed."[7]

A study in the journal *Small Group Research* identifies several characteristics of an *effective* virtual group, including:

- adequate resources (funding, people, skills, etc.) to achieve its goal
- appropriate and effective information technology and support
- adequate electronic communication skills training
- adequate remote coordination skills training
- members who serve as role models so others can learn from them in day-to-day interactions[9]

In this chapter, we examine challenges that arise when you work in virtual groups. As you read, keep in mind that the "convenience of electronic communication does not diminish the importance of face-to-face meetings. Relying totally on electronic communication often diminishes the bonding and synergy that happens when team members meet and work face-to-face."[10]

> ## Remember This
> "The survival of virtual teams depends on active and effective communication...."[8]

Virtual Groups

A Chapter-by-Chapter Review

Every chapter of this textbook includes a Virtual Groups feature. A review of their titles underscores the ways in which virtual groups have become an integral part of group work. As you prepare to work in a virtual group, review the material in the following chapters:

- Chapter 1: Using Technology to Communicate (synchronous and asynchronous communication)
- Chapter 2: Developmental Tasks (adapting to the forming, storming, norming, performing, and adjourning stages)
- Chapter 3: Confidence with Technology (computer anxiety and confidence)
- Chapter 4: Cultural Dimensions in Cyberspace (adapting to cultural dimensions)

- Chapter 5: Sharing Leadership Functions (leading virtual groups)
- Chapter 6: Expressing Emotions Online (using emoticons appropriately)
- Chapter 7: Listening Online (active listening versus faked attention)
- Chapter 8: Conflict in Cyberspace (politeness and civil behavior)
- Chapter 9: Adapting Decision-Making and Problem-Solving Methods (choosing appropriate technologies)
- Chapter 10: Think Critically about the Internet (testing Internet sources)
- Chapter 11: Meeting in Cyberspace (planning and conducting virtual meetings)

FTF Versus CMC

Academic researchers use the acronyms **FTF** and **CMC** as shorthand for describing face-to-face group meetings and groups working in computer-mediated communication environments. Much of their research examines how efficiently and effectively these two types of groups work to achieve their goals.

Many businesses, government agencies, and organizations embrace CMC groups because they save travel time and money by connecting geographically dispersed members, from as far away as other continents to as close as networked offices in one building. A study of *Meetings in America* found that "saving time and money" was the number-one reason for supporting virtual work and groups.[11] Ironically and despite corporate enthusiasm for virtual groups, face-to-face interaction has become more indispensable than ever. A study by Harvard economist Edward Glaeser notes that "...faxes, email, and videoconferencing were all supposed to eliminate the need for face-to-face-meetings, yet business travel has soared over the last 20 years.... [M]illions of years of evolution have made us into machines for learning from the people next to us."[12]

Are CMC groups as effective as FTF groups? Here's what some of the research says. When group tasks are complex, FTF groups usually perform better than groups using computer-mediated communication. However, when a group task is simple, CMC groups do just as well as FTF groups.[13] Depending on the complexity and nature of the task, CMC groups are less efficient than FTF groups in terms of communication effectiveness. They also use more time than FTF groups to complete their tasks.[14] CMC groups are simply more challenging to coordinate, which may explain why these groups are sometimes less efficient.[15] The bottom line is this: "More often than not, face-to-face groups outperformed computer mediated groups."[16] Even so, virtual groups are here to stay, making it imperative that we learn how to work effectively and manage virtual group work.

If possible, schedule an FTF meeting when a virtual group is formed, especially if members do not already know each other or are unfamiliar with the necessary technology.[17] An FTF meeting allows group members to get acquainted, understand the virtual group's protocols, and learn how to use technology effectively.

Face-to-Face Communication	Computer-Mediated Communication

Synchronous and Asynchronous Communication

As we note in Chapter 1, "Introduction to Group Communication," when group members use technology to interact simultaneously in real time, they engage in **synchronous communication**. Conference calls, videoconferences, and Internet chat rooms are examples of synchronous communication media. Because synchronous communication is spontaneous and dynamic, it works best for brainstorming and problem solving.

Theory in Groups

Media Richness and Media Synchronicity Theories

Media Richness Theory contends that when you use more communication channels (thereby making your communication "richer"), you will be more successful communicating with others. Thus, face-to-face groups are often more successful because members can (1) see and respond instantly to feedback, (2) use nonverbal communication to clarify and reinforce messages, (3) use a natural speaking style, and (4) convey personal feelings and emotions to other group members. In contrast, forms of computer-mediated communication such as email are quite the opposite: They only rely on the printed words and, in some cases, illustrations for sharing meaning.[18]

In short, FTF communication engages more of our senses and sensibilities than any other form of communication. Thus, it is important to keep in mind that media richness can make the difference between interpreting a comment as harsh criticism and perceiving it as constructive feedback.[19]

A more recent theory, **Media Synchronicity Theory,** expands Media Richness Theory by examining how group needs, group development, and member characteristics interact with media richness. It claims that "the key to effective use of media is to match the media capabilities to the fundamental communication processes required to perform the task." In other words, just because FTF may be the richest medium, it may not be the best way to achieve a group goal given differences in group development and the nature of the task. For example, a group that has worked together successfully on multiple projects may be more effective and efficient using email than by meeting face-to-face. However, the members of a newly formed group may need to work in FTF settings as they move through forming, storming, and norming before shifting to audioconferences or electronic meeting software to achieve their common goal.[20]

Asynchronous communication is the opposite of synchronous communication because, by definition, it does not take place in real time. During asynchronous communication, one person makes a statement and, for example, posts it online for the group to see. Group members, often at their convenience, look at the message and then post responses. Asynchronous communication does not require group members to hold a meeting. Instead, members read and respond to messages as their schedules permit. Email and bulletin boards are examples of asynchronous communication media. Figure 12.1 summarizes the advantages and disadvantages of these two types of virtual communication.

Figure 12.1 Advantages and Disadvantages of Synchronous and Asynchronous Communication

	Advantages	Disadvantages
Synchronous Communication	• Group cohesion and synergy • Spontaneous and dynamic interaction	• Typing speed is slower than speaking speed • Messages might be received out of order
Asynchronous Communication	• More time to compose responses • Facilitates document review and editing	• Lacks spontaneity • Linear rather than interactive

Groups in Balance...

Negotiate the Dialectics of Virtual Groups

Virtual groups experience the same dialectic tensions as face-to-face groups. The nature of virtual groups, however, can intensify dialectic tensions. Here, we examine two dialectics to illustrate some of the unique tensions in virtual groups: (1) conformity↔nonconformity and (2) conflict↔cohesion.

Psychologist Patricia Wallace explains that group interaction seems to intensify the viewpoints of individual group members and moves them toward extremes.[21] This tendency—known as **group polarization**—is quite strong in virtual groups because there are fewer nonverbal cues to moderate opinions and behavior. Thus, although the potential for flocking together with "birds of a feather" in virtual groups has advantages, it also "can lead to a false sense of security in one's point of view."[22] At the same time, virtual group members may feel more independent when contributing online because they cannot see one another's reactions. Virtual groups in balance understand that some level of group polarization can lead *to both* strong group agreement (conformity) *and* fruitful risk taking (nonconformity).

Virtual groups are often more successful in balancing conflict and cohesion because members feel more independent and are physically removed from the "dangers" of face-to-face conflict. Moreover, the content of messages in virtual groups tends to be "less controversial than is popularly believed: Conversations are more helpful and social than competitive. Interactive messages seem to be more humorous, contain more self-disclosure, display a higher preference for agreement and contain many more first-person-plural pronouns."[23] In short, virtual groups provide an environment that encourages *both* constructive conflict *and* genuine cohesion while avoiding the perils of false consensus and groupthink.

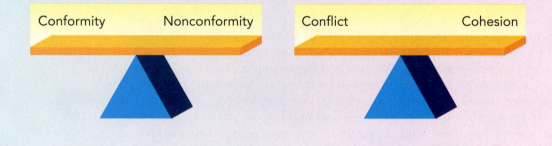

| Conformity | Nonconformity |

| Conflict | Cohesion |

Synchronous Groupware

The term **groupware** refers to computer-mediated methods and tools designed to support group collaboration, even though participants may not be together in either time or space.[24] Groupware combines two basic ideas: *group* + *ware*, or people + technology.[25] Synchronous groupware ranges from low-tech telephone conferences to high-tech electronic meeting systems. Here we offer guidelines for using voice-, video-, and text-based groupware as well as a meeting technology that combines all three types of virtual communication.

Audioconferences

When virtual groups use voice-only media to communicate, they engage in an **audioconference**. Audioconferences take two forms: conference calls (also known as teleconferences) and computer-based voice links. Conference calls only require a telephone with service that supports conference calling. Almost all business telephone services and some residential phone services have teleconference capabilities.

Audioconferencing is the easiest type of virtual group interaction to understand because we are familiar with the basic technology—the telephone or computer microphone. However, author and business executive Clyde Burelson offers the following advice: "Do not think of teleconferencing as talking on the telephone. This is a meeting."[27] A group should plan for an audioconference just as it would for a face-to-face meeting. This means developing an agenda and making all other preparations appropriate for the meeting. Figure 12.2 summarizes the advantages and disadvantages of audioconferences.

Use the following guidelines for planning, conducting, and participating in an audioconference:

- Limit participation to no more than five active participants.
- Make sure everyone has the agenda and any necessary documents well in advance.
- Take attendance and make introductions at the beginning of the meeting.
- Identify yourself by name whenever you speak.
- Keep your comments short, clear, and to the point.
- If someone must "sign off" before the end of the meeting, ask that member to inform the group when she or he is leaving.

Figure 12.2   Advantages and Disadvantages of Audioconferences

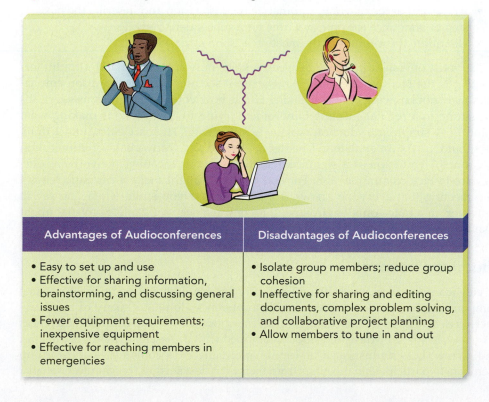

Advantages of Audioconferences	Disadvantages of Audioconferences
• Easy to set up and use • Effective for sharing information, brainstorming, and discussing general issues • Fewer equipment requirements; inexpensive equipment • Effective for reaching members in emergencies	• Isolate group members; reduce group cohesion • Ineffective for sharing and editing documents, complex problem solving, and collaborative project planning • Allow members to tune in and out

A group should plan for an audioconference just as it would for a face-to-face meeting. This means developing an agenda and making all other preparations appropriate for the meeting. What are some of the advantages and disadvantages of audioconference meetings?

- At the end of the meeting, summarize the discussion and describe the next step or announce the date and time for a subsequent meeting.
- Distribute the minutes of the meeting as soon as possible.

The most obvious difference between a voice-only conference and a traditional meeting is the fact that the participants cannot see one another. Burelson emphasizes that "not knowing who is speaking affects how you perceive the messages. It's like sitting in a regular meeting blindfolded, trying to guess who is making what point."[28] A simple introduction is usually sufficient: "This is Deidre, and I think we should…" As we explain in Chapter 6, "Verbal and Nonverbal Communication in Groups," you express a significant portion of your meaning nonverbally during face-to-face communication. For example, you might make a sarcastic remark in a meeting that everyone knows is a joke because you smile when you say it. However, in a voice-only environment, no one can see you smile. Someone might take your joke seriously.

Videoconferences

A **videoconference** is much like an audioconference with the addition of a visual component. The visual element of a videoconference eliminates many of the drawbacks associated with audioconferences. The most sophisticated videoconferences take place in specially designed studios equipped with professional lighting, cameras, and a crew. Less sophisticated and more affordable videoconferences allow group members to participate in meetings from their own desks using webcam technology.

Figure 12.3   Advantages and Disadvantages of Videoconferences

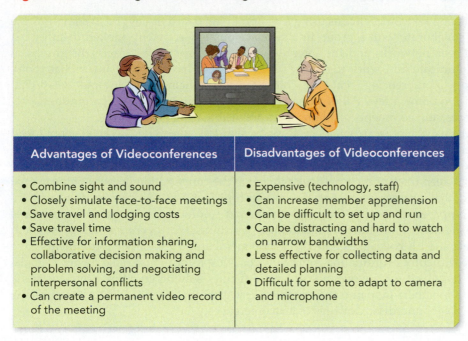

Advantages of Videoconferences	Disadvantages of Videoconferences
• Combine sight and sound • Closely simulate face-to-face meetings • Save travel and lodging costs • Save travel time • Effective for information sharing, collaborative decision making and problem solving, and negotiating interpersonal conflicts • Can create a permanent video record of the meeting	• Expensive (technology, staff) • Can increase member apprehension • Can be difficult to set up and run • Can be distracting and hard to watch on narrow bandwidths • Less effective for collecting data and detailed planning • Difficult for some to adapt to camera and microphone

Although videoconferences are becoming popular, the thought of being "on television" during this kind of conference can generate a great deal of communication apprehension. Figure 12.3 summarizes the advantages and disadvantages of videoconferencing.

Groups should address member anxieties well before the videoconference takes place by telling everyone how a videoconference works and what to expect. The more group members know about the process, the more comfortable they will be during the meeting. Here are several recommendations for preparing and conducting a videoconference:

- Brief all members about the operation of the videoconferencing system.
- Make sure everyone has the agenda and any necessary documents well in advance.
- When you talk to participants at other sites, look directly at the camera, not at their images on a television monitor.
- Use the microphone appropriately.
- Dress for the camera.

Always be aware of the microphone. Regardless of how the microphone is set up, remember that it is always listening. Avoid the temptation to lean over and whisper something to the person sitting next to you. Although the people across the room may not be able to hear you, everyone at the other end of the videoconference will.

Consider what you are going to wear to a videoconference. If your clothing is distracting, you will create a barrier to effective communication. Avoid clothes with narrow, contrasting stripes because video monitors can make stripes appear to pulsate. Also avoid wearing shiny or reflective clothing as well as jangling jewelry.

Textconferences

Think of a **textconference** as using a computer keyboard or keypad to communicate and collaborate with a group in a synchronous environment. Linked together via local area networks and the Internet, computers provide a "place" for groups to communicate and work together. Textconferences have many names: chat room, desktop conferencing, real-time computer conferencing, and Internet relay chat (IRC), to name a few. All of these variations occur in real time. The questions, responses, and comments of all members are visible to all participants.

At first glance, textconference sessions may *look* confusing. Because people read faster than they type, written comments may overlap, be highly repetitive, or seem irrelevant. Despite the presence of these multiple messages, participants "seem to be able to keep track of their particular thread in the conversation because of the textual record that is preserved as contribution after contribution is displayed on the screen."[29]

Compared to face-to-face interaction and audioconferencing, textconferences give members more time to prepare their responses. However, research by Kenneth Graetz and his colleagues note that group members in text-only environments have more difficulty coordinating input and verifying information, take longer to make decisions, and may experience greater difficulty solving complex problems. As a result, members may find the experience frustrating.[30] Figure 12.4 summarizes the advantages and disadvantages of textconferences.

Figure 12.4 Advantages and Disadvantages of Textconferences

Advantages of Textconferences	Disadvantages of Textconferences
• Save time, travel, and money • Effective for sharing and discussing ideas, information, and data, as well as resolving simple problems • Can create a permanent record of interaction • Distance and anonymity may increase honesty and participation by all members • Members have more time to prepare their responses.	• May lead to misunderstanding • Ineffective for solving complex problems, collaborative decision making and project planning, and resolving interpersonal problems • Limit participation by poor typists and writers • May frustrate members who like or need to talk through ideas and debate issues • Decrease social support for members

Several guidelines can help a virtual group take advantage of the freewheeling nature of textconferences:

- Plan the session carefully. Send participants an agenda and access to relevant information or documents well before the meeting begins.
- Make sure everyone has similar technology and the ability to use that technology.
- Appoint a facilitator or moderator to keep the discussion on track.
- Limit group size to keep the process under control.
- Monitor member participation and deal with nonparticipants and members assuming negative roles.
- Don't become sidetracked by irrelevant threads of conversation.
- Read messages carefully before sending to avoid potential misunderstandings.
- Summarize the meeting and distribute a written summary to all members.

Group Decision Support Systems

Group decision support systems (GDSS) use specialized software to help participants perform a variety of group tasks, such as brainstorming, problem solving, and decision making, by integrating the contributions of group members working at individual workstations.[31] Whether they are in the same room or miles apart, participants using a group decision support system can collaborate on a variety of group tasks. Most GDSSs include several capabilities:[32]

- *Generating ideas and brainstorming.* A GDSS resembles a chat room in which virtual group members present ideas and are able to see the ideas contributed by all other members on their monitors or on a projection screen.
- *Grouping and analyzing issues.* Collectively, group members can move ideas into discrete categories, identify ideas that merit further discussion, outline a plan, and finalize a list of ideas or issues for further development.
- *Creating and editing documents.* Members can write assigned sections of documents and comment on or revise material written by other members.
- *Voting.* Special voting features can assess the degree of consensus on ideas and decisions without pressuring members to make a final decision. GDSS software also can display voting results in total, graphic, or tabular form.

Consider the following examples of how two very different groups used GDSS to make important, far-reaching decisions:

Example 1: Corporate Risk Taking. Nine senior executives of a $2.5 billion transportation leasing company took less than four hours to brainstorm 52 risks to the corporation and then to identify the ten that presented the greatest risk to the company's achieving its strategic objectives and the ten that should receive the highest priority for an internal audit. After six months, the results of this four-hour meeting were still guiding the focus of both the senior executives and the internal audit staff.[33]

Example 2: Church Priorities. The members of the congregation filed into the church sanctuary, filling every seat in every pew. The top-ten priorities of each of the five church task forces were projected on five screens along the side wall. The task of the 467 people in the sanctuary was to choose, from among all 50 priorities, the ones on which the church should spend its limited resources. By using 467 keypads (a combination of handheld numeric keypads, computer software, and a projection screen), the members took only three hours to reach agreement on 13 priorities for the coming year.[34]

Guidelines for Using Group Decision Support Systems. In addition to the usual requirements for effective participation, group decision support systems

Groups in Balance...

Use Netspeak, Netlingo, and Leet Appropriately

Netspeak, Netlingo, and Leet are three names for Internet slang. Unless you are a *n00b* ("newbie"—as in "new and inexperienced" or "uninformed"), you're probably familiar with the new language forms used in email, text messages, and increasingly in everyday writing.

David Crystal, who writes about language, claims that "Netspeak is a development of millennial significance. A new medium of linguistic communication does not arrive very often in the history of the [human] race."[35] Consider these brief descriptions of three of these languages—Netspeak, Netlingo, and Leet:

Netspeak includes common typographic strategies used to achieve a more sociable, oral, and interactive communication style.

- *Letter homophones.* Examples: RU ("are you"), OIC ("oh, I see"), CUL8R ("see you later")
- *Capitalization or other symbols used for emphasis.* Examples: YES, *yes*
- *Onomatopoeic and/or stylized spelling.* Examples: cooooool, hahahahahah
- *Keyboard-generated emoticons.* Examples: :-) = "smile"; @>—;— = "rose"; ;-) = "winking"; ;-o = "shocked," "uh-oh," "oh-no"

Netlingo refers to a variety of language forms used in Internet communication, such as the familiar FYI (for your information) and FAQ (frequently asked questions):

- *Compounds and blends.* Examples: shareware, netiquette, e- and cyber- anything.
- *Abbreviations and acronyms.* Examples: BTW = "by the way," THX = "thanks," IRL = "in real life," F2F = "face-to-face," IMHO = "in my humble opinion," GMTA = "great minds think alike," BBL = "be back later," WDYT = "what do you think?"

- *Less use of capitalization, punctuation, and hyphenation.* Examples: internet and email.
- *Less use of traditional openings and closings.* Examples: *Hi* or *hey* instead of *dear* or using no greeting phrase at all.[36]

Leet, also known as *eleet* or *leetspeak*, uses an alternative alphabet to create words. In many cases the new alphabet's symbols visually resembles our standard alphabet. So *Leet* can become 133t, or 1337. *Leetspeak* becomes 133tspeek. Leet also uses common misspellings or letters and symbols that correspond to the sound of a word (as in *skillz* for "skills"), as well as a variety of symbols for sounds such as c@tL0vr, (47 £0v3r, and (@ L0 ≢ 3r for "cat lover."

Are you a skilled Internet slang user or a n00b? See if you can translate the following sentence:

> i g2g to da stor 2day c ya l8er LOLZ
> i @m 5o 1337 i pwn joo[37]

We urge you to be careful when using netlingo, netspeak, and especially Leet. Some readers may not understand it and will become confused or exasperated. The changing trends in Internet language even have some people in their twenties feeling old or slightly out of touch. As a 23-year-old technology consultant complained about his 12- and 19-year-old siblings, "I have no idea what they're saying.... I may not text in full sentences, but at least there's punctuation to get my point across. I guess I'm old school."[38]

If you send difficult-to-understand netspeak, netlingo, or Leet messages to people who will have to translate your "words" into recognizable English, they may not make the effort or ignore what you're saying. Don't load your messages with unnecessary or "show-off" symbols. Too many in one message can make reading difficult and annoying—and make your writing (and you) appear immature.[39]

---

require specialized software, compatible and specially networked hardware, and computer expertise to make the process work. A GDSS meeting usually requires a facilitator to keep the group moving through the process, a coach or trainer to help inexperienced or nonparticipating members, and a technician to solve technical problems. The best advice we can offer to participants in such a complex virtual group is this: Follow instructions and leave the rest to the hardware and software.

Deborah Duarte and Nancy Tennant Snyder, the authors of *Mastering Virtual Teams,* share a set of best practices for making GDSS meetings more effective:[40]

- Make sure that everyone's system is compatible and working properly.
- Make sure that everyone can access the software as well as any shared files.
- Develop and use a clear, focused agenda and set of technical instructions.
- Decide if and when input will be anonymous (e.g., brainstorming, voting).
- Rotate functions, such as sorting information and voting, to avoid fatigue.

Pros and Cons of Group Decision Support Systems.   Depending on the system and a group's technical expertise, members can move back and forth from the GDSS to other computer-based applications, such as word processing, spreadsheets, presentation software, and project management software. The GDSS can integrate other systems, such as desktop video, to capture the nonverbal and interpersonal dynamics of a meeting.[41] Projects that would otherwise have taken weeks or months to complete are finished in hours or days. Ideas flow, posted results lead to highly targeted discussions, and the final product can be of high quality.

Renting a GDSS facility can be prohibitive for many groups. In addition, a technician is often needed to make the process work. At the very least, a skilled facilitator is necessary to keep the group moving and to ensure that group members are using the software and hardware properly.

Fortunately, GDSS services have become available and more affordable via the Web. After downloading a peer-to-peer collaboration platform, groups pay a user fee to establish direct, instant communication and collaboration with other group members. Figure 12.5 summarizes the advantages and disadvantages of GDSS conferences.

Figure 12.5   Advantages and Disadvantages of Group Decision Support Systems (GDSS)

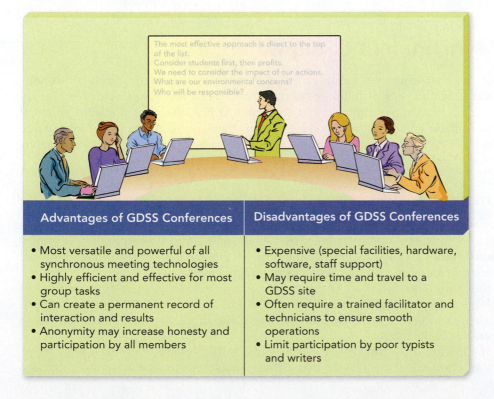

Advantages of GDSS Conferences	Disadvantages of GDSS Conferences
• Most versatile and powerful of all synchronous meeting technologies • Highly efficient and effective for most group tasks • Can create a permanent record of interaction and results • Anonymity may increase honesty and participation by all members	• Expensive (special facilities, hardware, software, staff support) • May require time and travel to a GDSS site • Often require a trained facilitator and technicians to ensure smooth operations • Limit participation by poor typists and writers

Groups in Balance...

Take Advantage of Collaborative Presentation Technology

When you see the term *presentation technology*, PowerPoint presentations may come to mind. We have added the word *collaborative* to this phrase in order to move beyond individual PowerPoint presentations and into the realm of technology-enhanced, interactive group presentations. **Collaborative presentation technology** projects an idea or graphic onto a screen, wall, or whiteboard so that both face-to-face and virtual participants can interact with the presentation.[42] Collaborative presentation tools make it possible to display information without being physically present with other group members. The use of these technologies also allows members to review, revise, edit, and finalize documents. Sophisticated meeting rooms now come fully equipped with the tools necessary for collaborative presentations: projection screens, LCD projectors, whiteboards, video cameras and monitors, laptop computers, and even old-fashioned flip charts and overhead projectors.

One of the most useful collaborative presentation technologies is the **interactive whiteboard.**
Computer-based electronic whiteboards allow members to work on the same document or drawing simultaneously. Anything written on the whiteboard is instantly digitized, stored, printed, and displayed in both local and remote locations. Thus, group members can sketch a flow chart or display a design on an interactive whiteboard that can be seen and altered by other group members, regardless of whether they are in the same room or located thousands of miles away. Group members can pose ideas, suggest modifications, draw links among ideas, edit text, and format documents. The primary advantage of using whiteboards is that they build on the team members' existing skills and meeting behaviors while also providing some sense of social presence. The primary disadvantage is that team members must have access to specially equipped conference rooms or desktop systems in order to participate.[43] When groups use interactive whiteboards in virtual or face-to-face settings along with audio and video capabilities, their potential for effective collaboration increases significantly.

Asynchronous Groupware

Although synchronous groupware has numerous advantages, an asynchronous group meeting has a double advantage: It is both less costly and more easily accessed from almost anywhere at any time. At first, you may not think of email and bulletin boards as groupware; however, they are the first types of groupware available to almost all groups and—despite the advantages of using synchronous groupware—they serve the needs of many groups efficiently and easily.

Email

As a worldwide, text-based, asynchronous medium, **email** lets group members interact from great distances and across time zones. In many corporate and professional settings, group members communicate via email more than they do on the phone or in person. In fact, some group members are able to express themselves better through email than in face-to-face meetings.[44] Even so, keep in mind that *Wall Street Journal* reporter Jonah Lehrer writes, "There is simply too much value in face-to-face contact, in all the body language and implicit information that doesn't translate to the Internet."[45]

One way of reaching every member of a virtual group with email is by using an electronic mailing service that delivers messages to everyone in the group.

Figure 12.6   Advantages and Disadvantages of Email Discussions

Advantages of Email Discussions	Disadvantages of Email Discussions
• Easy to use, accessible, and inexpensive • May make it easier for some members to discuss personal or controversial issues • Effective for sharing information; revising ideas, plans, and documents; defining and analyzing uncomplicated problems • Easy to transmit files • Can include many people	• Content subject to misinterpretation • Member may ignore messages, fake participation, or avoid difficult conversations and decisions • Ineffective for brainstorming and prioritizing, debating issues, making difficult decisions, and solving complex problems • Too many messages can waste time and discourage use • Not well suited for interpersonal conflict resolution

For example, you may have worked on a committee or had a course in which the chairperson or instructor used a listserv to send and receive messages to and from the entire group.[46]

The asynchronous nature of email means that you can receive a message that may have been sent days, hours, or just seconds ago. You respond to it when you can or by a designated deadline and hope that other members will do the same. Figure 12.6 summarizes the advantages and disadvantages of email discussions.

If you are going to participate in an email discussion, the following guidelines can help your group achieve its common goal:

- Make sure that all participants know what is expected of them. They should know the group's specific purpose, the deadlines and schedule for replying via email, and the amount of time expected for the task.
- Ask for confirmation that group members received your email.
- Develop a common system for editing documents, such as underlining, strikeovers, highlighting, or using the track changes feature in your software. Provide training for members who are unfamiliar with a computer system's email and editing features.
- Contact and encourage members who are not participating.
- Observe the basics of good writing, such as rules of capitalization, spelling, grammar, and formatting.
- Include a context for your reply. A message that says only "I disagree" may leave other members unsure about what you oppose.

Bulletin Boards

Like email, a **bulletin board** is an asynchronous, text-based communication medium. What distinguishes bulletin boards from email and synchronous textconferences is the size of the audience they attempt to reach and the manner in which members write and read messages. If you subscribe to a bulletin board, you send your message to a single address. The program or a designated moderator then sends your message to everyone else on the bulletin board.

Figure 12.7 Advantages and Disadvantages of Bulletin Boards

Advantages of Bulletin Boards	Disadvantages of Bulletin Boards
• Can save time • Easy to use, accessible, and inexpensive • Provide time to think before responding • Provide space for shared messages, display, and documents • Effective for brainstorming; discussing ideas, plans, and documents; collecting and sharing information • Use threaded discussions that allow complex interactions and analysis • Can create synergy and increase collaboration • Effective way to communicate with numerous group members	• Content subject to misinterpretation • Easy to ignore • Difficult to organize • Ineffective for debating, voting, prioritizing, and collaborative decision making, and problem solving • High message volume can waste time, discourage users, and result in information overload • Discussions can diverge from the topic or degenerate into nonproductive personal arguments

But unlike a real bulletin board, a computer-mediated bulletin board organizes incoming materials and posts subsequent messages as responses to specific issues, one right after another.[47] This system is called a *thread,* and it can continue and extend for as long as participants send submissions. Thus, a **threaded discussion** occurs when a series of related email messages about a specific issue appears on a bulletin board.

Generally, bulletin boards make fewer demands on participants than email does. Good bulletin boards become a source of information and a means of following the development of an argument, plan, or report. Figure 12.7 summarizes the advantages and disadvantages of bulletin board discussions.

The following guidelines can help groups use a bulletin board to post messages or respond to others:

- Determine whether someone will moderate the bulletin board or whether the program will accept and post all messages. If the group uses a moderator, the program should not permit anonymous input, particularly if virtual group members are responsible for the outcome.
- Organize your thoughts before you contribute to a bulletin board. State your point clearly. No one wants to read your ramblings.
- Be careful of being highly critical. Your written comments will become part of a permanent record.
- If you want to pursue an issue with only one or two members, contact them by email. Don't take up bulletin board space with a private conversation.

Group Diversity and the Digital Divide

In virtual groups, cultural, educational, geographical, and socioeconomic differences combine with technical differences that can result in unique challenges. For example, language differences are an obvious, but often overlooked, cultural difference among computer and Internet users.

Follow the Research

Internet Addiction

The phrase *Internet addiction* is no joke, although it began as one. In 1995, psychiatrist Ivan Goldberg lightheartedly posted a diagnosis for **Internet Addiction Disorder (IAD)**, which he described as "a maladaptive pattern of Internet use, leading to clinically significant impairment or distress."[48] Although Goldberg intended his "diagnosis" as a joke, it quickly became a popular term and a serious topic for study by mental health professionals. Today, researchers shun the word *addiction* and instead use labels such as *problematic* or *pathological* to describe excessive or disturbed patterns of Internet use, with symptoms that include mood alteration, inability to fulfill major role obligations, guilty feelings, and cravings for more.[49] Here are some general symptoms that can help identify group members with problematic Internet use:

- They feel a strong need to use the Internet and spend increasing amounts of time doing so to achieve satisfaction.
- They feel restless, moody, depressed, or irritable when attempting or forced to cut down or stop Internet use.
- They stay online longer than they originally intended.
- They have lied about or concealed the amount of time they spend on the Internet.
- They use the Internet as a way of escaping problems or relieving feelings of anxiety or depression.[50]

Internet addiction behavior can help explain a member's nonproductive or antisocial behavior. For example, are any of these behaviors characteristics of one or more group members?

- They prefer Internet interaction to face-to-face communication.
- They eagerly volunteer to do an Internet search for the group when, in fact, the issue does not require extensive research.
- They are reluctant to leave their computers for a meeting and may even bring a wireless laptop to meetings so that they have access to the Internet.

Groups are often sidetracked by computer-dependent members. Another version of this addiction is *crackberry*, a reference to people addicted to their BlackBerries. Be cautious, however, about drawing unwarranted conclusions about problematic Internet use or about discouraging members from using the Internet. As Andrew Goodman put it, "for every story about Internet addiction leading victims to ignore their families and become withdrawn, antisocial, and depressed, there is an [opposite] example of a person who has found a support group, employment prospects, or a community of like-minded topical enthusiasts through the 'net."[51] To that list, we would add group members who use the Internet effectively and responsibly to help a group achieve its common goal.

Those who rely on computers and Internet access at home, work, or school for a wide range of tasks may assume that everyone has the same opportunities and skills. Certainly members of virtual groups need to have access to compatible technology and possess comparable abilities in order to work efficiently and effectively. But those who "have" and "know a lot" about technology should recognize that they may be working in the same group as members who "do not have" and "do not know a lot."

Virtual groups may encounter the digital divide and its consequences. The phrase **digital divide** refers to inequalities in access to, distribution of, and use of information technology between two or more populations. For example, 94 percent of Americans with college degrees use the Internet compared to only 39 percent of Americans with less than a high school degree.[52] In 2001, the typical Internet user was young, white, urban, male, and relatively well educated. Today, the percentage of women using the Internet lags only slightly behind the percentage of men, but women under 30 and black women use the Internet *more* than their male peers. However, older women trail dramatically behind older men.[53] Equally interesting are the technology advances among racial and ethnic groups. Although 76 percent of whites are Internet users, 70 percent of blacks and 64 percent of Hispanics use the Internet.[54]

In terms of cell phone use, the image of the typical cell phone owner as affluent and white is a mistaken one, according to a 2011 report by the Pew Research Center's Internet and American Life Center. The study found that African-Americans and Hispanics continue to be *more* likely to own cell phones than whites and more likely to use their phones for a greater range of activities.[55]

These changing statistics may lead you to believe that the digital divide is shrinking and may soon disappear. Despite impressive gains, however, a 2010 survey of U.S. households found that "a significant proportion of residents—one in four households—completely lacked Internet connections, dial-up as well as broadband."[56] Unfortunately, there are still significant digital divide discrepancies in age, geography, and socioeconomic dimensions. All of these factors have a significant effect on the ability of virtual groups to achieve their common goal.

Ethics in Groups

The Ten Commandments for Computer Ethics

More than 20 years ago, Dr. Ramon C. Barquin recognized the need for a set of standards to guide and instruct people in the ethical use of computers.[57] He called for the use of the following "Ten Commandments for Computer Ethics," all of which are just as relevant today:

1. Thou shalt not use a computer to harm other people.
2. Thou shalt not interfere with other people's computer work.
3. Thou shalt not snoop around in other people's computer files.
4. Thou shalt not use a computer to steal.
5. Thou shalt not use a computer to bear false witness.
6. Thou shalt not copy or use proprietary software for which you have not paid.
7. Thou shalt not use other people's computer resources without authorization or proper compensation.
8. Thou shalt not appropriate other people's intellectual output.
9. Thou shalt think about the social consequences of the program you are writing or the system you are designing.
10. Thou shalt always use a computer in ways that ensure consideration and respect for your fellow humans.[58]

Barquin's commandments have been widely adopted by the computing industry as a starting point for ethics standards. However, most professionals recognize that specific circumstances may present ethical dilemmas.[59] For example, consider the third commandment, "Thou shalt not snoop around in other people's computer files." "What if the 'other people' are using the computer to do harm? Should we still refrain from interfering? Should computer files be private even if they are being used as part of a criminal conspiracy?"[60]

As is the case with many ethical issues, there are no easy answers to the questions that arise from these commandments. At the same time, Barquin's code is widely accepted and forms the basis for developing useful guidelines about the ethical use of computers, whether used by individuals or by virtual groups.

The digital divide results in inequalities in access to and use of technology. Group members from households with higher incomes are more likely to have the latest technology and easy access to the Internet. Whereas, other members may need to rely on the computers at work or at the public library to access the Internet and complete group tasks.

Age

In some virtual groups, older members embrace computer technology and excel in its use. Others fear or have avoided learning and using computer technology. The statistics are revealing: 93 percent of American 18- to 29-year-olds use the Internet compared to only 38 percent of those older than 65.[61] Whereas some older group members may be intimidated by the increasing complexity of computer technology, younger members have been brought up using it. In short, "one generation's technology is another generation's appliance."[62] In spite of such differences, however, most research concludes that multi-generational groups can and do work together effectively.[63]

Remember This

"Telecommunications, which in theory should bind us together, has often divided us in practice."[64]

Geography

Where we live and the type of Internet service available to us can divide us digitally. For example, if you live in a big city or wealthy Northeastern suburb, you have access to some of the fastest connectivity in the country. If you live in a smaller, rural, and less wealthy community, your Internet speed may be six times slower and reliant on dial-up access. "That means a hundred-fold disparity in connection speeds."[65]

Income

Income level may be the strongest determinant of a person's access to computer technology and the Internet. One government study on Internet use in the United States found that *urban* households earning incomes more than $75,000 a year are *twenty times* as likely to have home Internet access as rural households at the lowest income levels.[66] When asked which demographic groups of college students are less Web-savvy, Eszter Hargittal identifies socioeconomic status and its effects on women, Latin/Hispanic, and African American students whose parents have lower levels of education.[67]

Summary Study Guide

The Nature of Virtual Groups

- Technology allows virtual groups to collaborate across space and time.
- Media Richness Theory and Media Synchronicity Theory examine the relative advantages of using more communication channels as well as matching specific media channels to a group's needs and purpose.
- Virtual groups can interact synchronously (simultaneously in real time) or asynchronously (consecutively and without being interrupted).

Synchronous Groupware

- Groupware refers to computer-mediated methods and tools that support group collaboration, even though members may not be together in either time or location.
- Audioconferences are coordinated phone calls and computer voice links among three or more group members.
- Videoconferences can be as effective as face-to-face interaction, but they may require expensive equipment and technicians to run the meeting.
- Textconferences are very effective for sharing information and data, and resolving simple problems, but they can also lead to misunderstanding, frustration, and lack of social support for members.

- Group decision support systems are effective for group work, but they rely on expensive, networked equipment; staff support; and (in some cases) time and money to travel to a fully equipped GDSS site.

Asynchronous Groupware

- Email discussions are a highly accessible and inexpensive way for virtual groups to communicate, although written messages may be misinterpreted and members may ignore messages or fake participation.
- Bulletin board discussions make fewer demands on members than email and can be highly focused, although written messages may be misinterpreted and ignored.

Group Diversity and the Digital Divide

- The digital divide refers to inequalities in access to, distribution of, and use of information technology among different populations.
- Older group members, geographically isolated members, and members from low-income households may not have access to communication technology or may be less skilled and less comfortable with technology, particularly as an alternative to face-to-face meetings.

GroupWork

Match the Medium to the Message[68]

Directions: The left column of the following table lists six types of virtual groups discussed in this chapter. The column headings across the top of the table show common group tasks. Rate how well each type of virtual group matches the group tasks using the following scale:

1 = Very effective and useful
2 = Moderately effective and useful
3 = Ineffective

	Sharing and Analyzing Information	General Discussion and Brainstorming	Collaborative Decision Making and Problem Solving	Handling Interpersonal Problems and Conflict
Audioconferences				
Videoconferences				
Textconferences				
Electronic Meeting Systems (EMSs)				
Email				
Bulletin Boards				

Group Assessment

Virtual Meeting Evaluation

Directions: When you participate in an audioconference, videoconference, or textconference, use the following criteria to evaluate the success of your virtual meeting. Circle the number that best represents your assessment of each statement.

Audioconference

1. An audioconference was appropriate for this meeting.

Disagree	1	2	3	4	5	6	7	Agree

2. The sound quality was satisfactory.

Disagree	1	2	3	4	5	6	7	Agree

3. Members received and followed a meeting agenda.

Disagree	1	2	3	4	5	6	7	Agree

4. Members adapted to the oral-only medium.

Disagree	1	2	3	4	5	6	7	Agree

Videoconference

1. A videoconference was appropriate for this meeting.

Disagree	1	2	3	4	5	6	7	Agree

2. Members received and followed a meeting agenda.

Disagree	1	2	3	4	5	6	7	Agree

3. Members used the microphones effectively.

Disagree	1	2	3	4	5	6	7	Agree

4. Members dressed appropriately.

Disagree	1	2	3	4	5	6	7	Agree

Textconference

1. A textconference was appropriate for this meeting.

Disagree	1	2	3	4	5	6	7	Agree

2. Members received and followed a meeting agenda.

Disagree	1	2	3	4	5	6	7	Agree

3. Members typed clear and succinct messages.

Disagree	1	2	3	4	5	6	7	Agree

4. Members interacted frequently and met deadlines.

Disagree	1	2	3	4	5	6	7	Agree

Group Presentations

Chapter Outline

Case Study

Team Challenge

As the final project in their Media and Message Design course, student teams must develop and present their promotional campaigns for one of the college's academic departments. Each team must submit a written report as well as designs for a poster, a brochure, and web page. In addition, all group members must participate in a 30-minute team presentation that summarizes their research, campaign strategies, and media designs to an audience of class members, three communication professors, and faculty from the client department.

Brittany, Simon, Leah, Javier, and Enola have enlisted the theatre department as their client. After weeks of research, analysis, and intense discussions, the group drafts a promotional plan. Javier and Enola—two art majors—develop a creative design for the poster and brochure. The same design will also be used on the website. Leah writes the report and brochure content. Simon and Brittany prepare a new layout and copy for the website. Now the group faces the task of preparing their team presentation.

The group decides that Enola should serve as a moderator. Leah claims the task of presenting the group's research and analysis. Javier wants to present the poster on his own, but Enola objects, saying that even though she's the moderator, she has to make a presentation, too. Brittany and Simon watch Javier and Enola vie for the honor of presenting the poster and decide that they want to present the website together.

As the date of the team presentation approaches, the group realizes they are spending most of their time trying to decide who will do the presenting rather than focusing on finalizing the report and crafting the team presentation. They declare a moratorium on arguments about media and shift to discussing the overall presentation.

"Just remember," says Brittany, "our purpose is to get an A!"

"No," says Javier. "Our purpose is to present a brilliant promotional plan and designs to the audience—and if we do it well, we'll earn a good grade, too."

Leah asks the group to put aside concerns about grades and look at the presentation in a broader sense. "Aren't we supposed to demonstrate how our promotional plan and designs will help the theatre department attract more majors?"

The group agrees and decides to concentrate on organizing individual presentations into the team presentation. Enola says that as much as she would like to present the poster (and as long as Javier gives her credit as the co-designer), she'll open the team presentation by explaining the overall campaign plan. Leah interjects and insists that she should do that section because she did most of the research and writing.

By now the team is anxious. They're still arguing about who does what rather than what to do. "What if," says Brittany, "we look at this as members of the theatre department. What would they want to know? Why would they trust our judgment and recommendations?"

Simon adds, "You're right. But we also need to consider, how to 'perform' this presentation in a way that will impress the theatre department *and* our communication instructors."

The group looks at Brittany and Simon with gratitude. "I guess we're back to square one," says Leah. The group acknowledges and accepts the fact that they need to find an appropriate approach to planning their team presentation.

When you finish reading this appendix, you should be able to answer the following critical thinking questions.

1   What, in your opinion, is the team presentation's purpose or purposes?

2   How well did the group consider the needs of its audience—other students, the course instructor, and faculty members from the theatre department?

3   In what ways can the group enhance its credibility?

4   To what extent did the group follow the Seven-Step Team Presentation Planning Guidelines?

5   Which dialectic tensions are likely to affect whether the group's team presentation is successful?

Presentations in and by Groups

In her book *Keeping the Team Going,* Deborah Harrington-Mackin responds to a question frequently asked by her management clients:

QUESTION: I like the idea of having team members speak on panels and give presentations, but how can I trust that they will give the right answers when under pressure?

ANSWER: I'm always pleasantly surprised at how competent, composed, and prepared team members are when they sit on panels or give presentations. Remember, they're in the spotlight and want to look and act their best.[1]

In general, we agree with Harrington-Mackin, but we also know there's a lot more involved in an effective presentation than trusting it will turn out okay. This chapter focuses on preparing you for success in the three types of group presentations illustrated and explained in Figure A.1.

Figure A.1 Three Types of Group Presentations

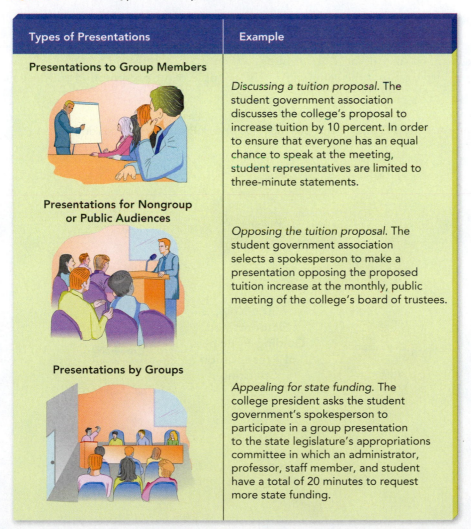

Types of Presentations	Example
Presentations to Group Members	*Discussing a tuition proposal.* The student government association discusses the college's proposal to increase tuition by 10 percent. In order to ensure that everyone has an equal chance to speak at the meeting, student representatives are limited to three-minute statements.
Presentations for Nongroup or Public Audiences	*Opposing the tuition proposal.* The student government association selects a spokesperson to make a presentation opposing the proposed tuition increase at the monthly, public meeting of the college's board of trustees.
Presentations by Groups	*Appealing for state funding.* The college president asks the student government's spokesperson to participate in a group presentation to the state legislature's appropriations committee in which an administrator, professor, staff member, and student have a total of 20 minutes to request more state funding.

Whether it is within a group, on behalf of a group, or by an entire group, **group presentations** occur whenever a member speaks, relatively uninterrupted, to other group members or audience members. All group members should know how to prepare and give a successful **presentation** adapted to the needs and characteristics of their group and its goals.

Presentation Guidelines

In this appendix, we introduce a set of seven guiding principles to help you make critical decisions about your presentation from the minute you find out you will have to speak to the minute you've said your last word. We have selected a single word to represent the key element in each guiding principle, as shown in Figure A.2. Are the principles represented by these seven words all you need to know about effective speaking? No. Rather, the seven key elements and guiding principles provide a framework for strategic decision making about the complex process of presentation speaking.[2]

Purpose

The first step in developing a successful presentation is identifying your purpose—much like the need for groups to identify and agree on a common goal. Your purpose is not the same thing as your topic. Your **presentation purpose** is

Figure A.2 Key Elements and Guiding Principles of Presentation Speaking

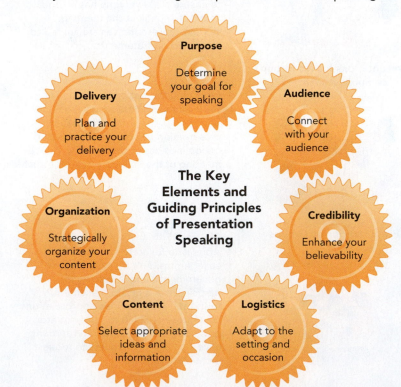

what you want your listeners to know, think, believe, or do as a result of your presentation. For example, a proposed tuition increase is the discussion topic for the student government association. A student speaker's purpose, however, may be to support or oppose the increase.

Dr. Terry Paulson, psychologist and author of *They Shoot Managers, Don't They?*, cautions speakers against making a presentation without a purpose:

> There are so many messages and memos hurled at [us] today…it's like sipping through a fire hydrant. Don't unnecessarily add to the stream by including unnecessary fill, fact, and fluff. Volume and graphs will not have a lasting impression: having a focus will. Ask yourself early in the process: What do I want them to remember or do three months from now? If you can't succinctly answer that question, cancel your presentation.[3]

Remember This

Having a clear purpose for your presentation does not necessarily mean that you will achieve it. But without a clear purpose, you may not accomplish anything.

Audience

After determining the purpose of your presentation, turn your attention to analyzing and adapting to your listeners—the members of your group or an outside audience. This process begins by seeking answers to two questions: What are your listeners' characteristics? What are their opinions?

Characteristics. Two types of audience characteristics demand your attention: demographic traits and individual attributes.

1. **Demographic traits** include age, gender, race, ethnicity, religion, educational level, and marital status. If you have been working in a group for a long time, you can easily catalog the demographic traits of group members. For a presentation to a new or a large audience, the task is more difficult. Take a good look at your listeners and note visible demographic traits, such as age, gender, and race. At the same time, assume that there is more diversity than similarity among your audience members.
2. **Individual attributes** take into account the distinct features of particular group members, such as job title and status, special interests, personality traits, relationships with other members, and length of group membership.

Demographic traits and individual attributes can affect how your listeners react to you and your message. For example, students who support themselves on limited incomes may oppose a tuition increase more strongly than students who can afford the increase.

Opinions. There can be as many opinions in an audience as there are members. Some members will agree with you before you begin your presentation, whereas others will disagree with you no matter what you say. Some will have no opinion about an issue and will accept a reasonable point of view. Effective presenters try to predict who or how many listeners will agree, disagree, or be undecided. Then they look for communication strategies that adapt to the diversity of opinions.

Follow the Research

Adapting to Audience Opinions

Marketing and persuasion research suggests several strategies for adapting to a variety of audience opinions, attitudes, beliefs, and values.

If most audience members agree with you or are undecided, your presentation should share new information, summarize important ideas and arguments, and motivate them to act. For example, if the members of the student government are universally opposed to a tuition increase, a speaker could focus on motivating the audience to show up at the college's board of trustees meeting and write letters to the editor of the college and community newspapers.

If audience members disagree with you, make sure you set realistic goals. Asking students to storm the president's office may get the administration's attention, but such an action may be too radical for most students to support. A second strategy is to find **common ground:** Find a belief or value that you share with those who disagree with you. Emphasizing shared ideas, feelings, history, and hopes can help you overcome resistance. For example, if a student speaker tells the board of trustees that the student government wants to help it find a solution to the financial crisis, the board may be more willing to listen to student concerns about the proposed tuition increase.

Finally, when you address a controversial issue, make sure you support your arguments with fair and reasonable evidence. If your arguments and evidence are weak, your opponents are likely to use those weaknesses against you. Chapter 10, "Critical Thinking and Argumentation in Groups," discusses methods for developing and presenting valid arguments.

Audience Adaptation Strategies

If the Audience Agrees with You, Is Undecided, or Has No Opinion	If the Audience Disagrees with You
• Present new information	• Make sure your goals are realistic
• Summarize important ideas	• Find common ground
• Motivate the audience to act	• Use fair and reasonable evidence

Credibility

Your **credibility** as a speaker represents the extent to which an audience believes you. No matter how much you know about the subject or how sincere you are about your purpose, your audience decides whether you seem competent and trustworthy.

Confident speakers are also more credible presenters. Chapter 3, "Group Membership," explains that the majority of speakers experience some level of communication apprehension when faced with doing a presentation. Chapter 3 also provides several effective strategies for reducing apprehension and building communication confidence.

Theory in Groups

Aristotle's Ethos

The concept of *speaker credibility* is more than two thousand years old. Even in ancient times, speech coaches (yes, there were speech teachers back then) recognized that the speaker was just as important as the speech. In *Rhetoric*, Aristotle wrote about **ethos**, a Greek word meaning "character": "The character [ethos] of the speaker is a cause of persuasion when the speech is so uttered as to make him worthy of belief.... His character [ethos] is the most potent of all the means to persuasion."[4] Aristotle's concept of *ethos* has evolved into what we now call speaker credibility—the extent to which an audience believes you and your message.

Numerous studies back up the importance of speaker credibility. In most of these studies, two different audiences listen to a recording or see a live performance of the same presentation. One audience is told that the speaker is a national expert on the topic. The other audience is told that the speaker is a college student. After listening to the presentation, each audience is asked for their reactions. Can you guess the results? The "national expert's" presentation persuaded more audience members to change their minds than the one by the "student"—even though both audiences listened to the same exact presentation. The only difference was the *perceived* credibility of the speaker.

Of the many factors researchers have identified as major components of credibility, three have an especially strong impact on the believability of a speaker: competence, character, and caring.

- **Competence** refers to your expertise and abilities.[5] If you are not a recognized expert on a subject, you must demonstrate that you are well prepared. There is nothing wrong with letting your audience know how much time and effort you have put into researching the topic or with sharing your surprise at discovering new information.

- **Character** reflects your trustworthiness. Are you honest and sincere? Do you put the group's goal above your own? "Do you make a special effort to be fair in presenting evidence, acknowledging limitations of your data and opinions, and conceding those parts of opposing viewpoints that have validity?"[6] If your audience or the members of your group don't trust you, it won't matter what you say.

- **Caring** refers to whether you seem to have listeners' interests at heart, demonstrate an understanding of others' ideas, and are empathic and responsive to audience responses.[7] Caring speakers let their actions speak louder than their words. Do you complain about higher tuition and cutbacks in student services, or do you write to your college's board of trustees expressing your concerns? By showing that you care about others, you can enhance your credibility.

Logistics

Logistics describes the strategic planning, arranging, and use of people, facilities, time, and materials relevant to your presentation. Adapting to the occasion and setting of a presentation requires more than taking a quick look at the seating arrangements for a meeting. Ask questions about *where* and *when* you will be speaking.

Where? Where will you be delivering your presentation—in a large conference room, an auditorium, a classroom, a meeting room? What are the seating arrangements? Are there any distracting sights or sounds? Will you need a microphone? Do you need special equipment to display your presentation aids? Once you have answered such questions, figure out how to adapt to the location. For example, requesting a microphone would be in order if a student government spokesperson learns that several hundred people will be attending the board of trustees meeting.

When? Will you be speaking in the morning or the afternoon? Are you scheduled to speak for five minutes, 20 minutes, or one hour? What comes before or after your presentation? The answers to such questions may require major adjustments to your presentation. If there is a time limit for the presentation, respect and adhere to that limit. Regardless of whether you have five minutes or one hour for your presentation, never add more than 5 percent to your allotted time. Even better, aim for 5 percent less.

Content

As soon as you know you have to make a presentation, start collecting relevant ideas and information. Gathering materials can be as simple as spending a few hours thinking about the purpose of your presentation or as complicated and time-consuming as spending days doing research. In Chapter 10, "Critical Thinking and Argumentation in Groups," we devoted a major section to evaluating various types of evidence. These recommendations also apply to gathering and assessing the content of a presentation.

Organization

Audiences react positively to well-organized presentations and speakers, and negatively to poorly organized ones.[8] Ask yourself whether there is a natural structure or framework for your message. What common ideas have appeared in most of your materials? What information seems most interesting, important, and relevant to the purpose of your presentation?

Your ability to organize a presentation also depends on whether you have selected appropriate ideas and information based on your analysis of purpose, audience, and logistics. Without well-thought-out content, you may have nothing substantive to organize.

Organizational Patterns. Even the most experienced speakers sometimes find it difficult to see how their content fits into an organizational pattern. If you're in a similar position, do not despair. Several commonly used organizational patterns can help you clarify your central idea and find an appropriate format for your presentation. Figure A.3 lists several common patterns.

Figure A.3 Organizational Patterns

Organizational Pattern	Example
Reason Giving	Three reasons why we should increase the dues are . . .
Time Arrangement	The college's hiring steps must be complied with in the following order . . .
Space Arrangement	The following membership increases occured in the East, South, West, and Central regions . . .
Problem–Solution	This research method avoids the problems we encountered last time . . .
Causes and Effects	Here's what could happen if we fail to increase our dues . . .
Stories and Examples	I've contacted four community associations in this county and here's what I found . . .
Compare–Contrast	Let's take a look at the two research methods we considered . . .

Outlining Your Presentation. Presentation outlines begin with a few basic building blocks. Use the following outline as a model for organizing almost any kind of presentation.

   I. Introduction
  II. Central Idea or Purpose (Preview of Main Points)
 III. Body of Presentation
     A. Main Point 1
        1. Supporting Material
        2. Supporting Material
     B. Main Point 2
        1. Supporting Material
        2. Supporting Material
     C. Main Point 3
        1. Supporting Material
        2. Supporting Material
 IV. Conclusion

Naturally, every outline will differ, depending on the number of main points you have and the amount and type of supporting material you use.

The introduction of a presentation is critical because, when well crafted, it gains audience attention and interest. An effective beginning should focus audience attention on you and your message. An interesting example, statistic, quotation, or story at the beginning of a presentation can "warm up" the members of your audience and prepare them for your message.

The "central idea or purpose" section of a presentation lets you state your purpose and preview your main points. This section should be brief, no more than a few sentences. The heart of your presentation is the "body" section. Here, you add your supporting material to each main point. No matter how many main points there are, each one should be backed up with at least one type of supporting material. If you can use several different types of material, your presentation will be more interesting and impressive.

The end of a presentation should have a strong and well-planned conclusion. An effective conclusion helps listeners remember the most important parts of your message. A quick summary, a brief story, a memorable quotation, or a challenge to the group can leave a strong final impression. Figure A.4, on the next page, shows one possible organizational structure, including notes, for a presentation by a student spokesperson to a college's board of trustees.

Delivery

By the time you ask questions about delivery, you should know what you want to say and have given a lot of thought to how you want to say it.

Forms of Delivery. In many group and public audience settings, you will speak **impromptu**—a form of delivery without advance preparation or practice. For example, a member of the board of trustees may ask a student spokesperson a question after a presentation. The student responds impromptu.

When you do have advance notice, you will be more effective if you speak extemporaneously. **Extemporaneous speaking**—the most common form of delivery—involves using an outline or notes to guide you

Remember This

How you speak can say more about what you really mean and also shape what listeners hear and understand.

Figure A.4 Sample Presentation Outline

OUTLINE

Hold the Line on Tuition

I.   Introduction

Story: Student who had to choose between buying shoes for her children and paying tuition for her nursing courses.

II. Central Idea or Purpose

Because a tuition increase will have a devastating effect on many students, we ask you to search for other ways to manage the college's financial crisis.

III. Body of Presentation

A. Another tuition increase will prevent students from continuing or completing their college education on schedule.

1. More students are becoming part-time rather than full-time students. (College statistics)

2. Students are taking longer to complete their college degrees. (College statistics)

3. Students are sacrificing important needs to pay their tuition bills. (Quotations and examples from college newspaper)

B. There are better ways to manage the college's financial crisis.

1. Consolidate areas and reduce the number of administrators and support staff. (Compare to college of same size that has less staff)

2. Seek more state and grant funding. (Statistics from national publication comparing funding levels and grants at similar types of colleges)

3. Re-evaluate cost and need for activities and services such as athletic teams, the off-campus homecoming and scholarship balls, intersession courses, and full staffing during summer sessions. (Examples)

IV. Conclusion

Money is a terrible thing to waste when students' hearts and minds are at stake. Let's work together to guarantee that all of our students become proud and grateful alumni.

through your presentation. Your notes can be a few key words on a small card or a detailed outline that includes supporting materials. These notes will reflect the decisions you have made during the preparation process, but they will also give you the flexibility to adapt your presentation to the audience and the occasion.[9]

Unless the situation is very formal or your words are intended for publication, avoid reading a manuscript version of your presentation. Even though your manuscript may be well written and well read, this delivery style is too formal for most settings. Moreover, reading from a script prevents you from observing listeners' reactions and modifying your presentation. If you must use a manuscript, write it as though you are speaking; that is, avoid long sentences, complex words, and formal term-paper grammar. Also, do not memorize your manuscript and try to deliver it without any notes. What if you forget or go blank? Unless you have the skills of a professional actor and can memorize a script and make it sound as if you just came up with the wording, forget about memorizing a presentation.

Vocal and Physical Delivery.   The key to a successful performance is practice. Once you begin your presentation, it's too late to make many delivery decisions. Moreover, the only way to predict the length of your presentation accurately is to practice it aloud and time it.

You can control, improve, and practice vocal characteristics such as volume, rate, pitch, articulation, and pronunciation. Rehearse your presentation in a strong, loud voice, but without shouting. Even in a small-group setting, a presentation requires more volume than you would use in everyday conversations. Also, monitor your speaking rate. Many listeners have difficulty following someone who speaks at a rate that exceeds 180 words per minute. The tolerable, all-purpose rate is 140 to 180 words per minute.[10]

Sometimes speakers are difficult to understand because their articulation is not clear. Poor articulation is often described as sloppy speech or mumbling. Generally, it helps to speak a little more slowly and a little louder and to open your mouth a little wider than usual. Similar problems can occur when words are mispronounced. Because it can be embarrassing to mispronounce a word or a person's name, look up any words you are not sure of in a dictionary or ask someone how to pronounce them correctly.

The single most important physical characteristic in an oral presentation is eye contact. Look directly at individual members of your audience, eye to eye. Even before a large audience, "the only kind of eye contact that successfully establishes the feeling of connection with members of the audience is a reasonably long, in-focus look at specific individuals."[11]

There is more to body movement than thinking about how you sit in a chair or stand before a group. Your gestures, appearance, and actions can add to or detract from your presentation. Your gestures and movements should be natural. At the same time, try to avoid distracting gestures such as pushing up eyeglasses, tapping the table with a pencil, or pulling on a strand of hair. Such movements draw attention away from the content of your presentation.

Virtual Groups

Mediated Presentations

Presentations are no longer the sole domain of people who speak, uninterrupted, to an audience that they can see and hear in real time. Groups use technology to communicate across time, distances, and organizational boundaries. Preparing and delivering effective virtual presentations are essential skills for anyone working in a virtual group.

In audioconferences, you must use your voice to communicate your meaning and emotions. Speak as clearly as you can. Use changes in rate, pitch, and inflection to emphasize particular ideas and to communicate your feelings. When you add video to the virtual mix, your appearance sends a powerful message to those who are watching. Dress appropriately: avoid busy patterns, noisy jewelry, and stark white or black clothing. If you are talking to an audience at another location, speak directly to the camera as though it were a group member instead of a machine. Try to keep your delivery natural and sincere. This isn't prime-time live; it's a group at work.

Group Presentations

The seven key elements and guiding principles—purpose, audience, logistics, content, organization, credibility, and delivery—apply to any presentation you make to your group or to external audiences. If however, you make a presentation as a member of a public group or as part of a team presentation, you must consider some additional factors.

Public Group Presentations

Chapter 1, "Introduction to Group Communication," describes public groups as including panel discussions, symposiums, forums, and governance groups. In all these situations, group members speak to a public audience. In addition to following the presentation guidelines described in this chapter, make sure you have considered the unique requirements of a presentation by a public group for a public audience. As a member of a public group, you have a responsibility to yourself, your group, and your audience.

When you are participating in a public group, remember that you are "on stage" all the time—even when you are not speaking. If you look bored while another member is speaking, the audience may wonder whether what that speaker is saying is worth sharing. During a presentation by a public group, an attentive audience will notice other group members' "gestures, facial expression, and posture. They deliberately look for unspoken disagreements or conflicts."[12] For example, if a member of the college's board of trustees rolls his eyes every time another board member speaks in support of student concerns, the audience will receive a mixed message about the board's commitment to serving student needs. Look at and support the other members of your group when they speak, and hope that they will do the same for you.

Team Presentations

When you, as an individual group member, prepare a presentation, you must make dozens of critical decisions. When an entire group prepares a team presentation, the task becomes more complex. A **team presentation** is a well-coordinated, persuasive presentation by a cohesive group of speakers who are trying to influence an audience of key decision makers. For example, team presentations are common in nonprofit agencies and international corporations.

- A professional football team seeking backing for a new stadium brings a well-rehearsed group of executives and players to a public meeting, at which they explain how the stadium will enhance the economic development and prestige of the community without adversely affecting the surrounding neighborhoods.
- Companies making the "short list" of businesses being considered for a lucrative government contract make team presentations to the officials who will award the final contract.
- In a presentation to the state legislature's appropriations committee, a state college's board chairperson, college president, academic vice president, and student representative have a total of 20 minutes to justify their request for more state funding.

A team presentation is *not* a collection of individual speeches; it is a team product. Team presentations influence decisions about whether the group or represented company is competent enough to perform a task or take on a major responsibility. They make every effort to present a united front when organizations are seeking support. Although a symposium is a coordinated presentation, symposium speakers do not necessarily present a unified front or have a persuasive goal as their purpose.

Groups that work well in the conference room may fall apart in the spotlight of a team presentation. Marjorie Brody, author of *Speaking Your Way to the Top,* writes:

> To be effective, team presentations must be meticulously planned and executed.... If a team works like a smooth, well-oiled machine, if one member's presentation flows into the next presentation, and if all members present themselves professionally and intelligently, the impression left is one of confidence and competence.[13]

As with any significant group task, the structure↔spontaneity dialectic comes into play when planning and delivering a team presentation. An effective team presentation is highly structured as well as flexible. Team members must be well-prepared with their own presentations *and* prepared to adapt to listeners' questions, a group member's misstep, or logistical problems. When preparing a team presentation, follow the guidelines in Figure A.5 below.

> **Remember This**
>
> In many ways, the team presentation is the ultimate group challenge because it requires both efficient and effective decision making and a coordinated performance.

Figure A.5   The Seven-Step Team Presentation Planning Guide

1. Purpose

    a. _____ Develop and agree upon a clear and common goal for the team presentation.

    b. _____ Begin discussing the kinds of individual presentations needed to support the group's goal.

    c. _____ Choose a chairperson who will moderate the team presentation and oversee the project.

    d. _____ Create a timetable of meetings for sharing, reviewing, assessing, and rehearsing individual presentations and the team presentation.

2. Audience

    a. _____ Conduct research about audience characteristics, opinion, expectations, and needs.

    b. _____ Develop strategies for adapting presentations to the specific audience.

3. Credibility

    a. _____ Ehance team credibility by emphasizing member expertise in individual presentations and transitions between speakers.

    b. _____ Remind team members to show interest in and enthusiasm for all of the individual presentations.

4. Logistics

    a. _____ Determine how long each member will speak.

    b. _____ Make sure the moderator has time to introduce the presentation and group members, provide transitions between speakers, and conclude with a summary.

    c. _____ Set strict deadlines for preparing and sharing individual presentations.

    d. _____ Decide whether the group will use visual aids and how they will be developed in a consistent design and style.

Figure A.5 Continued

5. Content

a. _____ Research and select appropriate supporting material for each presentation. Do not overwhelm listeners with unrelated details.

b. _____ Assess the quality and quantity of the group's content and supporting material.

c. _____ Review all presentation aids for effectiveness, consistency in style, and quality of content.

6. Organization

a. _____ Divide the team presentation into separate topics for individual group members.

b. _____ Determine the order of each presentation.

c. _____ Make sure individual presentations are well-organized.

d. _____ If possible, schedule the strongest speakers as the first and last speakers.

7. Practice

a. _____ Review, critique, and revise the content and delivery of individual presentations.

b. _____ Assess the team presentation as a whole to determine if there are unaddressed topics and ways to strengthen the overall presentation.

c. _____ Make final decisions about the logistics of the team presentation.

d. _____ Practice the team presentation at least three times including the moderator's introduction, transitions, and summary. Practice until the team's performance approaches perfection.

e. _____ Practice with all visual aids.

f. _____ Make sure the team presentation is well within the time limit.

g. _____ Prepare the team to look for and adapt to audience reactions.

Every group member should know every detail of a team presentation. The moderator should introduce each speaker, preview the importance of the topic, and bolster the speaker's credibility. In addition to describing the member's credentials, a brief story or humorous anecdote about the person gives the audience another reason to listen.[14]

Rosa Vargas, the human resources manager for the Topps Company in New York City, learned about team presentations in graduate school:

> During my MBA studies, I was part of a team, and our purpose was to launch a new product to market. I feel that preparation and rehearsal are key to a successful team presentation. I was nervous in the beginning of our presentation (we presented to a panel of professors and students), but as the presentation progressed, I relaxed a bit. Our group had practiced, and I know this helped us give a more focused presentation.[15]

Even though you have probably made individual presentations in other settings, doing a team presentation requires exceptional teamwork as well as a great deal of time, effort, and resources to prepare and present. The payoffs, however, are high. For instance, following team presentations by several companies, the Department of Energy awarded a $2.2 billion contract for environmental cleanup to a team headed by Fluor Corporation. Fluor made the best impression. "All the firms had capabilities, but how the team works as a team in the oral presentations is a key determining factor."[16] The awarding of a $2.2 billion contract should convince anyone who doubts the value of effective team presentations.

Groups in Balance...

Welcome and Encourage Questions

Once you or your team has completed a presentation, group or audience members may have questions or comments. The key to making a question-and-answer session a positive experience for everyone is to be prepared to answer a variety of questions and to know what to do when you don't have an answer.

Effective presenters use a variety of techniques to encourage audience members to ask questions. Never open a question-and-answer session with "Are there any questions?" If audience members do not have any questions in mind, they may just sit there. Instead, begin by asking a question that assumes that there are questions, such as "What are your questions?" or "Who has the first question?"

If no one answers at this point, pause and wait. Inexperienced presenters often feel uncomfortable waiting the several seconds it takes for audience members to come up with questions. Keep in mind that just as you may need a few seconds to organize your thoughts for an answer, audience members may need time to frame their questions. If you still don't get any questions after a significant pause, be prepared with some of your own, for example: "One of the questions our group often hears after our presentation is…" or "If I were in the audience, I'd want to know…"

Once an audience member asks the first question, you may find yourself facing the opposite situation: You may get an overwhelming number of questions and not have time to answer them all. As you near the end of your allotted time, or when you determine that the question-and-answer session has gone on long enough, bring the questioning to an end by saying, "I have time for two more questions." Then do just that: Answer two more questions and thank the audience for its participation.[17]

If there is a single rule, it is this: Answer the question. Practice for a question-and-answer session using these guidelines:

- *Be brief.* Respond to questions with no more than a few sentences.
- *Be honest.* If you don't know the answer to a question, admit it. Don't change the subject. The audience will know if you are avoiding the issue.
- *Be specific.* Provide appropriate information. Have some ready-made remarks, including interesting statistics, stories, examples, and quotations you can use in your answers.

If you run into difficult or hostile questions, remember that just because one listener disagrees with you doesn't mean everyone is against you. Follow the listening guideline "listen before you leap." Take your time before answering, and do not strike back in anger. Try to paraphrase the question to make sure you understand what the person is asking. If you are prepared for questions, you should have little difficulty dealing with the unexpected.

Questions   Answers

FEMA's Incident Management Assistance Teams (IMATs) participate in frequent training sessions to prepare for a variety of emergency situations. The team leader conducting the training session should encourage participants to ask questions. When answering audience questions remember to be brief, be honest, and be specific.

Presentation Aids

Presentation aids are supplementary audio and/or visual materials that help an audience understand and remember the content of a discussion or presentation. Effective presentation aids can make a dull topic interesting, a complex idea understandable, and a long presentation endurable. Studies sponsored by the 3M Corporation found that group "presenters who use visual aids are perceived as better prepared, more professional, more highly credible, and more interesting than those who do not."[18] At first, these findings may be difficult to believe. Can something as simple as an overhead transparency make that much difference? The answer is yes—but *only* if the presentation aid is clear, appropriate, and well designed.

Presentation aids are more than a pretty picture or a set of colorful computer slides. They serve three specific functions:

- *Gain Attention and Interest.* A clever cartoon, a dramatic photograph, or any other compelling aid can gain and hold listener attention.
- *Enhance Clarity and Comprehension.* Presentation aids can enhance comprehension when you present numbers and statistics, compare and contrast ideas and items, explain a complicated process, or talk about something visual (a map, a film, a painting) or auditory (music, bird calls, heartbeats).
- *Save Time.* A graph or chart can save time when summarizing a complex process or a set of statistics. Rather than writing on the board or a flip chart, speakers use computer-generated slides and handouts to save time.

As you consider the benefits and functions of presentation aids, keep in mind the most basic principle of all: *Presentation aids are only aids.* They are not your presentation.

Too often, business and professional presentations—whether they are in meetings, to clients, or before public audiences—are nothing more than narrated slide shows. The presenter simply reads what appears on a slide. By not taking time to connect with group members, clients, or audience members, such presenters miss the point of making live presentations in the first place. Before preparing any presentation aids, make sure you know what you want to say and what you want your listeners to understand and remember.

> **Remember This**
>
> Don't let your aids and their technical razzle-dazzle steal the show.

Creating Presentation Aids

The first question you should ask yourself about presentation aids is whether you need them. For some group meetings and members, presentation aids are unnecessary and a waste of time. In other group settings, a presentation aid can help listeners understand and remember critical ideas and information. If you conclude that you need presentation aids, ask a second question: Does it need to be digital?

In *The Non-Designer's Presentation Book*, Robin Williams writes that "although Apple's Keynote or Microsoft's PowerPoint is the first thing many people think of when they are asked to give a presentation, not all information is best presented digitally. Seriously consider your other alternatives so you know you are using the best method for the information you need to impart."[19]

Before punching up your slide software, consider whether other types of presentation aids are a better match for your presentation. Ask yourself whether any of the following types of presentation aids will work just as well or better than computer-generated slides:

- Flip chart
- Chalkboard or whiteboard
- Handouts or booklets
- Interactive activities or exercises
- Theatrical performance—a reading, a song, a physical demonstration

Before rejecting or ridiculing the above types of presentation aids, remember that none of them requires advanced technology. There is no computer or projector or screen necessary. If nothing else, consider these types of presentation aids as fall-back methods in case your technology fails.

Exercise Restraint. **Presentation software** offers such a dazzling array of graphics, fonts, colors, and other visual elements that you may be tempted to use them all. Resist the temptation. More often than not, a simple slide will be much more effective than a complex one.

Two recommendations can help you decide how much is just right for a presentation using computer-generated slides (as well as hand-drawn posters and flip charts):

1. *Make only one point on each slide.* Each slide should make only one point, and the title of the slide should state that

Figure A.6   **Presentation Aid Guidelines**

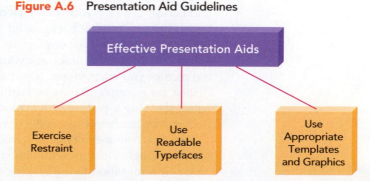

point. Everything else on the slide should support the main point. It takes less time to present two well-structured slides than to load up one slide with a muddled message.[20]

2. *In general, follow the six-by-six rule.* Aim for no more than six lines of text with six words per line. This allows your slide to contain the main heading and several bullet points without information overload.[21] Depending on your purpose, audience, logistics, and content, you may want less on each slide and use a four-by-four rule or even a one-sentence or one-phrase rule.

Today's **multimedia** technology allows you to go beyond the words on a slide. It is possible to create presentation aids so dazzling that group members remember more about the slide show than about you or your message. Your goal is to find a balance by creating clear and concise slides that will also interest your audience. Finding this balance depends on understanding not only the value of presentation aids, but also the pitfalls to avoid when adding technical "sizzle" to your presentation.[22]

Although animation or sound may sometimes enhance understanding, these multimedia components are frequently no more than window dressing that gets in the way of the message. The last thing you want is for your audience to leave a presentation wondering how you got the Tyrannosaurus rex to eat the pie chart (to the beat of the latest top-of-the-charts hit) instead of discussing the data represented in the pie chart.

> **Remember This**
>
> If you decide to include multimedia effects in a presentation, you should be able to articulate a reason for doing so other than "it's awesome."

Use Readable Typefaces.   After deciding what you want to put on a slide, select an appropriate typeface or font. "Users of presentation software have instant access to a veritable candy store of typefaces with tempting names like Arial, Calypso, Gold Rush, and Circus."[23] Again, exercise restraint. Using too many typefaces looks amateurish. As a rule, never use more than two different fonts on a single slide. Avoid the fancy, but difficult-to-read, fonts. You are better off choosing common typefaces such as Helvetica, Arial, or Times Roman.

Type size is as important as the font. The best way to determine if your type is large enough is to prepare a few sample slides and project them in the room where your group will be meeting. Generally, you should try to avoid type that is smaller than 24 points. If you have more text than will fit on a slide, don't reduce the size of the type. Two clear slides are always better than one cluttered slide.

Use Appropriate Templates and Graphics.   Use a consistent and simple style and background for your slides. Here, too, exercise restraint. In most cases, it is better to choose a modest background that will spruce up your slide but not compete with your words, charts, or graphics.

When choosing graphics, ask yourself whether group members really need to see the picture you want to use. If you are making a presentation about a new medical device, for example, it may be useful to show a picture of the device. On the other hand, showing a picture of a doctor would probably not be useful. A picture of a doctor does not help explain the device.

Artwork that doesn't have a specific purpose can get in the way of your presentation. Although most presentation software comes with numerous clip-art images, resist the temptation to use graphic elements just because you can. More often than

Figure A.7 Sample Presentation Slide

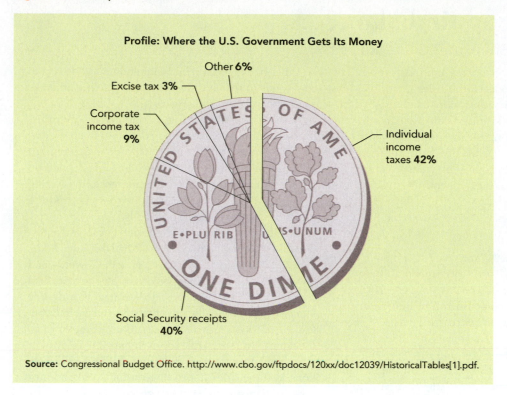

Profile: Where the U.S. Government Gets Its Money

Other **6%**

Excise tax **3%**

Corporate income tax **9%**

Individual income taxes **42%**

E·PLU RIB U S·U NUM

ONE DIME

Social Security receipts **40%**

Source: Congressional Budget Office. http://www.cbo.gov/ftpdocs/120xx/doc12039/HistoricalTables[1].pdf.

not, clip-art graphics get in the way of messages when the graphic is not the reason for the slide. See Figure A.7 for an example of an effective presentation slide.

The Pitfalls of PowerPoint

Many presenters use PowerPoint (or other brands of presentation software, such as Google Presentation) without thoroughly investigating whether it enhances the listeners' comprehension or helps speakers accomplish their purpose. Some corporations have even banned PowerPoint presentations by employees who have not had extensive training in visual design and its relationship to audience comprehension and reasoned analysis. The 3M Corporation discourages the use of PowerPoint because "it removes subtlety and thinking."[24]

Edward Tufte, author of several books on graphic design, notes:

Presentations largely stand or fall on the quality, relevance, and integrity of the content.... If your numbers are boring, then you've got the wrong numbers. If your words or images are not on point, making them dance in color won't make them relevant. Audience boredom is usually a content failure, not a decoration failure.... PowerPoint cognitive style routinely disrupts, dominates, and trivializes content. PowerPoint presentations too often resemble a school play: very loud, very slow, and very simple.[25]

A survey of college students concluded that students like technology in the classroom, but some gave professors failing grades when it came to using PowerPoint. They complained that many professors cram slides with text and then recite the

Groups in Balance...

Know When to Break the "Slide" Rules[26]

PowerPoint trade books and courses are full of rules. And, in many cases, the rules contradict one another from book to book and instructor to instructor. Effective speakers understand that the "rules" are a way of demonstrating guidelines such as exercising restraint or choosing appropriate type. Consider the following sets of rules. Would you feel comfortable breaking or bending any of these "rules"?

Slide Timing. Nancy Duarte extols the 3-second rule:

> Presentations are a "glance media"—more closely related to billboards than other media. It requires commuters to process quickly as they drive past. Imagine having a billboard full of bullets; drivers would crash trying to process the ads. Ask yourself whether your message on a single slide can be processed effectively within three seconds. The audience should be able to ascertain the meaning quickly before turning their attention back to the presenter.[27]

Other books recommend giving an audience up to 60 seconds to read a slide. We suggest giving an audience time to read a slide twice.

Rather than interpreting this advice as contradictory, consider the content and context of the presentation. The amount of text or data on and the amount of time it takes an audience to read a slide depend on the presentation's purpose, the audience, the setting and occasion, the complexity of the message, and the presenter's speaking style and skills.

Magic Number Rules. Rules about the amount of text on a slide include the rule of four items; the 5 × 5, 6 × 6, and 7 × 7 rules; the 1-7-7 rule; and the 3-word- and 6-word-per-slide rules. One book advocates no more than seven slides per presentation; another suggests a 10-slide limit. Again, consider the presentation's content and context. In his book *Presentation Zen*, Garr Reynolds illustrates the folly of rigid rules by examining the 1-7-7 rule.

As was the case with slide timing, there are exceptions to these rules depending on the speaker's purpose, audience, context, message, and delivery.

The 1-7-7 rule: What is it?

- Have only <u>one</u> main idea per slide
- Insert only <u>seven</u> lines of text maximum
- Use only <u>seven</u> words per line maximum
- The question is: does this work?
- Is this method really good advice?
- Is there really an appropriate, effective "visual"?
- This slide has just seven bullet points!

Garr Reynolds, *Presentation Zen: Simple Ideas on Presentation Design and Delivery*, p. 130.

Used to illustrate thr folly of rigid rules

Ethics in Groups

Respect Copyrights

Technology not only makes it easier to create professional-looking presentation aids, but it also makes it easier to appropriate the creative work of others in a presentation. When the creation of visual or audio images is a person's livelihood, the uncompensated use of such images raises ethical questions. Such unfair use may even be a violation of federal copyright laws. A discussion of whether a particular use of an image is illegal is far beyond the scope of this book; however, you should be aware of the legal and ethical implications of using unlicensed images.

A whole industry has developed to provide clip art and clip audio to computer users. A user who purchases such packages has the right to make copies of the images and use them in presentations. Likewise, the visual and audio images included with presentation software are free. On the other hand, if you create a computer image by scanning an image from another source or if you obtain an image from the Internet, your conscience and your knowledge of copyright law must act as your guide.

text during class, which some students say makes the delivery flatter than if the professor did not use the slides.[28] As one student put it: "The majority are taking their lectures and just putting them on PowerPoint.... With a chalkboard, at least the lights were on and you didn't fall asleep." One professor reported a 20 percent drop in attendance when he posted his PowerPoint slides on the Web. Now his slides are "riddled with blanks and missing information, which he fills in aloud during lecture."[29]

In many cases, paper handouts can show text, numbers, data, graphics, and images more effectively than slides can. Images on paper have a higher resolution. Content on paper can include more words and numbers. Thoughtfully planned, well-written handouts tell your audience that you are serious and thorough, that your message has consequences, and that you respect their attention and intelligence.[30]

Delivering Presentation Aids

Presentation aids can take many forms: handouts, posters, flip charts, overhead transparencies, computer-generated slides, and videos. The following list of dos and don'ts can help you avoid some common pitfalls when using any type of presentation aid.

- *Explain the point.* A presentation aid does not speak for itself. You may need to explain why you have chosen it and what it means.
- *Wait until it's time.* Prepare listeners for a presentation aid so that they will want to see it. Give them enough time to look at it so that they don't mind turning their attention back to you.
- *Don't talk to your aid.* You control the presentation aid; it shouldn't control you. Talk directly to the people in your audience, not to the poster, flip chart, or slide.
- *Be prepared to do without.* Presentation aids can be lost or damaged; equipment can malfunction. Have a backup plan. Be prepared to make your presentation without your aids.

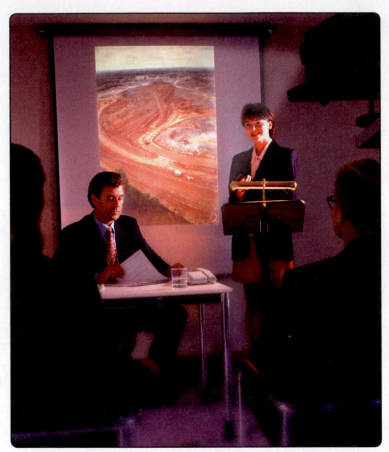

Computer-generated slides have become so common that many presenters feel helpless without them. Unfortunately, they are often used ineffectively. Just because someone always uses slides in staff meetings does not mean they are needed or that you have to play "follow the leader."

- *Handle handouts effectively*. Handouts are appropriate when your presentation contains a lot of technical information or if you want your audience to take notes. In general, distribute handouts before you begin speaking–but not if your handout is a word-for-word copy of your presentation.
- *Show and tell*. Audience members learn and remember more when a speaker's words and visuals are presented simultaneously rather than successively. In other words, *show* the audience a well designed visual and *tell* them about it at the same time.
- *Don't read your slides to the audience*. "Contrary to conventional wisdom and common practice, reading bullet points word-for-word from a screen actually hurts learning rather than helping it."[31]

Beyond these dos and don'ts, here is one more piece of advice: practice, practice, practice. Not only can practice improve your overall performance, it can also alert you to problems with your presentation aids. For example, we once watched a consultant put almost everything in her talk on slides. As soon as she projected something onto the screen, she would turn around and point out the numbers that she thought were important. Unfortunately, she stood right between the screen and the projector so that most of the information projected onto her back. If she had practiced in front of others before making the presentation, she could have avoided the problem.

Summary Study Guide

Presentations in and by Groups
- A group presentation occurs whenever a member speaks, relatively uninterrupted, to other group members or audience members.
- Group members make presentations within a group, on behalf of a group, or as part of a team presentation.

Presentation Guidelines
- The seven critical decision-making guidelines of presentation speaking revolve around the following key elements: (1) purpose, (2) audience, (3) credibility, (4) logistics, (5) content, (6) organization, and (7) delivery.
- The first and most important step in developing a successful presentation is to determine your purpose—what you want your listeners to know, think, believe, or do as a result of your presentation.
- Three major factors that enhance a speaker's credibility are perceived competence, character, and caring.
- Seek common ground with your audience by analyzing their demographic traits, individual attributes, and opinions.
- An effective presentation should have an interesting introduction, the statement of a central idea, a preview of key points, a well-organized body, and a memorable conclusion.

- Forms of delivery include impromptu, extemporaneous, manuscript, and memorized delivery.

Group Presentations
- A team presentation is a well-coordinated, persuasive presentation by a cohesive group of speakers who are trying to influence an audience of key decision makers.
- When you are the member of a group making a public presentation, remember that you are "on stage" at all times—even when you are not speaking.
- Use the Seven-Step Team Presentation Planning Guide to ensure team success.
- During a question-and-answer session, answer questions directly and as clearly as possible.

Presentation Aids
- Consider the following design elements when developing computer-generated slides: restraint, type, templates, graphics, and multimedia enhancements.
- When planning your presentation aids, make sure you can explain the point of the aid, know when to display it, know where to stand when using the aid, and are prepared to make the presentation without the aid.

Group Work

Re-envision the Visual

Directions: Use the design principles presented in this chapter to redesign one or both of the following slides. Explain why your design decisions produce a better slide than the examples. In addition to changing the design, you may change wording (add, subtract, substitute other words) but not the basic meaning.

Examples of Bad Slides

Slide #1

Common Cents

Save half a buck a day in loose change	$ 15
Drink 12 fewer cans of soda per month	6
Drink regular coffee instead of cappuccino	40
Avoid ATM fees and credit-card late charges	80
Eat out two fewer times a month	30
Borrow, rather than buy, a book or CD	15
TOTAL MONTHLY SAVINGS	186

Source: America Saves

Slide #2

Challenges We Face

We lost 3% of our market share last year

Our stock price is down by 7% from just a year ago.

Customer complaints are up by 14%

Retention of key people is down by five percent

Group Assessment

Team Presentation Evaluation

Directions: Use the Seven-Step Team Presentation Planning Guide to assess a team presentation. Check one of the four ratings to indicate your evaluation of the team presentation. Then identify two of the group's strengths and make two suggestions for improvement.

Team Name and/or Group Members: _____

_____

Team Presentation Planning Guidelines	Excellent	Good	Fair	Poor
1. **Purpose.** The purpose of individual presentations and the overall team presentation were clear.				
2. **Audience.** Individual presentations and the overall team presentation engaged, interested, and adapted to the audience.				
3. **Credibility.** Group members seemed well informed, trustworthy, and helpful.				
4. **Logistics.** Individual presentations and the overall team presentation adapted to the setting, time limits, and occasion.				
5. **Content.** Individual presentations and the overall team presentation offered valuable ideas and information.				
6. **Organization.** Individual presentations and the overall team presentation were well organized and easy to follow.				
7. **Delivery.** Individual presentations and the overall team presentation were well rehearsed and delivered.				
Group Presentation's Strengths	1. _____ _____ 2. _____ _____			
Suggestions for Improvement	1. _____ _____ 2. _____ _____			

Glossary

abdicrat A group member whose need for control is not met; an abdicrat is submissive and avoids responsibility.

abstract word A word that refers to an idea or concept that cannot be perceived by your five senses.

accommodation conflict style An approach to conflict in which a person gives in to other group members, even at the expense of his or her own goals.

achievement norm A norm that determines the quality and quantity of work expected from group members.

action item An item in the written minutes of a meeting that identifies the member responsible for an assigned task.

ad hominem attack The fallacy of making an irrelevant attack against a person's character rather than a substantive response to an issue or argument.

adjourning stage The group development phase in which a group has achieved its common goal and begins to disengage or disband.

A-E-I-O-U Model A conflict resolution model with five steps: Assume that other members mean well; Express your feelings; Identify your goal; clarify expected Outcomes; and achieve mutual Understanding.

affection need The need to express and receive warmth or to be liked.

affective conflict A type of conflict that reflects the emotions stirred by interpersonal disagreements, differences in personalities and communication styles, and conflicting core values and beliefs.

agenda An outline of the items to be discussed and the tasks to be accomplished at a meeting.

aggressiveness Critical, insensitive, combative, or abusive behavior that is motivated by self-interest at the expense of others.

aggressor A group member who puts down other members to get what she or he wants (a self-centered role).

agreeableness trait A Big Five Personality Theory trait that describes a cooperative, friendly, flexible, trusting, and tolerant personality.

amendment A modification or change to a motion under consideration in a meeting using parliamentary procedure.

analytical listening A type of listening that focuses on evaluating and forming opinions about a message.

antecedent phase The first phase of new member socialization in which the newcomer's beliefs and attitudes, culture, traits, and prior experiences are identified.

anticipatory phase The second phase of new member socialization in which group members determine if a newcomer meets the group's expectations in terms of characteristics and motives.

appeal to authority The fallacy of using the opinions of a supposed expert when in fact the person has no particular expertise in the area under consideration.

appeal to popularity The fallacy of claiming that an action or belief is acceptable because many people do it or believe it.

appeal to tradition The fallacy of claiming that people should continue a certain course of action because that is the way it has always been done.

arbitration A conflict resolution method that involves a third party who, after considering all sides in a dispute, decides how to resolve the conflict.

argument A claim supported by evidence and reasons for accepting it.

argumentation The use of critical thinking to advocate a position, examine competing ideas, and influence others.

argumentativeness The willingness to argue with others and take public positions on controversial issues.

assertiveness Speaking up and acting in your own best interests without denying the rights and interests of others.

assimilation phase The fourth phase of new member socialization in which a newcomer becomes fully integrated into the group and works toward the common group goal.

asynchronous communication Electronic communication that does not occur simultaneously or in real time; communication that is linear and not interactive.

Attribution Theory A theory that claims we make judgments about people's motives and characteristics that go beyond what we see and hear.

audioconference A voice-only communication medium that usually takes one of two forms: a teleconference or a computer-based voice link.

authority rule A situation in which a leader or an authority outside a group makes final decisions for the group.

autocrat A group member whose need for control is not met; an autocrat tries to dominate and control the group.

autocratic leader A leader who uses power and authority to strictly control the direction and outcome of group work.

avoidance conflict style A passive and nonconfrontational approach to conflict.

avoidant decision maker A person who feels uncomfortable and shuns making decisions.

backing The component of the Toulmin Model of Argument that provides support for an argument's warrant.

balance A state of equilibrium in which no significant factor dominates or interferes with other factors.

Big Five Personality Traits A theory that describes five factors (extraversion, agreeableness, conscientiousness, emotional stability, and openness to experience) that, taken together, describe a personality.

blocker A group member who stands in the way of progress and uses delaying tactics to derail an idea or proposal (a self-centered role).

brainstorming A technique that encourages group members to generate as many ideas as possible in a nonevaluative atmosphere.

bulletin board An asynchronous, text-based communication technology in which group members read one another's messages and that can be organized in a threaded discussion.

bylaws A document that specifies the rules governing how an organization is structured and how it conducts its official business.

bypassing A form of miscommunication that occurs when people have different meanings for the same words or phrases and miss each other with their meanings.

caring A major factor in determining a communicator's credibility that relies on listeners' perceptions of a person's willingness and ability to understand, show concern for, and empathize with others.

certainty Behavior that may contribute to a defensive communication climate in which members act as though only their ideas and opinions are absolutely correct and therefore refuse to consider or support other members' ideas and opinions.

chair or **chairperson** A person who has been appointed or elected to conduct a group meeting. In meetings using parliamentary procedures, the chair may be the president or may be referred to as the presiding officer.

channel The media (hearing, seeing, touching, smelling, and/or tasting) through which group members share messages.

Chaos Theory A theory that claims that, although certain behaviors in natural systems are not predictable, there is a pattern to their randomness.

character A major factor in determining a communicator's credibility based on listeners' perceptions of whether that person is trustworthy and honest.

charismatic power A type of personal power that relies on a leader's character, competence, and vitality.

civic group A group dedicated to worthy causes and that helps people within the group.

claim The component of the Toulmin Model of Argument that states the proposition or conclusion of an argument.

claim of conjecture An argument suggesting that something will or will not happen.

claim of fact An argument stating that something is true or false or that something did or did not occur.

claim of policy An argument advocating a specific course of action.

claim of value An argument evaluating whether something is good or bad, right or wrong, worthwhile or worthless.

clerk A group member or employee assigned to take minutes, track the status of motions, and record votes during a meeting or assembly.

climate The group atmosphere, characterized by the degree to which members feel comfortable interacting.

clown A group member who injects inappropriate humor into the discussion and seems more interested in goofing off than in working (a self-centered role).

CMC An acronym for computer-mediated communication.

co-culture A group of people who coexist within the mainstream society yet remain connected to one another through their cultural heritage.

codeswitching The ability to change from the language or dialect of your own culture and adopt the language or dialect of another cultural group.

coercive power A type of position power with the ability or authority to pressure or punish group members if they do not follow orders and directions.

cognitive restructuring A technique for reducing communication apprehension that analyzes worrisome, irrational, and nonproductive assumptions about speaking to and with others (cognitions) and seeks to modify those thoughts (restructuring).

cohesion The mutual attraction that holds the members of a group together.

collaboration conflict style An approach to conflict emphasizing the search for solutions that satisfy all group members and that also achieve the group's common goal.

collaborative presentation technology   Technology that enhances interactive group presentations by allowing members to project ideas or graphics onto a screen, wall, or whiteboard.

collectivism   A cultural value or belief in interdependence that places greater emphasis on the views, needs, and goals of the group than on the views, needs, and goals of individuals.

common ground   An identifiable belief, value, experience, or point of view shared by all group members.

communication apprehension   An individual's level of fear or anxiety associated with either real or anticipated communication with another person or persons.

competence   A major factor in determining a communicator's credibility based on listeners' perceptions about that person's expertise and abilities.

competition conflict style   An approach to conflict that is focused on achieving a person's own goals rather than the group's goals, even if this upsets the group and its members.

completer/finisher   A group member who emphasizes schedules, deadlines, and task completion and searches for errors (an action-oriented team role).

Complexity Theory   A theory that seeks patterns in complex systems by examining states of order, complexity, and chaos.

comprehensive listening   A type of listening that focuses on accurately understanding the meaning of spoken and nonverbal messages.

compromise conflict style   An approach to conflict that involves the concession of some goals in order to achieve others.

compromiser   A group member who helps minimize differences among group members and helps the group reach consensus (a maintenance role).

concrete word   A word that refers to something that can be perceived by the senses.

confirmation bias   Resistance to information that is inconsistent with a preconceived belief.

conflict   The disagreement and disharmony that occurs in groups when differences regarding group goals, member ideas, behavior, roles, or group procedures and norms arise.

conflict↔cohesion   A group dialectic in which the value of constructive conflict is balanced with the need for unity and cohesiveness.

conforming↔nonconforming   A group dialectic in which a commitment to group norms and standards is balanced with a willingness to accept differences and change.

conformity   The choice of behavior that is socially acceptable and favored by a majority of group members.

conscientiousness trait   A Big Five Personality Theory trait that describes a self-disciplined, organized, responsible, achievement-oriented personality.

consensus   A situation in which all group members have a part in shaping and are willing to support a group decision.

constructive conflict   An approach to disagreement in which group members express differences in a way that values everyone's contributions and promotes the group's goal.

constructive nonconformity   The act of resisting conformity to group norms and expectations while still working to achieve the group's goal.

context   The physical and psychological environment in which group communication takes place.

Contingency Model of Leadership Effectiveness   A leadership theory claiming that effective leadership depends upon an ideal match between the leader's style and the group's work situation.

control   Member behavior that may contribute to a defensive communication climate by imposing personal ideas, preferences, and solutions on others.

control need   The need to feel competent, confident, and free to make your own choices.

cooperative argumentation   A process of reasoned interaction intended to help members make the best assessments or decisions in a given situation.

coordinator   A group member who pulls ideas and suggestions together and tries to coordinate the activities of various members or subgroups (a task role).

coordinator-chairperson   A group member who clarifies group goals, helps allocate roles and duties, and articulates group conclusions (a people-oriented team role).

creativity   The nonjudgmental process and outcome of searching for, separating, and connecting thoughts to form new ideas.

credibility   The extent to which others believe you and your messages.

critical thinking   The kind of thinking used when analyzing something read, seen, or heard in order to arrive at a justified conclusion or decision.

cultural dimension   An aspect of a culture that can be measured relative to other cultures.

culture   The learned set of shared expectations about beliefs, values, and norms that affect the behaviors of a relatively large group of people.

decision making   The act of making a judgment, choosing an option, and making up one's mind about something.

Decreasing Options Technique (DOT)   A procedure for reducing and refining a large number of ideas or suggestions into more manageable categories.

deep diversity   Member characterisitics that are difficult to observe, such as knowledge, skills, and abilities related to the demands of a group's task.

defensive climate   A communication situation that triggers group members' instincts to protect themselves when physically or verbally attacked by someone.

definition   A statement that clarifies the meaning of a word, phrase, or concept.

democratic leader   A leader who practices social equality and shares the decision-making process with group members.

democratic member   A group member whose need for control is met and who has no problems dealing with power in groups.

demographic trait   An audience trait such as age, gender, race, ethnicity, religion, and marital status.

dependent decision maker   A person who seeks the advice and opinions of others before making a decision.

description   1. Member behavior that contributes to a supportive communication climate by making understanding and helpful statements and using *I* and *we* language. 2. A type of evidence that creates a mental image of a person, event, place, or object.

deserter   A group member who seems bored or annoyed with the discussion and stops contributing (a self-centered role).

designated leader   A leader selected by a group or an outside authority.

destructive conflict   Disagreement that is expressed through behaviors that create hostility and prevent achievement of the group's goal.

destructive nonconformity   Resistance to conforming to group norms and expectations without regard for the best interests of the group and its goal.

dialect   The distinct regional and cultural variations in vocabulary, pronunciation, syntax, and style that distinguish speakers from different ethnic groups, geographic areas, and social classes.

dialectics   Two seemingly opposing ideas or tensions in a relationship or group that may be resolved with a *both/and* approach.

digital divide   Inequalities in access to, distribution of, and use of information technology among different groups or populations.

discrimination   Acting out and expressing prejudice by excluding groups of people from the opportunities and rights granted to others.

diversity   The quality of being different.

documentation   The practice of citing sources of evidence.

dominator   A group member who tries to assert authority and prevents others from participating (a self-centered role).

early leaver   A person who disrupts a meeting or annoys others by leaving before a group meeting is over.

elaborator   A group member who helps explain ideas and suggestions by providing examples or summaries or by describing the consequences of a decision or action (a task role).

email   A worldwide, text-based, asynchronous technology that allows group members to interact from great distances.

emergent leader   A person who gradually achieves leadership status by interacting with group members and contributing to the achievement of the group's common goal.

emoticon   Typographical characters used to express emotion when communicating via computer.

emotional intelligence   The capacity for recognizing your own feelings and those of others, for motivating yourself, and for managing emotions in yourself and in various interpersonal relationships.

emotional stability trait   A Big Five Personality Theory trait that, when positive, depicts a calm, poised, and secure personality.

empathic listening   A type of listening that focuses on understanding a person's feelings, motives, and situation.

empathy   Member behavior that contributes to a supportive communication climate by expressing acceptance, caring, and understanding of others and their feelings.

empowerment   A shift in power or authority that allows group members to assume responsibility for their work.

encounter phase   The third phase of new member socialization in which a newcomer tries to fit in and adjust to the group.

encourager-supporter   A group member who praises and agrees with others, provides recognition, and listens empathically (a maintenance role).

energizer   A group member who motivates others to do their best and helps create enthusiasm for the task (a task role).

engaged↔disengaged   A group dialectic in which members' loyalty and labor are balanced with the group's need for rest and renewal.

equality   Member behaviors that contribute to a supportive communication climate by respecting everyone's ability to make useful contributions.

ethics   An understanding of whether group members' communication behaviors meet agreed-upon standards of right and wrong.

ethnocentrism   A mistaken belief that your culture is a superior culture with special rights and privileges that are or should be denied to others.

ethos   A Greek word meaning character that has evolved into the modern concept of credibility.

evaluation   Member behavior that may contribute to a defensive communication climate by making judgmental and disparaging statements about other group members.

evaluator-critic   A group member who assesses ideas, arguments, and suggestions; functions as the group's critical thinker; and diagnoses task and procedural problems (a task role).

evidence   The component of the Toulmin Model of Argument that provides facts, statistics, opinions, examples, or other material to support a claim.

example   A type of evidence that refers to a specific case or instance.

exit phase   The final phase of new member socialization in which a newcomer may leave an established group.

expert power   A type of power with the ability to motivate and persuade others by demonstrating special expertise or knowledge.

explicit norm   A norm that is written or stated verbally.

extemporaneous speaking   A form of presentation delivery in which the speaker has done prior preparations but uses limited notes while speaking.

extrinsic reward   A reward that comes from the external environment, such as money, benefits, and job perks.

extraversion trait   A Big Five Personality Theory trait that describes an outgoing, talkative, sociable, assertive, and active person.

extrovert, as a personality trait   A Myers-Briggs personality type who is outgoing, usually talks more than others, and is often enthusiastic and animated during a discussion.

face, as a cultural term   The positive image that a person tries to create or preserve that is also appropriate to a particular culture.

fact   A verifiable observation, experience, or event; something that is known to be true.

fallacy   An argument based on false or invalid reasoning.

false consensus   A situation in which members succumb to group pressure and accept a decision that they do not like or support.

faulty analogy   The fallacy of claiming that two things are similar when they actually differ with regard to relevant characteristics.

faulty cause   The fallacy of identifying the cause of an event before ruling out other possible causes.

feedback   The verbal or nonverbal response or reaction to a message.

feeler, as a personality trait   A Myers-Briggs personality type who wants everyone to get along and who will spend time with other group members to achieve harmony.

feminine value society   A culture in which gender roles overlap: Both men and women are supposed to be modest, tender, and concerned with the quality of life.

5M Model of Leadership Effectiveness   An approach to leadership that divides leadership tasks into five interdependent functions: (1) *Modeling* leadership behavior, (2) *Motivating* members, (3) *Managing* the group process, (4) *Making* decisions, and (5) *Mentoring* members.

floor   In parliamentary procedure, a reference to the right to speak before a group after being recognized by the chair, as in "I have the floor."

follower   A group member who supports the group and its members, accepts others' ideas and assignments, and serves as an attentive audience member (a maintenance role).

forming stage   The group development phase in which member and group goals are explored and interpersonal relationships are tested.

FTF   An acronym for face-to-face communication.

Functional Leadership Theory   An approach to leadership that claims that any capable group member can assume leadership functions when necessary.

Functional Perspective   A problem-solving theory claiming that a set of preparation, competence, and critical thinking/communication functions can explain and predict how well a group will solve problems.

Fundamental Interpersonal Relationship Orientation (FIRO) Theory   Will Schutz's theory that examines the extent to which the satisfaction of inclusion, control, and affection needs affects why people join groups and how well group members interact with one another.

gatekeeper   A group member who monitors participation and tries to regulate the flow of communication in a discussion (a maintenance role).

goal   The purpose or objective toward which a group's efforts are directed.

golden listening rule   The principle that you should listen to others as you would have them listen to you.

group communication   The interaction of three or more interdependent members working to achieve a common goal.

group decision support system (GDSS)   System using specialized software to help participants perform a variety of group tasks by integrating the contributions of group members working at individual workstations.

group dialectics The contradictory tensions groups experience as they work toward a common goal.

group polarization A tendency for group members (and especially virtual groups in which there are no visible nonverbal cues) to express more extreme opinions and take more extreme actions.

group presentation A relatively uninterrupted talk or speech by one or more group members within a group, on behalf of a group, or by an entire group.

groupthink The deterioration of group effectiveness and moral judgment that results from in-group pressure.

groupware Computer-mediated methods and tools that are designed to support group collaboration.

harmonizer A group member who helps resolve conflicts and promotes teamwork (a maintenance role).

hasty generalization The fallacy of using too few examples or experiences to support a conclusion.

help-seeker A group member who seeks sympathetic responses from the group and expresses insecurity, confusion, or inferiority (a self-centered role).

Hersey-Blanchard Situational Leadership® Model A model that links leadership style to whether group members are ready, willing, and able to contribute.

heterogeneous group A group composed of members who are different from one another.

hidden agenda An individual member's private motives and goals that differ from a group's common goal.

high-context culture A culture in which very little meaning is expressed through words; gestures, silence, facial expression, and relationships among communicators are more reliable indicators of meaning.

high power distance A cultural norm of accepting major differences in power and assuming that all people are *not* created equal.

homogeneous group A group composed of members who are all the same or very similar to one another.

homogeneous↔heterogeneous A group dialectic in which member similarities are balanced with member differences in skills, roles, personal characteristics, and cultural perspectives.

HURIER Listening Model A framework that identifies six interrelated components of listening processes: *H*earing, *U*nderstanding *R*emembering, *I*nterpreting, *E*valuating, and *R*esponding.

hyperpersonal communication An increase in confidence and a decrease in communication apprehension that occurs in computer-mediated rather than face-to-face communication.

illustration An extended or detailed example.

immediacy Nonverbal behaviors that communicate greater physical closeness to or liking of others.

implementer A group member who transforms ideas into action and develops action plans for members (an action-oriented team role).

implicit norm A norm that is rarely discussed or openly communicated.

impromptu A form of presentation delivery in which a person speaks without prior preparation or practice.

inclusion need The need to be accepted and affiliated with a group; the need to belong or be involved.

individual attributes Distinctive features of particular group members, such as personality traits, job titles, status, special interests, relationships with other members, and length of membership.

individual goals ↔ group goals A group dialectic in which members' personal goals are balanced with the group's common goal.

individualism A cultural value or belief that the individual is important, that independence is worth pursuing, that personal achievement should be rewarded, and that individual uniqueness is an important value.

informational power A type of position power with the ability to control and transmit information and sources.

information-getting meeting A meeting that provides an opportunity for members to provide reports or briefings to the chairperson and other members.

information giver A group member who provides and organizes relevant information (a task role).

information-giving meeting A meeting that provides the chairperson an opportunity to present information to members.

information seeker A group member who asks for needed information, requests explanations and clarifications, and makes the group aware of information gaps (a task role).

initiator-contributor A group member who proposes ideas and suggestions, provides direction for the group, and gets the group started (a task role).

innovator A group member who advances proposals, offers ideas, and provides insights on courses of action (a thought-oriented team role).

instructional meeting A meeting that provides members with training in a specific skill or knowledge area.

interaction Communication among group members who use verbal and nonverbal messages to generate meaning and establish relationships.

interaction norm A norm that determines how group members communicate with one another.

interactive whiteboard   A presentation technology that allows members to work simultaneously on the same document or drawing by instantly digitizing, storing, printing, and displaying members' work in both local and remote locations.

interdependence   The extent to which group members are affected and influenced by the actions of other members.

Internet Addiction Disorder (IAD)   A maladaptive pattern of Internet use that results in clinically significant impairment or distress.

interpersonal space   The psychological space surrounding each person that expands and contracts in different contexts.

interrupter   A person who speaks out during a meeting while other members are still talking.

intimate distance   Interpersonal space ranging from zero to 18 inches, typically reserved for close friends, family, and lovers.

intrinsic reward   A reward that is satisfying and energizing in itself.

introvert, as a personality trait   A Myers-Briggs personality type who needs time to think before speaking and who may prefer to work alone rather than in a group.

intuitive, as a personality trait   A Myers-Briggs personality type who likes to make connections and formulate big ideas but who may become bored with details.

intuitive decision maker   A person who makes decisions based on instincts and feelings.

jargon   The specialized or technical language of a profession.

judger, as a personality trait   A Myers-Briggs personality type who is highly structured and likes to plan ahead.

kinesics   The study of body movement and physical expression.

laissez-faire leader   A leader who lets the group take charge of all decisions and actions.

latecomer   A group member who disrupts a meeting by arriving late.

leader–member relations   A situational leadership factor that assesses how well a leader gets along with group members.

leadership   The ability to make strategic decisions and use communication to mobilize a group toward achieving a common goal.

leadership↔followership   A group dialectic in which effective and ethical leadership is balanced with loyal and responsible followership.

learning group   A group that helps its members acquire knowledge and develop skills by sharing information and experience.

leet   A language form common to electronic communication that uses an alternate alphabet to create words.

legitimate power   A type of power that resides in a job or position.

listening   The ability to understand, analyze, respect, and appropriately respond to spoken and/or nonverbal messages.

listening to evaluate   The ability to use critical thinking skills to analyze what is heard, also known as analytical listening.

listening to hear   The ability to make clear, aural distinctions among the sounds and words in a language.

listening to interpret   A factor in empathic listening involving the ability to recognize and appropriately respond to emotional meanings.

listening to remember   The ability to recall what is heard.

listening to respond   The ability to react verbally and nonverbally to what is heard such as asking a question, providing support, offering advice, or sharing an opinion.

listening to understand   The ability to focus on accurately grasping the meaning of spoken and nonverbal messages, also known as comprehensive listening.

logistics   The strategic planning, arranging, and use of people, facilities, time, and materials.

loudmouth   A person who talks so much that no one else gets a chance to speak during a group meeting.

low-context culture   A culture in which meaning is expressed primarily through language; people from a low-context culture tend to speak more, speak louder, and speak more rapidly than people from a high-context culture.

low power distance   A cultural perspective in which power distinctions are minimized.

main motion   In parliamentary procedure, a proposal for a new action or decision.

maintenance role   A positive role that affects how group members get along with one another while pursuing a common goal.

majority vote   The results of a vote in which more than half the members vote in favor of a proposal.

manipulation   Behavior in which people seek to influence and manage others, usually for self-centered reasons.

masculine value society   A culture in which men are supposed to be assertive, tough, and focused on material success, whereas women are supposed to be more modest, tender, and concerned with the quality of life.

Media Richness Theory   A theory that contends that communication will be more successful when more communication channels are used.

Media Synchronicity Theory   A theory that extends Media Richness Theory by matching media capabilities to the fundamental communication processes required to perform a group task.

mediation   A facilitated negotiation that employs the services of an impartial third party for the purpose of guiding, coaching, and encouraging disputants to a successful resolution and an agreement.

meeting   A scheduled gathering of group members for a structured discussion guided by a designated chairperson.

meetingthink   The failure of group members to think critically in meetings and, as a result, make faulty decisions.

member   Any individual whom other members recognize as belonging to the group.

member readiness   The extent to which a member is willing and able to contribute to achieving the group's goal.

message   An idea, information, opinion, and/or feeling that generates meaning.

minutes   The written record of a group's discussion and activities during a meeting.

mnemonic   A memory aid that is based on something simple, like a pattern or a rhyme.

monitor/evaluator   A group member who analyzes problems, monitors progress, assesses others' contributions, and explores options (a thought-oriented team role).

monochronic time (M time)   An approach to time that favors clear deadlines and the scheduling of one thing at a time.

motion   In parliamentary procedure, a formal, carefully worded proposal made by a member seeking the consideration and action of an assembly or group.

multimedia   Technology that enables you to combine words, charts, graphics, sounds, and animation in a single presentation.

Muted Group Theory   A theory that claims that power imbalances inhibit some female and minority group members from expressing themselves assertively and impede their ability to participate effectively in group work.

Myers-Briggs Type Indicator® (MBTI)   A widely used inventory that identifies specific personality types based on the ways in which people perceive the world around them and make judgments.

negotiation   A process of bargaining for the purpose of settling differences or reaching solutions.

netlingo   Language forms, such as abbreviations, acronyms, and less use of punctuation, that are common to communication via the Internet.

netspeak   Typographical strategies common to communication via the Internet that are used to achieve a more sociable and interactive style.

neutrality   Member behavior that may contribute to a defensive communication climate when members appear withdrawn, detached, and indifferent.

noise   Anything that interferes with or inhibits communication.

Nominal Group Technique (NGT)   A procedure in which members write and report suggested ideas, after which discussion and multiple votes are used to decide the priority or value of the listed suggestions.

nonconformity   A member's behavior that does not meet the norms or expectations of the group.

nonparticipant   A person who never or rarely contributes during a group meeting.

nonverbal communication   The behavioral elements of messages other than the actual words spoken.

norm   An expectation held by group members concerning what kinds of behavior or opinions are acceptable or unacceptable.

norming stage   The group development stage in which members resolve conflicts and work as a cohesive team to develop methods for achieving the group's goal.

observer-commentator   A group member who explains what others are trying to say, monitors and interprets feelings and nonverbal communication, expresses group feelings, and paraphrases other members' comments (a maintenance role).

offensive language   Terminology that demeans, inappropriately excludes, or stereotypes people.

open system↔closed system   A group dialectic in which external support and recognition are balanced with internal group solidarity and rewards.

openness to experience, as a personality trait   A Big Five Personality Theory trait that describes an imaginative, curious, broadminded, and artistically sensitive personality.

opinion   A personal conclusion regarding the meaning or implication of facts.

opinion giver   A group member who states personal beliefs and interpretations and offers analysis and arguments (a task role).

opinion seeker   A group member who asks for others' opinions (a task role).

optimal group experience   An experience in which all group members are caught up in the group's work and are performing at a high level of achievement.

oral citation   A comment that includes enough information to allow others to find the original source of any evidence.

orienter   A group member who summarizes what has been said and what has occurred and raises questions about the direction the discussion is taking in relation to the group agenda and goals (a task role).

overpersonal member A group member whose affection needs are not met and who is too talkative and overly personal.

oversocial member A group member whose inclusion needs are not met and who seeks attention as a way of compensating for feelings of inadequacy.

paraphrasing A form of feedback that uses different words to restate what a person has said as a way of indicating that the listener has understood what the speaker means and feels.

parliamentarian A person who advises the chair of a meeting on matters concerning parliamentary procedure.

parliamentary procedure A systematic method and set of formal rules used to determine the will of the majority through fair and orderly discussion and debate.

passive-aggressive Uncooperative and obstructive behavior that appears to be cooperative.

passivity Nonassertive behavior characterized by a lack of confidence and a reluctance to communicate.

perceiver, as a personality trait A Myers-Briggs personality type who is less rigid about deadlines and time constraints and who is flexible and willing to try new options.

performing stage The group development stage in which group members focus their energy on doing the work needed to achieve group goals.

personal distance Interpersonal space ranging from 18 inches to four feet, typically used for friends and acquaintances.

personal member A group member whose affection needs are met and who is comfortable interacting with group members.

personal power Power that stems from a member's individual character, competence, and earned status.

persuasive power A type of power that relies on effective communication skills.

point of order A statement that questions whether the rules and principles of parliamentary procedure are being followed correctly.

polychronic time (P time) An approach to time that allows many things to be done at once; schedules are flexible, and deadlines may be missed.

position power Power that depends on a member's job or status within an organization.

Post-Meeting Reaction (PMR) form A questionnaire designed to assess the success of a meeting by collecting written reactions from participants.

power The ability or authority to influence and motivate others.

power distance A cultural dimension that reflects the physical and psychological distance between those of different status.

precedence In parliamentary procedure, the rank, order, or priority governing the proposal and consideration of motions.

prejudice A negative attitude about other people that is based on faulty and inflexible stereotypes.

presentation A relatively uninterrupted talk or speech to a group of people.

presentation aid Supplementary audio and/or visual material used in a discussion or oral presentation.

presentation purpose What a speaker wants listeners to know, think, believe, or do as a result of a presentation.

presentation software Computer programs used to design presentation slides.

primary group A group of family members or friends who provide affection, support, and a sense of belonging.

primary tension The social unease and inhibitions experienced by group members during the getting-acquainted phase of a group's development.

privileged request In parliamentary procedure, a motion regarding the personal needs and rights of members.

problem orientation Member behavior that contributes to a supportive communication climate by focusing on solving a problem collaboratively rather than imposing a personal preference.

problem solving A complex process in which groups analyze a problem and develop a plan for solving it or reducing the harmful effects of the problem.

problem-solving meeting A meeting that provides an opportunity for all members to participate in solving a problem and/or making a decision.

procedural conflict A disagreement over what method or process a group should follow to accomplish its goal.

procedural norm A norm that dictates how a group will operate.

procedural technician A group member who assists with preparations for meetings, including suggesting agenda items, making room arrangements, and providing needed materials and equipment (a task role).

provisionalism Member behavior that contributes to a supportive communication climate by being open-minded and accepting, offering tentative suggestions, and avoiding unyielding claims.

proxemics The study of how people perceive and use personal space and distance.

public distance Interpersonal space beyond twelve feet, typically reserved for large audiences.

public group A group that discusses issues or makes presentations in front of or for the benefit of a public audience or key decision makers.

qualifier The component of the Toulmin Model of Argument that states the degree to which a claim may be true.

question In parliamentary procedure, a motion put before a group for a decision.

question of conjecture A decision-making question that asks whether something will or will not happen.

question of fact A decision-making question that asks whether something is true or false, or whether something did or did not occur.

question of policy A decision-making question that asks whether and how a specific course of action should be taken to solve a problem.

question of privilege In parliamentary procedure, a motion that focuses on conditions that affect the health, safety, and operation of the meeting.

question of value A decision-making question that asks the group to decide whether something is good or bad, right or wrong, or worthwhile or worthless.

quorum The minimum number or percentage of voting members who, according to a group's constitution or bylaws, must be present at a meeting in order to transact business legally.

rational decision maker A person who carefully weighs information and options before making a decision.

recognition seeker A group member who boasts about her or his accomplishments and tries to become the group's center of attention (a self-centered role).

recorder A group member who keeps and provides accurate written records of a group's major ideas, suggestions, and decisions (a task role).

referent power A type of power held by a person who is admired and respected.

Reflective Thinking Process A set of practical steps that a rational person should follow when solving a problem.

refutation The process of proving that an argument is false and/or lacks sufficient support.

Relational Dialectics Theory A theory that claims that relationships are characterized by ongoing, dialectic tensions among the multiple contradictions, complexities, and changes in human experiences.

relationship-motivated leader A leader who tends to establish close personal relations with group members.

religious literacy The ability to understand and use the religious terms, symbols, images, beliefs, practices, scripture, heroes, themes, and stories that are employed within a culture.

research A systematic search or investigation designed to find useful and appropriate evidence.

reservation The component of the Toulmin Model of Argument that recognizes the conditions under which a claim may not necessarily be true.

resource investigator A group member who explores opportunities, makes contacts, shares external information, and negotiates with outsiders (a people-oriented team role).

reward power A type of power that comes from the authority to give group members something that they value.

role A group member's unique set of skills or behavioral patterns that serve specific functions within the group.

second In parliamentary procedure, the endorsement of a motion for consideration by a second member.

secondary tension The frustrations and personality conflicts experienced by group members as they compete with one another for acceptance and achievement.

self-centered role A negative role in which individual needs are put ahead of the group's goal and other members' needs.

self-confessor A group member who seeks emotional support from the group, shares very personal feelings and problems, and uses the group for emotional support rather than contributing to the group's goals (a self-centered role).

self-help group A group that offers support and encouragement to members who want or need help with personal problems.

sensor, as a personality trait A Myers-Briggs personality type who focuses on details and prefers to concentrate on one task at a time.

sense of choice The shared feeling that the group has the power and ability to make decisions about how to organize and do its job.

sense of competence The shared feeling that the group is doing good, high quality work.

sense of meaningfulness The shared feeling that the group is pursuing a worthy task.

sense of progress The shared feeling that the group is accomplishing something.

service group A group dedicated to worthy causes that help people outside the group.

shaper A group member who seeks patterns in the group's work and pushes the group toward agreement and decisions (an action-oriented team role).

short-term memory The content a person remembers immediately after listening to a series of numbers, words, sentences, or paragraphs.

Single Question Format A problem-solving procedure that focuses group analysis on answering a single, agreed-upon question in order to arrive at a solution.

Situational Leadership Model See Hersey-Blanchard Situational Leadership® Model.

Situational Leadership Theory An approach to leadership that helps leaders improve their skills by carefully analyzing their attitudes, their group, and the circumstances in which they must lead.

skill In the context of group work, a specific ability that helps a group carry out or achieve its common goal.

social dimension A group's focus on the interpersonal relationships among group members.

social distance Interpersonal space ranging from four to twelve feet, typically reserved for new acquaintances and strangers.

social group A group in which members share common interests in a friendly setting or participate in common leisure activities.

social member A person whose inclusion needs are met and who enjoys working with other people but is comfortable working alone.

socialization The process by which an individual acquires the social knowledge and skills necessary to assume an organizational role.

special interest pleader A group member who speaks on behalf of an outside group or a personal interest and who tries to influence others to support nongroup interests (a self-centered role).

specialist A group member who is single-minded, dedicated, and provides unique expertise and skills (a thought-oriented team role).

spontaneity Member behavior that contributes to a supportive communication climate by being straightforward, appreciative, direct, open, encouraging, and honest.

spontaneous decision maker A person who is impulsive and makes decisions on the spur of the moment.

Standard Agenda A procedure that guides a group through problem solving by using the following steps: task clarification, problem identification, fact finding, solution criteria, solution suggestions, solution evaluation and selection, and solution implementation.

statistics Information presented in a numerical form.

status norm A norm that identifyies levels of influence among group members.

stereotype A generalization about a group of people that oversimplifies their characteristics and results in erroneous judgment about the entire group of people.

storming stage The group development stage in which members compete with one another to determine individual status and to establish group goals.

strategy 1. A method, guideline, or technique for dealing with issues or problems. 2. Member behavior that may contribute to a defensive communication climate by manipulating and controlling others as well as advancing hidden agendas.

structure ↔ spontaneity A group dialectic in which the need for structured procedures is balanced with the need for innovative and creative thinking.

Styles Leadership Theory An approach to leadership that identifies specific behaviors or styles that can be learned; these can be put into three categories: autocratic, democratic, or laissez-faire leadership.

substantive conflict A disagreement over ideas, issues, decisions, actions, or goals.

superiority Member behavior that may contribute to a defensive communication climate by implying that a member and his or her ideas and opinions are better than others.

supportive climate A communication context in which members feel free to share their opinions and feelings.

synchronous communication Communication that occurs simultaneously and in real time, either face to face or electronically.

synergy The cooperative interaction of several factors that results in a combined effect that is greater than the sum of individual contributions.

system A collection of interacting, interdependent elements working together to form a complex whole that adapts to a changing environment.

Systems Theory A group of theories that examine how interdependent factors affect one another.

task dimension A group's focus on achieving its goal.

task dimension↔social dimension A group dialectic in which the responsibility and motivation to complete tasks are balanced with promoting relationships among members.

task-motivated leader A leader whose major satisfaction comes from successfully completing the group task rather than from promoting positive interpersonal relationships with group members.

task role A positive role that affects a group's ability to do the work needed to achieve its goals.

task structure A situational leadership factor that assesses how a group must organize or plan a specific task.

team presentation A coordinated presentation by a group of speakers who are trying to influence an audience of decision makers.

Team-Role Theory R. Meredith Belbin's theory that claims group members will seek out and perform roles that are compatible with their personal characteristics and skills.

team talk Anne Donnellon's term to describe the nature of the language that group members use as they work together.

teamworker A member who gives personal support and help to others, is socially oriented, and serves as an in-group diplomat (a people-oriented team role).

tension releaser A group member who alleviates tension with friendly humor and tries to relax other group members (a maintenance role).

territoriality The sense of personal ownership attached to a particular space.

textconference A conference in which group members use their computer keyboards to communicate and collaborate with one another.

texter A person who disrupts a meeting or annoys others by checking and responding to messages rather than engaging in the meeting.

theory A principle that tries to explain or predict events and behavior.

thinker, as a personality trait A Myers-Briggs personality type who takes pride in thinking objectively and making difficult decisions.

third-party intervention The use of an impartial outsider to analyze and resolve conflict.

thought speed The speed (in words per minute) at which most people can think compared to the slower speed at which most people speak.

threaded discussion A series of email messages about a specific issue posted on an electronic bulletin board.

Toulmin Model of Argument A model developed by Stephen Toulmin that represents the structure of an argument.

Trait Leadership Theory An approach to leadership that tries to identify common characteristics and behaviors of effective leaders.

Tuckman's Group Development Stages A model of group development that identifies five stages in the life cycle of groups: forming, storming, norming, performing, and adjourning.

two-thirds vote The results of a vote in which at least twice as many group members vote in favor of a proposal as those who vote to oppose it.

underpersonal member A group member whose affection needs are not met and who has only superficial relationships with other group members.

undersocial member A group member whose inclusion needs are not met and who may withdraw from the group or feel unworthy.

valid Accurate, reasonable, and justifiable; refers to evidence that is considered reliable.

verbal communication The use of words and language to generate meaning.

videoconference A form of communication that combines audio and video media to provide both voice communication and video images.

virtual group A group that relies on technology to communicate synchronously and/or asynchronously, often across time, distance, and organizational boundaries.

visualization A technique for reducing communication apprehension that encourages positive thinking about communicating in groups by relaxing and imagining yourself succeeding.

warrant The component of the Toulmin Model of Argument that justifies how the evidence supports a particular claim.

whisperer A person who carries on confidential conversations with another group member during a meeting.

Whorf Hypothesis A theory that claims language reflects culture and influences how people think, act, and behave.

word stress The degree of vocal prominence given to a syllable within a word or to a word within a phrase or sentence.

work group A group responsible for achieving specific tasks or performing routine duties on behalf of a company, organization, association, agency, or institution.

working memory The memory subsystem used when we try to understand information, remember it, or use it to solve a problem or communicate with others.

Working Memory Theory A listening theory that claims that listening involves not just short-term memory but also engages one's working memory.

Notes

Chapter 1

1. Steve W. J. Kozlowski and Daniel R. Ilgen. "Enhancing the Effectiveness of Work Groups and Teams," *Psychological Science in the Public Interest*, 7, no. 3 (2006), p. 77.

2. Peter D. Hart Research Associates, *How Should Colleges Prepare Students to Succeed in Today's Global Economy?* (Washington, DC: Peter D. Hart Research Associates, December 28, 2006), p. 2. Also see Association of American Colleges and Universities, *College Learning for the New Global Age* (Washington, DC: Association of American Colleges and Universities, 2007).

3. Peter D. Hart Research Associates, 2006, p. 7.

4. National Association of Colleges and Employers, *Special Report: Job Outlook '96* (Bethlehem, PA: NACE, November 1995).

5. Rodney W. Napier and Matti K. Gershenfeld, *Groups: Theory and Experience*, 7th ed. (Boston: Houghton Mifflin, 2004), pp. 42–43.

6. Susan A. Wheelan, (2009) "Group Size, Group Development, and Group Productivity," *Small Group Research* 40, pp. 247–262.

7. Wheelan, pp. 247–262.

8. Wheelan, p. 260.

9. Malcolm Gladwell, "The Cellular Church," *The New Yorker*, September 12, 2005, pp. 61–63.

10. Based on the definition of communication developed at the Association for Communication Administration's 1995 Conference on the Discipline: "the field of communication focuses on how people use verbal and nonverbal messages to generate meanings within and across various contexts, cultures, channels, and media." See *Spectra*, the newsletter of the National Communication Association, October 1995, p. 12.

11. Anne Donnellon, *Team Talk: The Power of Language in Team Dynamics* (Boston: Harvard Business School Press, 1996), p. 28.

12. John A. Courtright, "Relational Communication: As Viewed from the Pragmatic Perspective," in *Explaining Communication: Contemporary Theories and Exemplars*, ed. Bryan B. Whaley and Wendy Samter (Mahwah, NJ: Lawrence Erlbaum Associates, 2007), p. 313.

13. Carl E. Larson and Frank M. J. LaFasto, *TeamWork: What Must Go Right/What Can Go Wrong* (Newbury Park, CA: Sage, 1989), p. 27.

14. Joe Sharkey, "Setbacks in the Air Add to Lure of Virtual Meetings," *The New York Times*, April 27, 2010, p. B6.

15. Jon R. Katzenback and Douglas K. Smith, *The Discipline of Teams: A Mindbook-Workbook for Delivering Small Group Performance* (New York: John Wiley, 2001), p. 41.

16. Susan B. Barnes, *Online Connections: Internet Interpersonal Relationships* (Cresskill, NJ: Hampton Press, 2001), p. 41.

17. Michael A. West, Felix C. Brodbeck, and Andreas W. Richter, "Does the 'Romance of Teams' Exist? The Effectiveness of Teams in Experimental and Field Settings." *Journal of Occupational and Organization Psychology*, 77 (2004), p. 471.

18. Mark D. Cannon and Brian A. Griffith, *Effective Groups: Concepts and Skills to Meet Leadership Challenges* (Boston: Pearson/Allyn and Bacon, 2007), p. 7.

19. Robert A. Cooke and John A. Kernaghan, "Estimating the Difference Between Group Versus Individual Performance on Problem-Solving Tasks," *Group and Organizational Studies*, 12 (1987), pp. 319–342.

20. Quoted in David W. Johnson, Roger T. Johnson, and Karl A. Smith, "Cooperative Learning Returns to College," *Change*, July/August (1998), p. 31.

21. Peter M. Senge et al., *The Fifth Discipline Fieldbook: Strategies and Skills for Building a Learning Organization* (New York: Doubleday, 1994), p. 51.

22. Lee Towe, *Why Didn't I Think of That? Creativity in the Workplace* (West Des Moines, IA: American Media, 1996), p. 8.

23. Donald J. Noone, *Creative Problem Solving*, 2nd ed. (Hauppauge, NY: Barron's, 1998), p. 132.

24. The National Communication Association (NCA) offers *Service-Learning and Communication: A Disciplinary Toolkit* on its website. This 74-page document provides excellent information on how to develop a comprehensive service learning program. Go to www.natcom.org. The instructor's manual for this textbook includes a detailed Service Learning Assignment with an Assessment component prepared by Shirlee Levin, emeritus professor of speech communication, College of Southern Maryland.

25. Sara Chudnovsky Weintraub, "Constructing Communication Courses with Service-Learning Projects" (paper presented at the Eastern Communication Association Convention, Pittsburgh, April 27–30, 2000).

26. 3M Meeting Management Team with Jeannine Drew, *Mastering Meetings: Discovering the Hidden Potential of Effective Business Meetings* (New York: McGraw-Hill, 1994), p. 12.

27. *The Week*, April 1, 2005, p. 36.

28. Warren Bennis, Jagdish Parikh, and Ronnie Lessem, *Beyond Leadership: Balancing Economics, Ethics and Ecology* (Cambridge, MA: Blackwell, 1994), p. 139.

29. Senge et al., pp. 28–31. *Note:* We have substituted the communication-based terms *strategies* for *methods* and *skills* for *tools* in Senge's model of theory, methods, and tools.

30. Leslie A. Baxter and Barbara M. Montgomery, *Relating: Dialogues and Dialectics* (New York: Guilford Press, 1996).

31. Baxter and Montgomery, p. 3.

32. The first edition of *Working in Groups* introduced the balance metaphor as a guiding principle for effective group communication. The nine dialectic tensions in this edition are an extension of this principle and are based on five major, contemporary sources: (a) relational dialectics in Baxter and Montgomery; (b) the dialectics of affect and instrumentality and judgment and acceptance in William K. Rawlins, *Friendship Matters: Communication, Dialectics, and the Life Course* (New York: Aldine De Gruyter, 1992); (c) the dialectic of groups in Michael W. Kramer, "Toward a Communication Theory of Group Dialectics: An Ethnographic Study of a Community Theater Group," *Communication Monographs* 71 (2004): pp. 11–332; (d) Larry A. Erbert et al., "Perceptions of Turning Points and Dialectical Interpretations in Organizational Team Development," *Small Group Research* 36 (2005), pp. 21–58; (e) Scott D. Johnson and Lynette M. Long, "Being a Part and Being Apart," in *New Directions in Group Communication,* ed. Lawrence Frey (Thousand Oaks, CA. Sage, 2002), pp. 25–41. Special thanks are extended to the faculty members participating in the group communication seminar at the 2005 NCA Hope Institute for Faculty Development at Luther College in Iowa. Participants helped consolidate dozens of group tensions into nine dialectics that closely resemble those presented in this textbook.

33. Harvey Robbins and Michael Finley, *The New Why Teams Don't Work: What Went Wrong and How to Make It Right* (Princeton, NJ: Peterson's/Pacesetter Books, 2000), pp. 27–29.

34. Larson and LaFasto, p. 128.

35. Marshall Scott Poole, "Procedures for Managing Meetings: Social and Technical Innovation," in *Innovative Meeting Management,* ed. Richard A. Swanson and Bonnie Ogram Knapp (Austin, TX: 3M Meeting Management Institute, 1990), pp. 54–55.

36. Alexander Hiam, *Motivating and Rewarding Employees: New and Better Ways to Inspire Your People* (Holbrook, MA: Adams Streetwise, 1999), p. 17.

37. Hiam, p. 17.

38. Richard L. Johannesen, *Ethics in Human Communication,* 5th ed. (Prospect Heights, IL: Waveland, 2002), p. 1.

39. Nicky Hayes, *Managing Teams: A Strategy for Success,* 2nd ed. (London: Thomson, 2002), p. 99.

40. Bradley L. Kirkman and Benson Rosen, "Beyond Self-Management: Antecedents and Consequences of Team Empowerment," *Academy of Management Journal* 42 (1999), pp. 58–74.

41. James M. Kouzes and Barry Z. Posner, *The Leadership Challenge,* 3rd ed. (San Francisco: Jossey-Bass, 2002), p. 282.

42. D. S. Hutchinson, "Ethics," in *The Cambridge Companion to Aristotle,* ed. Jonathan Barnes (Cambridge: Cambridge University Press, 1995), pp. 217–227.

43. Aristotle, *Nicomachean Ethics,* translated by William D. Ross; revised by James O. Urmson, in *The Complete Works of Aristotle: The Revised Oxford Translation,* ed. Jonathan Barnes (Princeton, NJ: Princeton University Press, 1984), p. 1176.

44. The NCA Credo for Ethical Communication was developed at the 1999 conference sponsored by the National Communication Association and facilitated by the authors of this textbook. The credo was adopted and endorsed by the Legislative Council of the National Communication Association in November 1999. www .natcom.org/aboutNCA/Policies/Platform.html.

Chapter 2

1. Artemis Chang, Julie Duck, and Prashant Bordia, "Understanding the Multidimensionality of Group Development," *Small Group Research* 37 (2006), p. 329.

2. "Famous Models: Stages of Group Development," http://www.chimaeraconsulting.com/tuckman.htm, 2001.

3. Chang, Duck, and Bordia, pp. 327–350.

4. Susan A. Wheelan, *Creating Effective Teams: A Guide for Members and Leaders* (Thousand Oaks, CA: Sage, 1999), p. 29.

5. Marshall Scott Poole and J. Roth, "Decision Making in Small Groups, V: Test of a Contingency Model," *Human Communication Research* 15 (1989), pp. 549–89. For more analysis of sequential group stage models, see Holly Arrow et al., "Time, Change, and Development: The Temporal Perspective on Groups," *Small Group Research* 35 (February 2004), pp. 73–105.

6. Bruce W. Tuckman and Mary Ann C. Jensen, "Stages of Small Group Development Revisited," *Group and Organizational Studies* 2 (1997), pp. 419–427.

7. B. Aubrey Fisher, "Decision Emergence: Phases in Group Decision Making," *Speech Monographs,* 37 (1970), pp. 53–66.

8. Wheelan, pp. 23–36, 93–132.

9. Bruce W. Tuckman, "Developmental Sequence in Small Groups," *Psychological Bulletin* 63 (1965), pp. 384–399. Tuckman's 1965 article is reprinted in *Group Facilitation: A Research and Applications Journal* 3 (Spring 2001), http://dennislearningcenter.osu.edu/references/ Group%20DEV%20ARTICLE.doc. See also Mark K. Smith, "Bruce W. Tuckman—Forming, Storming, Norming, and Performing in Groups," *The Encyclopaedia of Informal Education,* www.infed.org/thinkers/tuckman .htm, updated March 14, 2005; "Famous Models: Stages of Group Development" (Chimaera Consulting Limited), www.chimaeraconsulting.com/tuckman.htm, 2001; A. Paul Hare, "Theories of Group Development and Categories for Interaction Analysis," *Small Group Research* 41 (2009), pp. 124–126. Reprinted from *Small Group Behavior* (1973).

10. Tuckman and Jensen, pp. 419–427.

11. Chang, Duck, and Bordia, pp. 331, 337–338.

12. Harvey Robbins and Michael Finley, *Why Teams Don't Work: What Goes Wrong and How to Make It Right* (Princeton, NJ: Peterson's/Pacesetter Books, 1995), p. 26.

13. Ernest G. Bormann, *Small Group Communication: Theory and Practice*, 3rd ed. (Edina, MN: Burgess, 1996), pp. 132–135, 181–183.

14. Moira Burke, Robert Kraut, and Elizabeth Joyce, "Membership Claims and Request: Conversation-Level Newcomer Socialization Strategies in Online Groups," *Small Group Research*, 41 (2010), p. 4.

15. John Van Maanen and Edgar H. Schein. "Toward a Theory of Organizational Socialization," in *Research in Organizational Communication*, Barry M. Staw, ed. (Greenwich, CT: JAI Press, 1979), p. 211.

16. Carolyn M. Anderson, Bruce L. Riddle, and Matthew M. Martin, "Socialization Process in Groups," in *The Handbook of Group Communication Theory and Research*, ed. Lawrence R. Frey; assoc. eds. Dennis S. Gouran and Marshall Scott Poole (Thousand Oaks, CA: Sage, 1999), p. 155. See also Jennifer Waldeck and Karen Myers, "Organizational Assimilation Theory, Research, and Implications for Multiple Areas of the Discipline: A State of the Art Review," in *Communication Yearbook 31*, Christina S. Beck, ed. (New York, NY: Lawrence Erlbaum Associates, 2008), pp. 322–367; Michael W. Kramer, "Toward a Communication Model for the Socialization of Voluntary Members," *Communication Monographs*, 78 (2011), pp. 233–235.

17. Anderson, Riddle, and Martin, p. 139.

18. Burke, Kraut, and Joyce, pp. 28–30.

19. Bormann, pp. 135–139, 142–143.

20. Donald G. Ellis and B. Aubrey Fisher, *Small Group Decision Making: Communication and the Group Process*, 4th ed. (New York: McGraw-Hill, 1994), pp. 43–44.

21. Hare, p. 125.

22. Susan Wheelan and Nancy Brewer Danganan, "The Relationship Between the Internal Dynamics of Student Affairs Leadership Teams and Campus Leaders' Perceptions of the Effectiveness of Student Affairs Divisions," *Journal of Student Affairs Research and Practice*, 40 (2002), p. 27.

23. B. Aubrey Fisher, "Decision Emergence: Phases in Group Decision Making," *Speech Monographs*, 37 (1970), p. 160.

24. In 1997, Tuckman and Jensen proposed an updated model that includes a fifth stage: adjourning. Tuckman and Jensen, pp. 419–427.

25. Deborah L. Duarte and Nancy Tennant Snyder, *Mastering Virtual Teams: Strategies, Tools, and Techniques That Succeed*, 3rd ed. (San Francisco: Jossey-Bass, 2006), p. 190.

26. Anderson, Riddle, and Martin, p. 155.

27. "Famous Models: Stages of Group Development," 2001.

28. Carl E. Larson and Frank M. J. LaFasto, *TeamWork: What Must Go Right/What Can Go Wrong* (Newbury Park, CA: Sage, 1989), p. 27.

29. Larson and LaFasto, pp. 27–38.

30. Larson and LaFasto, p. 28.

31. Larson and LaFasto, p. 33.

32. David W. Johnson and Frank P. Johnson, *Joining Together: Group Theory and Group Skills*, 2nd ed. (Englewood Cliffs, NJ: Prentice Hall, 1982), p. 174.

33. Johnson and Johnson, p. 174.

34. Based on Edwin A. Locke and Gary P. Latham, *Goal Setting: A Motivational Technique That Works!* (Englewood Cliffs, NJ: Prentice-Hall, 1984), pp. 27–40; Johnson and Johnson, pp. 173–174.

35. Locke and Latham, also see Andrew J. DuBrin, *Leadership: Research Findings, Practice, and Skills*, 4th ed. (New York: Houghton Mifflin, 2004), pp. 297–298.

36. Locke and Latham, pp. 18–19.

37. Rodney W. Napier and Matti K. Gershenfeld, *Groups: Theory and Experience*, 7th ed. (Boston: Houghton Mifflin, 2004), p. 182.

38. Patricia H. Andrews, "Group Conformity," in *Small Group Communication: Theory and Practice*, 7th ed., eds. Robert S. Cathcart, Larry A. Samovar, and Linda D. Henman (Madison, WI: Brown & Benchmark, 1996), p. 185.

39. Nicky Hayes, *Managing Teams: A Strategy for Success* (London: Thomson, 2004), p. 31.

40. Hayes, p. 29.

41. Robert A. Baron, Donn Byrne, and Nyla R. Branscombe, *Social Psychology*, 11th ed. (Boston: Allyn & Bacon, 2006); Charles Pavitt and Ellen Curtis, *Small Group Discussion: A Theoretical Approach*, 2nd ed. (Scottsdale, AZ: Gorsuch, Scarisbrick, 1994), pp. 178, 339.

42. Napier and Gershenfeld, pp. 137–140.

43. For detailed descriptions of these classic studies, see Sharon S. Brehn, Saul M. Kassin, and Steven Fein, *Social Psychology*, 6th ed. (Boston: Houghton Mifflin, 2005), pp. 250–255, 472–475. For detailed description of Milgram's work, see Robert A. Baron, Donn Byrne, and Nyla R. Branscombe, *Social Psychology*, 11th ed. (Boston: Allyn & Bacon, 2006), pp. 364–369. Today, neither experiment would be conducted because an institution's research board must approve all research using human subjects to ensure that the study will not harm subjects.

44. Philip Zimbardo describes the famous Stanford prison study and its consequences as well as how it foreshadowed the abusive actions of U.S. military guards at Abu Ghraib prison in Iraq. See Philip G. Zimbardo, "Revisitng the Stanford Prison Experiment: A Lesson in the Power of Situation," *The Chronicle of Higher Education*, March 30, 2007, pp. B6–B7.

45. Bormann, pp. 270–274.

46. Bormann, pp. 286–288.

47. Jon R. Katzenbach and Douglas K. Smith, *The Discipline of Teams: A Mindbook-Workbook for Delivering Small Group Performance* (New York: Wiley, 2001), pp. 141–142.

48. Napier and Gershenfeld, pp. 147–148.

49. Kenneth W. Thomas, *Intrinsic Motivation at Work: Building Energy and Commitment* (San Francisco: Berrett-Koehler, 2000), pp. 6, 7.

50. Thomas, p. 44.

51. Alexander Hiam, *Motivating and Rewarding Employees: New and Better Ways to Inspire Your People* (Holbrook, MA: Adams Streetwise, 1999), p. 152.

52. Larson and LaFasto, pp. 39–58.

53. Michael Ramundo with Susan Shelly, *The Complete Idiot's Guide to Motivating People* (Indianapolis, IN: Alpha Books, 2000), p. 86.

Chapter 3

1. Rodney W. Napier and Matti K. Gershenfeld, *Groups: Theory and Experience,* 7th ed. (Boston: Houghton Mifflin, 2004), pp. 72–74.

2. Will Schutz, *The Human Element: Productivity, Self-Esteem, and the Bottom Line* (San Francisco: Jossey-Bass, 1994).

3. Schutz, p. 29.

4. Schutz, pp. 38–39.

5. In his more recent works, Schutz uses the term *openness* instead of *affection.* However, we find that students understand the third need better when we use Schutz's original term—*affection.*

6. Schutz, pp. 50–51.

7. Scott D. Johnson and Lynette M. Long, "Being a Part of Being Apart: Dialectics and Group Communication," in *New Directions in Group Communication,* ed. Lawrence R. Frey (Thousand Oaks, CA: Sage, 2002), p. 35.

8. Kenneth D. Benne and Paul Sheats, "Functional Roles of Group Members," *Journal of Social Issues* 4 (1948), pp. 41–49.

9. Benne and Sheats, pp. 41–49.

10. "Belbin's Team Roles," http://changingminds.org/explanations/preferences/belbin.htm, 2011. For more information, see R. Meredith Belbin, *Team Roles at Work* (Oxford: Butterworth/Heinemann, 1993); R Meredith Belbin, *Management Teams: Why They Succeed or Fail,* 3rd ed. (Oxford: Butterworth Heinemann, 2010); http://www.belbin.com

11. Eric Chong, "Role Balance and Team Development: A Study of Team Role Characteristics Underlying High and Low Performing Teams," *Journal of Behavioral and Applied Management,* 8 (2007), pp. 202–217.

12. "Belbin Team Roles and Descriptions," www.business-balls.com/personalitystylesmodels.htm#belbin%20team%20roles%2)descriptions

13. R. Meredith Belbin, *Management Teams* (London: Heinemann, 1981) and R. Meredith Belbin, *Team Roles at Work* (Oxford: Butterworth Heinemann, 1993). See also "Home to Belbin Team Roles," http://www.belbin.com and "Belbin's Team Roles, http://www.mindtools.com/pages/article/newLDR_83.htm

14. "Home to Belbin Team Roles," http://www.belbin.com/rte.asp?id=8

15. The table summarizes functions and characteristics from several sources: Belbin, 1993, p. 22; Nicky Hayes, *Managing Teams: Strategies for Success* (London: Thomson, 2004), p. 47; http://chimaeraconsulting.com/belbin.htm; "Home to Belbin Team Roles," http://www.belbin.com and "Belbin's Team Roles," http://www.mindtools.com/pages/article/newLDR_83.htm

16. Jeanne M. Plas, *Person-Centered Leadership: An American Approach to Participator Management* (Thousand Oaks, CA: Sage, 2000), p. 88.

17. Jon R. Katzenbach and Douglas K. Smith, *The Discipline of Teams: A Mindbook-Workbook for Delivering Small Group Performance* (New York: Wiley, 2000), pp. 20, 138.

18. Katzenbach and Smith, p. 138.

19. Elaine Sihera, The Definition of Confidence," http://ezinearticles.com/?The-Definition-of-Confidence&id=455084

20. James M. Kouzes and Barry Z. Posner, *The Leadership Challenge,* 3rd ed. (San Francisco: Jossey-Bass, 2002), p. 296. Also see the discussion of a leader's role in building group confidence in Frank M. J. LaFasto and Carl Larson, *When Teams Work Best* (Thousand Oaks, CA: Sage, 2001), pp. 121–130.

21. LaFasto and Larson, p. 71.

22. Virginia P. Richmond and James C. McCroskey, *Communication: Apprehension, Avoidance, and Effectiveness,* 4th ed. (Scottsdale, AZ: Gorsuch, Scarisbrick, 1995), p. 41.

23. Michael T. Motley, *Overcoming Your Fear of Public Speaking: A Proven Method* (Boston: Houghton Mifflin, 1997), p. 3; Virginia P. Richmond and James C. McCroskey, *Communication: Apprehension, Avoidance, and Effectiveness,* 5th ed. (Boston: Allyn & Bacon/Longman, 1998).

24. James C. McCroskey and Virginia P. Richmond, "Communication Apprehension and Small Group Communication," in *Small Group Communication: A Reader,* 6th ed., eds. Robert S. Cathcart and Larry A. Samovar (Dubuque, IA: Wm. C. Brown, 1992), p. 368. Also see Beth Bonniwell Haslett and Jenn Ruebush, "What Differences Do Individual Differences in Groups Make?" in *The Handbook of Group Communication Theory and Research,* ed. Lawrence R. Frey, assoc. eds. Dennis S. Gouran and Marshall Scott Poole (Thousand Oaks, CA: Sage, 1999), p. 124.

25. Richmond and McCroskey, 1995, p. 57.

26. Richmond and McCroskey, 1995, p. 43.

27. McCroskey and Richmond, p. 368.

28. Isa N. Engleberg and John A. Daly, *Presentations in Everyday Life: Strategies for Effective Speaking,* 3rd ed. (Boston: Pearson/Allyn & Bacon, 2009), p. 32.

29. Karen Kangas Dwyer, *Conquer Your Speech Anxiety,* 2nd ed. (Belmont, CA: Thomson Wadsworth, 2005), pp. 72–94; Richmond and McCroskey, 1995, pp. 102–105.

30. See Chapter 2, "Listening to the Cries and Whispers of the Articulate Body," in Randolph R. Cornelius, *The*

Science of Emotions: Research and Tradition in the Psychology of Emotions (Upper Saddle River, NJ: Prentice-Hall, 1996).

31. Delaine Fragnoli, "Fear of Lying," *Bicycling* 38 (1997), pp. 46–47.

32. Joe Ayres, Tim Hopf, and Debbie M. Ayres, "An Examination of Whether Imaging Ability Enhances the Effectiveness of an Intervention Designed to Reduce Speech Anxiety," *Communication Education* 43 (1994), pp. 252–258; Joe Ayres, Brian Heuett, and Debbie A. Sonandre, "Testing a Refinement in an Intervention for Communication Apprehension," *Communication Reports* 11 (1998), pp. 73–84.

33. Andrew F. Wood and Matthew J. Smith, *Online Communication: Linking Technology, Identity, and Culture* (Mahwah, NJ: Erlbaum, 2001), p. 15. For more information about writing apprehension, see Richmond and McCroskey, 1995.

34. Thomas Leso and Kyle L. Peck, "Computer Anxiety and Different Types of Computer Courses," *Journal of Educational Computing Research, 8* (1992): 469–478. See also Craig R. Scott and C. Erik Timmerman, "Relating Computer, Communication, and Computer-Mediated Communication Apprehension to New Communication Technology in the Workplace," *Communication Research,* 32 (2005), pp. 683–715.

35. Raafat George Saddé and Dennis Kira, "Computer Anxiety in E-Learning: The Effects of Computer Self-Efficacy," *Journal of Information Technology Education,* 8 (2009), p. 179.

36. Craig R. Scott and Steven C. Rockwell, "The Effect of Communication, Writing, and Technology Apprehension on Likelihood to Use New Communication Technologies," *Communication Education* 46 (1997), pp. 29–43.

37. Jill Nemiro, Michael Beyerlein, Lori Bradley, and Susan Beyerlein (eds.), *The Handbook of High-Performance Virtual Teams: A Toolkit for Collaborating Across Boundaries,* (San Francisco, CA: Jossey-Bass, 2008), p. 219.

38. Wood and Smith, p. 80.

39. Wood and Smith, pp. 88–90.

40. Ron Short, *A Special Kind of Leadership: The Key to Learning Organizations* (Seattle, WA: The Leadership Group, 1991), pp. 17, 26.

41. Sam R. Lloyd, *Leading Teams: The Skills for Success* (West Des Moines, IA: American Media, 1996), p. 57.

42. Joseph A. Bonito and Andrea B. Hollingshead, "Participation in Small Groups," in *Communication Yearbook,* 20, ed. Brant R. Burleson (Thousand Oaks, CA: Sage, 1997), p. 249.

43. Robert N. Bostrom and Nancy Grant Harrington, "An Exploratory Investigation of Characteristics of Compulsive Talkers," *Communication Education* 48 (1999), pp. 73–80.

44. Bostrom and Harrington, p. 76.

45. A more detailed definition and explanation of assertiveness can be found in Robert E. Alberti and Michael L. Emmons, *Your Perfect Right: Assertiveness and Equality in Your Life and Personal Relationships,* 8th ed. (Atascadero, CA: Impact, 2001).

46. Randy J. Paterson, *The Assertiveness Workbook: How to Express Your Ideas and Stand Up for Yourself at Work and in Relationships* (Oakland, CA: New Harbinger, 2000), p. 20.

47. © Isa N. Engleberg and Dianna Wynn, 2011.

48. Joshua D. Guilar, *The Interpersonal Communication Skills Workshop* (New York: AMACOM, 2001), p. 70.

49. Paterson, p. 149.

50. Paterson, p. 150.

51. Paterson, pp. 151–152.

52. The complete credo is available on the National Communication Association website at www.natcom.org/policies/External/EthicalComm.htm.

53. Suggestions based on advice from "How to Deal with a Manipulator," http://www.ehow.com/how_2106098_deal-manipulator.html

54. The PRCA-24 is reprinted with permission from the author. See James C. McCroskey, *An Introduction to Rhetorical Communication,* 6th ed. (Englewood Cliffs, NJ: Prentice-Hall, 1993), p. 37

Chapter 4

1. William Sonnenschein, *The Diversity Toolkit* (Chicago: Contemporary Books, 1997), p. 101.

2. Rushworth M. Kidder, "Trust: A Primer on Current Thinking," Institute for Global Ethics, www.globalethics.org/files/wp_trust_1222960968.pdf/21/.

3. James Leigh, "Teaching Content and Skills for Intercultural Communication: A Mini Case Studies Approach," *The Edge: The E-Journal of Intercultural Relations* 2 (Winter 1999), http://www.intercultural relations.com/v2ilWinter1999leigh.htm.

4. James Surowiecki, *The Wisdom of Crowds: Why the Many Are Smarter Than the Few and How Collective Wisdom Shapes Business, Economics, Societies, and Nations* (New York: Doubleday, 2004), p. 29.

5. Quoted in Surowiecki, p. 31.

6. Karen R. Humes, Nicholas A. Jones, and Roberto R. Ramirez, *Overview of Race and Hispanic Origin: 2010 Census Brief* (U.S. Census Bureau, March 2011), pp. 3, 4–5, 22. http://www.census.gov/prod/cen2010/briefs/c2010br-02.pdf

7. Humes, Jones, and Ramirez, p. 17.

8. U.S. Census Bureau, www.census.gov/population.

9. Myron W. Lustig and Jolene Koester, *Intercultural Competence: Interpersonal Communication across Cultures,* 6th ed. (Boston: Pearson/Allyn & Bacon, 2010), p. 25.

10. Intercultural authors use a variety of terms (*co-cultures, microcultures*) to describe the cultural groups that coexist within a larger culture. Using either of these terms is preferable to using the older, somewhat derogatory term *subcultures*. The combined co-cultures living in the United States will, by midcentury, make up the majority population.

11. Surowiecki, p. 30.

12. James R. Larson, Jr., "Modeling the Impact of Variability in Members' Problem-Solving Strategies on Group Problem-Solving Performance," *Small Group Communication*, 38, (2007), p. 413.

13. Larson, p. 433.

14. Larson, p. 415.

15. Diversity layers based on Lee Gardenswartz and Anita Rowe, *Diverse Teams at Work: Capitalizing on the Power of Diversity* (New York: McGraw-Hill, 1994), p. 18.

16. See David K. Shipler, *A Country of Strangers: Blacks and Whites in America*. New York: Alfred A Knopf, 1997; Thomas K. Nakayama and Judith N. Martin (Eds.) *Whiteness: The Communication of Social Identity* (Thousand Oaks: Sage, 1999); http://www.retirethechief.org/ Essays/stereotype0503.html#refs; http://answers .yahoo.com/question/index?qid=20081103220501 AAnCtaY.

17. Lustig and Koester, p. 156.

18. Lustig and Koester, p. 156.

19. Gardenswartz and Rowe, pp. 34–35.

20. Miranda A. G. Peeters et al., "The Big Five Personality Traits and Individual Satisfaction with Teams," *Small Group Research* 37 (2006), pp. 190–191.

21. Andrea B. Hollingshead et al., "A Look at Groups from the Functional Perspective," in *Theories of Small Groups: Interdisciplinary Perspectives*, eds. Marshall Scott Poole and Andrea B. Hollingshead (Thousand Oaks, CA: Sage, 2005), pp. 40–41. See also Miranda A. G. Peeters et al., "Designing in Teams: Does Personality Matter? *Small Group Communication* 39 (2008), pp. 438–467; Terry R. Halfhill, Tjai M. Nielsen, and Eric Sundstrom, "The ASA Field Study of Group Personality Composition and Group Performance in Military Action Teams," *Small Group Research* 39 (2008), pp. 616–635.

22. Hundreds of books and articles have been written about the Myers-Briggs Type Indicator®. The material in this chapter is based on Isa N. Engleberg's background and experience as a certified Myers-Briggs Type Indicator® trainer and a synthesis of materials from several MBTI resources: Isabel Briggs Myers (revised by Linda K. Kirby and Katharine D. Myers), *Introduction to Type*, 7th ed. (Palo Alto, CA: Consulting Psychologists, 1998); Isabel Briggs Myers with Peter B. Myers, *Gifts Differing: Tenth Anniversary Edition* (Palo Alto, CA: Consulting Psychologists, 1990); Otto Kroeger and Janet M. Thuesen, *Type Talk* (New York: Delacorte, 1988); Otto Kroeger and Janet M. Thuesen, *Type Talk at Work: How the 16 Personality Types Determine Your Success on the Job* (New York: Delta/Tilden Press, 1992); David Keirsey, *Please Understand Me II* (Del Mar, CA: Prometheus Nemesis, 1998); Sandra K. Hirsh, *Introduction to Type and Teams* (Palo Alto, CA: Consulting Psychologists, 1992); Larry Demarest, *Looking at Type in the Workplace* (Gainesville, FL: Center for Applications of Psychological Type, 1997).

23. Myers with Myers, p. 1.

24. Annie Murphy Paul, *The Cult of Personality* (New York: Free Press, 2004), pp. 125–127.

25. The Myers-Briggs Type Indicator® is for licensed use only by qualified professionals whose qualifications are on file and have been accepted by Consulting Psychologists Press, Inc.

26. The Myers-Briggs Type Indicator® (MBTI) uses the word *extravert*—with an *a* in the middle of the word—to describe this personality preference rather than *extrovert*. Some dictionaries and psychology textbooks use *extrovert* to note the alliterative similarities between *introvert* and *extrovert*. *Working in Groups* uses the term *extrovert* but here acknowledges the MBTI preference for *extravert*.

27. Robert E. Levasseur, *Breakthrough Business Meetings: Shared Leadership in Action* (Holbrook, MA: Bob Adams, 1994), p. 79.

28. Marti Olsen Laney, The Introvert Advantage: How to Thrive in an Extrovert World (New York: Workman, 2002), pp. 190–92.

29. Laney, pp. 190, 193–194.

30. J. M. Jaffe, "Of Different Minds," *Association Management* 37 (1985), pp. 120–124.

31. Renee Baron, *What Type Am I?* (New York: Penguin, 1998), pp. 20–21.

32. Carl E. Larson and Frank M. J. LaFasto, *TeamWork: What Must Go Right/What Can Go Wrong* (Newbury Park, CA: Sage, 1989), p. 63.

33. Baron, pp. 29–30.

34. Otto Kroeger and Janet M. Thuesen, *Type Talk* (New York: Delacorte, 1988), p. 80.

35. Kroeger and Thuesen, p. 114.

36. The following resources were used to develop the table of personality type motivators: Larry Damerest, *Looking at Type in the Workplace* (Gainesville, FL: Center for Applications of Psychological Type, 1997); Jean M. Kummerow, Nancy J. Barger, and Linda K. Kirby, *Work Types* (New York: Warner Books, 1997).

37. Geert Hofstede, *Cultures and Organizations: Software of the Mind* (New York: McGraw-Hill, 1997), p. 14. Also see Geert Hofstede, *Culture's Consequences*, 2nd ed. (Thousand Oaks, CA: Sage, 2001), p. 29. Hofstede identifies a fifth dimension: long-term versus short-term orientation, which relates to the choice of focus for people's efforts—either the future or the present. Cultures in Asia rank at the top of the list on long-term orientation, whereas those with a shorter-term orientation include English-speaking countries as well as Zimbabwe, the Philippines, Nigeria, and Pakistan. We have not included this fifth dimension in *Working in Groups* because fewer cultures have been thoroughly studied on this dimension.

38. Edward T. Hall, *The Silent Language* (Greenwich, CT: Fawcett, 1959); Edward T. Hall, *Beyond Culture* (New York: Anchor, 1976); Edward T. Hall, *The Dance of Life: The Other Dimension of Time* (New York: Doubleday, 1983); Edward T. Hall and M. R. Hall, *Understanding*

Cultural Differences: Germans, French and Americans (Yarmouth, ME: Intercultural Press, 1990).

39. Harry C. Triandis, *Individualism and Collectivism* (Boulder, CO: Westview, 1995).

40. Geert Hofstede, *Culture's Consequences*, 2nd ed., p. 215.

41. Harry C. Triandis, "The Self and Social Behavior in Different Cultural Contexts," *Psychological Review* 96 (1994): 506–520. Also see Triandis, *Individualism and Collectivism,* (Boulder, CO: Westview, 1995).

42. Triandis, p. 52.

43. Geert Hofstede, "The Cultural Relativity of the Quality of Life Concept," in *Cultural Communication and Conflict: Readings in Intercultural Relations*, 2nd ed., ed. Gary R. Weaver (Boston: Pearson, 2000), p. 139.

44. Hofstede, *Culture's Consequences*, quoted in Larry A. Samovar and Richard Porter, *Communication Between Cultures*, 5th ed. (Belmont, CA: Wadsworth, 2004), p. 65.

45. Hofstede, *Cultures and Organizations*, p. 84.

46. Hofstede, *Cultures and Organizations*, p. 84.

47. Hall and Hall, *Understanding Cultural Differences*, p. 6.

48. Dean Allen Foster, *Bargaining across Borders* (New York: McGraw-Hill, 1992), p. 280.

49. Hall, *The Dance of Life*, p. 42.

50. Lustig and Koester, p. 215.

51. Edward T. Hall, "Monochronic and Polychronic Time," in *Intercultural Communication: A Reader*, 10th ed., ed. Larry A. Samovar and Richard E. Porter (Belmont, CA: Wadsworth, 2002), p. 263.

52. Deborah L. Duarte and Nancy Tennant Snyder, *Mastering Virtual Teams*, 3rd ed. (San Francisco: Jossey-Bass, 2006), pp. 60–61, 118–119.

53. John Gray, *Men Are from Mars, Women Are from Venus* (New York: HarperCollins, 2005). Also see www.marsvenus.com.

54. Deborah Tannen, *You Just Don't Understand: Women and Men in Conversation* (New York: Morrow, 1990).

55. Janet Shibley Hyde, "The Gender Similarities Hypothesis," *American Psychologist* 60 (2005): p. 590, as quoted in Deborah Cameron, *The Myth of Mars and Venus* (Oxford: Oxford University Press, 2007), pp. 41–44.

56. Deborah Cameron, *The Myth of Mars and Venus* (Oxford: Oxford University Press, 2007), p. 43.

57. Rodney W. Napier and Matti K. Gershenfeld, *Groups: Theory and Experience*, 7th ed. (Boston: Houghton Mifflin, 2004), p. 29.

58. David Brown, "Stereotypes of Quiet Men, Chatty Women Not Sound Science," *The Washington Post*, July 6, 2007, p. A2. See also Donald G. McNeill, Jr. "Yada, Yada, Yada. Him? Or Her?" *The New York Times*, July 6, 2007, p. A13.

59. Sonnenschein, pp. 19–20.

60. Cheris Kramarae, "Muted Group Theory" in eds. Stephen W. Littlejohn and Karen A. Foss, *Encyclopedia of Communication Theory, Volume 2* (Los Angeles, CA: Sage, 2009), p. 667. Kramarae notes that muted group theory was initially developed by Edwin Ardener and Shirly Ardener.

61. Marianne Dainton and Elaine D. Zelley, *Applying Communication Theory for Professional Life* (Thousand Oaks, CA: Sage, 2005), p. 97.

62. Kramarae, p. 667.

63. Kramarae, pp. 667–668.

64. Marsha Houston and Cheris Kramarae, "Speaking from Silence: Methods of Silencing and of Resistance," *Discourse and Society*, 2 (1991), p. 389.

65. Interview with Cheris Karamarae in Katherine Miller, *Communication Theories: Perspectives, Processes, and Contexts* (Boston: McGraw Hill, 2002), p. 294.

66. Mayo Clinic, "Workplace Generation Gap: Understand Differences Among Colleagues," Special to CNN.com, http://www.cnn.com/HEALTH/library/WL/00045.html, July 6, 2005.

67. T. J. Wilhera, "Millennials Large and in Charge: Tech-Savvy Generation Taking Over," *Denver Post*, June 6, 2008, www.denverpost.com/opinion/ci_9494738; John Davidson, "We Invented the World You Live in, Kid," *Denver Post*, June 13, 2008, www.denverpost.com/search/ci_9570975.

68. Mayo Clinic, special to CNN.com, 2005.

69. David Stauffer, "Motivating Across Generations," in Harvard Business School Press, *Teams That Click* (Boston: Harvard Business School, 2004), p. 119.

70. Kelly Griffin, "You're Wiser Now," *The AARP Magazine*, September/October 2005, p. 77.

71. Stephen Prothero, *Religious Literacy: What Every American Needs to Know—and Doesn't* (New York: HarperSanFrancisco, 2007), p. 11. See also Prothero, pp. 27–28, 235–239.

72. Prothero, p. 23.

73. Laurie Goodstein, "On Basic Religion Test, Many Doth Not Pass," *The New York Times*, September 28, 2010, p. A17.

74. Questions are based on three sources: Robert Pollock, *The Everything World's Religions Book* (Avon, MA: Adams Media, 2002); Leo Rosen (ed.), *Religions of America: Fragment of Faith in an Age of Crisis* (New York: Touchstone, 1975); *Encyclopedia Britannica Almanac 2004* (Chicago: Encyclopedia Britannica, 2003).

75. Prothero, p. 30.

76. According to Richard L. Evans, a former member of the Council of Twelve of the Church of Jesus Christ of Latter-day Saints, "Strictly speaking, 'Mormon' is merely a nickname for a member of the Church of Jesus Christ of Latter-day Saints." When asked whether Mormons are Christians, he answered "Unequivocally yes." See "What Is a Mormon?" in Rosen; p. 187; Robert Pollock describes Mormonism as a "prevalent Christian faith" in Pollock, pp. 49–51.

77. J. Richard Hoel, Jr. "Developing Intercultural Competence," in *Intercultural Communication with Readings,* eds. Pamela J. Cooper, Carolyn Calloway-Thomas, and Cheri J. Simonds (Boston: Allyn & Bacon, 2007), p. 305.

78. Hoel, p. 305.

79. Gardenswartz and Rowe, p. 46.

80. Gardenswartz and Rowe, p. 46.

81. Judith N. Martin and Thomas K. Nakayama, *Experiencing Intercultural Communication*, 2nd ed. (New York: McGraw-Hill, 2005), p. 18.

82. Martin and Nakayama, pp. 20–22.

83. Note: The Myers-Briggs Type Indicator is for licensed use only by individuals whose qualifications are on file and have been accepted by Consulting Psychologists Press. This GroupWork activity uses a quick self-test that is not a licensed instrument.

Chapter 5

1. Eric Harper, David Cottrell, Al Lucia, and Mike Hourigan, *The Leadership Secrets of Santa Claus: How to Get Big Things Done in YOUR "Workshop" . . . All Year Long* (Dallas, TX: The Walk the Talk Company, 2003), pp. 78–79.

2. Robert S. Cathcart and Larry A. Samovar, "Group Leadership: Theories and Principles," in *Small Group Communication: A Reader*, 6th ed., eds. Robert S. Cathcart and Larry A. Samovar (Dubuque, IA: Wm. C. Brown, 1992), p. 364.

3. Antony Bell, *Great Leadership: What It Is and What It Takes in a Complex World* (Mountain View, CA: Davies-Black, 2006), pp. 87, 91.

4. Ron Heifetz, *Leadership without Easy Answers* (Cambridge, MA: The Belknap Press of Harvard University Press, 1994), pp. 126–128, 228.

5. Garry Wills, *Certain Trumpets: The Call of Leaders* (New York: Simon & Schuster, 1994), p. 13.

6. Carl E. Larson and Frank M. J. LaFasto, *Team Work: What Must Go Right/What Can Go Wrong* (Newbury Park, CA: Sage, 1989), p. 128.

7. Michael Z. Hackman and Craig E. Johnson, *Leadership: A Communication Perspective*, 5th ed. (Long Grove, IL: Waveland, 2009), p. 87.

8. Katrina Brooker, "Starting Over," *Fortune* (January 21, 2002), pp. 50–68.

9. Joseph R. Santo, "Where the Fortune 50 CEOs Went to College," *Time*, August 15, 2006, http://www.time.com/time/printout/0,8816,1227055,00.html.

10. Ivan G. Seidenberg, "Reference for Business," *Encyclopedia of Business*, 2nd ed., http://www.referenceforbusiness.com/biography/S-Z/Seidenberg-Ivan-G-1946.html.

11. Brenda Barnes, *Encyclopedia of World Biography*, http://www.notablebiographies, http://www.notablebiographies.com/newsmakers2/2007-A-Co/Barnes-Brenda-C.html. See also Brenda Barnes, *Bloomberg Businessweek*, http://investing.businessweek.com/businessweek/research/stocks/people/person.asp?personId=551751&ticker=SLE:US.

12. *Forbes Magazine*, 2010, http://www.forbes.com/2009/05/06/richest-black-americans-business-billionaires-richest-black-americans.html; http://billionaires.forbes.com/article/0eAPbmrcJhaSj/articles?q=billionaire+OR+billionaires+OR+billionaire%27s.

13. Sam R. Lloyd, *Leading Teams: The Skills for Success* (West Des Moines, IA: American Media, 1996), p. 13.

14. Edwin P. Hollander, *Leadership Dynamics: A Practical Guide to Effective Relationships* (New York: Macmillan, 1978), p. 53.

15. Hackman and Johnson, (2009), p. 191.

16. Andrew J. DuBrin, *Leadership: Research Findings, Practice, and Skills*, 6th ed. (Mason, OH: South-Western/Cengage Learning, 2010), p. 168.

17. DuBrin, p. 174.

18. The Center for Business Ethics at Bentley College, as described in DuBrin, p 176. See also James L. Bowditch and Anthony F. Buono, *A Primer on Organizational Behavior*, 5th ed. (New York: Wiley, 2001), p. 4.

19. Warren Bennis and Joan Goldsmith, *Learning to Lead: A Workbook on Becoming a Leader*, Updated Edition (Cambridge, MA: Perseus, 1997), p. 3.

20. Jorge Correia Jesuino, "Leadership: Micro-macro Links," in *Understanding Group Behavior*, vol. 2, eds. Erich H. White and James H. Davis (Mahwah, NJ: Lawrence Erlbaum Associates, 1996), pp. 93, 119.

21. Warren Bennis and Bruce Nanus, *Leaders: The Strategies for Taking Charge* (New York: HarperPerennial, 1985), p. 15.

22. Gary A. Yukl and Cecilia M. Falbe, "Importance of Different Power Sources in Downward and Lateral Relations," *Journal of Applied Psychology* 76 (1991), pp. 416–423.

23. Nicky Hayes, *Managing Teams: A Strategy for Success* (London: Thomson, 2004), p. 96.

24. Daniel Goleman, Richard Boyatzis, and Annie McKee, *Primal Leadership: Learning to Lead with Emotional Intelligence* (Boston: Harvard Business School Press, 2002), p. 23.

25. Michael Z. Hackman and Craig E. Johnson, *Leadership: A Communication Perspective*, 4th ed. (Prospect Heights, IL: Waveland, 2004), p. 127.

26. Bennis and Nanus, p. 4.

27. Thomas Carlyle, *On Heroes, Hero-Worship, and the Heroic History* (Boston, MA: Houghton Mifflin, 1841). See Centre of Research in Organisational Behaviour and Leadership, http://crob.dmst.aueb.gr/index.php?option=com_content&view=article&id=75&Itemid=89.

28. DuBrin, pp. 33–42.

29. Otto Kroeger with Janet M. Thuesen, *Type Talk at Work: How the 16 Personality Types Determine Your Success on the Job* (New York: Dell, 1992), p. 385.

30. Kurt Lewin, Ron Lippit, and R. K. White, "Patterns of Aggressive Behaviour in Experimentally Created Social Climates," *Journal of Social Psychology* 10 (1939), pp. 271–299.

31. Alan Dressler, *Voyage to the Great Attractor: Exploring Intergalactic Space* (New York: Alfred A. Knopf, 1994), pp. 193–194.

32. Jesuino, p. 99.

33. Lucy E. Garrick, "Leadership: Theory Evolution and the Development of Inter-Personal Leadership," Pacific

Northwest Organization Development Network, 2004 (Copyright 2004, Lucy Garrick, North Shore Group, LLC, Seattle, WA).

34. Richard J. Hackman, "What Makes for a Great Team? American Psychological Association," *Psychological Science Agenda* (June 2004), http://apa.org/science/about/psa/2004/06/hackman.aspx.

35. *Famous Models: Situational Leadership,* http://chimaeraconsulting.com/sitleader.htm.

36. Fred E. Fiedler and Martin M. Chemers, *Improving Leadership Effectiveness: The Leader Match Concept,* 2nd ed. (New York: Wiley, 1984). In addition to Fiedler's Contingency Model of Leadership Effectiveness, several other situational theories offer valuable insights into the ways in which leaders must find a match between their styles and the needs of their group. See Chapter 4 in Martin M. Chemers, *An Integrative Theory of Leadership* (Mahwah, NJ: Erlbaum, 1994), for a discussion and analysis of the following theories: House's Path-Goal Directive, Vroom and Yetton's Normative Decision Theory, and Hersey and Blanchard's Situational Leadership.

37. DuBrin, pp. 142–146.

38. Paul Hersey and Ken Blanchard, *Management of Organizational Behavior: Utilizing Human Resources,* 6th ed. (Upper Saddle River, NJ: Prentice-Hall, 1992).

39. Heifetz, pp. 126–127.

40. Jim Collins, *Good to Great: Why Some Companies Make the Leap…and Others Don't* (New York: HarperBusiness, 2001), p. 22.

41. Collins, p. 36.

42. Collins, p. 36.

43. James E. McGrath, Leadership Behavior: Some Requirements for Leadership Training (Washington, D.C.: U.S. Civil Service Commission, Office of Career Development, 1926) as quoted in Frederick P. Morgeson, D. Scott DeRue, and Elizabeth P. Karam, "Leadership in Teams: A Functional Approach to Understanding Leadership Structure and Processes," *Journal of Management Online First* (September 23, 2009), p. 4.

44. Based on J. Richard Hackman and Ruth Wageman (January 2007) "Asking the Right Questions About Leadership," *American Psychologists* 62 (January 2007), pp. 43–47; Richard J. Hackman, "What Makes for a Great Team? American Psychological Association, *Psychological Science Agenda* (June 2004), http://apa.org/science/about/psa/2004/06/hackman.aspx.

45. The 5M Model of Effective Leadership draws, in part, on Martin M. Chemers's integrative theory of leadership that identifies three functional aspects of leadership: image management, relationship development, and resource utilization. We have added a fourth and fifth function—decision making and mentoring members—and have integrated a stronger communication perspective into Chemers's view of leadership as a multifaceted process. Chemers, pp. 151–173.

46. Martin M. Chemers, *An Integrative Theory of Leadership* (Mahwah, NJ: Lawrence Erlbaum Associates, 1997), p. 154.

47. Orem Harari, *The Leadership Secrets of Colin Powell* (New York: McGraw-Hill, 2002), p. 249.

48. Mike Krzyzewski, "Coach K on How to Connect," *The Wall Street Journal*, July 16–17, 2011, p. C12.

49. Chemers, p. 155.

50. Chemers, p. 160.

51. Harvey A. Robbins and Michael Finley, *The New Why Teams Don't Work: What Goes Wrong and How to Make It Right* (San Francisco: Berrett-Koehler, 2000), p. 107.

52. Evan Rosen, *The Culture of Collaboration: Maximizing Time, Talent and Tools to Create Value in the Global Economy* (San Francisco: Red Ape, 2007), p. 37.

53. Jessica Lipnack and Jeffrey Stamps, *Virtual Teams,* 3rd ed. (New York: Wiley, 2006), p. 218.

54. Bell, p. 67.

55. James M. Kouzes and Barry Z. Posner, *Credibility: How Leaders Gain and Lose It, Why People Demand It* (San Francisco: Jossey-Bass, 1993), pp. 230–231.

56. Susan B. Shimanoff and Mercilee M. Jenkins, "Leadership and Gender: Challenging Assumptions and Recognizing Resources," in *Small Group Communication: Theory and Practice,* 7th ed., eds. Robert S. Cathcart, Larry A. Samovar, and Linda D. Henman (Madison, WI: Brown & Benchmark, 1996), p. 327.

57. Rodney Napier and Matti Gershenfeld, *Groups: Theory and Experience*, 7th ed. (Boston: Houghton Mifflin, 2004), p. 347.

58. Chemers, p. 150.

59. DuBrin, 415.

60. See http://www.grovewell.com/pub-GLOBE-precis.html. See also the homepage of The Global Leadership and Organizational Behavior Effectiveness Research Project, http://www.thunderbird.edu/sites/globe.

61. Chemers, p. 126.

62. Martin M. Chemers and Susan E. Murphy, *Leadership for Diversity in Groups and Organizations: Perspectives on a Changing Workplace* (Newbury Park, CA: Sage, 1995).

63. Fiedler and Chemers, pp. 17–42.

64. DuBrin, pp. 12–13. *Note:* We have changed a few words to keep the language consistent with the terminology in this textbook.

Chapter 6

1. Anne Donnellon, *Team Talk: The Power of Language in Team Dynamics* (Boston: Harvard Business School, 1996), p. 6.

2. Victoria Fromkin and Robert Rodman, *An Introduction to Language,* 6th ed. (Fort Worth, TX: Harcourt Brace, 1998), p. 3.

3. Nina-Jo Moore, Mark Hickson III, and Don W. Stacks, *Nonverbal Communication: Studies and Applications,* 5th New York: Oxford, 2010), p. 4.

4. Virginia P. Richmond, James C. McCroskey, and Mark L. Hickson, III, *Nonverbal Behavior in Interpersonal Relations,* 6th ed. (Boston: Pearson/Allyn & Bacon, 2008), p. 5.

5. Donnellon, p. 25.

6. Donnellon, p. 25.

7. Based on Donnellon, pp. 29–40. We have added qualifying phrases to Donnellon's categories to aid comprehension and recall.

8. Donnellon, p. 25.

9. Donnellon, p. 33.

10. Donnellon, pp. 40–41.

11. Mark Twain, "Letter to George Bainton, October 15, 1888," www.twainquotes.com/lightning.html.

12. Mike Kryzyewski, "Coach on K on How to Connect," *The Wall Street Journal*, 16–17 July 2001, p. C12.

13. Thomas J. Housel, "Foreword," in Arthur H. Bell, *You Can't Talk to Me That Way!* (Franklin Lakes, NJ: Career Press, 2005), p. 11.

14. Based on Arthur H. Bell, *You Can't Talk to Me That Way!* (Franklin Lakes, NJ: Career Press, 2005), pp. 24–25.

15. Based on Bell, pp. 192–200.

16. William V. Haney, *Communication and Interpersonal Relations: Text and Cases*, 6th ed. (Homewood, IL: Irwin, 1992), p. 269.

17. Haney, p. 290.

18. Vivian Cook, *Inside Language* (London: Arnold, 1997), p. 244.

19. William Lutz, *Doublespeak* (New York: HarperPerennial, 1990), p. 3.

20. Deborah Tannen, *You Just Don't Understand: Women and Men in Conversation* (New York: William Morrow, 1990).

21. Myron W. Lustig and Jolene Koester, *Intercultural Competence: Interpersonal Communication across Cultures*, 5th ed. (Boston: Allyn & Bacon, 2006), p. 200.

22. John McWhorter, *Word on the Street: Debunking the Myth of a "Pure" Standard English* (Cambridge, MA: Perseus, 1998), pp. 145–146.

23. McWhorter, p. 143.

24. Carley H. Dodd, *Dynamics of Intercultural Communication*, 4th ed. (Madison, WI: Brown & Benchmark, 1995), p. 151.

25. Geoffrey Finch, *Word of Mouth: A New Introduction to Language and Communication* (New York: Palgrave, 2003); http://www.aber.ac.uk/media/Documents/short/whorf.html; http://www.users.globalnet.co.uk/~skolyles/swh.htm.

26. Marcel Danesi and Paul Perron, *Analyzing Cultures: An Introduction and Handbook* (Bloomington: Indiana University Press, 1999), p. 61.

27. Moore, Hickson, and Stacks, p. 4; Albert Mehrabian, *Silent Messages: Implicit Communication of Emotions and Attitudes*, 2nd ed. (Belmont, CA: Wadsworth, 1981), p. 77.

28. Jessica L. Lakin, "Automatic Cognitive Processes and Nonverbal Communication," in *The Sage Handbook of Nonverbal Communication*, eds. Valerie Manusov and Miles L. Patterson, (Thousand Oaks, CA: Sage, 2006), p. 59.

29. Robert S. Cathcart, Larry A. Samovar, and Linda D. Henman, *Small Group Communication: Theory and Practice*, 7th ed. (Madison, WI: Brown & Benchmark, 1996), p. 236.

30. Virginia P. Richmond and James C. McCroskey, *Nonverbal Behavior in Interpersonal Relationships*, 5th ed. (Boston: Allyn & Bacon, 2004), p. 103.

31. Moore, Hickson, and Stacks, p. 128.

32. From The Federal Reserve Bank of St. Louis, *The Regional Economist*, April 2005, quoted in "Good Looks Can Mean Good Pay, Study Says," *The Sun*, April 28, 2005, p. D1.

33. Peter A. Andersen, "Nonverbal Communication in the Small Group," in *Small Group Communication: A Reader*, 6th ed., eds. Robert S. Cathcart and Larry A. Samovar (Dubuque, IA: Wm. C. Brown, 1992), p. 273.

34. Martin S. Remland, *Nonverbal Communication in Everyday Life* (Boston: Houghton Mifflin, 2000), p. 169.

35. Alan J. Fridlund and James A. Russell, "The Functions of Facial Expressions," in *The Sage Handbook of Nonverbal Communication*, eds. Valerie Manusov and Miles L. Patterson, (Thousand Oaks, CA: Sage, 2006), p. 315.

36. Lyle V. Mayer, *Fundamentals of Voice and Diction*, 13th ed. (Madison, WI: Brown & Benchmark, 2004), p. 229.

37. Sharon Begley, "Gesturing as You Talk Can Help You Take a Load Off Your Mind," *Wall Street Journal*, November 14, 2003.

38. Sandra M. Ketrow, "Nonverbal Aspects of Group Communication," in *The Handbook of Group Communication Theory and Research*, ed. Lawrence R. Frey; assoc. eds. Dennis S. Gouran and Marshall Scott Poole (Thousand Oaks, CA: Sage, 1999), p. 255.

39. Andersen, "Nonverbal Communication in the Small Group," p. 267.

40. Andersen, "The Touch Avoidance Measure," p. 62.

41. Joseph B. Walther and K. P. D'Addario, "The Impacts of Emoticons on Message Interpretation in Computer-Mediated Communication" (paper presented at the meeting of the International Communication Association, Washington, D.C., May 2001).

42. Thomas Mandel and Gerard Van der Leun, *Rules of the Net: Online Operating Instructions for Human Beings* (New York: Hyperion, 1996), p. 92.

43. See Judith K. Burgoon, "Spatial Relationships in Small Groups," in *Small Group Communication: Theory and Practice*, 8th ed., eds. Randy Y. Hirokawa, Robert S. Cathcart, Larry A. Samovar, and Linda D. Henman (Los Angeles: Roxbury, 2003), pp. 85–96.

44. Mark L. Knapp and Judith A. Hall, *Nonverbal Communication in Human Interaction*, 4th ed. (Fort Worth, TX: Harcourt Brace, 1997), p. 177.

45. Jeffrey Krasner, "Fistfights and Feng Shui," *Boston Globe*, July 21, 2001, pp. C1–C2.

46. Edward T. Hall, *The Hidden Dimension* (New York: Doubleday, 1982).

47. Andersen, "Nonverbal Communication in the Small Group," p. 269.

48. Judith A. Hall, "Women's and Men's Nonverbal Communication: Similarities, Differences, Stereotypes, and Origins," in *The Sage Handbook of Nonverbal Communication*, eds. Valerie Manusov and Miles L. Patterson, (Thousand Oaks, CA: Sage, 2006), p. 202.

49. Judith A. Hall, pp. 203–207.

50. Judith A. Hall, p. 209.

51. Judith A. Hall, pp. 207–208.

52. Guo-Ming Chen and William J. Starosta, *Foundations of Intercultural Communication* (Boston: Allyn & Bacon, 1998), p. 91.

53. Peter Suedfeld and G. Daniel Steel, "The Environmental Psychology of Capsule Habitats," *Annual Review of Psychology* 51 (2000), pp. 227–253; Peter Suedfeld, "Applying Positive Psychology in the Study of Extreme Environments," *Journal of Human Performance in Extreme Environments* 6 (2001), pp. 21–25.

54. Irwin Altman, "Research on Environment and Behavior: A Personal Statement of Strategy," *Perspectives on Environment and Behavior, ed. Daniel Stokols,* (New York: Plenum Press, 1977), p. 310.

55. Altman, p. 310.

56. Donelson R. Forsyth, *Group Dynamics*, 5th ed. (Belmont, CA: Wadsworth/Cengage Learning, 2010), p. 470.

57. Many websites provide detailed information about the ways in which the Chilean miners organized themselves into an effective group. For examples, see Alonso Soto and Irene Klotz, "Space, Oceans Hold Clues to Chile Miners' Survival," *Reuters*, http://www.reuters.com/assets/print?aid=USTRE67O05Q20100825, 2010; "Chilean Miners' Survival 'May Provide a Lesson in Human Resilience" *oneindia news*, http://news.oneindia.in/2010/10/17/chileanminers-survival-may-provide-a-lesson-in-humanresi.html October 17, 2010; 2010 Copiapo Mining Accident, http://en.wikipedia.org/wiki/2010_Copiap%C3%B3_mining_accident.

58. Jack R. Gibb, "Defensive Communication," *Journal of Communication* 2 (1961), pp. 141–148. Also see Jack R. Gibb, "Defensive Communication," in *Small Group Communication: A Reader,* 2nd ed., eds. Robert S. Cathcart and Larry A. Samovar (Dubuque, IA: Wm. C. Brown, 1974), pp. 327–333.

59. Martin S. Remland, "Uses and Consequences of Nonverbal Communication in the Context of Oganizational Life," in *The Sage Handbook of Nonverbal Communication*, eds. Valerie Manusov and Miles L. Patterson (Thousand Oaks, CA: Sage, 2006), p. 501.

60. Remland, p. 508.

61. Remland, p. 509.

62. James C. McCroskey, Virginia P. Richmond, and Linda L. McCroskey, "Nonverbal Communication in Instructional Contexts," in *The Sage Handbook of Nonverbal Communication*, eds. Valerie Manusov and Miles L. Patterson (Thousand Oaks, CA: Sage, 2006), p. 423.

63. Knapp and Hall, pp. 414–415.

Chapter 7

1. Patrice Johnson and Kittie Watson, "Managing Interpersonal and Team Conflict: Listening Strategies," in *Listening in Everyday Life: A Personal and Professional Approach*, 2nd ed., eds. Michael Purdy and Deborah Borisoff (Lanham, MD: University Press, 1997), pp. 121–32; also see Katherine W. Hawkins and Bryant P. Fillion, "Perceived Communication Skill Needs for Workgroups," *Communication Research Reports* 16 (1997), p. 168.

2. Richard Emanuel et al., "How College Students Spend Their Time Communicating," *International Journal of Listening* 22 (2008), pp. 13–28; Larry L. Barker et al., "An Investigation of Proportional Time Spent in Various Communication Activities by College Students," *Journal of Applied Communication Research* 8 (1980), pp. 101–109.

3. Andrew D. Wolvin and Carolyn G. Coakley, *Listening*, 5th ed. (Madison, WI: Brown and Benchmark, 1996), p. 15.

4. Michael Purdy, "The Listener Wins," http://featuredreports.monster.com/listen/overview.

5. Ralph G. Nichols, "Listening Is a 10-Part Skill," *Nation's Business* 75 (September 1987), p. 40.

6. S. S. Benoit and J. W. Lee, "Listening: It Can Be Taught," *Journal of Education for Business* 63 (1986), pp. 229–232.

7. Donald Carstensen, vice president for education services at ACT, quoted in Michael Purdy, "The Listener Wins"; available at http://featuredreports.monster.com/listen/overview. Also see http://www.act.org/workkeys/assess/listen/levels.html for information about ACT's listening assessment criteria.

8. Florence I. Wolff and Nadine C. Marsnik, *Perceptive Listening*, 2nd ed. (Fort Worth, TX: Harcourt Brace Jovanovich, 1992), pp. 9–16.

9. Edwin P. Hollander, *Leadership Dynamics: A Practical Guide to Effective Relationships* (New York: Macmillan, 1978), p. 53.

10. Carl E. Larson and Frank M. J. LaFasto, *TeamWork: What Must Go Right/What Can Go Wrong* (Newbury Park, CA: Sage, 1989), p. 90.

11. Quoted in Richard K. Bommelje, "I'm All Ears," *Current Magazine*, Council for Advancement and Support of Education (CASE), April 2005. See http://www.listen-coach.com/articles/CURRENTS%204-5-05%20IM%20ALL%20EARS.pdf.

12. Fran Rees, *How to Lead Work Teams*, 2nd ed. (San Francisco: Jossey-Bass, 2001), p. 41.

13. Stephen R. Covey, *The Seven Habits of Highly Effective People* (New York: Simon & Schuster, 1989), p. 47.

14. Covey, p. 47.

15. Isa N. Engleberg and Dianna R. Wynn, *Instructor's Manual for the Challenge of Communicating: Guiding Principles and Practices* (Boston: Pearson/Allyn & Bacon, 2008), pp. 90–91. Based on The Listen to Learn Survey in Margarete Imhoff, "What Makes a Good Listener? Listening Behavior in Instructional Settings," *International Journal of Listening* 12 (1998), pp. 81–105.

16. The list of poor listening habits is a summary of faculty listening behavior from a variety of sources including Judi Brownell, *Listening: Attitudes, Principles, and Skills*, 4th ed. (Boston: Pearson Allyn and Bacon, 2010); Madelyn Burley-Allen, *Listening: The Forgotten Skill*, 2nd ed. (New York: Wiley, 1995); Ralph G. Nichols, "Do We Know How to Listen? Practical Helps in a Modern Age," *Speech Teacher* 10 (1961); Ralph G. Nichols,

"Listening is a 10-Part Skill," Wolvin and Coakley, *Listening*.

17. Brownell, pp. 14–17.

18. Brownell, p. 16.

19. Brownell, pp. 16–17.

20. Brownell, p. 73.

21. Based on Tony Alessandra and Phil Hunsaker, *Communicating at Work* (New York: Fireside, 1993), pp. 76–77.

22. Samuel E. Wood, Ellen Green Wood, and Denise Boyd, *The World of Psychology*, 6th ed. (Boston: Pearson/Allyn & Bacon, 2008), p. 199.

23. Alan D. Baddeley and Robert H. Logie, "Working Memory: The Multiple-Component Model," in Akira Miyake and Priti Shah (Eds.) *Models of Working Memory* (Cambridge, UK: Cambridge University Press, 1999), pp. 28–61. See also http://cogweb.ucla.edu/Abstracts/Miyake_Shah_99.html#intro.

24. Laura Ann Janusik, "Building Listening Theory: The Validation of the Conversational Listening Span," *Communication Studies* 58 (2007): 142.

25. Janusik, 142.

26. Peter Desberg, *Speaking Scared Sounding Good* (Garden City Park, NY: Square One, 2007), p. 127.

27. Brownell, p. 168.

28. Based on Wolff and Marsnik, p. 100.

29. Wolff and Marsnik, pp. 101–102.

30. Based on Wolff and Marsnik, pp. 94–95.

31. David W. Johnson's Questionnaire on Listening and Response Alternatives in *Reaching Out: Interpersonal Effectiveness and Self-Actualization*, 7th ed. (Boston: Allyn & Bacon, 2000), pp. 234–239.

32. Michael P. Nichols, *The Lost Art of Listening* (New York: Guilford, 1995), p. 126.

33. Charles M. Kelly, "Empathetic Listening," in *Small Group Communication: A Reader*, 2nd ed., eds. Robert S. Cathcart and Larry A. Samovar (Dubuque, IA: Wm. C. Brown, 1974), p. 340.

34. Ralph G. Nichols, "Listening Is a 10-Part Skill," p. 40.

35. Ralph G. Nichols, "Listening Is a 10-Part Skill," p. 40.

36. Michael P. Nichols, *The Lost Art of Listening*, pp. 42, 43.

37. Wolvin and Coakley, pp. 135–138.

38. Burley-Allen, pp. 68–70.

39. See Peter A. Andersen, *Nonverbal Communication: Forms and Functions* (Mountain View, CA: Mayfield, 1999), pp. 1–2.

40. Nichols, "Do We Know How to Listen? Practical Helps in a Modern Age," p. 121.

41. Nichols, "Do We Know How to Listen? Practical Helps in a Modern Age," p.121.

42. Nichols, "Listening Is a 10-Part Skill," p.40.

43. Deborah Tannen, *You Just Don't Understand: Women and Men in Conversation* (New York: William Morrow, 1990), pp. 149–151.

44. Melanie Booth-Butterfield, "She Hears … He Hears: What They Hear and Why," *Personnel Journal* 44 (1984), p.39.

45. See Chapter 4, "Diversity in Groups" for a discussion of the Myers-Briggs Type Indicator.

46. Wolvin and Coakley, p. 125.

47. Myron W. Lustig and Jolene Koester, *Intercultural Competencies: Interpersonal Communication across Cultures*, 6th ed. (New York: Harper Collins, 2010), p. 226.

48. Elizabeth A. Tuleja, *Intercultural Communication for Business* (Mason, OH: Thomson Higher Education, 2005), p. 43.

49. The National Institute on Deafness and Other Communication Disorders, June 16, 2010, "Quick Statistics," http://www.nidcd.nih.gov/health/statistics/quick.htm.

50. Gallaudet Research Institute, Gallaudet University, June 6, 2010, "A Brief Summary of Estimates for the Size of the Deaf Population in the USA Based on Available Federal Data and Published Research," http://research.gallaudet.edu/Demographics/deaf-US.php.

51. Department of Education, West Virginia University, March 3, 2000, "Strategies for Teaching Students with Hearing Impairments," http: www.as.wvu.edu/~scidis.hearing.html.

52. Jamie Berke, "Lipreading (or Speechreading): It's Dad not Pad," *About.com: Deafness*, http://deafness.about.com/cs/communication/a/lipreading.htm.

53. Jamie Berke, "Lipreading (or Speechreading): It's Dad not Pad."

54. Alexander Solzhenitsyn, "A World Split Apart," *Vital Speeches* (September 1978), p. 680.

55. Brownell, pp. 355, 356.

56. Recommendations based on the Listener's Summarization Model in Madelyn Burley-Allen, *Listening: The Forgotten Skill*, 2nd ed. (New York: Wiley, 1995), p. 132.

57. Andrew Wolvin and Laura Janusik, "Janusik/Wolvin Student Listening Inventory," in *Communicating: A Social and Career Focus*, 9th ed., eds. Roy M. Berko, Andrew D. Wolvin, and Darlyn R. Wolvin (Boston: Houghton Mifflin, 2004), 129–131. *Note:* We have modified several questions in this inventory to ensure clarity and facilitate scoring.

Chapter 8

1. John O. Burtis and Paul D. Turman, *Group Communication Pitfalls: Overcoming Barriers to an Effective Group Experience* (Thousand Oaks, CA: Sage, 2006), p. 127.

2. John Gastil, *The Group in Society* (Los Angeles, Sage, 2010), p. 184.

3. Jim Billington, "The Three Essentials of an Effective Team," *Harvard Management Update* 2 (January 1997), p. 3.

4. William W. Wilmot and Joyce L. Hocker, *Interpersonal Conflict*, 7th ed. (Boston: McGraw-Hill, 2007), p. 45.

5. Peg Pickering, *How to Manage Conflict: Turn All Conflicts into Win-Win Outcomes*, 3rd ed. (Franklin Lakes, NJ: Career Press, 2000), p. 3.

6. Linda L. Putnam, "Conflict in Group Decision-Making," in *Communication and Group Decision-Making*, eds. Randy Y. Hirokawa and Marshall Scott Poole (Beverly Hills, CA: Sage, 1986), pp. 175–196. Also see Joseph P. Folger, Marshall Scott Poole, and Randall K. Stutman, *Working through Conflict*, 6th ed. (Boston: Allyn & Bacon, 2009), p. 16.

7. Dean C. Barnlund and Franklyn S. Haiman, *The Dynamics of Discussion* (Boston: Houghton Mifflin, 1960), p. 39.

8. Gastil, p. 177.

9. Putnam, p. 185.

10. Fritz Heider, *The Psychology of Interpersonal Relations* (New York: Wiley, 1958).

11. Dudley D. Cann and Ruth Anna Abigail, *Managing Conflict through Communication*, 3rd ed. (Boston: Pearson/Allyn & Bacon, 2007), pp. 138–139.

12. Joseph P. Folger, Marshall Scott Poole, and Randall K. Stutman, *Working through Conflict: Strategies for Relationships, Groups, and Organizations*, 6th ed. (Boston: Pearson/Allyn & Bacon, 2009), p. 60.

13. Kenneth Cloke and Joan Goldsmith, *Resolving Conflicts at Work: A Complete Guide for Everyone on the Job* (San Francisco: Jossey-Bass, 2000), p. 23.

14. Ronald T. Potter-Efron, *Work Rage: Preventing Anger and Resolving Conflict on the Job* (New York: Barnes & Noble Books, 2000), pp. 22–23.

15. Based on Stephen W. Littlejohn and Kathy Domenici, *Engaging Communication in Conflict: Systematic Practice* (Thousand Oaks, CA: Sage, 2001), pp. 94–103.

16. Folger, Poole, and Stutman, pp. 104–118.

17. See Kenneth W. Thomas and Ralph H. Kilmann, "Developing a Forced-Choice Measure of Conflict-Handling Behavior: The MODE Instrument," *Educational and Psychological Measurement* 37 (1977): 390–395. See also Pickering, pp. 35–41. Whereas Thomas and Kilmann classify conflict styles as avoidance, accommodation, competition, compromise, and collaboration, other researchers use different terms for similar categories, e.g., competing, avoiding, accommodating, compromising, and problem solving, as in Robert R. Blake and Jane S. Mouton, *The Managerial Grid* (Houston: Gulf, 1964).

18. Kenneth W. Thomas, *Intrinsic Motivation at Work: Building Energy and Commitment* (San Francisco: Berret-Koehler, 2000), p. 94.

19. "Full Apologies Deter Lawsuits, New Studies Find," *Newswise* (University of Nebraska), www.newswise.com/articles/view/500630/?sc=wire.

20. Cloke and Goldsmith, pp. 109–110; "When and How to Apologize," University of Nebraska Cooperative Extension and the Nebraska Health and Human Services System, http://extension.unl.edu/welfare/apology.htm.

21. Littlejohn and Domenici, p. 181.

22. Gary Harper, *The Joy of Conflict Resolution: Transforming Victims, Villains, and Heroes in the Workplace and at Home* (Gabriola Island, Canada: New Society, 2004), p. 121.

23. Thomas, p. 94.

24. Folger, Poole, and Stutman, pp. 123–124.

25. Deborah L. Duarte and Nancy Tennant Snyder, *Mastering Virtual Teams: Strategies, Tools, and Techniques That Succeed*, 3rd ed. (San Francisco: Jossey-Bass, 2006), p. 161.

26. Susan B. Barnes, *Online Connections: Internet Interpersonal Relationships* (Cresskill, NJ: Hampton Press, 2001), p. 46.

27. David Braga, Steve Jones, and Dennis Bowyer, "Problem Solving in Virtual Teams," in *The Handbook of High-Performance Virtual Teams: A Toolkit for Collaborating Across Boundaries*, eds. Jill Nemiro, Michael, Beyerlein, Lori Bradley, and Susan Beyerlein (San Francisco: John Wiley and Sons, 2008), p. 394.

28. Jerry Wisinski, *Resolving Conflicts on the Job* (New York: American Management Association, 1993), p. 27.

29. Wisinski, pp. 28–30.

30. Roger Fisher, William Ury, and Bruce Patton, *Getting to Yes: Negotiating Agreement without Giving In* (Boston: Houghton Mifflin, 1991), p. 15.

31. Wilmot and Hocker, p. 258.

32. Myra Warren Isenhart and Michael Spangle, *Collaborative Approaches to Resolving Conflict* (Thousand Oaks, CA: Sage, 2000), p. 58.

33. Jeffrey Z. Rubin, "Negotiation: An Introduction to Some Issues and Themes," in *Small Group Communication: A Reader*, 6th ed., eds. Robert S. Cathcart and Larry A. Samovar (Dubuque, IA: Wm. C. Brown, 1992), pp. 415–423.

34. William D. Kimsey, Rex M. Fuller, and Bruce C. McKinney, *Mediation and Conflict Management: General Mediation Manual* (Harrisonburg, VA: James Madison University Center for Mediation), p. 21.

35. Stephen B. Goldberg, "The Secrets of Successful Mediators," *Negotiation Journal* 3 (2005), p. 369.

36. D. S. Hutchinson, "Ethics," in *The Cambridge Companion to Aristotle*, ed. Jonathan Barnes (Cambridge, England: Cambridge University Press, 1995), pp. 217–227.

37. Aristotle, *Nicomachean Ethics*, translated by W. D. Ross; revised by J. O. Urmson, in *The Complete Works of Aristotle: The Revised Oxford Translation*, ed. Jonathan Barnes. (Princeton, NJ: Princeton University Press, 1984), p. 1776.

38. Paula S. Tompkins, *Practicing Communication Ethics: Development, Discernment, and Decision Making* (Boston: Pearson/Allyn & Bacon, 2011), p. 119.

39. Aristotle, p. 104. For a discussion of virtue ethics and Aristotle's virtues, see Tompkins, *Practicing*, pp. 118–121.

40. John W. Keltner, *The Management of Struggle: Elements of Dispute Resolution through Negotiation, Mediation, and Arbitration* (Cresskill, NJ: Hampton, 1994), p. 168.

41. Bren Ortega Murphy, "Promoting Dialogue in Culturally Diverse Workplace Environments," in *Innovation in Group Facilitation: Applications in Natural Settings,* ed. Lawrence R. Frey (Cresskill, NJ: Hampton, 1995), pp. 77–93.

42. Myron W. Lustig and Laura L. Cassotta, "Comparing Group Communication across Cultures: Leadership, Conformity, and Discussion Processes," in *Small Group Communication: Theory and Practice,* 7th ed., eds. Robert S. Cathcart, Larry A. Samovar, and Linda D. Henman (Madison, WI: Brown & Benchmark, 1996), pp. 316–326.

43. Russell Copranzano, Herman Aguinis, Marshall Schminke, and Dina L. Denham, "Disputant Reactions to Managerial Conflict Resolution Tactics: A Comparison Among Argentina, the Dominican Republic, Mexico, and the United States," *Group and Organization Management* 24 (1999), p. 131.

44. Laura E. Drake, "The Culture–Negotiation Link: Integrative and Distributive Bargaining Through an Intercultural Communication Lens," *Human Communication Research* 27 (2001): 321.

45. William R. Cupach and Daniel J. Canary, *Competencies in Interpersonal Conflict* (New York: McGraw-Hill, 1997), p. 133.

46. Myron W. Lustig and Jolene Koester, *Intercultural Competence: Interpersonal Communication across Cultures* (Boston: Pearson/Allyn & Bacon, 2010), pp. 269–270. Lustig and Koester summarize research by Stella Ting-Toomey and John G. Oetzel, *Managing Interpersonal Conflict Effectively* (Thousand Oaks, CA: Sage, 2002).

47. William W. Wilmot and Joyce L. Hocker, *Interpersonal Conflict,* 6th ed. (New York: McGraw-Hill, 2001), p. 31.

48. Deborah Tannen, *The Argument Culture: Moving from Debate to Dialogue* (New York: Random House, 1998), p. 196.

49. Ann Mayden Nicotera and Laura Kathleen Dorsey, "Individual and Interactive Processes in Organizational Conflict," in *The Sage Handbook of Conflict Communication* eds. John Oetzel and Stella Ting-Toomey (Thousand Oaks: Sage, 2006), p. 312.

50. Folger, Poole, and Stutman, p. 130.

51. Folger, Poole, and Stutman, p. 235.

52. Gastil, p. 181.

53. Marvin E. Shaw, "Group Composition and Group Cohesiveness," in *Small Group Communication: A Reader,* 6th ed., eds. Robert S. Cathcart and Larry A. Samovar (Dubuque, IA: Wm. C. Brown, 1992), pp. 214–220.

54. Based on Ernest G. Bormann and Nancy Bormann, *Effective Small Group Communication,* 6th ed. (Edina, MN: Burgess, 1996), pp. 137–139.

55. Daniel J. Beal et al., "Cohesiveness and Performance in Groups: A Meta-analytic Clarification of Construct Relations," *Journal of Applied Psychology*, 88 (2003), pp. 989–1004. Cited in Gastil, p. 181.

56. Karin Sanders and Aukje Nauta, "Social Cohesiveness and Absenteeism: The Relationships between Characteristics of Employees and Short-term Absenteeism within an Organization," *Small Groups Research*, 35 (2004), pp. 724–503.

57. Gastil, p. 182.

58. Irving L. Janis, *Groupthink: Psychological Studies of Policy Decisions and Fiascoes,* 2nd ed. (Boston: Houghton Mifflin, 1982), p. 9.

59. Donelson R. Forsyth, *Group Dynamics*, 5th ed. (Belmont, CA: Wadsworth/Cengage, 2010), p. 342.

60. Janis, p. 9.

61. James Surowiecki, *The Wisdom of Crowds: Why the Many Are Smarter Than the Few and How Collective Wisdom Shapes Business, Economies, Societies, and Nations* (New York: Doubleday, 2004), pp. 36–37.

62. Janis, pp. 174–175.

63. Gregory Moorhead, Richard Ference, and Christopher P. Neck, "Group Decision Fiascos Continue: Space Shuttle *Challenger* and a Groupthink Framework," *Human Relations*, 44 (1991), pp. 539–550, reprinted in *Small Group Communication: Theory and Practice,* 7th ed., eds. Robert S. Cathcart, Larry A. Samovar, and Linda D. Henman (Dubuque, IA: Brown & Benchmark, 1991), pp. 161–170. For a different perspective, see Diane Vaughan, *The Challenger Launch Decision: Risk Technology, Culture, and Deviance at NASA* (Chicago: University of Chicago, 1996).

64. Janis, pp. 174–175.

65. CBS News, May 8, 2011. President Obama on the raid that killed bin Laden: The president talks to *60 Minutes* in his first interview since the killing of terrorist leader Osama bin Laden. Transcript accessed 5/13/11 at http://www.cbsnews.com/stories/2011/05/08/60minutes/main20060876_page3.shtml?tag=contentMain;contentBody.

66. See Janis, R. J. W. Cline, "Groupthink and the Watergate Cover-Up: The Illusion of Unanimity," in *Group Communication in Context: Studies of Natural Groups,* ed. Lawrence R. Frey (Hillsdale, NJ: Erlbaum, 1994), pp. 199–223; 3M Meeting Management Team, *Mastering Meetings: Discovering the Hidden Potential of Effective Business Meetings* (New York: McGraw-Hill, 1994), p. 58.

67. Surowiecki, p. xix.

68. © Isa N. Engleberg and Dianna R. Wynn, 2010.

Chapter 9

1. Peter R. Drucker, *The Effective Executive* (New York: HarperBusiness, 1967), p. 143.

2. Marshall Scott Poole, "Procedures for Managing Meetings: Social and Technological Innovation,"

in *Innovative Meeting Management*, eds. Richard A. Swanson and Bonnie Ogram Knapp (Austin, TX: 3M Meeting Management Institute, 1990), pp. 73–74.

3. See Charles Pavitt and Ellen Curtis, *Small Group Discussion: A Theoretical Approach*, 2nd ed. (Scottsdale, AZ: Gorsuch, Scarisbrick, 1994), pp. 25–52; Robert S. Cathcart, Larry A. Samovar, and Linda D. Henman, *Small Group Communication: Theory and Practice*, 7th ed. (Madison, WI: Brown & Benchmark, 1996), pp. 102–03; Donald G. Ellis and B. Aubrey Fisher, *Small Group Decision Making: Communication and the Group Process*, 4th ed. (New York: McGraw-Hill, 1994), pp. 17–18.

4. Poole, pp. 73–74.

5. Julia T. Wood, "Alternative Methods of Group Decision Making," in *Small Group Communication: A Reader*, 6th ed., eds. Robert S. Cathcart and Larry A. Samovar (Dubuque, IA: Wm. C. Brown, 1992), p. 159.

6. Donald G. Ellis and B. Aubrey Fisher, *Small Group Decision Making: Communication and the Group Process*, 4th ed. (New York: McGraw-Hill, 1994), p. 142.

7. John R. Katzenbach and Douglas K. Smith, *The Discipline of Teams* (New York: Wiley, 2001), p. 112.

8. Katzenbach and Smith, p. 113.

9. Dennis S. Gouran, "Effective Versus Ineffective Group Decision Making," in *Managing Group Life: Communicating in Decision-Making Groups*, eds. Lawrence R. Frey and J. Kevin Barge (Boston: Houghton Mifflin, 1997), p. 139.

10. Dennis Gouran, *Discussion: The Process of Group Decision Making* (New York: Harper & Row, 1974), p. 72.

11. Suzanne G. Scott and Reginald A. Bruce, "Decision Making Style: The Development of a New Measure," *Educational and Psychological Measurement* 55 (1995), pp. 818–831.

12. Poole, pp. 54–55.

13. Pavitt and Curtis, p. 432.

14. John Dewey, *How We Think* (Boston: Heath, 1910).

15. Based on Kathryn Sue Young et al., *Group Discussion: A Practical Guide to Participation and Leadership*, 3rd ed. (Prospect Heights, IL: Waveland, 2001).

16. Randy Y. Hirokawa, "Communication and Group Decision-Making Efficacy," in *Small Group Communication: Theory and Practice*, 7th ed., eds. Robert S. Cathcart, Larry A. Samovar, and Linda D. Henman (Madison, WI: Brown & Benchmark, 1996), p. 108.

17. Susan Jarboe, "Procedures for Enhancing Group Decision Making," in *Communication and Group Decision Making*, 2nd ed., eds. Randy Y. Hirokawa and Marshall Scott Poole (Thousand Oaks, CA: Sage, 1996), p. 357.

18. Jarboe, p. 358.

19. Dennis S. Gouran and Randy Hirokawa, "The Role of Communication in Decision-Making Groups: A Functional Perspective," in *Communications in Transition: Issues and Debate in Current Research*, ed. Mary S. Mander (New York: Praeger, 1983), pp. 168–185; Dennis S. Gouran and Randy Hirokawa, "Functional Theory and Communication in Decision-Making and Problem-Solving Groups: An Expanded View," in *Communication and Group Decision Making*, 2nd ed., eds. Randy Y. Hirokawa and Marshall Scott Poole (Thousand Oaks, CA: Sage, 1996), pp. 55–80.

20. See Randy Y. Hirokawa and Roger Pace, "A Descriptive Investigation of the Possible Communication-Based Reasons for Effective and Ineffective Group Decision Making," *Communication Monographs* 50 (1983), pp. 363–79; Randy Y. Hirokawa and Dirk Scheerhorn, "Communication and Faulty Group Decision-Making," in *Communication and Group Decision-Making*, eds. Randy Y. Hirokawa and Marshall Scott Poole (Beverly Hills, CA: Sage, 1986), pp. 63–80.

21. Hirokawa, p. 108.

22. Hirokawa and Pace, pp. 363–367.

23. Frank LaFasto and Carl Larson, *When Teams Work Best* (Thousand Oaks, CA: Sage, 2001), pp. 84–85.

24. LaFasto and Larson, p. 85.

25. LaFasto and Larson, p. 88.

26. LaFasto and Larson, pp. 89–90.

27. LaFasto and Larson, p. 90.

28. Warren Bennis and Patricia Ward Biederman, *Organizing Genius: The Secrets of Creative Collaboration* (Reading, MA: Addison-Wesley, 1997), p. 17.

29. Bennis and Biederman, p. 20.

30. Based on Lee Towe, *Why Didn't I Think of That?* (West Des Moines, IA: American Media, 1996), p. 7.

31. Roger L. Firestein, "Effects of Creative Problem-Solving Training on Communication Behaviors in Small Groups," *Small Group Research* 21 (1990), pp. 507–521.

32. John Kao, *Jamming: The Art and Discipline of Business Creativity* (New York: HarperBusiness, 1997), p. 17.

33. Alex F. Osborn, *Applied Imagination: Principles and Procedures of Creative Problem Solving*, 3rd rev. ed. (New York: Scribner's, 1963).

34. Tom Kelley with Jonathan Littman, *The Art of Innovation: Lessons in Creativity from IDEO, America's Leading Design Firm* (New York: Currency, 2001), p. 55.

35. Some of the brainstorming guidelines are based on Tom Kelley with Jonathan Littman, *The Art of Innovation: Lessons in Creativity from IDEO, America's Leading Design Firm* (New York: Currency, 2001), pp. 56–59.

36. 3M Meeting Management Team with Jeannine Drew, *Mastering Meetings: Discovering the Hidden Potential of Effective Business Meetings* (New York: McGraw-Hill, 1994), p. 59.

37. Tudor Rickards, "Brainstorming Revisited: A Question of Context," *International Journal of Management Reviews*, 1, pp. 91–110; Tudor Rickards, in *Encyclopedia of Creativity*, Vol. 1 Ae–h, eds. Mark A. Runco and Steven R. Pitzker (San Diego: Academic Press, 1999), pp. 219–228.

38. Andre L. Delbecq, Andrew H. Van de Ven, and David H. Gustafson, *Group Techniques for Program Planning* (Glenview, IL: Scott, Foresman, 1975).

39. P. Keith Kelly, *Team Decision-Making Techniques* (Irvine, CA: Richard Chang Associates, 1994), p. 29.

40. Delbecq, Van de Ven, and Gustafson, p. 8.

41. Tudor Rickards, in *Encyclopedia of Creativity*, Vol. 1, Ae-h, eds. Mark A. Runco and Steven R. Pitzker (San Diego: Academic Press, 1999), p. 222.

42. Craig E. Johnson and Michael Z. Hackman, *Creative Communication: Principles and Applications* (Prospect Heights, IL: Waveland, 1995), pp. 129–30; Tudor Rickards, in *Encyclopedia of Creativity*, Vol. 1, Ae-h, eds. Mark A. Runco and Steven R. Pitzker (San Diego: Academic Press, 1999), pp. 219–228.

43. Johnson and Hackman, p. 131.

44. Delbecq, Van de Ven, and Gustafson, p. 8.

45. P. Keith Kelly, *Team Decision-Making Techniques* (Irvine, CA: Richard Chang Associates, 1994), p. 29.

46. The Decreasing Options Technique (DOT Method of Decision Making) was first introduced by name in Isa N. Engleberg and Dianna R. Wynn, *Working in Groups: Communication Principles and Strategies*, 3rd ed. (Boston: Houghton Mifflin, 2003), pp. 220–222.)

47. David Sibbet, *Visual Meetings: How Graphics, Sticky Notes, and Idea Mapping Can Transform Group Productivity* (Hoboken, NJ: Wiley, 2010).

48. Kao, p. 87.

49. Deborah L. Duarte and Nancy Tennant Snyder, *Mastering Virtual Teams*, 3rd ed. (San Francisco: Jossey-Bass, 2006), p. 171.

50. Duarte and Snyder, pp. 33–34 and 168.

51. Katzenbach and Smith, p. 167.

52. Rodney W. Napier and Matti K. Gershenfeld, *Groups: Theory and Experience*, 7th ed. (Boston: Houghton Mifflin, 2004), p. 327.

53. Duarte and Snyder, pp. 181–183.

54. Towe, p. 14.

55. Kao, p. 8.

56. Donald J. Noone, *Creative Problem Solving*, 2nd ed. (New York: Barron's, 1998), p. 60.

57. Bennis and Biederman, p. 216.

58. John Rawls, *A Theory of Justice* (Cambridge, MA: Harvard University Press, 1971).

59. James Gleick, *Genius: The Life and Science of Richard Feynman* (New York: Vintage, 1992), p. 208.

60. Towe, p. 77.

61. Donald J. Noone, *Creative Problem Solving*, 2nd ed. (New York: Barron's, 1998), p. 93.

62. Dirk Scheerhorn, Patricia Geist, and Jean-Claude Teboul, "Beyond Decision Making in Decision-Making Groups: Implications for the Study of Group Communication," in *Group Communication in Context: Studies of Natural Groups*, ed. Lawrence R. Frey (Hillsdale, NJ: Erlbaum, 1994), p. 256.

63. See Raymond. S. Nickerson, "Confirmation Bias: A Ubiquitous Phenomenon in Many Guises," *Review of General Psychology*, 2, pp. 175–220; Jane Risen and Thomas Gilovich, "Informal Logical Fallacies," in *Critical Thinking in Psychology*, eds. Robert J. Sternberg, Henry L. Roediger, and Diane E. Halpern (New York: Cambridge University Press, 2007), pp. 110–130.

64. See also Nicholas D. Kristoff, "Divided We Fall," *New York Times* (April 17, 2008), p. A27.

65. Frahad Manjoo, *True Enough: Learning to Live in a Post-Fact Society* (New York: John Wiley & Sons, 2008), p. 2.

66. See Naomi Oreskes (2004) "Beyond the Ivory Tower: The Scientific Consensus on Climate Change," *Science* 306 (5702), p. 1686. Based on research by the Intergovernmental Panel on Climate Change (IPCC) of the World Meteorological Organization and the United Nations Environmental Program, the American Meteorological Society, the American Geophysical Union, and the American Association for the Advancement of Science (AAAS), all of whom have issued statements in recent years concluding that the evidence for human modification of climate is compelling.

67. Manjoo, p. 23. For research on Americans' views about whether human activity is a significant cause of global warming, see *The Rasmussen Report*, http://www.rasmussenreports.com/public_content/politics/current_events/environment_energy/energy_update, December 10, 2010; Frank Newport, "Nearly Half of Americans Believe Climate Change Threat Is Exaggerated," *Gallup*, http://www.gallup.com/poll/126560/Americans-Global-Warming-Concerns-Continue-Drop.aspx?version, March 11, 2010; Jason Samenow, "Do Americans Think Global Warning Is Manmade?" http://voices.washingtonpost.com/capitalweathergang/2010/11/does_americans_think_global_wa.html, November 9, 2010.

68. Hirokawa and Pace, p. 379.

69. See www.uc.ie/careers/CMS/decision/student_skills_decision_styleex.html; www.acu.edu/campusoffices/ocad/students/exploration/assess/decision.html, updated August 24, 2005; and Suzanne Scott and Reginald Bruce, "Decision Making Style: The Development of a New Measure," *Educational and Psychological Measurement* 55 (1995): 818–831.

Chapter 10

1. D. Christopher Kayes, "From Climbing Stairs to Riding Waves: Group Critical Thinking and Its Development," *Small Group Research* 36 (2006), p. 615.

2. John Gastil, *The Group in Society* (Los Angeles: Sage, 2009), p. 73.

3. Renee A. Meyers and Dale E. Brashers, "Rethinking Traditional Approaches to Argument in Groups," in *New Directions in Group Communication*, ed. Lawrence R. Frey (Thousand Oaks, CA: Sage, 2002), p. 152.

4. David R. Seibold and Renee A. Meyers, "Group Argument: A Structuration Perspective and Research Program," *Small Group Research 38* (2007) p. *320.*

5. Josina M. Makau and Debian L. Marty, *Cooperative Argumentation: A Model for Deliberative Community* (Prospect Heights, IL: Waveland, 2001), p. 87.

6. Edward S. Inch and Barbara Warnick, *Critical Thinking and Communication: The Use of Reason in Argument* (Boston: Pearson/Allyn & Bacon, 2010), pp. 56–57.

7. Josina M. Makau, *Reasoning and Communication: Thinking Critically about Arguments* (Belmont, CA: Wadsworth, 1990), p. 54.

8. See Sandra M. Ketrow and Beatrice G. Schultz, "Using Argumentative Functions to Improve Decision Quality in the Small Group," in *Argument and the Postmodern Challenge: Proceedings of the Eighth SCA/AFA Conference on Argumentation,* ed. Raymie E. McKerrow (Annandale, VA: Speech Communication Association, 1993), pp. 218–225.

9. Gastil, p. 75.

10. Gastil, p. 75.

11. Toulmin, *The Uses of Argument* (London: Cambridge University, 1958), p. 94.

12. Toulmin, pp. 97–113.

13. Dominic A. Infante and Andrew S. Rancer, "A Conceptualization and Measure of Argumentativeness," *Journal of Personality Assessment* 46 (1982), pp. 72–80.

14. Meyers and Brashers, p. 143.

15. Dean C. Kazoleas and Bonnie Kay, "Are Argumentatives Really More Argumentative? The Behavior of Argumentatives in Group Deliberations over Controversial Issues" (paper presented at the meeting of the Speech Communication Association, New Orleans, LA, 1994).

16. Stephen Toulmin, p. 99.

17. Based on an example format in website notes provided by Evan Zakia O'Donnell, "The Toulmin Model," from the University of North Carolina Greensboro Speaking Center. Retrieved December 23, 2010, from http://speakingcenter.uncg.edu/resources/tipsheets/argumentation/thetoulminmodel.pdf.

18. "Americans Watching More TV Than Ever," Neilsonwire, May 20, 2009, http://blog.nielsen.com/nielsenwire/online_mobile/americans-watching-more-tv-than-ever.

19. "An American Original," *Vanity Fair,* October 6, 2010, http://www.vanityfair.com/politics/features/2010/11/moynihan-letters-201011. Excerpted from *Daniel Patrick Moynihan: A Portrait in Letters of an American Visionary,* edited and with an introduction by Steven R. Weisman, published by Public Affairs, 2010.

20. Warren Bennis and Burt Nanus, *Leaders: The Strategies for Taking Charge* (New York: HarperPerennial, 1985), p. 21.

21. *USA Today,* quoted in *The Week,* January 6, 2006, p. 16.

22. Adam Liptak, "Inmate Count in U.S. Dwarfs Other Nations,'" *The New York Times,* April 23, 2008, p. A1.

23. For more information on testing evidence, see Isa N. Engleberg and John A. Daly, Think Public Speaking (Boston: Pearson, 2013), pp. 133–136.

24. Quoted from *Chronicle of Higher Education,* August 1, 1997, A44, in Ann Raimes, *Keys for Writers,* 2nd ed. (Boston: Houghton Mifflin, 2000), p. 73.

25. Dominic A. Infante and Andrew S. Rancer, *Arguing Constructively* (Prospect Heights, IL: Waveland, 1988), p. 57.

26. For articles about the cardiac benefits of red wine, see http://circ.ahajournals.org/cgi/content/full/111/2/e10 from the American Heart Association and http://www.ynhh.org/online/nutrition/advisor/red_wine.html from the Yale–New Haven Hospital.

27. Renee A. Meyers, Dale Brashers, LaTonia Winston, and Lindsay Grob, "Sex Differences and Group Arguments: A Theoretical Framework and Empirical Investigation," *Communication Studies* 48 (1997), p. 33.

28. Karyn Charles Rybacki and Donald Jay Rybacki, *Advocacy and Opposition: An Introduction to Argumentation,* 3rd ed. (Boston: Allyn & Bacon, 1995), pp. 10–13. Subsequent editions of Rybacki and Rybacki do not include these four responsibilities but do discuss ethical standards for argumentation.

29. Meyers, Brashers, Winston, and Grob, pp. 35–36.

30. Myron W. Lustig and Jolene Koester, *Intercultural Competence: Interpersonal Communication across Cultures,* 6th ed. (Boston: Allyn & Bacon, 2011), p. 229.

31. Based on Daniel Goleman, *Working with Emotional Intelligence* (New York: Bantam, 1998), p. 318. Also see Henrie Weisinger, *Emotional Intelligence at Work* (San Francisco: Jossey-Bass, 1998), pp. xix–xxii.

32. Daniel Goleman, p. 182.

33. Daniel Goleman, p. 165.

34. Goleman, pp. 27–28. See also Antonio R. Damasio, *Descartes' Error: Emotion, Reason, and the Human Brain* (New York: Quill, 2000).

35. Daniel Goleman, p. 28. See also Antonio R. Damasio, *Descartes' Error: Emotion, Reason, and the Human Brain* (New York: Quill, 2000); Antonio Damasio, *The Feeling of What Happens: Body and Emotion in the Making of Consciousness* (San Diego: Harvest/Harcourt, 1999).

36. Daniel Goleman, p. 317.

37. Meyers and Brashers, p. 152.

38. Many excellent argument examples for the Toulmin model can be found on academic websites. The first argument is based on an example from LeTourneau University, http://owlet.letus.edu/contenthtml/research/toulmin.html. The second argument is based on an example from the Dr. L. Kip Wheller website at Carson-Newman College, http://web.cn.edu/kwheeler/documents/Toulmin.pdf. For more examples, search: Toulmin Model of Argument.

39. Dominic A. Infante and Andrew Rancer, "Argumentativeness Scale," from *The Journal of Personality Assessment,* 1982. Reprinted by permission of Lawrence Erlbaum Associates and the scale authors.

Chapter 11

1. Jeff Davidson, *The Complete Idiot's Guide to Getting Things Done* (New York: Alpha Books, 2005), p. 232.
2. Quoted in The 3M Meeting Management Team with Jeannine Drew, *Mastering Meetings: Discovering the Hidden Potential of Effective Business Meetings* (New York: McGraw-Hill, 1995), p. 1. From Dave Barry, *Claw Your Way to the Top* (Emmaus, PA; Rodale Press, 1986), p. 25.
3. Tyler Cowen, "On My Mind: In Favor of Face Time," October 1, 2007, www.members.forbes.com/forbes/2007/1001/030.html.
4. Shri Henkel, *Successful Meetings: How to Plan, Prepare, and Execute Top-Notch Business Meetings* (Ocala, FL: Atlantic Publishing Group, 2007), p. 146.
5. *The Week,* April 2, 2005, p. 35. Study reported in CNNMoney.com.
6. Nicholas C. Romano, Jr., and Jay F. Nunamaker, Jr., "Meeting Analysis: Findings from Research and Practice," *Proceedings of the 34th Hawaii International Conference on System Sciences* (2001), p. 1.
7. Steven G. Rogelberg, Joseph A. Allen, Linda Shanock, Cliff Scott, and Marissa Shuffler, "Employee Satisfaction with Meetings: A Contemporary Facet of Job Satisfaction," *Human Resource Management* 49 (2010), pp. 164–165.
8. Matthew Gilbert, *Communication Miracles at Work: Effective Tools and Tips for Getting the Most from Your Work Relationships* (Berkeley, CA: Conari Press, 2002), p. 173.
9. Henkel, pp. 22–24; Donald L. Kirkpatrick, *How to Conduct Productive Meetings: Strategies, Tips, and Tools to Ensure Your Next Meeting Is Well Planned and Effective* (Alexandria, VA: American Society for Training and Development, 2006), pp. 104–106.
10. Kirkpatrick, pp. 104–105.
11. Rogelberg, Allen, Shanock, Scott, and Shuffler, p. 168.
12. Karen Anderson, *Making Meetings Work: How to Plan and Conduct Effective Meetings* (West Des Moines, IA: American Media, 1997), p. 17.
13. Kirkpatrick, pp. 2–5.
14. Barbara Streibel, *The Manager's Guide to Effective Meetings* (New York: McGraw-Hill, 2003), p. 165.
15. Henkel, p. 47.
16. Henkel, p. 35; Glenn Parker and Robert Hoffman, *Meeting Excellence: 33 Tools to Lead Meetings That Get Results* (San Francisco; CA: Jossey-Bass, 2006), p. 6.
17. Parker and Hoffman, p. 52.
18. Henkel, p. 78
19. Robert Heller and Tim Hindle, *Essential Manager's Manual* (New York: DK, 1998), p. 471.
20. Heller and Hindle, p. 445.
21. Heller and Hindle, p. 444.
22. *Running Meetings: Expert Solutions to Everyday Challenges* (Boston: Harvard Business School Publishing, 2006), p. 20.
23. Irving L. Janis, *Groupthink: Psychological Studies of Policy Decisions and Fiascoes,* 2nd ed. (Boston: Houghton Mifflin, 1982).
24. Kelly M. Quintanilla and Shawn T. Wahl, *Business and Professional Communication: Keys for Workplace Excellence* (Los Angeles: Sage, 2011), pp. 129–131.
25. Quintanilla and Wahl, p. 129.
26. Quintanilla and Wahl, p. 129.
27. Quintanilla and Wahl, p. 130.
28. Bobbi Linkemer, *How to Run a Meeting That Works* (New York: American Management Association, 1987), p. 42.
29. 3M Meeting Management Team, with Jeannine Drew, *Mastering Meetings: Discovering the Hidden Potential of Effective Business Meetings* (New York: McGraw-Hill, 1995), p. 78.
30. Streibel, p. 65.
31. Heller and Hindle, pp. 470–471.
32. Kelly A. Lambing, "Increasing Meeting Effectiveness for Internal Auditors," St. Louis Chapter of the Institute for Internal Auditors Research Committee, 2007, www.theiia.org/download.cfm?file=65972, http://www.theiia.org/RFR/index.cfm?iid=593&catid=0&aid=3003.
33. "How to Be a Good Facilitator," from *How to Make Meetings Work* by Michael Doyle and David Straus, copyright © 1976 by Michael Doyle and David Straus. Used by permission of Berkley Publishing Group, a division of Penguin Group (USA) Inc.
34. Glenn Parker and Robert Hoffman, *Meeting Excellence: 33 Tools to Lead Meetings That Get Results* (San Francisco: Jossey-Bass, 2006), p. 42.
35. Deborah L. Duarte and Nancy Tennant Snyder, *Mastering Virtual Teams: Strategies, Tools, and Techniques That Succeed,* 3rd ed. (San Francisco: Jossey-Bass, 2006), p. 165.
36. Heller and Hindle, p. 429.
37. Henry M. Robert III, William J. Evans, Daniel H. Honemann, and Thomas J. Balch, *Robert's Rules of Order: Newly Revised,* 10th ed. (New York: HarperCollins, 2000). See also O. Garfield Jones, *Parliamentary Procedure at a Glance, New Edition* (New York: Penguin, 1971); Alice Sturgis, *The Standard Code of Parliamentary Procedure,* 3rd ed. (New York: McGraw-Hill, 1988).
38. Robert. Evans, Honemann, and Balch, p. xliv.
39. Bud A. McClure, *Putting a New Spin on Groups: The Science of Chaos* (Mahwah, NJ: Lawrence Erlbaum Associates, 1998), p. 3.
40. Based on a lecture by M. Mitchell Waldrop, *Complexity: The Emerging Science at the Edge of Order and Chaos* (New York: W. W. Norton, 1989).
41. McClure, p. 82.

Chapter 12

1. "Nomads at Last," *The Economist,* online, April 10, 2008. www.economist.com/surveys/displaystory.cfm?story_id=10950394.
2. Jonathan Strickland, "What Are the Most Wired Countries in the World and Why?" *How Stuff Works,* http://computer.howstuffworks.com/most-wired-countries-in-world1.htm; "The World's Most Wired Countries," *RealClearWorld,* July 29, 2010, http://www

.realclearworld.com/2010/07/29/the_worlds_most_wired_countries_113804.html.

3. Jared Bilski, "Employers Predict Big Increases in Virtual Workers Next Year: Do You?" *CFO Daily News*, November 17, 2010, http://www.cfodailynews.com/employers-predict-big-increases-in-virtual-workers-next-year-do-you.

4. RW3 Culture Wizard, "The Challenges of Working in Virtual Teams: Virtual Teams Survey Report—2010," http:/rw-3.com/VTSReportv7.pdf.

5. Stacey L. Connaughton and Marissa Shuffler, "Multinational and Multicultural Distributed Teams: A Review and Future Agenda," *Small Group Research* 38 (2007): 387, 388. Connaughton and Shuffler cite a variety of research findings in the introduction to their article.

6. L. L. Martins, L. Gilson, and M. Maynard, "Virtual Teams: What Do We Know and Where Do We Go from Here?" *Journal of Management*, 30 (2004): 805–835. Quoted in A. H. Anderson, R. McEwan, J. Bal, and J. Carletta, "Virtual Team Meetings: An Analysis of Communication and Context," *Computers and Human Behavior*, 23 (September 2007), p. 2558.

7. James Creighton and James W. R. Adams, *Cyber Meeting: How to Link People and Technology in Your Organization* (New York: AMACOM, 1998), p. ix.

8. Thomas A. O'Neill, Rhys J. Lewis, and Laura A. Hambly, "Leading Virtual Teams: Potential Problems and Simple Solutions," in *The Handbook of High Performance Virtual Teams: A Toolkit for Collaborating Across Boundaries*, eds. Jill Nemiro, Michael Beyerlein, Lori Bradley, and Susan Beyerlein (San Francisco: John Wiley & Sons, 2008), p. 222.

9. D. Sandy Staples and Jane Webster, "Exploring Traditional and Virtual Team Members' 'Best Practices,'" *Small Group Research* 38 (February 2007), pp. 90, 91.

10. Fran Rees, *How to Lead Work Teams* (San Francisco: Jossey-Bass/Pfeiffer, 2001), pp. 114–115.

11. Modalis Research Technologies, *Meetings in America III: A Study of the Virtual Workforce in 2001*, p. 16. http://e-meetings.mci.com/meetingsinamerica/pdf/MIA3.pdf.

12. Excerpt from Edward Glaeser, *Triumph of the City: How Our Greatest Invention Makes Us Richer, Smarter, Healthier and Happier* (New York: Penguin Press, 2011), http://books.google.com/books?id=-yWTIKsWGm4C&q=business+conferences#v=onepage&q=email&f=false;, See also Jonah Lehrer, "Social Networks Can't Replace Socializing," *The Wall Street Journal*, August 6–7, 2011, p. C12.

13. Shu-Chu Sarrina Li, "Computer-Mediated Communication and Group Decision Making," *Small Group Research* 38 (2007), pp. 596–597.

14. Sarrina Li, 609. See also Jamonn Campbell and Garold Stasser, "The Influence of Time and Task Demonstrability on Decision-Making in Computer-Mediated and Face-to-Face Groups," *Small Group Research* 37 (2006), pp. 271–294.

15. O'Neill, Lewis, and Hambly, p. 221.

16. John Gastil, *The Group in Society* (Los Angeles, CA: Sage 2010), p. 84.

17. Trina Hoefling, "The Three-Fold Path of Expanding Emotional Bandwith in Virtual Teams," in *The Handbook of High Performance Virtual Teams: A Toolkit for Collaborating Across Boundaries*, eds. Jill Nemiro, Michael Beyerlein, Lori Bradley, and Susan Beyerlein (San Francisco: John Wiley & Sons, 2008), p. 95.

18. See Richard L. Daft and Robert H. Lengel, "Information Richness: A New Approach to Managerial Behaviour and Organizational Design," in *Research in Organizational Behavior*, eds. Barry M. Staw and Larry L. Cummings (Greenwich, CT: JAI Press, 1984), pp. 355–366; Richard L. Daft, Robert H. Lengel, and Linda K. Trevino, "Message Equivocality, Media Selection, and Manager Performance: Implications for Information Systems," *MIS Quarters* 11 (1987): 355–366; Linda K. Trevino, Robert K. Lengel, and Richard L. Daft, "Media Symbolism, Media Richness, and Media Choice in Organizations," *Communication Research* 14 (1987), pp. 553–574.

19. O'Neill, Lewis, and Hambly, p. 218.

20. Alan R. Dennis and Joseph S. Valacich, "Rethinking Media Richness: Towards a Theory of Media," *Proceedings of the 32nd Hawaii International Conference on System Sciences*, 1999, p. 9. See also Dorrie De Luca and Joseph S. Valacich, "Virtual Teams In and Out of Synchronicity," *Information Technology and People*, 19 (2006), pp. 323–344.

21. Patricia Wallace, *The Psychology of the Internet* (Cambridge, England: Cambridge University Press, 1999), p. 75.

22. Crispin Thurlow, Laura Lengel, and Alice Tomic, *Computer Mediated Communication: Social Interaction and the Internet* (London: Sage, 2004), p. 63.

23. Sheizaf Rafaeli and Fay Sudweeks, "Networked Interactivity," *Journal of Computer-Mediated Communication* 2 (1997). www.december.com/cmc/mag/current/toc.html. Cited in Crispin Thurlow, Laura Lengel, and Alice Tomic, *Computer Mediated Communication: Social Interaction and the Internet* (London: Sage, 2004), p. 67.

24. For a brief history and explanation of the term *groupware*, see David Coleman (ed.), *Groupware: Collaborative Strategies for Corporate LANs and Intranets* (Upper Saddle River, NJ: Prentice-Hall, 1997), pp. 1–2.

25. Gerald O'Dwyer, Art Giser, and Ed Lovett, "Groupware and Reengineering: The Human Side of Change," in *Groupware: Collaborative Strategies for Corporate LANs and Intranets*, ed. David Coleman (Upper Saddle River, NJ: Prentice-Hall, 1997), p. 566.

26. Harvard Business School, *Leading Virtual Teams: Expert Solutions to Everyday Challenges* (Boston: Harvard Business Press, 2010), p. 42.

27. Clyde Burelson, *Effective Meetings: The Complete Guide* (New York: Wiley, 1990), p. 168.

28. Burelson, p. 171.

29. Andrew F. Wood and Matthew J. Smith, *Online Communication: Linking Technology, Identity, and Culture* (Mahwah, NJ: Erlbaum, 2001), p. 13.

30. Kenneth A. Graetz, "Information Sharing in Face-to-Face, Teleconferencing, and Electronic Chat Groups," *Small Group Research* 29 (1998), pp. 714–743.

31. Gastil, p. 84.

32. Deborah L. Duarte and Nancy Tennant Snyder, *Mastering Virtual Teams: Strategies, Tools, and Techniques That Succeed,* 3rd ed. (San Francisco: Jossey-Bass, 2006), pp. 37, 71.

33. W. A. Flexner and Kimbal Wheatley, in *Groupware: Collaborative Strategies for Corporate LANs and Intranets,* ed. David Coleman (Upper Saddle River, NJ: Prentice-Hall, 1997), p. 193.

34. Flexner and Wheatley, p. 194.

35. David Crystal, *Language and the Internet* (Cambridge, England: Cambridge University Press, 2001), pp. 238–239. Cited in Crispin Thurlow, Laura Lengel, and Alice Tomic, *Computer Mediated Communication: Social Interaction and the Internet* (London: Sage, 2004), p. 123.

36. Thurlow, Lengel, and Tomic, pp. 124–125.

37. Urban Dictionary, http://www.urbandictionary.com/define.php?term=netspeak.

38. Matt Richtel, "In Youthful World of Messaging, Email Gets Instant Makeover," *The New York Times,* December 21, 2010, p. B4.

39. For additional examples and warnings about overuse of symbols, see Deborah Jude-York, Lauren D. David, and Susan L. Wise, *Virtual Teams: Breaking the Boundaries of Time and Place* (Menlo Park, CA: Crisp Learning, 2000), pp. 91–92.

40. Duarte and Snyder, p. 185.

41. Duarte and Snyder, pp. 36–37.

42. Coleman (ed.), p. 266.

43. Duarte and Snyder, pp. 36, 38–39.

44. Wood and Smith, p. 80.

45. Jonah Lehrer, "Social Networks Can't Replace Socializing," *The Wall Street Journal,* August 6–7, 2011, p. C12.

46. Wood and Smith, p. 12.

47. Wood and Smith, p. 11.

48. For a summary discussion of Internet addiction issues, see Thurlow, Lengel, and Tomic, pp. 148–154. See also the following websites: Anne Federvisch, "Internet Addiction?" *Nurseweek/Healthweek,* www.nurseweek.com/ features/97-8/iadct.html; Ivan Goldberg message posted to the *Psychology of the Internet,* available at www.rider.edu/suler/ psychberg/psycyber.html; Leonard Holmes, "Internet Addiction— Is It Real?" http://mentalhealth.about.com/cs/sexaddict/a/interaddict.html, March 10, 1997; Leonard Holmes, "What Is 'Normal' Internet Use?" http://mentalhealth.about.com/cs/sexaddict/a/normalinet.htm, March 10, 1997.

49. Janet Morahan-Martin and Phyllis Schumacher, "Incidence and Correlates of Pathological Internet Use Among College Students," *Computers in Human Behavior* 16 (2000), p. 14.

50. Kimberly S. Young, "Internet Addiction: The Emergence of a New Disorder," *CyberPsychology and Behavior* 1 (1998), pp. 237–244.

51. Andrew Goodman, "Online Communities Endure as Platforms Come and Go," April 28, 2001, www.traffick.com/story/2001-04/online_community.asp.

52. Lee Rainie, "Internet, Broadband, and Cell Phone Statistics," *Pew Internet,* January 5, 2010, http://www.pewinternet.org/Reports/2010/Internet-broadband-and-cell-phone-statistics/Report.aspx.

53. Deborah Fallows, "How Women and Men Use the Internet," *Pew Internet & American Life Project,* Pew Research Center, December 28, 2005, http://www.pewinternet.org/Reports/2005/How-Women-and-Men-Use-the-Internet.aspx.

54. Rainie, "Internet, Broadband, and Cell Phone Statistics," January 5, 2010.

55. Joshua Brustein, "Mobile Web Use and the Digital Divide," *Pew Research Center's Internet and American Life Center,* July 7, 2010, http://bits.blogs.nytimes.com/2010/07/07/increased-mobile-web-use-and-the-digital-divide.

56. Wendy David, "Report: 'Digital Divide' Great as Ever, Media Post, November 9, 2010, http://www.mediapost.com/publications/?fa=Articles.showArticle&art_aid=139248.

57. The Ten Commandments of Computer Ethics were created in 1992 by the Computer Ethics Institute as a means to create a set of standards to guide and instruct people in the ethical use of computers. See Ramon C. Barquin, "In Pursuit of a 'Ten Commandments' for Computer Ethics," Computer Ethics Institute, Washington Consulting Group and Computer Ethics Institute, May 7, 1992, http://www.brookings.edu/its/cei/papers/Barquin_Pursuit_1992.htm.

58. Computer Ethics Institute, Computer Professionals for Social Responsibility (CPSR), The Ten Commandments for Computer Ethics, updated August 11, 2008, http://cpsr.org/issues/ethics/cei

59. N. Ben Fairweather, "Commentary on the 'Ten Commandments' for Computer Ethics," February 11, 2004, www.ccsr.cse.dmu.ac.uk/resources/professionalism/codes/cei_command_com.htm.

60. Fairweather, "Commentary on the 'Ten Commandments' for Computer Ethics," February 11, 2004.

61. Rainie, "Internet, Broadband, and Cell Phone Statistics," January 5, 2010.

62. Emanuel Brady and Lori Bradley, "Generational Differences in Virtual Teams," in *The Handbook of High Performance Virtual Teams: A Toolkit for Collaborating Across Boundaries,* eds. Jill Nemiro, Michael Beyerlein, Lori Bradley, and Susan Beyerlein (San Francisco: John Wiley & Sons, 2008), p. 265.

63. Brady and Bradley, p. 265.

64. Susan P. Crawford, "The New Digital Divide," *New York Times,* December 4, 2011, p. SR 1.

65. Stacey Higginbotham, "The Digital Divide Will Ensure a Broadband Ghetto," *Gigaom.com*, May 27, 2010, http://gigaom.com/2010/03/27/the-digital-divide-will-ensure-a-broadband-ghetto.

66. "'Digital Divide' Widening at Lower Income Levels," www.clickz.com/stats/sectors/geographics/article.php/5911_569351.

67. Eszter Hargittal, "Linked in with. . . ." *The Chronicle of Higher Education,* May 2, 2008, p. A13.

68. The categories are adapted from a more extensive analysis of strengths and weaknesses for several types of groupware in Deborah L. Duarte and Nancy Tennant Snyder, *Mastering Virtual Teams: Strategies, Tools, and Techniques That Succeed,* 3rd ed. (San Francisco: Jossey-Bass, 2006), pp. 30–48. Duarte and Snyder's recommended ratings are in the *Instructor's Manual* accompanying this textbook.

Appendix

1. Deborah Harrington-Mackin, *Keeping the Team Going: A Tool Kit to Renew and Refuel Your Workplace Teams* (New York: AMACOM, 1996), pp. 88–89.

2. Based on Isa N. Engleberg and John A. Daly, *Presentations in Everyday Life: Strategies for Effective Speaking,* 3rd ed. (Boston: Pearson/Allyn & Bacon, 2009), pp. 6–8 and 76–89.

3. Quoted in Lilly Walters, *Secrets of Successful Speakers* (New York: McGraw-Hill, 1993), pp. 3–4.

4. Lane Cooper, *The Rhetoric of Aristotle* (New York: Appleton-Century-Crofts, 1932), pp. 8–9.

5. Engleberg and Daly, pp. 135–136.

6. Jo Sprague and Douglas Stuart, *The Speaker's Handbook,* 6th ed. (Belmont, CA: Wadsworth, 2003), p. 255.

7. James C. McCroskey and Jason J. Teven, "Goodwill: A Reexamination of the Construct and Its Measurement," *Communication Monographs* 66 (1999): 90–103. McCroskey and Tevan note that Aristotle envisioned ethos as composed of three elements: intelligence, character, and goodwill. The results of McCroskey and Tevan's research establish that goodwill is a primary dimension of the ethos/source credibility construct.

8. Some of the best research on the value of organizing a presentation was done in the 1960s and 1970s. See Ernest C. Thompson, "An Experimental Investigation of the Relative Effectiveness of Organizational Structure in Oral Communication," *The Southern Speech Journal* 26 (1960): 59–69; Ernest C. Thompson, "Some Effects of Message Structure on Listeners' Comprehension," *Speech Monographs* 34 (1967): 51–57; James McCroskey and R. Samuel Mehrley, "The Effects of Disorganization and Nonfluency on Attitude Change and Source Credibility," *Communication Monographs* 36 (1969): 13–21; Arlee Johnson, "A Preliminary Investigation of the Relationship between Organization and Listener Comprehension," *Central States Speech Journal* 21 (1970): 104–107; Christopher Spicer and Ronald E. Bassett, "The Effect of Organization on Learning from an Informative Message," *Southern Speech Communication Journal* 41 (1976), pp. 290–299.

9. Engleberg and Daly, pp. 314, 315.

10. Authors of voice and articulation textbooks generally agree that a useful, all-purpose speaking rate is around 145 to 180 words per minute. See Lyle V. Mayer, *Fundamentals of Voice and Articulation,* 13th ed. (Boston: McGraw-Hill, 2004); Jeffrey C. Hahner, Martin A. Sokoloff, and Sandra L. Salisch, *Speaking Clearly: Improving Voice and Diction,* 6th ed. (New York: McGraw-Hill, 2002); Ethel C. Glenn, Phillip J. Glenn, and Sandra Forman, *Your Voice and Articulation,* 4th ed. (Boston: Allyn & Bacon, 1998).

11. Marya W. Holcombe and Judith K. Stein, *Presentations for Decision Makers: Strategies for Structuring and Delivering Your Ideas* (Belmont, CA: Wadsworth, 1983), p. 169.

12. Holcombe and Stein, p. 178.

13. Marjorie Brody, *Speaking Your Way to the Top: Making Powerful Business Presentations* (Boston: Allyn & Bacon, 1998), p. 81.

14. Judith Filek, "Tips for Seamless Team Presentations—A Baker's Dozen," Impact Communications Inc. *Face-to-Face Communications Skills Newsletter,* September 2006.www.impactcommunicationsinc.com/pdf/nwsltr_2006/ICINwsltreff0609.pdf.

15. Engleberg and Daly, p. 483.

16. Thomas Leech, *How to Prepare, Stage, and Deliver Winning Presentations* (New York: AMACOM, 1993), p. 288.

17. Engleberg and Daly, p. 461.

18. 3M Meeting Management Team, with Jeannine Drew, *Mastering Meetings: Discovering the Hidden Potential of Effective Business Meetings* (New York: McGraw-Hill, 1994), p. 140.

19. Robin Williams, *The Non-Designer's Presentation Book: Principles for Effective Presentation Design* (Berkeley, CA: Peachpit Press, 2010), p. 4.

20. RAND, *Guidelines for Preparing Briefings* [online] (1996). www.rand.org/pubs/corporate_pubs/2005/CP269.pdf.

21. William J. Ringle, *TechEdge: Using Computers to Present and Persuade* (Boston: Allyn & Bacon, 1998), p. 125.

22. Ringle, pp. 125, 135.

23. S. Hinkin, "Designing Standardized Templates: First You Choose It, but How Do You Get Them to Use It?" *Presentations* 8 (August 1994): 34.

24. "Microsoft PowerPoint," Wikipedia, http://en.wikipedia.org/wiki/PowerPoint.

25. Edward R. Tufte, *The Cognitive Style of PowerPoint* (Cheshire, CT: Graphics Press, 2003), p. 24.

26. Several trade books on using PowerPoint and preparing presentations using computer-generated slides and animation were reviewed to develop the list of rules in this

section, including: Rick Altman, *Why Most PowerPoint Presentations Suck and How You Can Make Them Better* (Pleasanton, CA: Harvest Books, 2007); Cliff Atkinson, *Beyond Bullet Points: Using Microsoft Office Power Point 2007 to Create Presentations That Inform, Motivate, and Inspire* (Redmond, WA: Microsoft Press, 2008); Nancy Duarte, *Slide:ology: The Art and Science of Creating Great Presentations* (Sebastopol, CA: O'Reilly Media, 2008); Garr Reynolds, *Presentation Zen: Simple Ideas on Presentation Design and Delivery* (Berkeley, CA: New Riders, 2008); Gene Zelazny, *Say It with Presentations: Revised and Expanded* (New York: McGraw-Hill, 2006); Gene Zelazny (edited by Sara Roche and Steve Sakson), *The Say It with Charts Complete ToolKit* (New York: McGraw-Hill, 2007).

27. Nancy Duarte, *Slide:ology: The Art and Science of Creating Great Presentations* (Sebastopol, CA: O'Reilly Media, 2008), p. 140.

28. Jeffrey R. Young, "When Good Technology Means Bad Teaching," *Chronicle of Higher Education* (November 12, 2004): A31–A32.

29. Young, A32.

30. Tufte, p. 24.

31. Cliff Atkinson, *Beyond Bullet Points* (Redmond, WA: Microsoft Press, 2008), p. 47.

Index

Credits

Front Matter: p. vi: Gallo Images/Alamy; p. vii: Jupiterimages/Thinkstock; p. viii: Megapress/ Alamy; p. ix: Jim West/Alamy; p. x: U.S. Air Force photo by Senior Airman Andrew Lee; p. xi: juice images/Corbis; p. xii: Ed Edahl/FEMA; p. xiii: Iain Cooper/Alamy; p. xiv: Jeff Greenberg/PhotoEdit; p. xv: David Bacon/The Image Works; p. xvi: Bill Bachman/Alamy; p. xvii: Syracuse Newspapers/ Gloria Wright/The Image Works; p. xviii: Bob Daemmrich/The Image Works; p. xix: Erwin Wodicka/ Shutterstock.

Chapter 1: p. 1: Gallo Images/Alamy; p. 2 (both): Pearson Education; p. 6: Aaron M. Sprecher/Icon SMI 952/Aaron M. Sprecher/Icon SMI/Newscom; p. 16: Bob Daemmrich/The Image Works; p. 17: Richard Lord/The Image Works.

Chapter 2: p. 25: Jupiterimages/Thinkstock; p. 26 (both): Pearson Education; p. 33: Greg Epperson/age footstock; p. 38: Chuck Painter/Stanford News Service; p. 41: HBSS/Crush/Corbis.

Chapter 3: p. 47: Megapress/Alamy; p. 48 (both): Pearson Education; p. 51: Claude Beaubien/ Shutterstock; p. 61: Matsunaka Takeya/Aflo/Glow Images; p. 64: Reprinted by permission of the publisher, from The Interpersonal Communication Skills Workshop by Joshua D. Guilar © 2001 Joshua Guilar, AMACOM, division of American Management Association, New York, NY. All rights reserved. www .amacombooks.org.

Chapter 4: p. 70: Jim West/Alamy; p. 71 (both): Pearson Education; p. 84: OJO Images Ltd/Alamy; p. 89: Fancy/Alamy; p. 91: AP Photo/GemunuAmarasinghe.

Chapter 5: p. 98: U.S. Air Force photo by Senior Airman Andrew Lee; p. 99 (both): Pearson Education; p. 110: Purestock/Superstock; p. 118: Corbis; p. 119: David Fine/FEMA.

Chapter 6: p. 123: juice images/Corbis; p. 124 (both): Pearson Education; p. 134: The Star-Ledger/ Tony Kurdzuk/The Image Works; p. 136: Holly Harris/Stone/Getty Images; p. 137: Masterfile; p. 141: REUTERS/Government of Chile/Pool/Landov ; p. 121: "GroupWork: The Least-Preferred-Coworker Scale," in Adapted from A Theory of Leadership Effectiveness, Edition 2, Author: Fred E. Fiedler, © 1967, pp. 17-42. Reprinted with permission; p. 122: From DUBRIN. LEADERSHIP, 4E, 4E. © 2004 South-Western, a part of Cengage Learning, Inc. Reproduced by permission. www.cengage.com/ permissions.

Chapter 7: p. 148: Ed Edahl/FEMA; p. 150 (both): Pearson Education; p. 153: Reprinted with permission from Franklin Covey; p. 163: Digital Vision/Jupiter Images.

Chapter 8: p. 171: Iain Cooper/Alamy; p. 173 (both): Pearson Education; p. 178: Mitch Wojnarowicz/The Image Works; p. 189: z03/ZUMA Press/Newscom.

Chapter 9: p. 193: Jeff Greenberg/PhotoEdit; p. 195 (both): Pearson Education; p. 207: Elizabeth Crews/ The Image Works; p. 210: Blend images/Alamy.

Chapter 10: p. 221: David Bacon/The Image Works; p. 223 (both): Pearson Education; p. 229: Florida Senate; p. 238: Richard A. Cooke/Corbis.

Chapter 11: p. 243: Bill Bachman/Alamy; p. 245 (both): Pearson Education; p. 254: image110/Alamy; p. 257: © 1994 John McPherson/Dist. by UNIVERSAL UCLICK. Reprinted with permission. All rights reserved; p. 260: Mitch Wojnarowicz/Amsterdam Recorder/The Image Works.

Chapter 12: p. 266: Syracuse Newspapers/Gloria Wright/The Image Works; p. 268 (both): Pearson Education; p. 274: Exactostock/SuperStock; p. 285 (left): Paul/Mayall/Alamy; p. 285 (right): Jeff Greenberg/ Alamy.

Appendix : p. 289: Bob Daemmrich/The Image Works; p. 310: paul king/Alamy.